The Islamic Threat

THE
ISLAMIC
THREAT

Myth or Reality?

Third Edition

John L. Esposito

New York   Oxford
OXFORD UNIVERSITY PRESS

Oxford University Press

Oxford New York
Athens Auckland Bangkok Bogotá Buenos Aires Calcutta
Cape Town Chennai Dar es Salaam Delhi Florence Hong Kong Istanbul
Karachi Kuala Lumpur Madrid Melbourne Mexico City Mumbai
Nairobi Paris São Paulo Singapore Taipei Tokyo Toronto Warsaw

and associated companies in
Berlin Ibadan

First published by Oxford University Press, Inc.
198 Madison Avenue, New York, New York 10016

First issued as an Oxford University Press paperback, 1992

Oxford is a registered trademark of Oxford University Press, Inc.

Library of Congress Cataloging-in-Publication Data
Esposito, John L.
The Islamic threat : myth or reality? / John L. Esposito. — 3rd ed.
p. cm.
Includes bibliographical references and index.
ISBN 0-19-513076-6
1. Islam—20th century. 2. Islamic countries—Relations—Europe.
3. Europe—Relations—Islamic countries. I. Title.
BP60.E84 1999   327.4017'671—dc21   99-28443

7 9 8

Printed in the United States of America

For my parents,
John and Mary Esposito

Contents

Preface to the
Third Edition

Relatively little time has elapsed since the last edition of *The Islamic Threat: Myth or Reality?* was published, but many changes have occurred since then. The government of Turkey, influenced by the military, forced its nation's first Islamist prime minister to resign and suppressed the Welfare Party. The Taliban swept across Afghanistan and gained control of 90 percent of the country. Violence and intolerance in Bosnia spread into Kosovo, where Serbian forces massacred ethnic Albanians. American military forces in Saudi Arabia and American embassies in Kenya and Tanzania were bombed. In retaliation for the bombings in Africa and to prevent or discourage future attacks, the United States undertook a preemptive strike against sites and camps in Sudan and Afghanistan allegedly supported by Osama bin Laden, whom the United States held responsible for the promotion and support of global terrorism. Israeli and Palestinian officials often blamed Hamas for acts of terrorism that undermined the peace process. Iran felt the winds of change with President Khatami's election, marked by new initiatives to build a civil society and engage the West through a civilizational dialogue. However, Khatami's reformism was countered by more conservative supporters of Ayatollah Khamenei, Iran's supreme religious leader (*faqih*). Muslims in the United States and Europe continued to be more visible participants at every level of society, but they also faced questions regarding their loyalty to their new homeland and their connections to militant groups overseas.

The problem today is putting into perspective relations between Islam and the West, as it was when the first edition of this book appeared. If some have spoken of the need for civilizational dialogue, others have warned of a clash of civilizations. Talk of a political and cultural conflict could be seen not only in fears of confrontation but also in assertions that Islam is incompatible with democracy and modernity. The charge that political Islam is inherently militant became an excuse for suppressing movements and closing the door to democratization in many Muslim countries. These beliefs and attitudes affected the policies of governments and the actions of Islamic activists in the Muslim world and in the West. At the dawn of the twenty-first century, placing global events and fears within a balanced context has never been more important.

Over the years many colleagues and friends in the Muslim world and the West have provided insights and encouragement. Space does not permit me to thank them all by name. I am especially indebted to John Voll, Yvonne Haddad, and James Piscatori, with whom I have worked closely over the years. Abdullah Alireza and I have shared stimulating days and evenings discussing many of the issues in this volume. The primary mover in the creation of the Center for Muslim-Christian Understanding, Hasib Sabbagh, along with Leo J. O'Donovan, S. J., President of Georgetown University, who shared his vision, helped establish a locus at which many of the concerns addressed in this volume can be addressed more fully and systematically. Patricia Gordon, the Center's administrative officer, has been a key partner from the beginning. My research assistants—Bettina Prado, Ewan Stein, and, most especially, Natana De Long Bas and Muqtedar Khan—were extremely helpful. Cynthia Read remains a major reason why publishing with Oxford is a pleasure. Finally, as always, Jeanette Esposito, my partner and wife of thirty-four years, my parents, and my brothers remain my inspiration.

John L. Esposito
Washington, D.C.
October 1998

Preface to the
Second Edition

Events in the Muslim world and in the West continue to highlight the issue of an "Islamic threat" and of the role of Islam in international affairs. The secretary general of NATO caused a stir when he spoke of Islam as the new communism, a remark that brought criticism and a hasty retraction. The Islamic republics of Iran and Sudan, labeled terrorist by the United States, are portrayed as exporters of revolutionary Islam. In Turkey, long regarded as a secular, democratic model and an alternative to the Iranian model, the Islamist Welfare Party emerged as a powerful political force, sweeping municipal elections in Istanbul and Ankara, its capital. Prime Minister Tansu Ciller predicted that should the Islamists succeed in Turkey the "last fortress" would fall and "there will be a confrontation in the world."[1]

From Morocco and Egypt to Saudi Arabia and Malaysia, governments denounced religious extremism, both domestic and international. Muslim rulers as diverse as Egypt's President Hosni Mubarak and Libya's Muammar Qaddafi, Saudi Arabia's King Fahd and Malaysia's Prime Minister Dr. Mahathir Mohamad, all challenged domestically by Islamic opposition, were critical of radical Islamist movements. Many Muslim leaders warned of the betrayal of moderate Islam by those who manipulated and distorted its true teachings. Dr. Mahathir, on the occasion of Id al-Fitra, the feast marking the end of Ramadan, declared that Islam practices moderation and not force, warning that " 'Muslims should be wary of fanatics who may appear to be promoting Islam . . . fanatics merely help to weaken Muslims and their countries. . . . Fanaticism is not the Islamic way. Islam practices moderation and places great appreciation on intellectual capabilities. And force is not the way to spread Islam.' "[2]

From Algeria and Bosnia to Central Asia, Pakistan and Kashmir, Islam continues to be a factor in international politics. Islamic organizations and political parties in Algeria, Egypt, Jordan, Turkey, and Kuwait have proven to be their countries' most potent political opposition. In Afghanistan, where mujahidin militias had successfully defeated Soviet occupation but then engaged in a seemingly endless fratricidal war, the *Taliban*, a new Islamic militia of mullahs and seminary (*madrasa*) students, mysteriously emerged and quickly won popular support in their quest to "purify" and restore peace and security.

Militants have continued to challenge governments and society. Islamists in Algeria (the Armed Islamic Group) and Egypt (the Gamaa Islamiyya) have been locked in confrontations with government militia and security forces. In the West Bank and Gaza, attacks by Hamas and Jihad have threatened the PLO–Israeli Peace Accords. Radical groups in Algeria, Egypt, Israel/Palestine, and Pakistan have waged battles in which other Muslims and non-Muslim citizens as well as foreigners have been victims, killed in streets and cafés, schools, and mosques.

In Europe and America, fear of the export of "Islamic fundamentalism" and its threat to domestic security has captured media attention and at times reinforced the image of Islam as a demographic threat. Among the more prominent incidents have been the convictions in the 1993 World Trade Center bombing and the subsequent trial of Shaykh Umar Abd al-Rahman and alleged co-conspirators, charged in New York with plotting to wage a war of urban terrorism against the United States; the hijacking of an Air France plane in Algeria and alleged plan to blow it up over Paris; the arrest of some fifty activists, reputedly linked to Algerian extremists who "were planning a terrorist attack somewhere in Europe."[3] Western fears of militant Islam seemed further confirmed by Samuel Huntington's "The Clash of Civilizations" in *Foreign Affairs*, which was also published in a one page synopsis as an op-ed article in prominent newspapers such as *The New York Times* and *The International Herald Tribune*.[4] The debate over a clash of civilizations has received widespread attention not only in the United States and Europe but also, and especially, in the Muslim world, where many saw this publication by a prominent member of the academic establishment as yet further proof of the West's true attitude toward Islam and the Muslim world. The topic remains a major theme in the media and in conferences across the Muslim world and in Muslim communities in the West.

Western governments have continued to be criticized by many Muslims for their double standard in promoting democracy with enthusiasm in the West but very selectively in the Muslim world. The impotence of Western responses to Bosnia and Chechnya seemed to overshadow that of Muslim governments and the Organization of the Islamic Conference in the rhetoric of Muslim critics. European and American leaders were often caught between the demands and expectations of Muslim allies and their Islamist opposition: the Algerian military, Hosni Mubarak, and Tunisia's Zeine Abedin Ben Ali versus the Islamic Salvation Front, the Muslim Brotherhood, and the Renaissance Party. Western policymakers continued to struggle with the policies of the past and the need to forge a political vision which incorporates both entrenched ruling elites and authentic populist opposition.

This second edition of *The Islamic Threat: Myth or Reality?* is occasioned by the continued relevance of the debate over the nature of political Islam, and its strength and significance in Muslim politics and in international affairs. In particular, it incorporates a new case study on Algeria in chapter 5 and a more extended assessment of Islam and the West in light of continued talk of an Islamic threat and of the implications of a clash of civilizations domestically and internationally.

The need for better understanding of Islam and of Muslim politics is as great as ever. In the midst of explosive headline events and acts of violence not only in the Muslim world but also now in the West, the temptation remains to view Islam through the prism of religious extremism and terrorism. The demonization of a great religious tradition due to the perverted actions of a minority of dissident and distorted voices remains the real threat, a threat that not only impacts on relations between the Muslim world and the West but also upon growing Muslim populations in the West itself.

Publication of this Second Edition provides the opportunity to acknowledge the importance of two institutions. Both in the development and completion of *The Islamic Threat* and in that of *The Oxford Encyclopedia of the Modern Islamic World*, the College of the Holy Cross and Georgetown University have provided supportive contexts for my work. The creation of the Center for Muslim–Christian Understanding: History and International Affairs in the Edmund A. Walsh School of Foreign Service at Georgetown University in 1993 through the insight of Hasib Sabbagh and the Fondation pour l'Entente entre Chretiens et Muslmans, Geneva and the commitment of President Leo J. O'Donovan, S. J. of Georgetown University has made possible a more systematic and programmatic approach to understanding the historic relationship of Islam and Christianity, the Muslim world and the West. The strong support of Georgetown's Dean Peter F. Krogh and Dr. Patrick A. Heelan, A. J., Executive Vice President as well as Sana Sabbagh and Basel Aql of the Foundation has been critical to our success. Through its teaching, research, and public affairs programs, the Center brings together scholars and students, government officials and policymakers, religious and corporate leaders, the media and general public. It explores Muslim–Christian relations and the role of religion in international affairs, countering those who would demonize Islam and strengthening bridges of understanding and communication between the Muslim world and the West.

Washington, D.C.
March 1995

NOTES

1. John Darnton, "Islamic Fundamentalism is on the Rise in Turkey," *International Herald Tribune*, March 3, 1995, p. 2.
2. "PM: Be Wary of Fanatics," *New Straits Times*, March 3, 1994.
3. "Muslim Activists Held in London," *New Straits Times* (Malaysia), March 3, 1993, p. 22.
4. For a discussion and critique of Huntington's position, see chapter ix.

Preface to the
Paperback Edition

In the time that has elapsed since the publication of *The Islamic Threat: Myth or Reality?*, much has happened. In Bosnia, Serbian militias have overrun Bosnia and Herzegovina in a war that has witnessed the use of "ethnic cleansing" and rape of Muslim women as political weapons while the outside world stood by seemingly impotent. In India, Hindu "fundamentalists" destroyed a disputed mosque in Avodya, triggering widespread rioting and Hindu-Muslim communal bloodshed throughout India. Some 396 members of Hamas (the Islamic Resistance Group) were expelled from Gaza by Israel to survive in a no-man's-land in southern Lebanon.

Fear of a growing Islamic threat has become more common both in response to political events and as a rationale for state actions. The Serbian leader Slobodan Milosevic spoke of Serbia's defense today, as in the past, against the spread of Islam across Europe. Israeli leaders maintain that as Israel had been a defense against the spread of communism, so today its strategic importance is as a bulwark against the spread of Islamic radicalism or fundamentalism. Israel's Prime Minister Yitzak Rabin declared, "We stand first today in the line of fire against the danger of extremist Islam."[1] Governments in the Muslim world give voice to similar concerns about a regional and global "fundamentalist threat." These concerns have been a major item on the agenda of Arab rulers and their interior ministers, particularly in Algeria, Tunisia, and Egypt, where a more coordinated strategy both in rhetoric and security measures has been attempted against what Tunisia's President Zine Abidine Ben Ali has called the "fundamentalist international" which, it is charged, is financed through Iran and Sudan.[2]

The Egyptian government used a major show of force against extremists (al-Gamaa al-Islamiya, the Islamic Group) who are said to have received inspiration from the teachings of Shaykh Umar Abd al-Rahman, a religious leader tried but acquitted for involvement in the assassination of Anwar Sadat. These extremists have killed Coptic Christians, vandalized and burned their churches and property, and attacked foreign tourists in an attempt to cripple Egypt's economy and thus hasten the fall of the Mubarak government.

Government nervousness at the growing strength of political Islam has often blurred its previously held distinction between moderate and extremist groups. The electoral victory of Egypt's Muslim Brotherhood in professional syndicates, especially the long-time liberal-dominated Lawyer's Syndicate, reinforced the fears of the government and many Egyptian elites that the growing strength of the Brotherhood as a social and political force could eventually lead to another Algeria. Tunisia and Algeria continued to pursue a policy of mass arrests to crush their Islamic opposition, drawing stiff criticism from international human rights organizations. Both governments held mass trials of Islamic activists in the summer of 1992, sentencing many to prison while human and legal rights groups denounced the conduct of the trials.

American awareness and concern about an Islamic threat took a major turn in March 1993. In New York, the bombing of the World Trade Center brought charges that Muslim fundamentalists, inspired by Shaykh Umar Abd al-Rahman who had left Egypt and was living in the New York area, committed their act with support from Iran. For the first time it seemed as if the wrath of the Islamic threat had been brought to the shores of the "Great Satan."

While some warned of the danger of projecting an Islamic threat, many academic analysts and political commentators in Israel and the U.S. increasingly warned of the global threat of Islamic fundamentalism to the West and questioned the compatibility of Islam and Arab culture with democracy, in articles such as: "Beware of Religious Stalinists,"[3] "By Peace or the Sword,"[4] "Israel Sees Self Defending West Again,"[5] "Wishful Thinking About Islamic Fundamentalism,"[6] "Fundamental Questions About Islam,"[7] "Islam vs. Democracy,"[8] and "Islam and Liberal Democracy."[9] Some columnists echoed Israeli and Egyptian charges that the U.S. and the West had become bases for Muslim extremists: "Britain and the U.S.— have become bases for extremists seeking to turn Islam into an aggressive political movement."[10] Others charged that Iran was the "center of the world's new Comintern" and that this "new threat is as evil as the old Evil Empire."[11] The House Republican Research Committee produced a report, "Task Force on Terrorism & Unconventional Warfare," which seemed to epitomize the hysteria of the times, asserting that the Bosnian president was a member of a worldwide radical Islamic movement which enjoyed support from Iran, that Bosnian youth were trained in schools for "radical mullahs" in the Middle East, that Belgrade in the 1980s had recognized that it too had become a base for Islamic terrorism, and that the growing Muslim populations of Europe signaled future acts of terrorism by European Islamists who "have good organization and state support."[12]

The World Trade Center bombing and attacks on Egyptian tourists eclipsed the plight of Muslims in Bosnia and other parts of the world and brought a new focus on the dangers of "Islamic fundamentalism" as a global threat as many speculated about future attacks in America and Europe. The fallout has again been a tendency to equate violence with Islam, to fail to distinguish between illegitimate use of religion by individuals and the faith and practice of the majority of the world's Muslims who, like their fellow believers in other religious traditions, believe in a religion of peace. Many failed to make the same distinctions with regard to Islam and Islamic organizations between the actions of a radical minority and the mainstream majority that were made so easily when, at roughly the same time, the world watched the Branch Davidian sect, an extremist "Christian" group in Waco, Texas, kill FBI agents and, protected by an astonishing arsenal of weapons, hold off federal authorities for weeks.

Religious extremism remains a threat today as in the past, but it is not restricted to or inherent in any one religion. The spector of attacks by terrorists motivated by ethnic, religious, or ideological beliefs and grievances is real. The challenge today, as in the past, is to avoid the easy answers yielded by stereotyping or the projection of a monolithic threat, to distinguish between the beliefs and activities of the majority (whether they be Hindus, Muslims, and Sikhs, Christians and Jews, Arabs and Israelis, Tamils and Buddhists) and a minority of extremists who justify their aggression and violence in the name of religion, ethnicity, or political ideology. It is equally important to distinguish between the aspirations and demands of legitimate political opposition groups and those of extremist groups.

There are lessons to be learned from a past in which fear of a monolithic Soviet threat often blinded us to the humanity, values, and aspirations and diversity of the majority; led to uncritical support for regimes as long as they remained allies in the Cold War; enabled an easy acceptance of authoritarianism and the suppression of the legitimate dissent of any whose governments and security forces labeled them communist or socialist. The Muslim world like many parts of the world is diverse and in a period of transformation. The conduct and record of governments and elites are often challenged from within as well as without. The reassertion of Islam in public life and politics seemingly challenges many of the secular presuppositions and political alliances of the past. If we are to understand and respond to the challenge of political Islam, its diverse manifestations must be seen within the multiplicity of intellectual and political contexts in which it occurs. While the threats of extremism and violence must be countered forcefully and effectively, the long-term relations of the West with the Muslim world—like the legitimacy of governments within the Muslim world—will hinge on its response to the emergence of new social and political forces and its respect for their legitimate aspirations for greater political participation, social justice, and human rights.

I wrote *The Islamic Threat: Myth or Reality?* to address a significant issue in the political development of the Middle East and in relations between the Muslim world and the West. I also hoped to initiate a dialogue among scholars and policymakers. I am grateful to those who have in their comments and reviews indicated the usefulness of the book and equally to those critics who have responded to my desire to elicit a discussion of issues that are important to us all.

Wayland, Mass.   J. L. E.
June 1993

NOTES

1. Clyde Haberman, "Gunfire Stops Arab Deportees From Going Back to the Israeli Zone," *The New York Times*, December 22, 1992, p. A 1.

2. Youssef Ibrahim, "Arabs in North Africa Wage Deadly Fight With Islamic Militants," *The International Herald Tribune*, August 4, 1992, p. 1.

3. Morton Zuckerman, "Beware of Religious Stalinists," *U.S. News and World Report*, March 22, 1993, p. 80.

4. E. McQuaid, "By Peace or the Sword," *The Jerusalem Post*, December 16, 1992.

5. Michael Parks, "Israel Sees Self Defending West Again," *Los Angeles Times*, January 2, 1993, p. A 22.

6. Amos Perlmutter, "Wishful Thinking About Islamic Fundamentalism," *The Washington Post*, January 19, 1991, p. 16.

7. Daniel Pipes, "Fundamental Questions About Islam," *The Wall Street Journal*, Oct. 30, 1992, p. A 11.

8. Martin Kramer, "Islam vs. Democracy," *Commentary* 95, no. 1 (January 1993).

9. Bernard Lewis, "Islam and Liberal Democracy," *Atlantic Monthly*, February 1993, pp. 89–94.

10. William Safire, "Islam Under Seige," *The New York Times*, March 18, 1993, p. A 23.

11. Charles Krauthammer, "Iran: Orchestrator of Disorder," *Washington Post*, January 1, 1993, p. A 19.

12. *Task Force on Terrorism & Unconventional Warfare*, House Republican Research Committee, September 1992, p. 3.

Preface

This is a book I never intended to write. However, over the years I have become increasingly aware that a series of world events—particularly those stretching from the Ayatollah Khomeini and the Iranian revolution to Saddam Hussein and the Gulf War—have reinforced mutually destructive stereotypes in the Muslim world and in the West. The underlying presuppositions in many of the questions put to me at conferences and speaking engagements across the country and in various media exemplified this problem. Whether in university lectures, community talks, or government briefings on Islam or on Muslim politics, images of a militant Islam would surface, of a faith that is regarded as particularly prone to religious extremism, fanaticism, and warfare. For many, the Ayatollah Khomeini and Saddam Hussein epitomized a decade of radical Islamic fundamentalism, militant and anti-Western, seen as part of a centuries-long historical pattern. This popular attitude was also reflected in articles by prominent political commentators. As I looked toward the postwar period and the inevitable issue of the creation of a New World Order as well as the growing populist calls within the Muslim world for greater political liberalization and democratization, I felt a pressing need to address the issue of an Islamic threat and to place it in historical perspective.

Although I have published many books, this one has been both the easiest and most difficult to write: easy because it grows out of and builds upon previous studies of contemporary Islam in general and Islamic revivalism or fundamentalism in particular; difficult because the mere mention of the topic conjures up strongly held convictions, deep resentments, and fears. Like it or not, the history of relations between Muslims and Christians, between the Muslim world and the West, both in the past and the present, has been marked by episodes of confrontation and conflict.

This book will have its admirers and detractors, with few readers not taking sides.

For many in the West for whom Islam self-evidently refers to an aggressive, hostile, and anti-American religious tradition and people, this volume will appear too uncritical, seemingly unaware of the "Sword of Islam." For others, who dismiss all negative judgments about Muslim activities as simply the result of neoimperialism and anti-Islamic sentiment, the highlighting of authoritarianism and violence in the name of Islam will be disturbing.

The reader should be forewarned that a certain selectivity of coverage and a degree of generalization are unavoidable. Since the purpose of this book is to address the question of whether there is an Islamic threat to the West and to explore related questions—the sources of confrontation and conflict; the nature of Islamic fundamentalism; the reasons for the perception of Islam as a threat to the West and of the West as a threat to the Muslim world, and its impact and implications for U.S. policy—this study will necessarily look at those aspects of Islamic religion, history, and politics that are directly relevant. Thus in discussing the historical record of confrontation and conflict between Islam and Christianity, or between the Muslim world and the West, I will rarely focus on the positive history of Muslim–Christian relations. At many points generalizations and stereotypes will be employed simply because they are part of the history and perceptions of two world civilizations. Sadly, both in the past and the present, religious and secular biases and historical experiences have produced a set of stereotypes that resurface in times of conflict, Crusader versus jihadist, or the modern, developed, secular, rational Western mind versus the traditional, underdeveloped, religious, emotional, irrational Muslim mind.

I will argue throughout this book that we must move beyond a monolithic worldview that sees Muslims and the Muslim world (both governments and social movements) as a unity. Similarly, Europe or the West should also be appreciated in their diversity and complexity. Yet since both sides tend to consider and talk about each other as a bloc, the language of "Islam" and the "West" will of necessity be employed at times.

A number of colleagues have been generous with their time in reviewing earlier drafts of this book. James P. Piscatori, Yvonne Y. Haddad, John O. Voll, and Tamara Sonn read the entire manuscript. John Entelis and David Long commented on chapter 6. Although they bear no responsibility for my opinions and judgments, all played a significant role in offering advice and encouragement. The College of the Holy Cross once again provided a much-needed year-long research grant. Cynthia A. Read is the kind of editor every author hopes for. She and her colleagues at Oxford University Press embody the highest standards of excellence. My wife, Jean, has been both a constant source of encouragement throughout the years and my most demanding critic.

In the coming decade Muslim politics will remain fragile and combustible, as will Muslim relations with the West. The Muslim world continues to expand beyond the more than forty-five Muslim nations. In addition, Muslim populations continue to grow in the former Soviet Union, China, India, Europe, and the United States. In an increasingly interdependent world, it becomes even more imperative to deal with political realities dispassionately and constructively and to transcend stereotypes.

Wayland, Mass.   J. L. E.
January 1992

The Islamic Threat

Introduction

> There are a good many people who think that the war between communism and the West is about to be replaced by a war between the West and Muslims.
>
> WILLIAM PFAFF, "Help Algeria's Fundamentalists,"
> *The New Yorker*, January 28, 1991

Are Islam and the West on an inevitable collision course? Are Islamic fundamentalists medieval fanatics? Are Islam and democracy incompatible? Is Islamic fundamentalism a threat to stability in the Muslim world and to American interests in the region? These are critical questions for our times that come from a history too often marked by mutual distrust and conflict.

From the Ayatollah Khomeini to Saddam Hussein and the Taliban in Afghanistan, for almost two decades the vision of Islamic fundamentalism or militant Islam as a threat to the West has gripped the imaginations of Western governments and the media. Khomeini's denunciation of America as the "Great Satan," chants of "Death to America," the condemnation of Salman Rushdie and his *Satanic Verses*, and Saddam Hussein's call for a jihad against foreign infidels reinforced images of Islam as a militant, expansionist religion, rabidly anti-American and intent upon war with the West.

Despite many common theological roots and beliefs, throughout history Muslim–Christian relations have often been overshadowed by conflict as the armies and missionaries of Islam and Christendom have struggled for power and for souls. This confrontation has involved such events as the defeat of the early Byzantine (Eastern Roman) empire by Islam in the seventh century; the fierce battles and polemics of the Crusades during the eleventh and twelfth centuries; the expulsion of the Moors from Spain and

1

the Inquisition; the Ottoman threat to Europe; European (Christian) colonial expansion and domination in the eighteenth and nineteenth centuries; the political and cultural challenge of the superpowers (America and the Soviet Union) in the latter half of the twentieth century; the creation of the state of Israel; the competition of Christian and Muslim missionaries for converts today; and the contemporary reassertion of Islam in politics.

"Islamic fundamentalism" has often been regarded as a major threat to the regional stability of the Middle East and to Western interests in the broader Muslim world.[1] The Iranian Revolution, attacks on Western embassies, hijackings and hostage taking, and violent acts by groups with names like the Army of God (Jund Allah), Holy War (al-Jihad), the Party of God (Hizbullah), and Salvation from Hell have all signaled a militant Islam on a collision course with the West. Uprisings in the Muslim republics of the former Soviet Union, in Kosovo in Yugoslavia, in Kashmir, in Sinkiang in China, and on the West Bank and in Gaza, and Saddam Hussein's attempted annexation of Kuwait, have reinforced images of an expansive and potentially explosive Islam in global politics.

With the triumph of the democratization movement in Eastern Europe and the breakup of the Soviet empire, Islam constitutes the most pervasive and powerful transnational force in the world, with one billion adherents spread out across the globe. Muslims are a majority in some 56 countries ranging from Africa to Southeast Asia, and they exist in growing and significant numbers in the United States, the former Soviet Union, and Europe. For a Western world long accustomed to a global vision and foreign policy predicated upon superpower rivalry for global influence if not dominance—a U.S.–Soviet conflict often portrayed as a struggle between good and evil, capitalism and communism—it has been all too tempting to identify another global ideological menace to fill the "threat vacuum" created by the demise of communism.

However diverse in reality, the existence of Islam as a worldwide religion and ideological force embracing more than one-fifth of the world's population, and its continued vitality and power in a Muslim world stretching from Africa to Southeast Asia, will continue to raise the specter of an Islamic threat. At the dawn of the twenty-first century it is important that the vacuum created by the end of the Cold War not be filled by exaggerated fears of Islam as a resurgent "evil empire" at war with the New World Order and a challenge to global stability: "No matter how and when the war ends, Islamic rage already threatens the stability of traditionally pro-Western regimes from Morocco to Jordan to Pakistan."[2] Belief that a clash of worldviews, values, and civilizations is leading to an impending confrontation between Islam and the West is reflected in headlines and articles with ominous titles like these: "Still Fighting the Crusades,'' "The New Crescent in Crisis: The Global Intifada,'' "Rising Islam May Overwhelm the West,'' "The Roots of Muslim Rage,'' "The Islamic War Against Modernity,'' and the "Arc of Crisis: The Clash of Civilizations.'' While such phrases capture public attention and the popular imagination, they exaggerate and distort the nature of Islam, the political realities of the Muslim world and its diverse relations with the West. They also reinforce an astonishing degree of ignorance and cultural stereotyping of Arabs and Islam. For many in the West it has been axiomatic that Arabs are nomads or oil shaykhs, denizens of the desert and harems, an emotional, combative, and irrational people. Islam is often equated with holy war and hatred, fanaticism and violence, intolerance and the oppression of women.

As Western leaders attempted to forge the New World Order, transnational Islam increasingly came to be regarded as the new global, monolithic enemy of the West: "To some Americans, searching for a new enemy against whom to test our mettle and power, after the death of communism, Islam is the preferred antagonist. But, to declare Islam an enemy of the United States is to declare a second Cold War that is unlikely to end in the same resounding victory as the first.''[3] Fear of the Green Menace (green being the color of Islam) may well replace that of the Red Menace of world communism.

Islam and Islamic movements constitute a religious and ideological alternative or challenge and in some instances a potential danger to Christianity and the West. However, distinguishing between a religious or ideological alternative or challenge and a direct political threat requires walking the fine line between myth and reality, between the unity of Islam and the diversity of its multiple and complex manifestations in the world today, between the violent actions of the few and the legitimate aspirations and policies of the many. Unfortunately, American policymakers, like the media, have too often proved surprisingly myopic, viewing the Muslim world and Islamic movements as a monolith and seeing them solely in terms of extremism and terrorism. While this is understandable in light of events in Iran and Lebanon and the Gulf crisis of 1990–91, it fails to do justice to the complex realities of the Muslim world and can undermine relations between the West and Islam.

The Islamic Threat: Myth or Reality? will place the challenge or threat of Islam in perspective, and discuss the vitality of Islam as a global force and the history of its relations with the West. Case studies of Muslim countries and Islamic movements will demonstrate the diversity in geography, politics, ideological and organizational orientation, tactics, and foreign policy of the Islamic resurgence.

Finally, the issues facing Islam and the West in the nineties and the potential challenge or threat of Islam to the West will be explored in light of the Salman Rushdie affair, the Gulf War of 1990–91, the New World Order, and the challenge of democratization in the Muslim world. Do the West and the Muslim world share common interests and values or does a clash of worldviews loom on the horizon? Is the drive for liberalization and democracy in the Muslim world by Islamic movements merely a tactical means to an end? What would the implications of Islamic societies be with regard to pluralism, human rights, and the status of women and minorities? How can U.S. policy transform the specter of an Islamic threat into the pursuit of a common global future?

The Economist put these issues in perspective in 1990 in an imaginary dialogue between a Christian and a Muslim religious leader who spoke as follows:

> It distresses me that so many people seem to think the next period of history will be a fight between your part of the world and mine. It is true that we live elbow to elbow with each other . . . it is also true that our elbows have banged painfully together many times in the past. But almost 2,000 years after the birth of your Jesus, and more than 1,400 years after the birth of our Muhammad, let me start by asking whether it really has to happen all over again.[4]

1

Contemporary Islam:
Reformation or Revolution?

Much of the reassertion of religion in politics and society has been subsumed under the term *Islamic fundamentalism*. Although "fundamentalism" is a common designation, in the press and increasingly among academics it is used in a variety of ways. For a number of reasons it tells us everything and yet, at the same time, nothing. First, all those who call for a return to foundational beliefs or the fundamentals of a religion may be called fundamentalist. In a strict sense this could include all practicing Muslims, who accept the Quran as the literal word of God and the Sunnah (example) of the Prophet Muhammad as a normative model for living.

Second, our understanding and perceptions of fundamentalism are heavily influenced by American Protestantism. *Webster's Tenth New Collegiate Dictionary* defines the term *fundamentalism*—as "a movement in 20th century Protestantism emphasizing the literally interpreted Bible as fundamental to Christian life and teaching." For many liberal or mainline Christians, "fundamentalist" is pejorative or derogatory, being applied rather indiscriminately to all those who advocate a literalist biblical position and thus are regarded as static, retrogressive, and extremist. As a result, fundamentalism often has been regarded popularly as referring to those who are literalists and wish to return to and replicate the past. In fact, few individuals or organizations in the Middle East fit such a stereotype. Indeed, many fundamentalist leaders have had the best education, enjoy responsible positions in society, and are adept at harnessing the latest technology to propagate their views and create viable modern institutions such as schools, hospitals, and social service agencies.

Third, "fundamentalism" is often equated with political activism, extremism, fanaticism, terrorism, and anti-Americanism. Yet while some engage in radical religiopolitics, most, as we shall see, work within the established order.

Perhaps the best way to appreciate the facile use of "fundamentalism" and its inadequacy (the many faces and postures of fundamentalism) is to consider the following. This term has been applied to the governments of Libya, Saudi Arabia, Pakistan, and Iran. Yet what does that really tell us about these states other than the fact that their rulers have appealed to Islam to legitimate their rule or policies? Muammar Qaddafi has claimed the right to interpret Islam, questioned the authenticity of the traditions of the Prophet Muhammad, silenced the religious establishment as well as the Muslim Brotherhood, and advocated a populist state of the masses. The rulers of Saudi Arabia, by contrast, have aligned themselves with the *ulama* (clergy), preached a more literalist and rigorous brand of Islam, and used religion to legitimate a conservative monarchy. Qaddafi's image as an unpredictable, independent supporter of worldwide terrorism stands in sharp relief beside the low-key, conservative, pro-American King Fahd. Similarly, contrast the foreign policy of the clerically run Shii state of Iran with the military, lay regime (1977–88) which implemented Pakistan's Islamic system (*nizam-i-Islam*) under Gen. Zia ul-Haq. Iran under the Ayatollah Khomeini was highly critical—even condemnatory—of the West, often at odds with the international community, and regarded as a radical terrorist state, while Pakistan under the Islamically oriented Zia ul-Haq was a close ally of the United States who enjoyed warm relations with the West and the international community and was generally regarded as moderate.

I regard "fundamentalism" as too laden with Christian presuppositions and Western stereotypes, as well as implying a monolithic threat that does not exist; more fitting general terms are "Islamic revivalism" or "Islamic activism," which are less value-laden and have roots within the Islamic tradition. In recent years, the terms "political Islam" and "Islamism" have become more common usage. Islam possesses a long tradition of revival (*tajdid*) and reform (*islah*) which includes notions of political and social activism dating from the early Islamic centuries to the present day.[1] Thus I prefer to speak of Islamic revivalism and Islamic activism rather than of Islamic fundamentalism.

The Resurrection of Religion:
Modernization and Development Theory Confounded

Just as European imperialism and colonialism had been based upon and legitimated by a modernity that was Western in its origins and forms, so too the development of non-Western regions including the Muslim world was based upon a theory of modernization that equated development with the progressive Westernization and secularization of society. In particular, secularization was regarded as a sine qua non for modernization: "Political development includes, as one of its basic processes, the secularization of polities, the progressive exclusion of religion from the political system."[2] Both the indigenous elites, who guided government development programs in newly emerging Muslim states, and their foreign patrons and advisers were Western-oriented and Western-educated. All proceeded from a premise that equated modernization with Westernization. The clear goal and presupposition of development was that every day and in every way things should become more modern (i.e., Western and secular), from cities, buildings, bureaucracies, companies, and schools to politics and culture. While some warned of the need to be selective, the desired direction and pace of change were unmistakable. Even those Muslims who spoke of selective change did so within a context which called for the separation of religion from public life. Western analysts and Muslim experts alike tended to regard a Western-based process of modernization as necessary and inevitable and believed equally that religion was a major hindrance to political and social change in the Muslim world.

The conceptual world which resulted was one of clear dichotomies: tradition versus change, fundamentalism versus modernism, stagnation versus progress and development. Science and technology were seen as powerful aids in this process of secular development. However, the reality proved to be far different from the ideal. Modernization as Westernization and secularization remained primarily the preserve of a small minority elite of society. Most important, the secularization of processes and institutions did not easily translate into the secularization of minds and culture. While a minority accepted and implemented a Western secular worldview, the majority of most Muslim populations did not internalize a secular outlook and values. Daniel Crecelius's perceptive observation regarding Egypt, long regarded as among the more modern Muslim societies, ran counter to the prevailing wisdom but proved true for most Muslim countries:

> Most studies on the process of modernization or secularism recognize the necessity for all systems by which man lives, the psychological and intellectual, no less than the political and economic, to undergo transformation. We do not find this change in Egypt, whether at the level of the state or society, except among a small minority of Westernized individuals. Traditional beliefs, practices, and values reign supreme among Egypt's teeming village population and among the majority of its urban masses. It should

be emphasized that adherence to tradition is not confined to any single class
or group of occupations, but is characteristic of a broad spectrum of all
Egyptian social classes.''[3]

For many, the contemporary revival of Islam challenged the received
wisdom and seemed to deal a death blow to reason and common sense.
The most forceful manifestations of the Islamic resurgence have occurred
in the more advanced and ''modernized'' (seemingly secular) countries of
the Muslim world such as Egypt, Iran, Lebanon, and Tunisia. In a very
real sense, Islamic revivalism has often been seen and experienced as a
direct threat to the ideas, beliefs, practices, and interests of Muslim secular
elites as well as Western governments and multinational corporations. This
clash of worldviews has reinforced the Western tendency to see Islamic
activism as extremism and fanaticism, as an antimodern return to the past
rather than the projection of an alternative vision for society. Because it
does not conform to modern secular presuppositions, to the West's most
cherished beliefs and values, Islamic activism is regarded as a dangerous,
irrational and countercultural movement.

Yet Islamic organizations have attracted the educated and professionals
(teachers, engineers, lawyers, scientists, bureaucrats, the military). Many
of the leaders of Islamic organizations are graduates of major universities
from faculties of medicine, science, and engineering. Modern technology
has been harnassed by conservative clergy and political activists alike to
organize and mobilize mass support as well as disseminate their message
of religion and sociopolitical activism. The widespread use of radio, television, audio and videocassettes, computers, and fax machines has made
for a more effective communication of Islam nationally and transnationally. Thus technology and communications have purveyed not simply a
modern secular culture but also a revitalized and, at times, transnational
Islam. Religious leaders, who were initially resistant, have come to depend
upon modern technology. Village Muslims no longer live in relatively
isolated worlds solely dependent upon their local religious leaders for
knowledge of Islam. Television, radio, and audiocassettes now expose
them to a diversity of voices (preachers) and messages or interpretations
of Islam. Just as Christian televangelists can now preach their messages
not just to those in their parishes but to audiences from rural Oregon to
New York City and to peoples throughout the world, so too modern science and technology have been harnessed to preach the message of Islam.
Whereas in the past people were limited by the realities of time and space
and of language and government censorship, today Muslims throughout
the world have available to them inexpensive translations and recordings
of Islamic materials. They can be broadcast legally or easily shipped across

borders, as witnessed by the spread of the writings and sermons of Khomeini throughout Iran during the Shah's rule, or the availability of the writings and cassettes of popular preachers and activists throughout the world. Thus modernization has not simply led to progressive secularization but instead has been a major factor in the resurgence of Islam in Muslim societies.

The Islamic Resurgence

Islam reemerged as a potent global force in Muslim politics during the 1970s and 1980s.[4] The scope of the Islamic resurgence has been worldwide, embracing much of the Muslim world from the Sudan to Indonesia. Heads of Muslim governments as well as opposition groups increasingly appealed to religion for legitimacy and to mobilize popular support. Islamic activists have held cabinet-level positions in Jordan, the Sudan, Iran, Malaysia, and Pakistan. Islamic organizations constitute the leading opposition parties and organizations in Egypt, Tunisia, Algeria, Morocco, the West Bank and Gaza, and Indonesia. Where permitted, they have participated in elections and served in parliament and in city government. Islam has been a significant ingredient in nationalist struggles and resistance movements in Afghanistan, the Muslim republics of the former Soviet Central Asia, and Kashmir, and in the communal politics of Lebanon, India, Thailand, China, and the Philippines.

Islamically oriented governments have been counted among America's staunchest allies (Saudi Arabia and Pakistan) and most vitriolic enemies (Libya and Iran). Islamic activist organizations have run the spectrum from those who work within the system—such as the Muslim Brotherhoods in Egypt, Jordan, and the Sudan—to radical revolutionaries like Egypt's Society of Muslims (known more popularly as Takfir wal-Hijra, Excommunication and Flight) and al-Jihad (Holy War), or Lebanon's Hizbullah (Party of God) and Islamic Jihad, which have resorted to violence in their attempts to overthrow prevailing political systems.

Yet to speak of a contemporary Islamic revival can be deceptive, if this implies that Islam had somehow disappeared or been absent from the Muslim world. It is more correct to view Islamic revivalism as having led to a higher profile of Islam in Muslim politics and society. Thus what had previously seemed to be an increasingly marginalized force in Muslim public life reemerged in the seventies—often dramatically—as a vibrant sociopolitical reality. Islam's resurgence in Muslim politics reflected a growing religious revivalism in both personal and public life that would sweep across much of the Muslim world and have a substantial impact on the West in world politics.

The indices of an Islamic reawakening in personal life are many: increased attention to religious observances (mosque attendance, prayer, fasting), proliferation of religious programming and publications, more emphasis upon Islamic dress and values, the revitalization of Sufism (mysticism). This broader-based renewal has also been accompanied by Islam's reassertion in public life: an increase in Islamically oriented governments, organizations, laws, banks, social welfare services, and educational institutions. Both governments and opposition movements have turned to Islam to enhance their authority and muster popular support. Governmental use of Islam has been illustrated by a great spectrum of leaders in the Middle East and Asia: Libya's Muammar Qaddafi, Sudan's Gaafar Muhammad Nimeiri, Egypt's Anwar Sadat, Iran's Ayatollah Khomeini, Pakistan's Zia ul-Haq, Bangladesh's Muhammad Ershad, Malaysia's Muhammad Mahathir. Most rulers and governments, including more secular states such as Turkey and Tunisia, becoming aware of the potential strength of Islam, have shown increased sensitivity to and anxiety about Islamic issues. The Iranian Revolution of 1978–79 focused attention on "Islamic fundamentalism" and with it the spread and vitality of political Islam in other parts of the Muslim world. However, the contemporary revival has its origins and roots in the late sixties and early seventies, when events in such disparate areas as Egypt and Libya as well as Pakistan and Malaysia contributed to experiences of crisis and failure, as well as power and success, which served as catalysts for a more visible reassertion of Islam in both public and private life.

The Experience of Failure and the Quest for Identity

Several conflicts (e.g., the 1967 Arab–Israeli war, Chinese–Malay riots in Malaysia in 1969, the Pakistan–Bangladesh civil war of 1971, and the Lebanese civil war of the midseventies) illustrate the breadth and diversity of these turning points or catalysts for change. For many in the Arab and broader Muslim world, 1967 proved to be a year of catastrophe as well as a historic turning point. Israel's quick and decisive defeat of Arab forces in what was remembered as the Six-Day War, the Israeli capture and occupation of the Golan Heights, Sinai, Gaza, the West Bank, and East Jerusalem, constituted a devastating blow to Arab/Muslim pride, identity, and self-esteem. Most important, the loss of Jerusalem, the third holiest city of Islam, assured that Palestine and the liberation of Jerusalem would not be regarded as a regional (Arab) issue but rather as an Islamic cause throughout the Muslim world. The defense of Israel is dear to many Jews throughout the world. Likewise, for Muslims who retain a sense of membership in a transnational community of believers (the *ummah*), Palestine and the liberation of Jerusalem are strongly seen as issues of Islamic solidarity. As anyone who works in the Muslim world can attest, Israeli control of the West Bank, Gaza, and Jerusalem as well as U.S.–Israeli relations are topics of concern and bitter debate among Muslims from Nigeria and the Sudan to Pakistan and Malaysia, as well as among the Muslims of Europe and the United States.

The aftermath of the 1967 war, remembered in Arab literature as the "disaster," witnessed a sense of disillusionment and soul-searching that gripped both Western-oriented secular elites as well as the more Islamically committed, striking at their sense of pride, identity, and history.[5] Where had they gone wrong? Both the secular and the Islamically oriented sectors of society now questioned the effectiveness of nationalist ideologies, Western models of development, and Western allies who had persisted in supporting Israel. Despite several decades of independence and modernization, Arab forces (consisting of the combined military might of Egypt, Jordan, and Syria) had proved impotent. A common critique of the military, political, and sociocultural failures of Western-oriented development and a quest for a more authentic society and culture emerged— an Arab identity less dependent upon the West and rooted more indigenously in an Arab/Islamic heritage and values. Examples from Malaysia, Pakistan, and Lebanon reflect the turmoil and soul-searching that occurred in many parts of the Muslim world.

Because Islam is often equated with the Middle East, we tend to forget that the largest Muslim populations are to be found in Asia (Indonesia, Pakistan, Bangladesh, and India). Asia too proved to be a major theater for the growth of Islamic revivalism. In Southeast Asia, Chinese–Malay communal riots in Kuala Lumpur in 1969 signaled growing Malay Muslim discontent and alienation. Though dominant politically, Malay Muslims lagged behind the more prosperous urban-based Chinese (non-Muslim) minority. In response to charges that the Chinese enjoyed disproportionate economic and educational advantages, a perceived threat to Malay status and identity, the Malaysian government responded by implementing an affirmative action–like plan (*bhumiputra*, sons of the soil) of incentives and quotas to strengthen Malay Muslim life. Greater emphasis on Malay identity, language, values, and community contributed to the attraction and growth of Islamic revivalism in a culture where many regard it as axiomatic that to be Malay is to be Muslim.

The Pakistan–Bangladesh civil war in 1971 changed the map of South Asia when the Islamic Republic of Pakistan, established in 1947 as a

Muslim homeland, lost its eastern section. The loss of East Pakistan and its re-creation as Bangladesh raised serious questions about the nature (or perhaps better, the failure) of Pakistan's Islamic identity and ideology. At the same time Pres. Zulfikar Ali Bhutto, a secular socialist, for economic and strategic reasons increasingly appealed to Islam in the seventies to establish Pakistan's ties with its oil-rich Arab/Muslim brothers in the Gulf states, who offered economic aid, and revenue in the form of wages of Pakistani military and laborers hired to work in the Gulf. This tilt toward the Gulf unleashed a process in which Islam moved from the periphery to center stage as both the government and the opposition used it to legitimate their competing claims and to gain popular support.

In Lebanon the Shii Muslims, long a minority in a Christian-dominated system, increasingly called for greater political representation and socioeconomic reforms to better reflect demographic changes which had resulted in a Muslim majority. A charismatic religious leader, Imam Musa Sadr, appealed to Shii identity, history, and symbols to organize and mobilize members of the Shii community into what in the midseventies would become the Movement for the Dispossessed, more commonly known today as AMAL. In the aftermath of the Iranian revolution, Lebanon would see the rise of more radical Islamic groups such as Hizbullah (Party of God), equally concerned with issues of identity and power.

The forms that the Islamic revival has taken have varied almost infinitely from one country to another. However, there are recurrent themes: a sense that existing political, economic, and social systems had failed; a disenchantment with, and at times a rejection of, the West; a quest for identity and greater authenticity; and the conviction that Islam provides a self-sufficient ideology for state and society, a valid alternative to secular nationalism, socialism, and capitalism.

The experience of failure triggered an identity crisis which led many to question the direction of political and social development and to turn inward for strength and guidance. The Western-oriented policies of governments and elites appeared to have failed. The soul-searching and critique of the sociopolitical realities of the Arab and Muslim world, which followed the 1967 war and the crises in Pakistan, Malaysia, and Lebanon, extended to other Muslim areas, embraced a broad spectrum of society, and raised many questions about the direction and accomplishments of development. More often than not, despite the hopes aroused by independence, the mixed record of several decades of existence was a challenge to the legitimacy and effectiveness of modern Muslim states. A crisis mentality fostered by specific events and the general impact and disruption of modernity spawned a growing disillusionment, a sense of failure.

Politically, modern secular nationalism was found wanting. Neither liberal nationalism nor Arab nationalism/socialism had fulfilled its promises. Muslim governments seemed less interested and successful in establishing their political legitimacy and creating an ideology for national unity than in perpetuating autocratic rule. The Muslim world was still dominated by monarchs and military or ex-military rulers, political parties were banned or restricted, and elections were often rigged. Parliamentary systems of government and political parties existed at the sufferance of rulers whose legitimacy, like their security, depended on a loyal military and secret police. Many were propped up by and dependent upon foreign governments and multinational corporations as well.

Charges of corruption and of concentration and maldistribution of wealth found a ready reception as one looked at individual countries and the region. The disparity between rich and poor was striking in urban areas, where the neighborhoods and new suburbs of the wealthy few stood in stark contrast to the deteriorating dwellings and sprawling shantytowns of the many. The vast chasm between rich and poor was even more pronounced between Arab oil states, which ironically tended to be among the least populated countries (Kuwait, Saudi Arabia, the Emirates) and the greater number of poor, densely populated countries (Egypt, Syria, Pakistan, Bangladesh). Both Western capitalism and Marxist socialism were rejected as being part of the problem rather than the solution, as having failed to redress widespread poverty and maldistribution of wealth. Capitalism was regarded as the system of special interests and new elites which produced a society more driven by materialism and conspicuous consumption than concern for equity and social justice. Marxism was dismissed as a godless alternative which struck at the heart of religion, substituting the material for the spiritual. Young people in particular found themselves in a world of shattered dreams which offered a dim future. In many countries idealism, study, and hard work were rewarded by unemployment or underemployment, housing shortages, and a lack of political participation which increased the sense of frustration and hopelessness.[6]

Socioculturally and psychologically, modernization was seen as a legacy of European colonialism perpetuated by Western-oriented elites who imposed and fostered the twin processes of Westernization and secularization. Just as dependence on Western models of development was seen as the cause of political and military failures, so, too, some Muslims charged, blind imitation of the West and an uncritical Westernization of Muslim societies which some called the disease of "westoxification" led to a cultural dependence which threatened the loss of Muslim identity. The resultant process of secular, "valueless" social change was identified as the cause of sociomoral decline, a major contributor to the breakdown of the Muslim family, more permissive and promiscuous societies, and spiritual malaise.

The psychological impact of modernity, and with it rapid sociocultural change, cannot be forgotten. Urban areas had undergone physical and institutional changes, so that both the skylines and the infrastructure of cities were judged to be modern by virtue of their Western profile and façade. To be modern was to be Western in dress, language, ideas, education, behavior (from table manners to greetings), architecture, and furnishings. Urban areas became the primary locations and showplaces for work and living. Modern governments and companies as well as foreign advisers and investors focused on urban areas, so that the results of modernization only trickled down to rural areas. Rapid urbanization therefore meant the migration of many from outlying villages and towns. The hopes of the poor for a better life were often undermined by the realities of poverty in urban slums and shantytowns. Psychological as well as physical displacement occurred. Loss of village, town, and extended family ties and traditional values were accompanied by the shock of modern urban life and its Westernized culture and mores. Many, swept along in a sea of alienation and marginalization, found an anchor in religion. Islam offered a sense of identity, fraternity, and cultural values that offset the psychological dislocation and cultural threat of their new environment. Both the poor in their urban neighborhoods, which approximated traditional ghettos in the midst of modern cities, and those in the lower middle class who took advantage of the new educational and job opportunities of the city and thus experienced culture shock more profoundly and regularly, found a welcome sense of meaning and security in a religious revivalism. Islamic organizations' workers and message offered a more familiar alternative which was consistent with their experience, identified their problems, and offered a time-honored solution.

Finally, American ignorance of and hostility toward Islam and the Middle East, often critiqued as a "Christian Crusader" mentality influenced by Orientalism and Zionism, were blamed for misguided U.S. political-military policies: support for the "un-Islamic" Shah of Iran, massive military and economic funding of Israel, and the backing of an unrepresentative Christian-controlled government in Lebanon.

These crises and failures reinforced a prevailing Muslim sense of inferiority, the product of centuries of European colonial dominance, which left a legacy of both admiration of Western power, science, and technology and resentment of Western dominance, penetration, and exploitation.[7] The failures of the modern experience stood in sharp contrast to an Islamic ideal which linked the faithfulness of the Islamic community with worldly success, as witnessed by the memory of a past history in which Islam was a dominant world power and civilization.

From Failure to Success

During the seventies Islamic politics seemed to explode on the scene, as events in the Middle East (the Egyptian–Israeli war and the Arab oil embargo of 1973, as well as the Iranian Revolution of 1978–79) shocked many into recognition of a powerful new force that threatened Western interests. Heads of state and opposition movements appealed to Islam to enhance their legitimacy and popular support; Islamic organizations and institutions proliferated.

In 1973 Egypt's Anwar Sadat initiated a "holy war" against Israel. In contrast to the 1967 Arab–Israeli war which was fought by Gamal Abdel Nasser in the name of Arab nationalism/socialism, this war was fought under the banner of Islam. Sadat generously employed Islamic symbols and history to rally his forces. Despite their loss of the war, the relative success of Egyptian forces led many Muslims to regard it as a moral victory, since most had believed that a U.S.-backed Israel could not be beaten.

Military vindication in the Middle East was accompanied by economic muscle, the power of the Arab oil boycott. For the first time since the dawn of colonialism, the West had to contend with and acknowledge, however begrudgingly, its dependence on the Middle East. For many in the Muslim world the new wealth, success, and power of the oil-rich countries seemed to indicate a return of the power of Islam to a community whose centuries-long political and cultural ascendance had been shattered by European colonialism and, despite independence, by second-class status in a superpower-dominated world. A number of factors enhanced the Islamic character of oil power. Most of the oil wealth was located in the Arab heartland, where Muhammad had received the revelation of the Quran and established the first Islamic community-state. The largest deposits were found in Saudi Arabia, a self-styled Islamic state which had asserted its role as keeper of the holy cities of Mecca and Medina, protector of the annual pilgrimage (*hajj*), and leader and benefactor of the Islamic world. The House of Saud used its oil wealth to establish numerous international Islamic organizations, promote the preaching and spread of Islam, support Islamic causes, and subsidize Islamic activities undertaken by Muslim governments.

No event demonstrated more dramatically the power of a resurgent Islam than the Iranian Revolution of 1978–79. For many in the West and

the Muslim world, the unthinkable became a reality. The powerful, modernizing, and Western-oriented regime of the Shah came crashing down.
This was an oil-rich Iran whose wealth had been used to build the best-
equipped military in the Middle East (next to Israel's) and to support an
ambitious modernization program, the Shah's White Revolution. Assisted
by Western-trained elites and advisers, the Shah had governed a state
which the United States regarded as its most stable ally in the Muslim
world. The fact that a revolution against him and against the West was
effectively mounted in the name of Islam, organizing disparate groups and
relying upon the mullah–mosque network for support, generated euphoria
among many in the Muslim world and convinced Islamic activists that
these were lessons for success to be emulated. Strength and victory would
belong to those who pursued change in the name of Islam, whatever the
odds and however formidable the regime.

For many in the broader Muslim world, the successes of the seventies
resonated with an idealized perception of early Islam, the Islamic paradigm
to be found in the time of the Prophet Muhammad, the Golden Age of
Islam. Muhammad's successful union of disparate tribal forces under the
banner of Islam, his creation of an Islamic state and society in which social
justice prevailed, and the extraordinary early expansion of Islam were
primal events to be remembered and, as the example of the Iranian Revolution seemingly verified, to be successfully emulated by those who adhered to Islam. Herein lies the initial attraction of the Iranian Revolution
for many Muslims, Sunni and Shii alike. Iran provided the first example
of a modern Islamic revolution, a revolt against impiety, oppression, and
injustice. The call of the Ayatollah Khomeini for an Islamic revolution
struck a chord among many who identified with his message of anti-
imperialism, his condemnation of failed, unjust, and oppressive regimes,
and his vision of a morally just society.

By contrast, the West stood incredulous before this challenge to the
Shah's "enlightened" development of his seemingly backward nation, and
the resurrection of an anachronistic, irrational medieval force that threatened to hurtle modern Iran back to the Middle Ages. Nothing symbolized
this belief more than the black-robed, bearded mullahs and the dour coun-
tenance of their leader, the Ayatollah Khomeini, who dominated the media,
reinforcing in Western minds the irrational nature of the entire movement.

The Ideological Worldview of Islamic Revivalism

At the heart of the revivalist worldview is the belief that the Muslim world
is in a state of decline. Its cause is departure from the straight path of

Islam; its cure, a return to Islam in personal and public life which will ensure the restoration of Islamic identity, values, and power. For Islamic political activists Islam is a total or comprehensive way of life as stipulated in the Quran, God's revelation, mirrored in the example of Muhammad and the nature of the first Muslim community-state, and embodied in the comprehensive nature of the Sharia, God's revealed law. Thus the revitalization of Muslim governments and societies requires the reimplementation of Islamic law, the blueprint for an Islamically guided and socially just state and society.

While Westernization and secularization of society are condemned, modernization as such is not. Science and technology are accepted, but the pace, direction, and extent of change are to be subordinated to Islamic belief and values in order to guard against the penetration of Western values and excessive dependence on them.

Radical movements go beyond these principles and often operate according to two basic assumptions. They assume that Islam and the West are locked in an ongoing battle, dating back to the early days of Islam, which is heavily influenced by the legacy of the Crusades and European colonialism, and which today is the product of a Judaeo-Christian conspiracy. This conspiracy is the result of superpower neocolonialism and the power of Zionism. The West (Britain, France, and especially the United States) is blamed for its support of un-Islamic or unjust regimes (Egypt, Iran, Lebanon) and also for its biased support for Israel in the face of Palestinian displacement. Violence against such governments and their representatives as well as Western multinationals is legitimate self-defense.

Second, these radical movements assume that Islam is not simply an ideological alternative for Muslim societies but a theological and political imperative. Since Islam is God's command, implementation must be immediate, not gradual, and the obligation to do so is incumbent on all true Muslims. Therefore individuals and governments who hesitate, remain apolitical, or resist are no longer to be regarded as Muslim. They are atheists or unbelievers, enemies of God against whom all true Muslims must wage jihad (holy war).

Exporting the Revolution

The success of the Iranian Revolution fired the imagination of the Muslim world and made Muslim governments tremble. Postrevolutionary Iran influenced Islamic activists throughout the world. In the aftermath of the revolution, delegations of Muslim leaders came from North America, the Middle East, and Southeast Asia to Teheran to congratulate Khomeini.

Sunni as well as Shii activist organizations, extending from Egypt (the moderate Muslim Brotherhood and radical al-Jihad) to Malaysia (ABIM, or the Malaysian Youth Movement, and the militant PAS) drew inspiration from the example of Iran. The Iranian Revolution provided lessons "to awaken Muslims and to restore their confidence in their religion and their adherence to it, so that they may assume the reins of world leadership of mankind once again and place the world under the protection of the esteemed Islamic civilization."[8] The Iranian Revolution served as a reminder that Islam is a comprehensive way of life which regulates worship and society: "It is religion and state, governance and politics, economics and social organization, education and morals, worship and holy war."[9]

Long-quiescent Shii minority communities in Sunni-dominated states like Saudi Arabia, the Gulf, and Pakistan aggressively asserted their Shii identity and rights and were emboldened to express discontent with ruling regimes. At the same time, threatened Muslim rulers increasingly branded their Islamic opposition as Khomeini-like or accused Iran of exerting undue influence on their domestic politics.

Gulf rulers were particularly nervous about the appeal of Iran's revolutionary example and rhetoric. In Iraq, where Shii constitute 60 percent of the population, the government of Saddam Hussein, a nominally Sunni Muslim ruler, was shaken by eruptions in the Shii cities of Karbala, Najaf, and Kufa (June 1979). Khomeini denounced Saddam Hussein as an atheist and called for the overthrow of his regime. Saddam Hussein countered by vilifying Khomeini and appealing to Iran's minority Arab population to revolt. The government suspected Iranian influence within Iraq's Shii activist groups—in particular, in the Islamic Call Society (al-Dawa) and the newly formed (1979) Mujahidin.[10] The Ayatollah Muhammad Baqir al-Sadr, one of Iraq's most prominent and influential Shii activist clerics, who had befriended Khomeini during his exile in Iraq, welcomed Iran's revolution and Khomeini's Islamic government. Saddam Hussein acted decisively. Shii leaders were arrested. Baqir al-Sadr, who had declared Iraq's Baathist regime un-Islamic and forbidden any dealings with it, was executed (April 1980), and al-Dawa was outlawed. In an atmosphere in which both Iraq and Iran played upon centuries-long Arab–Persian and Sunni–Shii rivalries and hostilities, the situation deteriorated. In September 1980 Iraq invaded Iran, initiating a war that would last eight years.

Khomeini was particularly critical of the Saudi and Gulf governments. He denounced them as "un-Islamic" monarchies, disdainfully characterizing their military and economic ties with the United States as "American Islam." Audiotapes of Khomeini and revolutionary leaflets were smuggled

into these Sunni-dominated states, and daily Arabic broadcasts from Teheran were explicit in their critique and their agenda:

> The ruling regime in Saudi Arabia wears Muslim clothing, but it actually
> represents a luxurious, frivolous, shameless way of life, robbing funds from
> the people and squandering them, and engaging in gambling, drinking par-
> ties, and orgies. Would it be surprising if people follow the path of revo-
> lution, resort to violence and continue their struggle to regain their rights
> and resources?[11]

The worst fears of Gulf rulers and of the West—that Iran's Revolution
would prove contagious—seemed to be coming true in the first years after
the revolution. In November 1979 Saudi Arabia was rocked by two explosive events. On November 20, as Muslims prepared to usher in the
fifteenth century of Islam, the Grand Mosque at Mecca was seized and
occupied for two weeks by Sunni militants who denounced the Saudi
monarchy. Khomeini's accusation that Americans had been behind the
mosque seizure led to attacks against American embassies and the destruction by fire of the American embassy in Islamabad, Pakistan.

While still reeling from the seizure of the Grand Mosque, on November
27 the house of Saud saw riots break out among the 250,000 Shii Muslims
in the oil-rich Eastern Province (Al-Hasa) where Shii constitute 35 percent
of the population.[12] Pent-up emotions and grievances among Shii, who felt
discriminated against by their Sunni rulers and cheated by an unfair distribution of oil wealth and government services, had exploded earlier in
the year in response to Iran's revolution and the triumphant return of
Khomeini.

Events in the early eighties did nothing to lessen concern among governments in the Gulf, the wider Muslim world, and the West. Statements
by the ruling ayatollahs in Iran, who called for an aggressive, expansionist
policy, exacerbated the situation. President Khamenei called upon prayer
leaders from forty countries to turn their mosques into houses of ''prayer,
cultural and military bases [to] . . . prepare the ground for the creation of
Islamic governments in all countries.''[13] The Iran–Iraq war, which officially began with Iraq's invasion of Iran on September 22, 1980, inflamed
relations between Iran and its neighbors. The Gulf states organized the
Gulf Cooperation Council (GCC) and threw their substantial financial support to Iraq. Khomeini called upon the GCC to ''return to the lap of Islam,
abandon the Saddam Hussein regime in Baghdad, and stop squandering
the wealth of their peoples.''[14]

During the same period Bahrain and Kuwait were also threatened by
Shii unrest.[15] In 1981 the government of Bahrain foiled an Iranian-inspired
coup by the Shii Front for the Liberation of Bahrain. Kuwait, 30 percent

of whose population is Shii, was hit by car bombings of the American and French embassies (1983) and was forced to crack down on Shii unrest in 1987 and 1989.

Iran frequently used the annual *hajj* to Mecca to propagate its revolutionary message. The Ayatollah Khomeini and other senior clerics rejected the Saudi claim to be the keepers of the holy sites and maintained that the *hajj* had a rightful political dimension. Iranian pilgrims, displaying posters of Khomeini and chanting slogans against the United States, the Soviet Union, and Israel, clashed with Saudi security in June 1982. The tensions continued during subsequent years and climaxed in 1987 when more than four hundred people were killed in a confrontation between Iranian pilgrims and Saudi security forces.

Despite these sporadic disturbances and government fears of massive unrest, Iran's export of its revolution proved in the end to be surprisingly unsuccessful in rallying Iraqi Shii as well as the populations of the Gulf states. By and large, most Iraqi (Arab) Shii were swayed more by nationalist than religious ties to their (Persian) coreligionists in Iran. Pockets of Shii militancy in the Gulf states did not translate into significant revolutionary movements. To thwart their growth, governments successfully used a combination of carrot and stick, addressing socioeconomic grievances while increasing security and imprisoning and deporting dissidents.

Lebanon provides the clearest and boldest example of the direct impact of Iran's Revolution. After the revolution Iran sent a contingent of its Revolutionary Guards to Lebanon who influenced the development there of Shii militant organizations, in particular Hizbullah and al-Jihad, supplying training, material, and money. In contrast to the more moderate Shii AMAL, which fought for a more representative reapportionment of power within the existing state structure, the goal of Iranian-inspired organizations was the eventual creation of an Islamic state. Iran was suspected of attempting to further that end through everything from bombings of Western embassies to car bomb attacks and the taking of hostages.

From the Periphery to the Center: Mainstream Revivalism

While the exploitation of Islam by governments and by extremist organizations has reinforced the secular orientations of many Muslims and cynicism in the West, a less-well-known and yet potentially far-reaching social transformation has also occurred in the Muslim world. In the nineties Islamic revivalism has ceased to be restricted to small, marginal organizations on the periphery of society and instead has become part of mainstream Muslim society, producing a new class of modern-educated but Islamically oriented elites who work alongside, and at times in coalitions with, their secular counterparts. Revivalism continues to grow as a broad-based socioreligious movement, functioning today in virtually every Muslim country and transnationally. It is a vibrant, multifaceted movement that will embody the major impact of Islamic revivalism for the foreseeable future. Its goal is the transformation of society through the Islamic formation of individuals at the grass-roots level. *Dawa* (call) societies work in social services (hospitals, clinics, legal-aid societies), in economic projects (Islamic banks, investment houses, insurance companies), in education (schools, child-care centers, youth camps), and in religious publishing and broadcasting. Their common programs are aimed at young and old alike.

A more pronounced Islamic orientation is now to be found among the middle and lower classes, educated and uneducated, professionals and workers, young and old, men, women, and children. A new generation of Islamically oriented leaders have appeared in Egypt, the Sudan, Tunisia, Jordan, Iran, Malaysia, Kuwait, Saudi Arabia, and Pakistan. Islamic activists have become an accustomed part of the political process, participating in national and local elections, scoring an impressive victory in Algeria's municipal elections, emerging as the chief opposition parties or groups in Egypt, Tunisia, and Jordan, and serving in cabinet positions in the Sudan, Jordan, Pakistan, Iran, and Malaysia.

For many who have nurtured visions of Islamic activism as the work of a small band of radicals and terrorists, the reality of Islam's strength, its expanding spheres of influence in mainstream politics and society, are both bewildering and menacing. How is one to make sense of the growth and prominence of Islamic activism in much of the Muslim world? What are the roots of the Islamic resurgence? Is Islamic fundamentalism simply a form of religiously motivated terrorism and extremism? If so, why does it enjoy such widespread support? Why is Islam so prominent in Muslim politics? Where and how has Islam been reasserted in politics and society? Why has Islamic revivalism proved to be so strong in those countries long regarded as among the most Westernized—Egypt, Lebanon, Iran, and Tunisia? How could Saddam Hussein, the most secular and un-Islamic of leaders, have appealed to Islam in the 1991 Gulf War? Finally, to what extent is there an "Islamic threat"?

Saddam Hussein's attempt to rally populist Muslim opinion for yet another holy war between Islam and the West is but the most recent episode in a long history of confrontation between Islam and the West. Muslim–Christian relations have often seemed a history of confrontation, with each side regarding the other as a historic threat from the rise of Islam to the present. Early encounters and confrontations, theological and political, provide the images and folklore which sustain the mutual stereotypes, images, and suspicions that continue to fuel fears and biases and perpetuate a vision of Islam against the West or of the West against Islam.

2

Islam and the West:
Roots of Conflict, Cooperation,
and Confrontation

Despite common theological roots and centuries-long interaction, Islam's relationship to the West has often been marked by mutual ignorance, stereotyping, contempt, and conflict. Ancient rivalries and modern conflicts have so accentuated differences as to completely obscure the shared theological roots and vision of the Judeo-Christian–Islamic tradition. Both sides have focused solely on and reinforced differences, and have polarized rather than united these three great interrelated monotheistic traditions.

Islam's early expansion and success constituted a challenge theologically, politically, and culturally which proved a stumbling block to understanding, and a threat to the Christian West. Both Islam and Christianity possessed a sense of universal message and mission which in retrospect were destined to lead to confrontation rather than mutual cooperation. Because of a long history in which Christendom often vilified the Prophet and grossly distorted Islam, and a recent history in which Islam has often been equated with radicalism and terrorism, some understanding of Islam is necessary before moving on to the history of relations between the West and the Muslim world. Moreover, some awareness of the Quran, the Prophet Muhammad, and the early Islamic period is indispensable for understanding Islam, since they have continued to provide a paradigm for emulation by Muslims and Islamic movements in every age. As we struggle to move beyond stereotypes and the tendency to confine our images of Islam and Muslims to demonstrators shouting ''Death to America'' or ''Holy war against the infidels,'' it is important to remember that men and women of every race and color, social class, and educational background across the world and down through the ages have found in Islam a faith that nourishes and transforms their lives, one that offers a sense of community, solidarity, and peace.

The Origins and Nature of Islam

Although the origins of the Muslim community date back to Muhammad and the seventh century of the common era, Muslims, like Jews and Christians, also trace the origins of their religious tradition (Islam) to the one true God (Allah, "the God") through a long line of prophetic messengers. Thus Muslims emphasize that the Judeo-Christian tradition is more accurately the Judaeo-Christian–Islamic tradition because all three are children of Abraham, the first prophet to receive God's revelation. They share an Abrahamic faith with its common belief in God, prophets, revelation, a divinely mandated community, and moral responsibility.[1] While Jews and Christians trace their lineage through Isaac to Abraham and Sarah, Muslims do so through Ishmael, the first-born son of Abraham and his servant Hagar.

Much as the sacred story of the Hebrew people records the triumph of a monothesim revealed to Adam, Abraham, and Moses in a polytheistic world, so Islamic history recounts a similar process of uncompromising monotheism, prophecy, and divine revelation within a tribal, polytheistic social setting.[2] As Jews have the Hebrew scriptures or Torah, and Christians the Bible, so Muslims possess their sacred scripture or book, the Quran. Muslims believe that God first sent His revelation to the Jews and then to the Christians, but that the revelation became distorted through human intervention and interpolation of the scriptures, resulting in such beliefs as the incarnation, crucifixion, death, and resurrection of Jesus, and the doctrine of redemption. The Hebrew Bible or Old Testament and the Christian New Testament are believed to be flawed versions of the original, pristine divine revelation. God subsequently sent down his revelation one more time through Muhammad, the last and final prophet. This, then, is the basis for the Muslim belief that the Quran, which Muslims view as the perfect, complete, and literal word of God, supersedes Jewish and Christian scriptures.

Muhammad: Messenger of God

The Quran and the Prophet Muhammad provide the sacred sources and guidance for the development of faith in both past and present. As the followers of Muhammad turned to him during his lifetime, so today devout Muslims across the world look to revelation and the teachings of the Prophet for direction in their lives.

Born in Arabia (roughly, modern-day Saudi Arabia) in 570, Muhammad ibn Abdullah (570–632) had a profound religious experience at the age of forty which transformed his life and initiated a community that some fourteen centuries later would become the second largest of the world's religious, spanning the globe and numbering approximately one billion adherents. In comparison to most prophets or founders of the world's great religious traditions, whose lives remain undocumented, a significant number of early documents provide information on the Prophet's life and work: the Quran, prophetic traditions (Hadith, reports about what the Prophet said and did), and an early biography by ibn-Ishaq (d. circa 768).[3] However, we know little of Muhammad's early years. He was orphaned as a child and raised by relatives. Muslim tradition tells us that as a young man of twenty-five he married a wealthy widow. Khadija was the owner of the caravan for which he was business manager and was some fifteen years older than Muhammad. Religiously inclined, Muhammad often retreated to a quiet place to reflect and meditate. In 610 C.E., on a night which Muslims commemorate as the "Night of Power and Excellence," Muhammad the caravan leader became Muhammad the Messenger of God, receiving the first of many revelations through the angel Gabriel: "Recite in the name of your Lord who has created, created man out of a germ-cell. Recite for your Lord is the Most Generous One who has taught by the pen, taught man what he did not know!" (Quran 96:1–5). Coming over the period from 610 to 632, the revelations would be fully compiled after the Prophet's death and constitute Islam's sacred scripture, the Quran.

Muslim tradition portrays an initially confused and somewhat reluctant prophet who, like the biblical Hebrew prophets, was overwhelmed by the experience—confused as to its meaning and worried about the reception of his special claims by others. As the history of the prophetic tradition demonstrates, those called to be a warner or messenger from God do not have an easy life. Prophets who claim to be a divinely inspired conscience of society, who denounce the waywardness and infidelity of the community, and who challenge the establishment and prevailing culture often faced derision, rejection, and persecution. Muhammad was no exception.

For ten years he preached a message of religious and social reform in Mecca. Muhammad and the Quran proclaimed one true God, rejecting the prevailing polytheism of Arabia, and denounced social injustice. Muhammad did not claim to bring a new religion but to purify and restore the one true religion of Abraham. His message was one of reformation and restoration of a wayward and faithless community. Like Amos and Jere-

which led to

purify & restore

miah before him, Muhammad was a messenger sent from God who denounced the impiety of his society and called upon his hearers to repent and obey God, for the final judgment was near: "Say: 'O men, I am only for you a warner.' Those who believe and do deeds of righteousness—theirs shall be forgiveness and generous provision. And those who strive against our signs to avoid them—they shall be inhabitants of Hell" (Quran 22:49–50).

Muhammad called upon Meccan society to worship the one true God and to abandon its polytheistic cult and practices. Arabia was no stranger to monotheism. However, while there were Jewish and Christian communities as well as indigenous Arabian monotheists (Hanifs), a vast array of tribal gods and goddesses dominated Arabian society. Muhammad preached a return to the faith of Abraham: belief in the one true God, the creator, sustainer, and judge of the universe. Muhammad and the Quran taught that human beings were accountable and that they would be judged and eternally rewarded or punished for their actions on Judgment Day. The call to Islam was a call to turn away from the path of unbelief and return to the straight path (Sharia) or law of God. This conversion meant membership in a community dedicated to the worship of the one true God, the implementation of His will, and thus the creation of a socially just community.

The Quranic message was a challenge to the prevailing sociopolitical as well as religious order. Mecca was a center not only of religious pilgrimage but also of trade and commerce, caught in the transition from a semi-Bedouin tribal to a commercial urban society. Obedience to God and his Prophet, a brotherhood of believers, alms for the poor, and struggle (jihad) against oppression were prescribed. The Quran condemned the exploitation of the poor, orphans, and women; forbade corruption, fraud, cheating, false contracts in business, the flaunting of wealth and arrogance; and prescribed strict punishments for slander, stealing, murder, the use of intoxicants, gambling, and adultery. Muhammad's claim to prophetic authority, his denunciation of injustices in Meccan society, and insistence that all believers belonged to a single universal community undermined tribal political authority. His rejection of polytheism seriously threatened the economic interests of the Meccans who controlled the Kaaba, a sacred shrine that housed the tribal idols and was the site of a great annual pilgrimage and fair, the source of Meccan religious prestige and revenue.

After ten years Muhammad enjoyed limited success. By worldly standards he would have been regarded as a failure. Although protected by his influential uncle, abu-Talib, and by his kinsman of the Banu Hashim, he himself lacked the power and prestige to overcome widespread opposition from the Meccan aristocracy, led by the Quraysh, the dominant merchant/trader clan in Mecca. By 619, with the passing of both his wife and his uncle, Muhammad had lost the pillars of his personal support and protection and was even more alone and vulnerable. His small band of followers was increasingly persecuted by the Meccan aristocracy, who regarded Muhammad's claim to prophecy and reformist agenda, with its implicit criticism of the political and socioeconomic status quo, as a challenge to their leadership and interests. For these reasons, when invited by leaders of the neighboring city of Medina, an agricultural oasis, to serve as its arbitrator, he and a band of his Meccan followers migrated in 622 and established there the first Muslim community (ummah).

The Islamic Community   MEDINA

The importance of the *hijra* (hegira), the emigration of Muhammad and his companions from Mecca to Medina, cannot be overestimated. The *hijra* constitutes the beginning of the Muslim community and was of such religious and historical significance that it became the basis for reckoning Muslim history, the first year of the Islamic calendar. Muhammad's move to Medina signaled a major transformation in history from a pre-Islamic pagan past to a divinely guided and centered world in which tribal kinship was to be superseded by membership in a community (ummah) bound together by common religious belief.

The community at Medina consisted of many clans, including several Jewish clans. Over the course of time Muhammad was able to consolidate his power and authority, converting the pagan clans to Islam. Muhammad was at last both Prophet and leader of a community.[4] Islam did not know a sharp cleavage between sacred and profane, between religion and society, individual and community. Islam's orientation was symbolized in the recurrent Quranic command, "Obey God and His Prophet." The Prophet received and transmitted a revelation that both guided and responded to the dynamics of the community's history. At the same time he oversaw and governed its affairs, serving as its political and military leader, judge and social reformer. Religion was integral to the leadership, life, and fabric of society, providing norms for worship (duties to God) and social life (duties to society). If Islam means submission to the will of God, the Muslim is one who submits, that is, follows or actualizes God's will in both individual and community life.

Medina reflected the integral relationship of religion and state in Islam, an ideal that influenced the development of the Islamic community both then and now. The state was led by Muhammad, the Prophet of God, and guided by divine revelation. Muhammad exercised executive, legislative, and judicial roles as head of state. He oversaw domestic and foreign affairs, the military, and the collection of taxes, and he settled disputes. The Islamic community was obliged not only to follow but also to spread God's word and rule. Muhammad combined diplomacy and military action. He returned in triumph to Mecca and by the time of his death in 632 had consolidated the disparate tribes of Arabia.

Muhammad brought more than simply a new synthesis or interpretation of existing religious ideas and customs (Arabian, Jewish, Christian). He fashioned a new order and community, a religious and political (more accurately, a religiopolitical) community rooted in and united by a religious vision or bond.[5] Old ideas and institutions were adopted and transformed in light of Islamic norms, as a new sense of identity, solidarity, community, and authority were fashioned. At the heart of the movement was a "new religion," a special understanding of the meaning and implications of Islam's monotheistic vision and way of life: the oneness of a transcendent and all-powerful God; His all-encompassing will for creation, which impacted on personal and public life; the requirement of obedience to that will; the mission of each Muslim as an individual and as a member of a religious community to realize and spread God's rule; and the completeness and correctness of the Quranic revelation and the finality of Muhammad's prophethood. It was this vision that was to transform the tribes of Arabia and bring about a major world historical and cultural transformation.

Islamic Government and Society

Muhammad's death precipitated a crisis of leadership in the community whose resolution would see the creation of the caliphate and also sow the seeds for the later emergence of Islam's two major branches, Sunni and Shii Islam. With Muhammad's death, the Muslim community faced the selection of a successor. Two opinions emerged. The majority believed that Muhammad had not designated a successor and accepted the selection of his successor (caliph) by Muhammad's senior companions. The caliph was to be the political leader of the community with no claim to the prophetic mantle of the Prophet. However, a minority believed that Muhammad had designated Ali who, as his cousin and son-in-law, was the senior male in Muhammad's family. For these followers of Ali (Shii or "partisans" of Ali), leadership of the Islamic community was to stay within the house of the Prophet. Ali and his descendants were to be the religiopolitical leaders (Imams) of the community. Though not a prophet, the Shii Imam, in contrast to the office of caliph, enjoyed a very special religious status as a religiously inspired and sinless leader.

The majority Sunni opinion prevailed. The Islamic community was organized and governed under a caliphal state which was quickly transformed into a central, imperial, dynastic caliphate.[6] The first six centuries of Islam can be neatly divided into three major periods: the Four Rightly Guided Caliphs at Medina (632–61), so called because, in conjunction with the era of Muhammad, their rule is regarded as the ideal formative and normative period of Islam; the Umayyad Caliphate (661–750) at Damascus; and the Abbasid Caliphate (750–1258) at Baghdad.

The worldview that prevailed during the caliphate period was deeply indebted to religion. While rulers relied upon their armies for security and conquest, Islam provided the ideological framework for state and society, a source of legitimacy and authority. Whatever the character of the ruler or how he came to power, all sought legitimacy in their caliphal title as successors to the Prophet, as the "commander of the believers," whose task it was to defend and spread the faith and assure that society was governed by God's law. The world was divided into Islamic territory (the *dar al-Islam*, abode of peace) and the non-Islamic world (the *dar al-harb*, abode of war). Citizenship, taxation, and issues of war and peace were determined by religious belief. Muslims enjoyed full citizenship and paid certain taxes, while Jews and Christians (People of the Book) were designated "protected people" and paid a special poll or head tax, in exchange for which they were to be defended by the Muslim military.

The Spread and Conquests of Islam

Within one hundred years of the death of the Prophet Muhammad, the successors (caliphs) of Muhammad had established an empire greater than Rome at its zenith. The shock to the international order and more specifically to Christendom was incalculable. That the tribes of Arabia could be united, let alone spill out of Arabia, overcome the Byzantine (Eastern Roman) and Persian (Sassanid) empires, and by the end of a century create an Islamic caliphate extending from North Africa to India, seemed unthinkable.

There are many reasons for the rapidity and success of Arab expansion: the mutual exhaustion of the Byzantine and Persian empires after years of war, the dissatisfaction of indigenous populations with their imperial rulers, the skill of Bedouin warriors, the lure of booty. However, the critical factors were the rise of the state and the role of Islam in uniting disparate tribes and providing a greater sense of purpose and meaning:

> Islam . . . provided the ideological underpinnings for this remarkable breakthrough in social organization. . . . In this sense, the conquests were truly an *Islamic* movement. For it was Islam—the set of religious beliefs preached by Muhammed, with its social and political ramifications—that

ultimately sparked the whole integration process and hence was the ultimate cause of the conquests' success.[7]

The perception or belief that this was indeed an Islamic movement remains prevalent today among many Muslims as a source of inspiration and emulation. Because of the tendency in our secular age to downplay religion as a major factor in sociopolitical development, it is useful to bear in mind a similar comment regarding the central importance of Islam in the conquests from a work by two Western, non-Muslim historians.

> Even the secular historian . . . must regard Islam as the decisive factor in the expansion of the Arabs. That bedouin tribes, which constantly for centuries had engaged in warfare with each other and were known to prize their independence, should have suddenly placed themselves obediently under the order of Muslim commanders is inconceivable apart from Islam. It was Islam that provided the necessary rallying cry and instilled in the bedouin warriors a sense that they were fighting in a grand cause. Whatever may have been the original material motives of the bedouin . . . [they found themselves] caught up in a movement greater than anything they had dreamt of, a movement not of their own making, which they could explain only in terms of a divine intervention in human affairs.[8]

During subsequent centuries Islam would spread across much of the world. While the centralized caliphate disintegrated, it was replaced by individual states (sultanates) which extended from Africa to Southeast Asia, from Timbuktu to the southern Philippines.[9] In addition, great Muslim cities existed in what today are the Central Asian republics of the former Soviet Union, China, Eastern Europe, Spain, southern Italy, and Sicily.

Jihad

The rapid spread of Islam proved a double threat to Christendom, both religious and political. The armies and merchants of Islam were its missionaries, bringing both Muslim faith and imperial rule. Islam was used to bind together, inspire, and mobilize the tribes as well as to provide a rationale for expansion and conquest. The Quranic notion of jihad, striving or self-exertion in the path of God, was of central significance to Muslim self-understanding and mobilization. The term jihad has a number of meanings which include the effort to lead a good life, to make society more moral and just, and to spread Islam through preaching, teaching, or armed struggle. Muslim jurists distinguished ways "in which the duty might be fulfilled: by the heart, by the tongue, by the hands and by the sword."[10]

In its most generic meaning, "jihad" signifies the battle against evil and the devil, the self-discipline (common to the three Abrahamic faiths) in which believers seek to follow God's will, to be better Muslims. It is the lifelong struggle to be virtuous, to be true to the straight path of God. This is the primary way in which the observant Muslim gives witness to or actualizes the truth of the first pillar of Islam in everyday life. The spread of Islam through "tongue" and "hands" refers to the Quranically prescribed obligation of the Muslim community "to enjoin good and forbid evil" (3:110). Finally, "jihad" means the struggle to spread and to defend Islam. Just as the example of the Prophet offers a paradigm and the basis for the fusion of religion and state, so too Muhammad's movement readily supplies the model for all Islamic movements in their struggle to reform society and the world. The world is a battleground on which believers and unbelievers, the friends of God and the enemies of God or followers of Satan, wage war: "The believers fight in the way of God, and the unbelievers fight in the idol's way. Fight you therefore against the friends of Satan" (4:76). The mission of the Islamic community is to spread the rule or abode of Islam globally much as Muhammad and his followers expanded Islamic rule through preaching, diplomacy, and warfare, and to "defend" it. Islamic law stipulates that it is a Muslim's duty to wage war against polytheists, apostates, and People of the Book who refuse Muslim rule, and those who attack Muslim territory. To die in battle is the highest form of witness to God and to one's faith. The very Arabic word for martyr (*shahid*) comes from the same root as the profession of faith (*shahada*). As in Christianity, the reward for martyrdom is paradise.

Islamic Civilization

As Muslims spread their rule and faith, they proved to be great learners as well as doers. Politically, Muslim rulers recognized their own limitations and the advanced development of many of the kingdoms and cultures that their armies conquered. Local institutions, ideas, and personnel were assimilated or retained, and adopted or adapted to Islamic norms, as Muslim masters learned from their more advanced subjects. Great libraries and translation centers were established; the great books of science, medicine, and philosophy of the West and the East were collected and translated, often by Christian and Jewish subjects, from Greek, Latin, Persian, Coptic, Syriac, and Sanskrit into Arabic. Thus the best works of literature, science, and medicine were made more accessible.

The age of translation was followed by a period of great creativity, as a new generation of educated Muslim thinkers and scientists now built upon their received knowledge and made their own contributions to learning. "The process of Islamicizing the traditions had done more than integrate and reform them. It had released tremendous creative energies. The High Caliphal Period was one of great cultural florescence."[11] This was the age of great masters of philosophy and science: ibn-Sina (Avicenna), ibn-Rushd (Averroës), al-Farabi. Major urban centers of learning with vast libraries emerged in Cordova, Palermo, Nishapur, Cairo, Baghdad, Damascus, and Bukhara to eclipse a Europe mired in the Dark Ages. The political and cultural life of Muslims and non-Muslims alike in Islamic empires and states, despite tribal and religious differences, were brought within the framework of Islamic faith and Arabic language. New ideas and practices were Arabized and Islamized. Islamic civilization was the product of a dynamic, creative process of change in which Muslims borrowed freely from other cultures. It demonstrated a sense of openness and self-confidence that came from being masters not servants, colonizers rather than the colonized. In contrast to the twentieth century, Muslims then enjoyed a sense of control and security. They felt free to borrow from the West, since their identity and autonomy were not threatened by the specter of political and cultural domination. As they borrowed, so too they provided a legacy to the West. The earlier cultural traffic pattern was reversed when Europe, emerging from the Dark Ages, turned to Muslim centers of learning to reappropriate much of its lost heritage and to learn from Muslim advances in mathematics, medicine, and science.

Islamic Law: The Path of God

If the Muslim vocation was to follow or obey God's will, then knowing God's will was imperative. Whereas dogma or doctrine epitomized the essential statement of Christian belief, Islam, like Judaism, found its central expression in law.[12] Law rather than theology was the dominant discipline for defining or delineating faith. For Muslim jurists, God's revelation and prophetic example were the starting points for discerning and applying God's will to every aspect of life. Both the message of the Quran and the traditions of the Prophet reveal the comprehensiveness of Islam's way of life, its individual and corporate dimensions. Within several centuries of the death of the Prophet, Muslims had codified their way of life. Pious Muslims concerned about the unfettered powers of Muslim rulers and the infiltration and uncritical assimilation of foreign practices, sought to delineate God's law in order to preserve the true path of God and to limit the powers of the caliph.

Based on the Quran and the example of the Prophet and utilizing custom and reason, the work of individual jurists gave birth to schools (communities of scholars) of law which sprang up in many of the great cities of

Islam: Medina, Mecca, Damascus, Baghdad, Kufa. Though united in purpose and based upon the same revealed sources, their conclusions often bore the mark of differing geographic contexts and customs as well as intellectual orientations. Of the many law schools which sprang up, several (the Hanafi, Maliki, Shafii, Hanbali, and Jafari) would survive and endure.

Islamic law provided the blueprint of the good society, the Islamic ideal. The Sharia or path of God was therefore a set of divinely revealed general principles, directives, and values from which human beings developed detailed rules and regulations which were in turn to be applied by judges (*qadis*) in Sharia courts.

The scope of Islamic law was comprehensive, including regulations which governed ritual and worship and defined the social norms of the community. Central to the faith are the five pillars, or basic duties, which are incumbent upon all believers.

> 1. The Profession of Faith (*shahada*) which marks entrance into or membership in the Islamic community: "There is no God but the God and Muhammad is the messenger or prophet of God."
> 2. Prayer (*salat*) five times each day at fixed times, and attendance at the Friday congregational prayer.
> 3. Almsgiving (*zakat*) a two-and-a-half percent tithe on a Muslim's accumulated wealth, which is to be distributed to the poor not as charity but as a religious obligation of all Muslims toward the less fortunate brothers and sisters of the community.
> 4. Fasting (*sawm*) from dawn to dusk during the month of Ramadan.
> 5. Participating in the annual pilgrimage (*hajj*) to Mecca at least once in one's life, a duty incumbent upon all who have the health and economic resources to do so.

The five pillars combine a sense of individual responsibility, social awareness, and collective consciousness or membership in the broader community of Islam.

The social dimension of the law is embodied in a set of regulations or norms that govern family, criminal, contract, and international law. Here in particular one sees the impact of Islam on both personal and community life. A vast body of laws regulated marriage, polygamy or polygyny, divorce, inheritance, theft, adultery, drinking, and issues of war and peace.

While it possessed an underlying essential unity, Islamic law reflected the diversity of the geographical contexts, with their differing customs, in which it developed, as well as differences due to human interpretation or judgment. Islamic law, then, was neither rigid nor closed but instead manifested dynamism, flexibility, and diversity. It remained responsive to new circumstances in the hands of legal experts (*muftis*) who served as advisers to the courts. Their interpretations (legal opinions or decrees, *fatwas*) either on the finer points of law or on new situations or questions, often guided the findings of the court. By the tenth century, however, Islamic law did tend to become more fixed as many jurists concluded that the essentials of God's law had been adequately delineated in legal texts. Thus there was a tendency to restrict substantive interpretation (ijtihad) and instead emphasize the obligation to simply follow or imitate (taqlid) Islamic legal texts. New practices or doctrines were condemned as deviations (bida) from God's revealed law, unwarranted innovation often regarded as akin to heresy. As a result, over time the distinction between God's immutable law as found in revelation and many of the legal regulations which were the product of fallible human reasoning or local custom became blurred and forgotten. The question of Islamic law and change would become a major issue in the nineteenth and twentieth centuries, as Muslims responded to the impact of modernization and development.

Islamic Mysticism and Spirituality

Given the prescriptive role of Islamic law in defining official Islam and the tendency in recent years to focus on political Islam, it has been easy to lose sight of the rich mystical and spiritual tradition (Sufism) which has nourished the lives of Muslims and accounts for the effective spread of Islam throughout much of the world. The formal, legal tradition, with its specific guidelines and punishments, has always been accompanied by an inner-directed quest and path. The letter of the law was offset by an emphasis on the inner spirit or heart of Islamic faith and belief.

Sufism began as a reform movement.[13] For some pious Muslims the splendor and wealth of the conquests, the transformation of the relative simplicity of life in Arabia into the imperial court life of Damascus, threatened the pristine faith and moral fiber of the community. The kingdom of man, with its focus on this world, seemed to have overwhelmed and obscured the kingdom of God, the true focus and center of Muslim life. In Sufi eyes, Islam triumphant had become an Islam endangered. Calling for a refocusing on the truths of the next life rather than the pleasures and rewards of this life, the Sufis preached a message of simplicity and detachment from the things of this world. To this early austerity was added a strain of spirituality that emphasized love of God. Sufism offered an affective, devotional path to God whose selfless love and service to God complemented and sometimes challenged the more legalistic, scripturalist approach. Thus the good Muslim was not only one who followed God's will through observance of the law, but also the believer who sought through various means including recollection, and sometimes song and dance, to draw closer to the divine, to experience the presence of God.

to experience the presence of God

The fusion of asceticism and devotionalism transformed Sufism from a relatively small urban elite movement into a broad-based populist movement whose communities attracted followers from all social classes and educational backgrounds. Groups of Sufis, gathered around a spiritual leader or master (a *pir* or shaykh), formed brotherhoods or orders. From the twelfth to the fourteenth centuries, Sufi brotherhoods were transformed from small voluntary associations into organized brotherhoods with an international network of centers spreading across the Muslim world. They became the great missionaries of Islam, responsible for its effective spread. In Africa and Southeast Asia Islam was spread primarily by Sufi brotherhoods and merchants rather than the armies of Islam. Sufism brought a message of Islam whose mystical doctrines and practices proved attractive to many and was open to linkages with local religious traditions and customs. Whereas official Islam often emphasized strict observance of the letter of the law, Sufism presented an alternative tradition flexible and open to assimilation and synthesis. Outside influences were absorbed from Christianity, Neoplatonism, Hinduism, and Buddhism. As Sufism became a mass movement, it came into conflict with the official Islam of the *ulama*, whose authority in the community was challenged by Sufi popularity and success as the *ulama* and Sufi *pirs* often vied for influence.

Islam and the West

The rapid rise and expansion of the Islamic empire and the flourishing of Islamic civilization posed a direct danger to Christendom's place in the world both theologically and politically. As Maxime Rodinson has observed, "The Muslims were a threat to Western Christendom long before they became a problem."[14]

The very theological similarities of Christendom and Islam put the two on a collision course. Each community believed that its covenant with God was the fulfillment of God's earlier revelation to a previous community that had gone astray. Each believed in the history of God's revelation and that its revelation and messenger marked the end of revelation and prophecy. Thus while Christians assumed a position of superiority and therefore had little problem with their supercessionist views toward Judaism, a similar attitude and claim by Muslims regarding Christianity was unthinkable and, more than that, a threat to the uniqueness and divinely mandated role of Christianity to be the sole representative of God and the only means to salvation. Islam was at best a heresy preached by a deluded or misguided prophet, and at worst a direct challenge to Christian claims and mission: "the combination of fear and ignorance produced a body of

theology that sets Christians against Muslims

legends, some absurd and all unfair: Muslims were idolaters worshipping a false trinity. Muhammad was a magician, he was even a Cardinal of the Roman Church who, thwarted in his ambition to become Pope, revolted, fled to Arabia and there founded a church of his own.''[15]

Both Christianity and Islam claimed a universal mission; each was a transnational community based upon common belief and a vocation to be an example to the nations of the world, the vehicle for the spread and triumph of God's kingdom. However, the challenge of Islam was not at the level of theological discourse and debate. The success of Muslim armies and missionaries was experienced as a force which seemed to come out of nowhere to challenge the very existence and foundations of Christendom. Although Muslims were initially a minority in the conquered territories, in time they became a majority, owing largely to mass conversions of local Christians.[16] In addition, those who remained Christian were Arabized, adopting Arabic language and culture. The response of Western Christendom was, with few exceptions, defensive and belligerent. Islam was a danger to be reckoned with. A seemingly impregnable Byzantine empire had buckled and risked being swept away during the seventh and eighth centuries. Muslim armies overran the Persian empire as well, conquered Syria, Iraq, and Egypt, and swept across North Africa and parts of southern Europe until they ruled most of Spain and the Mediterranean from Sicily to Anatolia. Ancient historical and theological affinities went unnoticed as the Christian West, Church and State, faced the onslaught of an enemy which it found easier to demonize and to dismiss as barbarian and infidel than to understand.

Non-Muslims in the Islamic State

The indigenous peoples in the conquered areas belonged to one of three major ''scriptural'' communities (People of the Book, *ahl al-kitab*): Christian, Jewish, and Zoroastrian. For many non-Muslim populations in Byzantine and Persian territories already subjugated to foreign rulers, Islamic rule meant an exchange of rulers, the new ones often more flexible and tolerant, rather than a loss of independence. Many of these populations now enjoyed greater local autonomy and often paid lower taxes. The Arab lands lost by Byzantium exchanged Graeco-Roman rule for new Arab masters, fellow Semites with whom the populace had closer linguistic and cultural affinities. Religiously, Islam proved a more tolerant religion, providing greater religious freedom for Jews and indigenous Christians. Most of the local Christian churches had been persecuted as schismatics and heretics by a ''foreign'' Christian orthodoxy. For these reasons, some Jew-

[margin note: domination of Islam]

[margin note: Christians and Jews under conquering Muslims]

ish and Christian communities had actually aided the invading Muslim armies. Francis Peters has observed:

> The conquests destroyed little: what they did suppress were imperial rivalries and sectarian bloodletting among the newly subjected population. The Muslims tolerated Christianity but they disestablished it; henceforth Christian life and liturgy, its endowments, politics, and theology, would be a private not a public affair. By an exquisite irony, Islam reduced the status of Christians to that which the Christians had earlier thrust upon the Jews, with one difference. The reduction in Christian status was merely judicial; it was unaccompanied by either systematic persecution or blood lust, and generally, though not everywhere and at all times, unmarred by vexatious behavior.[17]

Just as Muslim rulers tended to leave the government institutions and bureaucracy intact, so too religious communities were free to practice their faith and be governed in their internal affairs by their religious laws and leaders. As previously mentioned, religious communities were required to pay a poll or head tax, in exchange for which they were entitled to peace and security; thus they were known as "protected people." The Islamic ideal was to fashion a world in which, under Muslim rule, idolatry and paganism would be eliminated, and all people of the book could live in a society guided and protected by Muslim power. While Islam was regarded as the final and perfect religion of God, others were to be invited, through persuasion first rather than the sword, to convert to Islam. Thus non-Muslims were offered three choices: (1) conversion to Islam and full membership in the community; (2) retention of one's faith and payment of a poll tax; or (3), if they refused Islam or "protected" status, warfare until Islamic rule was accepted.

The Crusades

Few events had a more shattering and long-lasting effect on Muslim–Christian relations than the Crusades. Two myths pervade Western perceptions of the Crusades: first, that Christendom triumphed; second, that the Crusades were simply fought for the liberation of Jerusalem. For many in the West, the specific facts regarding the Crusades are but dimly known.[18] Indeed, many do not know who started the Crusades, why they were fought, or how the battle was won. For Muslims, the memory of the Crusades lives on as the clearest example of militant Christianity, an earlier harbinger of the aggression and imperialism of the Christian West, a vivid reminder of Christianity's early hostility toward Islam. If many re-

[margin note, left: militant christianity]

[margin note, right: misconceptions of the Crusades]

gard Islam as a religion of the sword, Muslims down through the ages have spoken of the West's Crusader mentality and ambitions. Therefore, for Muslim–Christian relations, it is less a case of what actually happened in the Crusades than how they are remembered.

The Crusades, which take their name from the "cross" (*crux* in Latin), were a series of eight military expeditions extending from the eleventh to the thirteenth centuries which pitted Christendom (the Christian armies of the Franks) against Islam (the Muslim armies of the Saracens). The eleventh century marked a turning point in the relationship of the West to the Islamic world.

> Up till 1000 the West was a poor, backward and illiterate region, precariously defending itself against the assaults of barbarous nations by land and sea. . . . All this while for four centuries, Islam enjoyed an internal peace and security, untroubled save for domestic wars, and thus was able to build up a brilliant and impressive urban culture. Now the situation was dramatically transformed. . . . Trade and commerce revived [in the West], towns and markets sprang up; the population increased . . . and the arts and sciences were cultivated on a scale unknown since the days of the Roman Empire.[19]

The West, emerging from the Dark Ages, mounted a counteroffensive to drive the Muslims out of Spain, Italy, Sicily, and the Mediterranean at a time when the Islamic world had experienced an upsurge in political and religious strife.

When his forces were decisively defeated by the Abbasid army in the late eleventh century, Byzantine Emperor Alexius I, fearing that Muslim armies would sweep across Asia and capture the imperial capital at Constantinople, appealed to the West. He called upon fellow Christian rulers and the Pope to turn back the Islamic tide by undertaking a "pilgrimage" to liberate Jerusalem and its environs from Muslim rule.

Jerusalem was a city sacred to all three Abrahamic faiths. It had been captured by Muslim armies in 638 during the period of Arab expansion and conquest. Under Muslim rule, Christian churches and populations were left unmolested. Christian shrines and relics had become popular pilgrimage sites for Christendom. Jews, long banned from living there by Christian rulers, were permitted to return, live, and worship in the city of Solomon and David. Muslims built a shrine, the Dome of the Rock, and a mosque, the al-Aqsa, near the Wailing Wall, the last remnant of Solomon's Temple, and thus a site especially significant to Judaism. Five centuries of peaceful coexistence were now shattered by a series of holy wars which pitted Christianity against Islam and left an enduring legacy of distrust and misunderstanding.

The Crusades were initiated by Pope Urban II's response to Emperor

Alexius's plea. In 1095 Urban called for the liberation of the Holy Land from the infidel, appealing to an already established tradition of holy war. For the Pope, the call to the defense of the faith and Jerusalem provided an ideal opportunity to gain recognition for papal authority and its role in legitimating temporal rulers, and to reunite the Eastern (Greek) and Western (Latin) churches.

The Pope's battle cry "God wills it!" initially proved successful. The appeal to religion captured the popular mind and engaged the self-interest of many, producing a reinvigorated and relatively united Christendom. Christian rulers, knights, and merchants were driven by the political, military, and economic advantages that would result from the establishment of a Latin kingdom in the Middle East. Knights from France and other parts of Western Europe, moved by both religious zeal and hope of plunder, rallied and united against the "infidel" in a war whose ostensible goal was the liberation of the holy city. "God may indeed have wished it, but there is certainly no evidence that the Christians of Jerusalem did, or that anything extraordinary was occurring to pilgrims there to prompt such a response at that moment in history."[20]

The Crusades drew inspiration from two Christian institutions, pilgrimage and holy war: liberation of the holy places from Muslim rule partook of the character of both. Pilgrimage played an important role in Christian piety. Visiting sacred sites, venerating relics, and penance brought (its critics would say "bought") indulgences which promised the remission of sins. Jerusalem, central to the origins of Christian faith, was a symbol of the heavenly city of God and thus a major pilgrimage site. At the same time, the notion of holy war transformed and sacralized medieval warfare, and its notions of honor and chivalry. Warriors were victorious whether they won their earthly battles or not. To rout the enemy meant honor and booty; the indulgences earned by all who fought in the Crusades guaranteed the remission of sins and entrance into paradise. To fall in battle was to die a martyr for the faith and gain immediate access to heaven despite past sins.

Caught off guard and divided, the initial Muslim response was ineffectual; the armies of the First Crusade reached Jerusalem and captured it in 1099. But Christian success was short-lived: "The Crusaders were . . . a nuisance rather than a serious menace to the Islamic world."[21] By the middle of the twelfth century, Muslim armies mounted an effective response. Under the able leadership of Saladin (Salah-al-Din, d. 1193), one of Islam's most celebrated rulers and generals, Jerusalem was reconquered in 1187. The tide had turned and the momentum would remain with Muslim forces. By the thirteenth century the Crusades had degenerated into intra-Christian wars, wars against enemies whom the papacy denounced as heretics and schismatics. Finally, the very fear that had initiated the Christian holy war, with its call for a united Christendom to turn back the Islamic tide, was realized in 1453 when the Byzantine capital, Constantinople, fell and, renamed Istanbul, became the seat of the Ottoman empire. A dream of Muslim rulers and armies originating in the seventh century had been fulfilled. Conversely, Christian fears and the continued threat of a powerful, expansive Islam now extended to Eastern Europe, much of which was brought under Ottoman rule.

The legacy of the Crusades depends upon where one stands in history. Christian and Muslim communities had competing visions and interests, and each one cherishes memories of its commitment to faith, and heroic stories of valor and chivalry against "the infidel." For many in the West, the assumption of a Christian victory is predicated on a romanticized history celebrating the valor of Crusaders, as well as a tendency to interpret history through the experience of the past two centuries of European colonialism and preeminent American power. Each faith sees the other as militant, somewhat barbaric and fanatical in its religious zeal, determined to conquer, convert, or eradicate the other, and thus an obstacle and threat to the realization of God's will. Their contention continued during the Ottoman period, through the next wave of European colonialism, and finally into the superpower rivalry of the twentieth century.

The Ottoman Empire: The Scourge of Europe

No sooner had the Crusades passed when Europe was once again faced with the power and might of the Muslim threat embodied in the Ottoman empire. The Ottoman empire was one of the three great imperial medieval Muslim sultanates: Ottoman, Safavid in Iran, and Mogul in India. As C. E. Bosworth has noted, more than any other empire since the early period of Arab conquest and expansion, "the Ottoman Turks struck terror into the hearts of Christian Europe, so that the Elizabethan historian of the Turks, Richard Knollys, described them as 'the present terror of the world.'"[22] Having taken Constantinople in 1453, the Ottomans proceeded to build a vast and extremely well-organized, hierarchical, and efficient state. The imperial capital at Istanbul, with a population that grew to 700,000—twice that of its European counterparts—became an international center of power and culture.[23] The Ottomans became the great warriors of Islam, creating a world empire that incorporated major Muslim centers like Cairo, Baghdad, Damascus, Mecca, and Medina. They threatened the heart of Europe for almost two centuries.

An unusual series of capable sultans (which included the celebrated Mehmet the Conqueror, 1451–81, and Suleiman the Magnificent, 1520–

66), led Ottoman armies and navies that dominated much of the Mediterranean and the Indian Ocean. They created an empire whose size, prosperity, government, and culture rivaled that of the Abbasids. The Ottomans overpowered and subdued the Christian Balkan states, as well as much of the Middle East and North Africa. As in the early Arab conquests, their flexible policy toward Orthodox Christians and other religious minorities was often well received by the subject populations: "This live-and-let-live policy was in striking contrast to the fanatical bigotry of Christian states at the time. Balkan peasants in Mehmet's times used to say, 'Better the turban of the Turk than the tiara of the Pope.' "[24] But if many in the Balkans saw the Ottomans as liberators, the heartland in Europe seemed traumatized.

[margin note: Success of the early Empire]

> Authors and clerics revived and refurbished the diatribes against the infidel which had characterized the period of the Crusades. . . . Cardinal Bessarion, writing to the Doge of Venice after the fall of Constantinople, set the tone for a century of abuse: "A city which was so flourishing . . . the splendour and glory of the East . . . the refuge of all good things, has been captured, despoiled, ravaged and completely sacked by the most inhuman barbarians . . . by the fiercest of wild beasts. . . . Much danger threatens Italy, not to mention the other lands, if the violent assaults of the most ferocious barbarians are not checked."[25]

[margin note: demonizing the Muslims by Europeans]

Invective and propaganda were popularized by Bartholomew Gregevich of Croatia's best-selling work, *Miseries and Tribulations of the Christians Held in Tribute and Slavery by the Turks*.[26] The convenient, hostile stereotype and caricature of the Turks, informed more by passion than by reason, prevailed over the minority voices of those diplomats and scholars who had actually seen or dispassionately studied the Turks and, like the French political philosopher Jean Bodin, could observe:

> The King of the Turks, who rules over a great part of Europe, safeguards the rites of religion as well as any prince in this world. Yet, he constrains no one, but on the contrary permits everyone to live as his conscience dictates. What is more, even in his seraglio at Pera he permits the practice of four diverse religions, that of the Jews, the Christian according to the Roman rite, and according to the Greek rite, and that of Islam.[27]

The Ottoman threat contributed to the development of "Europe" as the focus of a common identity and bond within a European Christendom torn apart by the Reformation, so that "Erasmus exhorted the 'nations of Europe'—no longer addressing them as the constituent powers of Christendom—to crusade against the Turks."[28]

[margin note: union of Europe]

Ottoman power and glory rested upon the development of a system for training young men for military and administrative service. It produced a first-class bureaucracy and military which relied heavily upon its religious scholars (the *ulama*) and a corps of elite slave soldiers and officials, the Janissaries. Young Christian males were taken from conquered populations of the Balkans, and later from Anatolia, converted to Islam, and sent to special schools which trained and produced generations of Ottoman officials. The combination of extremely capable rulers and a well-trained and disciplined military able to use gunpowder to advantage enabled the Ottomans to conquer large areas of Arab and European territory: "It was the discipline and firepower of these troops (the Ottoman army made use of artillery and hand-guns . . .) which did much to create in Europe the image of Ottoman ferocity and invincibility."[29] Some eight hundred years after the first Arab threat to Europe, Islam, now in the hands of the Turks, seemed even more of a menace. Having subdued the Balkans, they seemed poised to engulf Western Europe. From the fifteenth to the seventeenth century Ottoman forces seemed invincible to European Christians. Yet the Ottoman naval defeat at Lepanto in 1571 was a turning point, hailed as a victory of Christian Europe over the Muslim Turks, and the successful defense of Vienna in 1683 confirmed the decline of the Ottoman threat and the shift in power to a revitalized and now self-confident Europe. The "Scourge of Christendom" would soon become the "sick man of Europe."[30]

The Crusades and the Ottoman empire clearly show that, despite the theological roots and affinities of Christianity and Islam, competing religious and political interests produced a history of confrontation and warfare in the course of which Christian Europe for centuries often found itself on the defensive against Muslim armies, seeming at times to be fighting for its very existence.

European Images of Islam

The negative fallout from events in Christian–Muslim history is reflected in the view of Islam that emerges from Western literature and thought. Although there were moments of contact, mutual knowledge, and constructive exchange, by and large the Muslim expansion into Europe, ranging from the Arab conquests through the Crusades and the Ottoman empire, produced alienation and distrust of Islam, which was primarily viewed as a threat to Christendom. This legacy, as Albert Hourani has noted, is "still present in the consciousness of Western Europe, still feared and still, in general, misunderstood."[31] Fear and disdain, coupled with European ethnocentrism, produced distorted images of Islam and Muslims and dissuaded scholars from serious study of Islam's contributions to Western thought. "[I]t was not until the years between the two World

Wars that a serious effort was made to understand the contribution of Islam to the development of Western thought, and the effect on Western society of the neighborhood of Islam.''[32]

As with the seventh-century Arab conquests, Christendom again experienced Islam as a double threat, both theological and political. The Crusades had for the first time made Islam all too familiar in medieval Europe, though not necessarily understood. R. W. Southern notes: "Before 1100 I have found only one mention of the name of Mahomet in medieval literature outside Spain and Southern Italy. But from the year 1120 everyone in the West had some picture of what Islam meant, and who Mahomet was. The picture was brilliantly clear, but it was not knowledge. . . . Its authors luxuriated in ignorance of triumphant imagination."[33]

This ignorance reflected not only lack of knowledge but also the all-too-common human tendency among educated and uneducated alike to denigrate and dehumanize the enemy, to assume a superior posture and dismiss that which challenges and threatens one's deepest beliefs or interests by labeling it inferior, heretical, fanatical, or irrational. Distorted portraits or caricatures of Muhammad and Islam were created—more accurately, fabricated—with little concern for accuracy. Often beliefs and practices such as polytheism, eating pork, drinking wine, and sexual promiscuity—which run directly counter to its most basic beliefs—were attributed to Islam and the Prophet. Muhammad was vilified as an impostor and anti-Christ who used magic and promiscuity to try to destroy the Church. As the non-Muslim author of an early biography of the Prophet produced in the West confessed, "It is safe to speak evil of one whose malignity exceeds whatever evil can be spoken."[34] The great epics of the times perpetuated ignorance and distortions, featuring idolatrous Muslims worshiping their chief god, Muhammad, "in synagogues (thereby bringing Islam closer to the equally unacceptable Jewish belief) or in 'mahomeries.' " Maxime Rodinson has observed: "Pure fiction, whose only object was to spur the reader's interest, was mixed in varying proportions with misrepresentations of belief which inflamed hatred of the foe."[35]

By the time of the Reformation, after centuries of fear and hostility, Islam proved a convenient tool in polemical attacks among Christians, a symbol of the dangers of the anti-Christ. Martin Luther saw Islam "in the medieval way, as a movement of violence in the service of the anti-Christ; it cannot be converted because it is closed to reason; it can only be resisted by the sword, and even then with difficulty."[36]

In later centuries Islam continued to be used as a foil for authors who championed Enlightenment principles and virtues. Voltaire's *Fanaticism, or Muhammad the Prophet* portrayed the Prophet as a theocratic tyrant, and Ernest Renan, in an oft-cited lecture, championed science, reason, and human progress by dismissing Islam as incompatible with science, and the Muslim as "incapable of learning anything or of opening himself to a new idea."[37] These stereotypes of a static, irrational, retrogressive, antimodern religious tradition were to be perpetuated by scholars and development theory in the twentieth century.

Though the Islamic and Christian worlds take enormous pride in their faith and rich traditions of learning and civility, the historical dynamics of Christian–Muslim relations often found the two communities in competition, and locked at times in deadly combat, for power, land, and souls. As a result they were often enemies, rather than People of the Book striving in a common quest to obey and serve their Lord. For Christendom, Islam proved a double threat, religious and political, which often threatened to overrun Europe, first at Poitiers and finally at the gates of Vienna. It was not in jest that some historians noted that had Muslim armies not been turned back at Poitiers, the language of Oxford, as indeed of Europe itself, might have been Arabic! A Christian Church convinced of its possession of truth and its preordained mission to save the world legitimated papal and imperial designs. Moreover, it fostered a sense of superiority and righteousness which provided a rationale for the denigration of the infidel religiously, intellectually, and culturally. These same attitudes made the successes of Muslim armies and the rapid spread of Islam by soldiers, traders, and missionaries that much more of a challenge to Christian faith and power. If the first ten centuries seemed a lopsided contest in which Christendom was more often than not literally or figuratively under siege, the dawn of European colonialism signaled a shift in power: thereafter, colonialism would dominate the history and psyche of Muslims, and continues seriously and at times dramatically to affect relations between Islam and the West today. As the Iranian Revolution of 1978–79 and, more recently, the Gulf War of 1991 have revealed, images of Christian Crusaders and Western imperialism remain a living legacy, an experience very much alive in Muslim consciousness and political rhetoric.

3

The West Triumphant: Muslim Responses

Two themes dominate the first half of twentieth-century Muslim history: European imperialism, and the struggle for independence from colonial rule. Few events were more far-reaching and influential in the relationship of Islam to the West than the experience of European colonialism. The theme of European colonialism and imperialism, their impact in the past and their continued legacy, remains alive in Middle East politics and throughout the Muslim world from North Africa to Southeast Asia. Intertwined with colonial rule was the emergence of nationalist movements in the decades-long battle for independence. In the post-independence period political elites in emerging Muslim states turned to liberal nationalism and Arab socialism in nation building. These experiments failed, damaging the credibility of nationalism and contributing to the Islamic resurgence. Issues of foreign domination and dependence remain a bitter memory as well as a continued threat in the eyes of many Muslims today.

Colonialism quite literally altered the geographic and institutional map of the Middle East, or perhaps more accurately, it often drew the boundaries and appointed the leaders for much of the modern Muslim world. It replaced or transformed indigenous political, social, economic, legal, and educational institutions and explicitly as well as implicitly challenged Muslim faith and culture. Countries that welcomed European trade missions in the sixteenth and seventeenth centuries found themselves transformed by the nineteenth century into European colonies or protectorates.

The image of Islam as both a potential threat to the Christian West and a retrogressive force and thus a source of Muslim backwardness and decline dominated the worldview of European colonialism. It provided a ready-made rationale for "crown and cross." Colonial officials and Christian missionaries became the footsoldiers of Europe's expansion and imperial hegemony in the Muslim world. The British spoke of the "white man's burden" and the French of their "mission to civilize." As the balance of power and leadership shifted from the Muslim world to Europe, modernity was seen as the result not simply of conditions that produced the Enlightenment and the industrial revolution, but also of Christianity's inherent superiority as a religion and culture.

> This was Civilization, as proud, imperial-trivial nineteenth-century Europe called it, demeaning everything non-European with an insensitivity.... (Was it triumphalism, lack of experience, a parvenu spirit, and too abrupt an entrance into the wider field of human civilization?) ... Europe did not become aware of how original its civilization was until it compared it with that of others. ... Then the internal disparities faded from view and the white man affirmed himself and closed ranks in solidarity against everything outside.[1]

Lord Cromer, British consul in Cairo from 1883 to 1907 during Britain's occupation of Egypt, epitomized this outlook. Albert Hourani has summarized Cromer's attitude as a "benevolent" imperialism. Islam is seen as a

> "noble monotheism," but as a social system it "has been a complete failure": Islam keeps women in a position of inferiority, it "crystallizes religion and law into an inseparable and immutable whole, with a result that all elasticity is taken out of the social system"; it permits slavery; its general tendency is towards intolerance of other faiths; it does not encourage the development of the power of logical thought. Thus, Muslims can scarcely hope to rule themselves or reform their societies; and yet Islam can generate a mass feeling which, in a moment, can break whatever brittle bonds the European reformer has been able to establish with those he is trying to help. The fear of the "revolt of Islam" is never far from Cromer's thoughts.[2]

European colonialism posed both a political and a religious challenge. It abruptly reversed a pattern of self-rule in the Muslim world which had existed from the time of the Prophet. By and large, the vast majority of the Muslim community had possessed a sense of history in which Islam had remained triumphant. Despite past divisions, civil wars, and revolts as well as invasion and occupation, Islam had prevailed—Muslims had ruled Muslims. To be a Muslim was to live in a state which at least nominally was a Muslim community guided by the laws and institutions of Islam. Even the seemingly catastrophic end of the Abbasid Caliphate with the fall of Baghdad to the Mongols in 1258 was followed by the conversion of the Mongol conquerors and the continuance of an Islamic world order composed of Muslim sultanates which extended from Africa to Southeast Asia. However, this sense of Muslim history and belief now seemed to be unraveling, owing to internal as well as external threats to the identity and fabric of Islamic society. Muslim communities had already been struggling with internal problems. The external challenge and threat of subjugation by Europe came on the heels of a powerful wave of Muslim religious revivalism in the eighteenth century which had addressed the internal sociomoral decline of the community. The political challenge of European colonialism was intensified by the threat posed by the wave of Christian missionary activity which sought to win souls for Christ and openly questioned the viability of Islam in the modern world.

> The degraded state of the Muslim world made it an obvious target for Christian missionaries. The proselytizing crusade was launched with renewed vigor and quickly spread. . . . In keeping with the common beliefs of their time and normal human inclinations, the missionaries credited the triumphs of European nations to Christianity while blaming the misfortunes of the Muslim world on Islam. The perception was that, if Christianity was inherently favorable to progress, then Islam must, by its nature, encourage cultural and developmental stagnation.[3]

The external threat to Muslim identity and autonomy intensified profound religious as well as political questions for many in the Muslim world. What had gone wrong? Why had Muslim fortunes been so thoroughly reversed? Was it Muslims who had failed Islam or Islam that had failed Muslims? How were Muslims to respond?

Islamic Renewal and Reform

Although modern Islamic reform is often simply presented as a response to the challenge of the West, in fact its roots are both Islamic (its revivalist tradition) and Western (a response to European colonialism).

Islam possesses a rich, long tradition of Islamic revival (*tajdid*) and reform (*islah*).[4] Down through the ages, individuals (theologians, legal scholars, Sufi masters, and charismatic preachers) and organizations undertook the renewal of the community in times of weakness and decline, responding to the apparent gap between the Islamic ideal and the realities of Muslim life. As with all things, a return to Islam—that is, to the fundamentals: the Quran, the life of the Prophet, and the early Islamic community—offered the model for Islamic reform.

During the eighteenth and nineteenth centuries, revivalist leaders and movements had sprung up across the Islamic world: the Mahdi (1848–85) in the Sudan, the Sanusi (1787–1859) in Libya, the Wahhabi (1703–92)

in Saudi Arabia, the Fulani in Nigeria (1754–1817), the Faraidiyyah of
Hajji Shariat Allah (1764–1840) in Bengal, the militant movement of Ahmad Brelwi (1786–1831) in India, and the Padri in Indonesia (1803–37).[5]

Most revivalist movements were primarily internally motivated; they
responded to a decline whose root cause was identified as being within
the Islamic world. The powerful revivalist spirit that gripped the Islamic
world during the eighteenth century was a response to economic and sociomoral decline, military defeats, and political divisions within the imperial sultanates (Ottoman, Safavid, and Mogul) and beyond. Despite differences, all were movements whose goal was the moral reconstruction of
society. They diagnosed their societies as being internally weak and in
decline politically, economically, and religiously. The cause was identified
as Muslim departure from true Islamic values brought about by the infiltration and assimilation of local, indigenous, un-Islamic beliefs and practices. The prescribed cure was purification through a return to "true Islam." Each movement resulted in the formation of organizations, a society
of "true believers" within the broader society, that combined religious
commitment with militant political activism in order to purify Muslim
communities. The process of Islamic renewal and reform was based upon
a return to the fundamental sources of Islam. In time, several of these
movements led to the creation of new states: the Mahdi in the Sudan, the
Sanusi in Libya, the Fulani in Nigeria, and the Wahhabi in Saudi Arabia.

Emulating the example of the prophet Muhammad, revivalist movements transformed their societies through a religiously legitimated and
inspired sociopolitical movement. The ideological worldview of revivalist
movements had an impact not only on their societies but also on Islamic
politics in the twentieth century. The key ideological components of their
program were: (1) Islam was the solution; (2) a return to the Quran and
the Sunnah (model, example) of the Prophet was the method; (3) a community governed by God's revealed law, the Sharia, was the goal; and (4)
all who resisted, Muslim or non-Muslim, were enemies of God. Members
of the community, like the early Muslims of the seventh century, were
trained in piety and military skills as these movements spread God's rule
through preaching and jihad.

European Colonialism

By the nineteenth century a clear shift of power had occurred, as the
decline of Muslim fortunes reversed the relationship of Islam to the West.
Increasingly, Muslims found themselves on the defensive in the face of
European expansion. Whereas the primary challenge to Islamic identity

and unity in the eighteenth and nineteenth centuries was generally seen as internal, the real threat of the West was not experienced until the late nineteenth and early twentieth century. It constituted a singular challenge to Islam politically, economically, morally, and culturally. European colonialism and imperialism threatened Muslim political and religiocultural identity and history. The impact of Western rule and modernization raised new questions and challenged time-honored beliefs and practices. With the dawn of European domination of the Muslim world, the image, if not always the reality, of Islam as an expansive worldwide force had been shattered.

The map of the Muslim world after World War I revealed the extent of foreign dominance: the French in North, West, and equatorial Africa and the Levant (Lebanon and Syria); the British in Palestine, Transjordan, Iraq, the Arabian Gulf, and the Indian subcontinent; and in Southeast Asia, the British in Malaya, Singapore, and Brunei, and the Dutch in Indonesia. Where Muslims retained power, in Turkey and Iran, they were constantly on the defensive against the political and economic ambitions of the British, French, and Russians, whose inroads and machinations threatened their independence and stability. Given the overwhelming presence and political, military, and economic superiority of Europe, it is not surprising that, as John Voll has observed, "[t]he old-fashioned Western imperialist [Lord Cromer] could complacently conclude that Islam's 'gradual decay cannot be arrested by any modern palliatives however skillfully they are applied.' "[6]

Muslim views of the West and responses to its power and ideas varied from rejection and confrontation to admiration and imitation. However, the prevailing mood was one of conflict and competition. For many, colonialism conjured up memories of the Crusades; the European challenge and aggression was but another phase of militant Christianity's war with Islam; Europe was the enemy that threatened both the faith of Islam and the political life of the Muslim community. The political crisis precipitated by European colonialism was accompanied by a spiritual one: "The fundamental spiritual crisis in Islam in the twentieth century stems from an awareness that something is awry between the religion which God has appointed and the historical development of the world which He controls."[7]

Muslim images of a Crusader West were reinforced by the policies of colonial powers. Colonialism was experienced as a threat to Muslim identity and faith. Implicit in its policies and explicit in the statements of many government officials and missionaries was the belief that Europe's expansion and domination were due to its inherent Christian cultural superiority. Educating the "natives" in the language, history, and sciences of the West and Christian virtues was part of an "enlightened" policy to civilize. One did not have to look far for statements which substantiated the worst Muslim fears. As a result, the struggle against European colonialism often appropriated the rhetoric of a war between Christendom and Islam. While French apologists spoke of the "battle of the Cross against the Crescent," a defeated Algerian Muslim officer declared, "We have fought to this day in defense of our liberties and religion."[8] The master–servant relationship inherent in a good deal of European colonial rule generated mutual stereotypes and distrust that reflected an adversarial relationship:

> The Egyptian, as viewed by the British, was a portly parody of a petty French official, a boastful coward, a turbaned Muslim fanatic, a noisy agitator blind to the benefits British rule had given the country, or a "wog" (for "wily Oriental gentleman") selling dirty postcards in the bazaar. The Egyptians saw the British as coldhearted, exclusive (it was a sore point that, for many years, the only Egyptians that could enter Cairo's posh Gezira Sporting Club were servants), mercenary, and power-mad.[9]

Europe came not only with its armies of bureaucrats and soldiers but also with its Christian missionaries. The double threat of colonialism was that of the crown and the cross. The mutual relationship between the clergy and the government and military was proclaimed by France's Marshal Bugeaud, who praised their "grands rapports," commenting that the clergy "gain for us the hearts of the Arabs whom we have subjected to force of arms."[10] The preachers and missionary institutions (churches, schools, hospitals, and publishing houses) were regarded by many Muslims as an arm of imperialism, one aspect of a policy that displaced indigenous institutions, supplanted local languages and history with Western curricula, and seduced souls through schools and social welfare. The French seizure of the Grand Mosque of Algiers and its conversion into the cathedral of Saint-Philippe, with the French flag and the cross on its minaret, symbolized the threat of Christianity. France's patronizing disdain was boldly articulated by the archbishop of Algiers when he stated that the Church's mission was to convert Arab Muslims from "the vices of their original religion generative of sloth, divorce, polygamy, theft, agrarian communism, fanaticism, and even cannibalism."[11]

Muslim Responses to the Challenge of Colonialism

Four diverse Muslim responses to the West took shape: rejection; withdrawal; secularism and Westernization; and Islamic modernism.

Rejection and Withdrawal

For many Muslims, the Prophet's response to his Meccan detractors was the answer—emigration (*hijra*) or sacred struggle (jihad): leaving a territory no longer under Muslim rule, or fighting to defend and defeat the infidel. Although Christians had always been regarded as believers, People of the Book, European Christian colonizers were now rejected as infidels, the enemies of Islam. While resistance or confrontation initially proved attractive, emigration proved impractical for large numbers of people and, given the superior military strength of Europe, holy war was doomed to defeat. For many religious leaders, the alternative was simply to refuse to deal with their colonial masters, to shun their company, schools, and institutions. Any form of cooperation was regarded as capitulation to the enemy or treason. Modern European education was condemned as alien, superfluous, and a threat to religious belief. Muslims did not have to look far to find Europeans whose statements reinforced their fears; said one English author: "The luxuriant religions of Asia shrivel into dry sticks when brought into contact with the icy realities of Western sciences."[12]

Secularism and Westernization

However, Muslim responses varied. If some preached rejection and resistance, others were eager to learn from and emulate the strength of Europe, to modernize. The conclusion of one scholar regarding Muslim reactions in the Indian subcontinent is generally true for much of the Muslim world: "Muslim reaction to English education was by no means uniform . . . the Muslim reaction to modernity varied from blind and self-defeating hostility to reasonable cooperation with British educational policy."[13] For many, the realities of European ascendancy had to be acknowledged and dealt with, and its lessons discerned in order to survive.

Muslim rulers in the Ottoman empire, Egypt, and Iran looked to the West to develop military, economic, and political modernization programs based upon European learning and technology. They sought to emulate the strength of the West, to develop a modern trained and equipped military and bureaucracy, and to appropriate the science that provided modern weapons. European teachers and schools were imported. Educational missions were sent to Europe, where Muslims studied languages, science, and politics. Translation bureaus and printing presses were established to translate and publish Western works. A new intellectual elite was born—modern, educated, and Western-oriented. However, change through emulation came from above, initiated and imposed by rulers, in reaction to the external threat of European expansionism and not as a response to internal societal pressures. The state initiated this change, and a small elite implemented and were the primary beneficiaries of reform. Though Islamic rationales were employed by some to legitimate the transformation, implicit in this process was the gradual acceptance of a secular outlook that restricted religion to personal life while turning to the West for development models in public life. The result was a series of military, administrative, educational, economic, legal, and social reforms, strongly influenced and inspired by the West, to "modernize" Muslim societies. The traditional Islamic basis and legitimacy of Muslim societies were slowly altered as the ideology, law, and institutions of the state, indebted to imported models from the West, were increasingly secularized.

The modernization through Western models initiated by Muslim rulers was primarily motivated by a desire to strengthen and centralize their power, not to share it. Political participation was not a government priority. The rulers' primary interest was in military, bureaucratic, and technological reform, not in substantive political change. Thus for example, though the Ottoman sultan Abdulhamid II promulgated the First Ottoman Constitution in 1876, and the Shah in Iran capitulated to pressure and established a National Consultative Assembly in 1906, in both cases attempts to bring about serious constitutional reforms limiting the absolute power of the rulers were thwarted or crushed.

A major result of modernization was the emergence of new elites and a growing bifurcation of Muslim society, epitomized in its legal and educational systems. The coexistence of traditional religious and modern secular schools, each with its own curriculum, teachers, and constituencies, produced two classes with divergent worldviews: a modern Westernized elite minority and a more traditional, Islamically oriented majority. The process also eroded the traditional bases of power and authority of religious leaders, as new classes of modern trained elites assumed positions of importance in government, education, and law, positions which had always been the province of the *ulama*.

Islamic Modernism

A fourth response to the challenge of the West, the Islamic modernist movement, sought to bridge the gap between Islamic traditionalists and secular reformers. Islamic modernists incorporated the internal community concerns of eighteenth-century revivalism with the need to respond to the threat of European colonialism and the demands of modernity.[14] Like secular reformers, Islamic reformers responded to European colonialism and were influenced by their perception of the "Success of the West." The

West was strong and successful; Muslims were weak and subject to domination and dependence. Thus they believed that the sources of the West's strength must be accommodated and assimilated. In the latter half of the twentieth century, this posture would stand in sharp contrast to Islamic activism (fundamentalism), with its denunciation of the "neocolonialism of the superpowers" and its emphasis on the "Failure of the West" and the autonomy and self-sufficiency of Islam.[15]

Islamic modernism, like much of the modern Muslim response to the West in the twentieth century, had an ambivalent attitude toward the West, a simultaneous attraction and repulsion. Europe was admired for its strength, technology, and political ideals of freedom, justice, and equality, but often rejected for its imperialist goals and policies. Reformers like Jamal al-Din al-Afghani and Muhammad Abduh in Egypt, Morocco's Allal al-Fasi, Tunisia's Abd al-Aziz al-Thalabi, Algeria's Abd al-Hamid Ibn Badis, and Sayyid Ahmad Khan and Muhammad Iqbal in the Indian subcontinent, argued the compatibility of Islam with modern science and the best of Western thought. They preached the need and acceptability of a selective synthesis of Islam and modern Western thought; condemned unquestioned veneration and imitation of the past; reasserted their right to reinterpret (*ijtihad*) Islam in light of modern conditions; and sought to provide an Islamically based rationale for educational, legal, and social reform to revitalize a dormant and impotent Muslim community. In contrast to eighteenth-century revivalist movements, Islamic modernism did not seek to restore a pristine past but instead wished to reformulate its Islamic heritage in response to the political, scientific, and cultural challenge of the West. It provided an Islamic rationale for accepting modern ideas and institutions, whether scientific, technological, or political (constitutionalism and representative government). For most of these reformers, the renaissance of the Muslim community was the first step to national independence or liberation from the hated yoke of colonialism—the restoration of Muslim power. Muslims, they believed, must look to Islam, their source of strength and unity, but learn the secrets of Western power in order to cast off foreign rule and regain their identity and autonomy.

Jamal al-Din al-Afghani (1838–97) epitomized the concerns and program of Islamic modernism. Born and educated in Iran and then in British India, Afghani was a teacher and tireless political activist who roamed the Muslim world from Egypt to India, calling upon Muslims to arise from their lethargy and reclaim their God-ordained purpose and identity. While he taught in Egypt, served as an adviser to the Shah of Iran, and traveled in Europe, he preached a message that challenged both Muslim and European authorities, citing "the danger of European intervention, the need for national unity to resist it, the need for a broader unity of the Islamic peoples, the need for a constitution to limit the ruler's power."[16] These themes of anti-imperialism, Arab unity, Pan-Islam (Islamic solidarity), and constitutionalism were a major part of his legacy.

Afghani proved a thorn in the side of Muslim and British rulers alike. He and his disciples were involved in the Urabi nationalist revolt against British and French influence in Egypt in 1882. Afghani was subsequently deported from Iran in 1891 for his instigation and support of the Tobacco Protest. Later, after being invited to Istanbul by the Ottoman sultan Abdulhamid, Afghani was placed under virtual house arrest in 1896 when Iran's Nasir al-Din Shah was assassinated by a reputed follower of Afghani's.

Afghani blamed the ills of the Muslim world, its political decline and religious stagnation, on European expansionism, autocratic rulers, and the religious establishment. Critical of the *ulama* and their retrogressive interpretation of Islam, Afghani preached a message of renewal and change. Formulated in response to Europe and its criteria for modernity, it sounded very much like a "Protestant Islam." Indeed, Afghani believed that Islam, like Christianity before it, needed a Martin Luther and a reformation.[17] Islam was the religion of progress and change, of reason and science, a religion with a strong work ethic. Reformers argued that these characteristics were integral to Muslim history, the source of Islam's past strength and glory. Muslims had produced and possessed a rich Islamic civilization; thus, Afghani argued, reason, philosophy, and science were not foreign to Islam, were not simply products of the West. Similarly, Islam had provided the social bond which unified and guided a once triumphant community. Muslim unity, like anti-imperialism, remained a prerequisite for political and cultural independence.

For Afghani the revitalization of a subjugated community could not be achieved by ignoring or rejecting the West but by active engagement and confrontation. The West was both the problem and part of the solution. On the one hand, Europe had subdued and threatened the identity and autonomy of the community. On the other hand, the Islamic community nationally and transnationally must learn from the West, identity and harness the sources of its power. Thus in addition to science and technology, Afghani appropriated political ideas such as constitutionalism and political participation through elected assemblies. The revitalization of Islam and Muslim solidarity were the keys to attain the ultimate goal, independence from the West and the restoration of Muslim fortunes.

If Afghani was primarily a political activist, his protégé Muhammad Abduh (1849–1905) was the developer of the intellectual and social reformist dimensions of Islamic modernism. Abduh's Salafiyya movement sought legitimacy through identification of its Islamic modernist reformism with the elders (*salafi*) of the early Muslim community, those who followed the example of the Prophet. Abduh was an Egyptian trained as a religious scholar, a member of the *ulama*. He taught at al-Azhar University, the oldest center of Islamic learning, and at Dar al-Ulum, a new college that incorporated a modern curriculum to prepare Azhar graduates for government positions. The most enthusiastic of Afghani's early students, Abduh worked closely with Afghani, publishing articles on sociopolitical reform, and was exiled to Paris with Afghani for his participation in the Urabi revolt. In France they formed a secret society and published a newspaper that continued to preach Afghani's message of Islamic reform and anticolonialism.

After his return from exile, Abduh turned away from political activism and focused on intellectual, religious, educational, and social reform. His published works included the journal *al-Manar* (*The Beacon* or *Lighthouse*), which treated Quranic exegesis and theology. He preached the compatibility of revelation and reason, condemned the blind following of tradition (*taqlid*), championed the legitimacy of and need for a reinterpretation of Islam to respond to the demands of modern life. Abduh worked to reform the *ulama*, in particular the curriculum of al-Azhar University, and the religious courts. He provided a rationale for the reform of Islamic law, arguing that while laws concerned with worship of God were immutable, Islam's social legislation was capable of substantive change. As mufti (chief religious leader) of Egypt, Abduh's official opinions covered a broad range of reforms from the permissibility of European attire to banking interest, marriage, and divorce.

Muhammad Abduh was also an early champion of legal and educational reforms to improve the status of Muslim women. A critic of polygamy and its negative effect on the Muslim family, he argued that it had been permitted as a concession to prevailing social conditions in Arabia at the time of the Prophet. Abduh offered a modernist interpretation of the Quran which concluded that the Quranic ideal (Quran 4:3 and 4:129) was in fact monogamy, since the Quran's permission for more than one wife was contingent upon equal justice and impartiality, both of which were a practical impossibility. Muhammad Abduh's Quranic interpretation was adopted by most Islamic reformers and provided the modernist rationale for many governments' Muslim family-law reforms restricting polygamy.

However, it was Abduh's associate Qasim Amin (1863–1908), a lawyer and judge, who developed the feminist dimension of Islamic modernism. In two controversial books (*The Emancipation of Women* and *The New Woman*) he denounced the subjugation of Muslim women as un-Islamic and a major cause for the deterioration of the family and society. Amin linked the emancipation of women to the nationalist cause. The bondage of women retarded national development. He argued the equality of the sexes in Islam, denounced veiling and social seclusion as un-Islamic, criticized the ills of arranged marriages, and a male's unfettered right to divorce and a wife's inability to do so. Although criticized and attacked by many religious and nationalist leaders who accused him of aping the West, Amin became an inspiration to Egyptian feminists like Huda Shaarawi a generation later.

While Islamic modernists like Jamal al-Din al-Afghani in the Middle East and Sir Sayyid Ahmad Khan (1817–98) in the Indian subcontinent shared a modern reformist agenda, they differed in their political orientation and goals, in particular their attitude toward the West. In contrast to Afghani, whose anticolonialist ideas and actions were so influential in the Middle East, Ahmad Khan was a British loyalist. Ahmad Khan, who had lived through the Mutiny of 1857 (which nationalists would later call the first war of independence), committed his life to the survival of the Muslim community in British India. He had two goals: to restore a debilitated and defeated Muslim community, and to reassure the British that Islam itself was not a threat to British interests. He called for a new theology to respond to modern change. His writings and activities contributed to this process of reinterpretation and reform. Ahmad Khan concentrated specifically on producing a new generation of Muslim leaders through educational reforms. He created the Anglo-Muhammadan Oriental College (in 1920 renamed the Aligarh Muslim University), modeled on Cambridge University. At the same time Ahmad Khan sought to counter both the *ulama* who dismissed the British as "enemies of Islam," and the British who regarded the Muslims as an inherent political threat because of their allegiance to Islam. Thus he opposed the Muslim tendency to advocate a policy of withdrawal and, contrary to prevailing British belief, argued that Muslims could be loyal citizens in a non-Muslim state. Despite his accomplishments, his close identification with the West condemned him in the eyes of those who chafed under colonial rule. Ahmad Khan's strong affinity for the West, symbolized by his decision to wear Western clothing, adopt a European life-style, and accept knighthood by Queen Victoria, brought strong criticism from many *ulama* and anticolonialists who dismissed his loyalism and reformism as political and cultural capitulation.

Muhammad Iqbal (1875–1938) in India and Taha Husayn (1889–1973) in Egypt represented the next stage in modernist reform, in which nationalist movements grew and a more secular orientation emerged. They exemplify the dual winds of change: Islamic modernist and secular nationalist.

Iqbal combined a traditional upbringing with an intimate knowledge of the West. He studied in Germany and England, earning a doctorate in philosophy at Munich and a law degree at London. Though a lawyer by profession, he is remembered as the great poet–philosopher of southern Asia. Iqbal combined what he thought to be the best of the East and the West, his Islamic heritage and Western philosophy (Hegel, Bergson, Fichte, and Nietzsche), to produce his own synthesis and reinterpretation of Islam. The reformist thrust of his thinking and its openness to Western thought was summarized in *The Reconstruction of Religious Thought in Islam*:

> No wonder then that the younger generation . . . demand a fresh orientation of their faith. With the reawakening of Islam, therefore, it is necessary to examine, in an independent spirit, what Europe has thought and how far the conclusions reached by her can help us in the revision, and if necessary reconstruction of theological thought in Islam.[18]

Like Afghani, Iqbal spoke of the need for an Islamic reformation like that which Christianity had undergone: "We are today passing through a period similar to that of the Protestant Reformation in Europe and the lesson which the rise and outcome of Luther's movement teaches should not be lost on us."[19]

Iqbal borrowed from the West but was not uncritical of it. He leveled sharp criticism at European colonialism and imperialism. Though an admirer of the accomplishments of the West, its dynamic spirit, intellectual tradition, and technology, he denounced the excesses of colonialism and imperialism, the exploitation of capitalism, the atheism of Marxism, and the moral bankruptcy of secularism. Like Ahmad Khan, Iqbal argued that, contrary to the Western caricature of Islam as a "religion of holy war," Islam was a religion of peace: "All forms of political and social disturbance are condemned . . . the ideal of Islam is to secure social peace at any price."[20] In contrast to Ahmad Khan and more like Afghani, Iqbal wanted to resuscitate the Muslim community so that it could reclaim its political independence and rightful place in history. Iqbal attempted to develop alternative Islamic models for modern Muslim societies. Drawing on Islamic traditions, he sought to "rediscover" Islamic principles and values that would provide the basis for Islamic versions of Western concepts and institutions such as democracy and parliamentary government.

Although Iqbal believed that nationalism was antithetical to the Islamic ideal of a transnational community, or Pan-Islam, he nevertheless accepted its practical necessity and utility. Muslims must gain independence and rebuild their local and regional communities. In contrast to Sir Sayyid Ahmad Khan's loyalism, Iqbal was an early voice both for independence from Britain and for Muslim nationalism in the subcontinent. Though originally an Indian nationalist, his concern for the identity and welfare of a Muslim minority in a Hindu-dominated state led Iqbal to turn from the dream of a united India, join the Muslim League, and call for a separate Muslim state.

In contrast to Iqbal's Islamic reformism, Taha Husayn, a former student of Muhammad Abduh, exemplifies the secular European drift of a new generation of Egyptian youth. His life and upbringing reflect the bifurcation of education and the split identity in Egyptian society. Although blind from an early age, he attended a village religious school, then was educated at Cairo's two premier institutions of higher learning, al-Azhar University, the famed Islamic center of learning, and the Egyptian (Cairo) University, the new modern national university. This was followed by four years (1915–19) of study in France, where he earned a doctorate from the Sorbonne. Husayn became an internationally known writer and educator and served as minister of education (1950–52).

Taha Husayn represents that group of Abduh's disciples who became leaders in politics and intellectual life but believed that the modern needs of society would best be served by the separation of religion and politics. Perhaps no book better represents the cultural crossroads that Muslims faced in the early twentieth century, and the Western orientation of many emerging Muslim elites, than Husayn's *Future of Culture in Egypt*. It embodies the rationale of those who concluded that future strength was best achieved not by a return to an Islamic past or the path of Islamic modernism, but rather by aggressive pursuit of Western-oriented liberal, secular reform. Although he was careful to speak of selective borrowing, the enormous pull of the West as a model for success was obvious in both his discourse and the degree of his reliance on Western models of development.

Taha Husayn and many of his generation were not critics of the West, but its unabashed admirers. Though he fought for political independence from Europe, he maintained that the roots of Egypt (as well as its future) and the roots of Islam were inextricably bound to the West. Indeed, he argued that Egypt was not of the East but of the West! He stressed their shared common religious and geographic origins (the one God, the Mediterranean). Just as Europe did not become Western when it embraced Christianity, whose roots were in the Middle East, so too Egypt did not become Eastern when it hastened to accept Islam. Similarly, Husayn maintained that the "essence and source of Islam are the essence and source of Christianity. . . . No, there are no intellectual or cultural differences to be found among the peoples who grew up around the Mediterranean and were influenced by it."[21] Husayn asserted that secularism had long been part of Egypt's tradition: "From earliest times Muslims have been well aware of the now universally acknowledged principle that a political system and a religion are different things, that a constitution and a state rest, above everything else, on practical foundations.''[22] Thus, he concluded, it was only natural that modern Egyptians should adopt European customs and institutions from table manners and railroads to political, legal, and educational systems.[23]

In many ways, the secular drift of Taha Husayn (and other former disciples of Afghani and Abduh) is symptomatic of the mixed legacy of Islamic modernism. It was both a success and a failure. Modernists did provide Islamically based rationales for modern reform. They did offer an alternative to the rejectionist tendencies of many religious leaders and the uncritical assimilationist proclivities of secularists. Through the modernists' writings, publications, teaching, and the establishment of educational and social institutions, Islamic modernist ideas and values became part of Muslim discourse and would in time become part of mainstream Muslim thought. Afghani and Abduh's legacy influenced not only the Arab heartland and North Africa but also distant Indonesia. Ahmad Khan and Iqbal were major cultural and intellectual forces throughout southern Asia and beyond. However, modernist leaders themselves failed to produce organizations that would systematically develop and implement their ideas. Nowhere is this more evident than in the tendency of many of their disciples to turn toward a more secular path. Taha Husayn is a prime example of this tendency, as is Saad Zaghlul, the great Egyptian nationalist leader.

Islamic modernism was primarily an intellectual movement. While it did not produce a unified movement or enduring organizations, its legacy was substantial in its influence on the Muslim community's development and its attitude toward the West: Islamic modernism reawakened Muslims to a sense of past power and glory; reinterpreted and produced a modern ideological interpretation of Islam; and demonstrated the compatibility of Islam with modern Western sociopolitical reform. Most reformers distinguished between adopting Western ideas and technology and rejecting Western imperialism; indeed, they promoted the ideas of anticolonialism and Muslim unity, autonomy, and independence. For these reasons, men like Jamal al-Din al-Afghani and Muhammad Iqbal came to be remembered as fathers of Muslim nationalism.

Nationalist Movements and the Long March to Independence

The period between the two world wars was dominated by two interrelated issues, national identity (nationalism) and independence. Ironically, secular and Islamic reformers saw the West as being at one and the same time

e and negative force. On the one hand, nationalism was a reaction
rn imperialism, to European colonial rule. On the other hand, it
was in a sense also the product of a century of Westernizing reform. Many
of those who led nationalist and independence movements owed their
training to the West and were influenced by the liberal nationalist beliefs
and ideals of the French Revolution (liberty, equality, fraternity) and, more
specifically, modern Western political values and institutions such as democracy, constitutional government, parliamentary rule, individual rights,
and nationalism. In contrast to the traditional Islamic ideal in which political loyalty and solidarity rest in a transnational Islamic community (*ummah*) based upon common belief, modern nationalism represented the notion of national communities based not upon religion but upon common
language, territory, ethnic ties, and history.

Islam played an important role in the development of anticolonial independence movements and modern nationalism. It proved a factor to
varying degrees in the development of local and regional nationalisms:
Arab, Egyptian, Algerian, Tunisian, Moroccan, Iranian, Pakistani, Malaysian, and Indonesian. However, if religion was one factor, it was far from
the only one. The appeal to Islam varied regionally and from country to
country, conditioned by local contexts. In some areas Islam was a prominent ingredient in nationalism, while in others it was subordinated to
secular nationalism. In many parts of the Muslim world, Islamic reformism
(the modernist movement) and nationalism joined together to form a potent force. The major themes of Islamic reformism inspired and complemented nationalist concerns: the preservation of Muslim identity and re-
juvenation of the Islamic community in the face of the threat of political
and cultural assimilation; the achievement of Muslim unity and solidarity
to attain autonomy and independence. In North Africa, Iran, and South
Asia, Islam provided a common identity and allegiance, ideology and symbols, leadership and mosque-based centers for organization and communications. Traditional calls to the defense of Islam (Islam in danger!) and
"Allahu Akbar" (God is most great) proved effective rallying cries among
many. Islamic leaders and organizations were often key actors in independence and nationalist movements.

The Arab East

Islam played a less prominent role in the early development of Arab and
Egyptian nationalism. The first stirrings of Arab nationalism emerged in
reaction to Ottoman rule rather than as a response to the West. The Arab
Christian Literary Movement's emphasis on Arabic language, with its
sense of a community identity rooted in literature and history rather than

in religion, and the Young Turks' Turkification program, which shifted emphasis from Ottoman to Turkish ethnic and linguistic identity, fostered nascent nationalist sentiments among Arab and religious and ethnic minorities (Balkan, Greek, Syrian) over issues of language, identity, and political autonomy during the late nineteenth and early twentieth centuries.[24] Traditional transnational Islamic and imperial or sultanate forms of government experienced the stirrings of modern forms of nationalism based on common language, territory, and ethnic ties.

However, Arab and Egyptian nationalism did not really take shape and function as an effective tool in the struggle for independence from European hegemony until after World War I. Two factors were particularly important, reflecting both the persistent threat of the West and the growth of Muslim resistance. In 1920, in retribution for Ottoman support for Germany during World War I, the Allies broke up the Ottoman empire and carved out a number of modern nation-states. Under the Treaty of Sèvres Britain and France set up a mandate system which gave Britain control over Palestine (including modern-day Jordan) and Iraq, while France governed Syria (including modern-day Lebanon), and the Hejaz (part of Saudi Arabia) remained independent. At the same time, the struggle against European imperialism intensified with the development of nationalist movements of independence within which Islam was a factor to varying degrees.

While Arab and local nationalists often found it necessary to acknowledge their Islamic heritage, Islam was subordinated to more secular forms of nationalism whose primary emphasis was on other factors such as common language, history, traditions, and territory. Thus for example, in Egypt former students of Afghani and Abduh like the Egyptian nationalist leader Saad Zaghlul (d. 1927) and Taha Husayn pursued a more secular Egyptian nationalist path.

This secular turn of Afghani and Abduh's disciples was countered by Rashid Rida (d. 1935), who carried on the reformist tradition of Muhammad Abduh. However, the political realities of the post–World War I period pushed Rida toward a more conservative and anti-Western position. While maintaining the transnational Islamic ideal and identity of Muslims, he pragmatically and reluctantly accepted the reality of modern states and nationalism, though he would subordinate them to membership and solidarity in the broader Islamic community. The progressive secular bent of Egyptian modernists, especially former students of Afghani and Abduh, influenced Rida's growing admiration for Saudi Arabia's self-proclaimed Islamic state and his alignment with religious leaders (*ulama*) whose conservatism he had previously criticized. Thus Rida in later life reacted to the secularization and Westernization of Muslim society, which he saw as outcomes of modern rationalism. He increasingly moved away from Islamic modernism's openness to cultural synthesis. Instead, he emphasized the self-sufficiency and comprehensiveness of Islam and took a more critical attitude toward the threat of the West. Rida's more defensive and polemical posture both reflected the failure of Islamic modernism to secure a firm middle ground between rejection and cultural assimilation, and heralded the appearance of activist Islamic organizations—the Muslim Brotherhood in Egypt and the Jamaat-i-Islami (Islamic Society) in Pakistan—which possessed a more anti-Western and consciously self-sufficient Islamic ideology.

The Arab West (North Africa, Maghreb)

In North Africa Islamic reformism, inspired ideologically by Afghani and Abduh's Salafiyya movement, became closely allied with the nationalist movement after World War I. North African reformers countered French rule and the dangers of cultural assimilation, preached the need for a revival of their Arabic and Islamic identity and heritage, and advocated a modernist interpretation of Islam. Islamic reformers were among the founders and leaders of early nationalist organizations and parties which emphasized independence and a national identity based upon an Arab–Islamic heritage: Allal al-Fasi who led Morocco's religiously oriented Istiqlal (Independence) party in 1946; Abd al-Aziz al-Thalibi, founder of Tunisia's Destour (Constitution) party after World War I; and Abd al-Hamid Ibn Badis (Ben Badis, 1889–1940), who organized the Association of Algerian Ulama in 1931.

Religion was employed by religious and secular-minded Muslims alike who recognized its ability to transcend local religious (sectarian and Sufi) differences, and ethnic and tribal differences, to achieve mass mobilization. Islam was used as a symbol of national unity and identity with respect to French rule and the threat of cultural assimilation. It proved an effective means to mobilize popular support and to bridge the gap between Arab and Berber in Morocco and Algeria.

Iran

Iran differed from most of the Arab world and South Asia in retaining its independence. However, it remained vulnerable to British and Russian imperial designs: the British in southern Iran and the Russians in the north threatened Iranian sovereignty. Two events proved formative in the development of Iranian nationalism, the Tobacco Protest (1891–92) and the Constitutional Revolution (1905–11). Each represented a different response to Western influence. The former was motivated by the desire to protect Iran from foreign infiltration and economic dependence, and the latter by the need to limit the arbitrary powers of the Shah through Western-inspired constitutional reform.

When the Shah in 1890 gave a British company a monopoly over the sale and export of tobacco, a nationwide boycott and strikes were organized, led in large part by merchants and Muslim religious leaders. The protesters received support from Jamal al-Din al-Afghani, an adviser to the Shah, who warned that economic concessions were a major step toward foreign rule. Ayatollah Hasan al-Shirazi, a leading cleric, issued an Islamic decree or ruling (*fatwa*) which forbade smoking, and leading mosques provided sanctuary for protesters. Fearing Russian intervention, the Shah gave in to the protesters' demands.

The success of the Tobacco Protest and the desire to limit the arbitrary acts of their rulers emboldened religious leaders, using their mosques as centers of resistance and asylum, to again join with other sectors of society—landlords, merchants, army officers—in the Constitutional Revolution. Although the Shah initially resisted demands for a Western-style constitution, public protests as well as pressure from Britain and Russia led to the creation of a national assembly in 1906. However, Iranian nationalist gains evaporated over the following years when a change of rulers occurred, and Britain and Russia were able to carve out their own spheres of influence. Yet as a result of its experience in the late nineteenth and early twentieth century, Iranian nationalism had begun to counter foreign influence and domination with a strong reaction that included an Islamic component.

South Asia

In southern Asia both Pan-Islamic and Muslim nationalist movements developed in reaction to European colonialism. Despite sporadic anti-British Muslim riots, Muslims did not follow the Ottoman empire's alignment with Germany during World War I but instead generally remained pro-British. However, in the aftermath of the war, concern in the Muslim world that the Allies would dismember the Ottoman empire and abolish the caliphate led to a growth of Pan-Islamic sentiment which in the Indian subcontinent expressed itself in the formation of the Caliphate Movement in 1919. Within a year of its founding, Muslim fears were realized with the partition of the Ottoman empire in 1920, which ushered in the mandate period. The Caliphate Movement continued until 1924, when Kemal Ataturk, the ruler of Turkey, formally abolished the caliphate. However, its spirit of anti-European imperialism and national independence was carried over into the Indian National Congress, the major nationalist movement in India, whose membership cut across communal boundaries and thus included leaders from all of India's major religious groups.

By the thirties, however, Muslim separatism had increased. Growing conflict between Hindu and Muslim communities and the results of provincial elections in 1937 convinced Muhammad Ali Jinnah and Muhammad Iqbal of the Muslim League that the tendency in India to vote along communal lines threatened the identity of the Muslim community and might well lead to its domination by the Hindu majority in an independent India. The Muslim League increasingly demanded a separate Muslim state and became the chief proponent of Muslim nationalism. Despite Jinnah's secular disposition and Western life-style, the more secular-oriented leadership of the Muslim League placed greater emphasis on Islam so as to overcome its lackluster track record. Islamic slogans and symbols proved effective in mobilizing disparate Muslim groups in the demand for a Muslim homeland.

Ironically, the Islamic politics of the Muslim League proved surprisingly ineffective among religious leaders. Most religious leaders refused to support the League's call for a separate Muslim state, maintaining that nationalism and Islam were antithetical. The reasons for their condemnation of nationalism varied, influenced by anti-Europeanism and local politics as much as religious belief. Nationalism was regarded as a Western concept whose narrow particularism was contrary to Islamic universalism and divisive. Abul Hasan Ali Nadwi, a religious scholar and community leader, maintained that nationalism was "a narrow national feeling, racial prejudice, and an exaggerated regard for geographical division [which] are the characteristics of the Western mind."[25] Mawlana Abul Ala Mawdudi, another prominent religious leader and the founder of the Jamaat-i-Islami, noted: "Be it in the sphere of economics or politics, or civics or legal rights and duties, those who accept the principles of Islam are not divided by any distinction of nationality, of class, or country."[26]

Although much has been made of Islam's incompatibility with nationalism, the objections of Indian religious leaders to Muslim nationalism were motivated as much by their opposition to the leadership of Muhammad Ali Jinnah, whom they considered part of the Western secular elite, as by ideological conviction. Most were convinced that the Muslim nationalism of the Muslim League was motivated solely by a hypocritical attempt to win votes, and that it disguised Jinnah's intention to create a secular rather than Islamic state in the newly proposed Muslim homeland of Pakistan.

The peoples of the Indian subcontinent finally gained independence in 1947. Two states were carved out: a secular India that was overwhelmingly Hindu but with a significant Muslim minority, and Pakistan, a Muslim homeland where Muslim nationalism, it was hoped, would unite West and East Pakistan (presently Bangladesh), which were separated by a thousand miles of Indian territory.

Emerging States and the West:
From Emulation to the Failure of Liberal Regimes

In the aftermath of independence, the relationship of Islam to the West was less one of conflict than of grand emulation. As newly emerging states struggled to establish themselves, the West proved a necessary and often popular source and model. Although the independence struggle left deep resentment and scars, most rulers appropriated their colonial institutional legacy and ties. Modernization was imposed from above by governments and Westernized elites. European languages remained the second (and, among modern elites, often their preferred) language. In some countries European languages were the official language of government, the courts, and university education. Modern bureaucratic, educational, and legal systems continued intact, as did trade and commerce. Islamic law was generally confined to the area of personal status or family law. Thus, for example, French language and culture remained influential in North Africa and Lebanon, and English in southern Asia and Malaysia. Individuals, countries, cities, and institutions judged themselves, and were judged, to be modern by the degree to which they were Westernized—in language, dress, manners, knowledge, organizational structure and values, architecture, and infrastructure. America, in particular, enjoyed a certain pride of place, since it lacked the negative baggage of European colonial powers.

The Western orientation of development and modernization theory and its application in the Muslim world set the stage for decades of educational and technical exchange as well as political, economic, and military alliances. Few questioned the accepted wisdom that modernization meant the progressive Westernization and secularization of society. Admiring the West for its democratic ideals, military power, and technology, students in many Muslim countries prized a modern Western education at home and especially abroad. Such an education was often the surest ticket to responsible positions in government, business, and academia. Close international ties were formed between governments, the military, oil companies, and banks. Thus, for example, Habib Bourguiba, the "Great Combatant" exiled by France during the nationalist struggle, increasingly aligned Tunisia with France and French culture. French, not Arabic, was the language of higher education and culture. King Hussein of Jordan and

the Shah of Iran became close allies of the United States. Pakistan remained a member of the British Commonwealth, and English served as
the language of government and higher education.

However, during the fifties and sixties widespread dissatisfaction with
the track record of Western-inspired liberal nationalism took its toll, as
monarchs and governments tumbled from power in Egypt, Libya, the Sudan, Iraq, and Algeria. Egypt's growing disillusionment with Europe was
not atypical.

> World War I, the political strife of the inter-war years, the Great Depression,
> and finally, World War II exposed Egyptians to the failings of the consti-
> tutional and liberal governments of Europe, the ruthlessness of the powers,
> their indifference to principle in manipulating non-European peoples, and
> their contempt for their subjects. These events shook the confidence of many
> Egyptians and the future belonged to the West, and left others disappointed
> and alienated. Furthermore, the failure of the liberal regime . . . to deal eq-
> uitably with the country's political and economic problems also undermined
> faith in parliamentary regimes and in the value of individualism.[27]

Two ideological orientations or movements emerged, both of them populist: the Islamic activism of the Muslim Brotherhood and the Arab na-
tionalism/socialism of Gamal Abdel Nasser. Both emphasized indigenous
Arab–Islamic roots and sources, stressed Arab unity, and were critical of
the failures of liberal nationalism and the West. Both the Brotherhood and
Nasser would not only capture the imagination of Egyptians but also impact the Arab world and beyond. While Arab nationalism attempted to
subsume Islam, Islamic activism asserted the primacy of Islam and called
for an Islamic order—a political system guided by Islamic law—as the
basis for Arab unity and solidarity.

Modern Islamic Neorevivalist Movements
and the "Failure of the West"

Islamic reform and Muslim responses to European colonialism and the
West took a significant ideological turn in the thirties and forties with the
creation of two modern Islamic organizations, the Muslim Brotherhood of
Egypt and the Jamaat-i-Islami (Islamic Society) in the Indian subcontinent.
Both embodied a growing ambivalence toward the penetration of Western
culture, the threat of secular nationalism, and the continued political presence of Western imperialism.

> The West surely seeks to humiliate us, to occupy our lands and begin de-
> stroying Islam by annulling its laws and abolishing its traditions. In doing

this, the West acts under the guidance of the Church. The power of the Church is operative in orienting the internal and foreign policies of the Western bloc, led by England and America.[28]

Both the Brotherhood and the Jamaat emphasized Islam's ideological self-sufficiency, and were less accommodationist, and far more critical of the West. Whereas Islamic modernism had sought to learn from and emulate the success of the West, the Muslim Brotherhood and the Jamaat emphasized the failure of both the West (capitalism) and the East (Marxism) as models for development in the Muslim world. They denounced the Westernization and secularization of Muslim societies, the divisiveness of nationalism, and the excesses of capitalism, as well as the materialism and godlessness of Marxism. Muslims were told to remember that they possessed a third way, an alternative to foreign models and systems—Islam.

Their desire to transform society invariably led to involvement in politics and, at times, confrontation with their national governments. Activists and national regimes accused each other of violence and sedition. At various times the activist leaders were arrested and their organizations suppressed. Hassan al-Banna was assassinated in 1949, and Brotherhood leaders were executed and the Muslim Brotherhood officially repressed and dissolved in the late sixties. While Mawlana Mawdudi and Jamaat leaders were imprisoned and even condemned to death on one occasion, the Jamaat-i-Islami was able to participate in the political process more freely than their Egyptian counterparts.

The significance of the Muslim Brotherhood and the Jamaat-i-Islami extended far beyond their national homelands and in time took on transnational significance. The Brotherhood inspired the establishment of similar organizations in the Sudan, Syria, Jordan, the Gulf, and Africa. The Jamaat developed sister organizations in India, Bangladesh, Afghanistan, and Kashmir. The writings of the Brotherhood's Hassan al-Banna and of Sayyid Qutb and Mawlana Mawdudi of the Jamaat-i-Islami would in time become widely translated and disseminated throughout much of the Islamic world. Their vision of Islam as an alternative ideology for state and society and the example of their organizations and activities provided a model for future generations of Muslims. As such, for many they constituted a link between the traditional religious heritage and the realities of modern life.

Arab Nationalism/Socialism and the West

Arab nationalism/socialism and the figure of Gamal Abdel Nasser dominated much of the Arab world and challenged Western powers from the midfifties on. As the influence of European colonialism diminished, the United States and the Soviet Union emerged as superpowers. Western capitalism, Marxism, and socialism were contending forces in a Cold War that seemed to force developing nations to choose between the West or communism. Liberal nationalism seemed exhausted or discredited as regimes were toppled by Arab socialist movements. New governments advocating Arab socialism came to power in Egypt, Syria, Iraq, Libya, the Sudan, and Algeria. Nasserism, Egypt's Gamal Abdel Nasser's Pan-Arab nationalism/socialism, inspired the revolutions of Libya's Muammar Qaddafi and the Sudan's Gaafar Muhammad Nimeiri in the late sixties; the Arab socialism of the Baath ("Resurrection") party in Syria and Iraq; and the Arab–Islamic socialism of Algerian independence (1962).

All new governments shared a worldview prevalent among many Third World countries. They indicted European imperialism for its invasion and occupation, as well as its policies which divided by creating states and drawing artificial national boundaries, thus debilitating the Arab and Muslim world. They espoused a continuing struggle against colonialism, exacerbated by the West's role in the creation and support of a Western colony, Israel, in the Arab homeland, and denounced the failures of the traditional Arab political leadership and its Western liberal nationalism. They condemned the radical individualism of capitalism, called for Arab unity and solidarity, and promised the creation of a new social order to alleviate the plight of the masses in Arab societies.

Perhaps no modern Arab leader captured the imagination of the Arab world and the Third World more than Gamal Abdel Nasser (1918–70). Nasser's memory cast a long shadow over political development in the Middle East. His name came to be associated with the two confrontations that epitomized the anti-imperialist mood and politics of the period: Suez and Palestine. A charismatic leader whose ability to sway a crowd was the envy of every Arab politician and the bane of his enemies, Nasser fired the imaginations and mobilized the emotions of Arabs and Muslims far beyond the borders of Egypt. Wishing to establish his leadership throughout the Arab world, Nasser broadened Egyptian nationalism into an Arab nationalism/socialism rooted in the region's common Arab–Islamic heritage. Although he competed with the Hashemites of Iraq and Jordan as well as the House of Saud for leadership in the Arab world, among the peoples of that world he was unrivaled in popularity, the object of a personality cult matched by very few Arab or Muslim rulers except perhaps the Ayatollah Khomeini. There were Nasserite parties in Arab countries and active student organizations in Lebanon, Syria, and Jordan. Nasser's picture adorned the walls of homes and the streets of cities and villages in many countries. He was seen as the savior of the Arabs and Palestinians.

Nasser, the man and his message, had many facets. He will long be remembered for his call for Arab unity, his defiance of the West and assertion of Arab independence from Western dominance in the Suez. He asserted Egypt's claim to leadership of the Arab world, championed the struggle for the liberation of Palestine, and espoused "positive neutrality" in the Cold War between the United States and the Soviet Union. He became the architect of Arab socialist reform.

The overthrow of the British-dominated regime of Egypt's King Farouk by Nasser and the Free Officers in the July 1952 coup was cast as a repudiation of European colonial influence, the failed policies of Western liberal nationalism and capitalism, and the ignominy of Egypt's defeat in Palestine in 1948. Nasser's nationalist and anti-imperialist (often inter-preted as anti-Western) credentials and his transnational popularity and leadership in the Arab and Third worlds were solidified by his defiance of the West over control of the Suez Canal and by his creation, with India's Nehru and Indonesia's Sukarno, of the Alliance of Nonaligned Nations.

When the United States withdrew its promised loan for building the Aswan Dam in 1956, Nasser seized control of the Suez. He nationalized the Suez Canal Company, dramatically proclaiming to a tumultuous crowd: "O Americans, may you choke to death in your fury!"[29] He stood his ground as Britain's Prime Minister Anthony Eden denounced him as a Hitler (much as George Bush would later denounce a would-be successor to Nasser, Saddam Hussein). Assisted by Israel, which the Arabs regarded as a colony of Europe and the United States, France and Britain invaded Egypt in 1956, while Israel occupied the Sinai. Although it was U.N. intervention and pressure from the United States against this violation of international law that forced Britain, France, and Israel to withdraw, Nasser was credited in the Arab, Muslim, and broader Third World with this singular defeat of European colonialism. In the eyes of many Western governments, Nasser's defiance of the West at Suez—coupled with his impassioned denunciation of Western imperialism, his wars with Israel, and his doctrine of "positive neutrality" (he accepted arms from the Soviet Union and recognized the People's Republic of China)—branded him as simply anti-Western. However, for much of the Third World he became the symbol of anti-imperialism.

The emergence of the Arab nationalism/socialism of Nasser and the Baath party signaled a period in which local or state nationalism was transformed into or equated with a transnational, Pan-Arab nationalist sentiment that stressed Arab political unification and independence from foreign domination. Both Nasserism and the Baath blamed European colonialism and the rivalry for power among pro-Western Arab monarchs for the ills of the Arab world. The artificial façade of modern nation-states and societies, whose boundaries were often arbitrarily drawn by Europe and whose European-appointed or dependent leaders lacked political legitimacy, had produced a fractured Arab nation. These divisions, they argued, had perpetuated Arab weakness and dependence upon the West and rendered the Arab world incapable of thwarting the creation of Israel.

The program of Arab nationalism was idealistic, revolutionary, and ambitious. It affirmed an ideal rather than a reality—the existence of an Arab nation that possessed a political and economic unity. Arab unity and solidarity were rooted in a transnational Arab identity based upon common language, history, and territory. Arab socialism promised the creation of a new social order, based upon state planning and control of major industries, financial institutions, and utilities. Arab socialism was to be a third alternative to capitalism and communism, eschewing the capitalist evils of individualism (the concentration of economic power and wealth) and consumerism as well as Marxism's atheism and theory of class conflict. Arab regimes were denounced for their failure to respond to the needs of the predominantly poor masses of workers and peasants. This failure was attributed to economic systems controlled either by the indigenous feudalism of a few privileged elites or by capitalism, which was equated with Western ownership or economic dependence. Arab socialism promised a more socially just society through state control of national resources and production, a more equitable distribution of wealth, and social services.

The union of Egypt and Syria in 1958 through the formation of the United Arab Republic, with Nasser elected its first president, and a Baathist coup in Iraq in 1963 seemed to signal the incorporation of these three major countries in a new Arab order. It was, however, a short-lived promise, for Nasser and the Baathists failed to resolve differences over leadership of the new state. But the failure of Arab leaders and of Arab socialism to create a transnational political union was offset by their rhetorical and political opposition to Israel. Palestine proved an effective symbol and rallying post.

Palestine

The creation of Israel in 1948 was seen as the boldest example of the duplicity of European colonialism and its desire to keep the Arabs divided and weak. Israel itself was considered a European–American colony in the midst of the Arab nation. The Arab defeats in the 1948 and 1956 wars were a further humiliation. For Arab leaders, Palestine provided a no-lose cause (not threatening class, political, or religious interests) that each could exploit domestically and internationally as rulers competed in the force of their denunciations. Military leaders and monarchs, the educated and the uneducated, the landed and the peasants, the secular and the Islamically oriented—all could identify with the plight of the Palestinians. The struggle against Israel symbolized the battle against imperialism, provided a common cause and sense of unity, and distracted from the failures of regimes and of Arab nationalism/socialism. As in the nationalist struggle, both the secular and the religiously oriented, Arab nationalists and Islamic activists, found common ground in regarding the liberation of Palestine as a great jihad against Western imperialism.

Arab Nationalism and Islam

While Arab nationalism was primarily secular in orientation, it did acknowledge the Islamic component of Arab identity and history. Arab nationalism had an affinity (linguistic, historical, and religious) with Islam. Arabic is the language of revelation and official prayer in Islam; Arab and Islamic history are intertwined (early heroes, conquests, and accomplishments); the homeland and early centers of power and culture were located in the Arab world. Moreover, Arab nationalists and the Muslim Brotherhood, active in Egypt and Syria, shared common concerns such as anti-imperialism, the need for Arab unity and solidarity, and the liberation of Palestine. However, although the Muslim Brotherhood in Egypt had initially backed Nasser and the Free Officers, the Brotherhood went over to the opposition when it became clear that Nasser did not intend to establish an Islamic government. Nasser's government clashed violently with the Brotherhood and suppressed it in 1954 and again in 1965, after abortive attempts to assassinate Nasser; thousands were imprisoned, and a number of its key leaders executed.

Though Nasser would brook no Islamic opposition, the realities of Egyptian and Arab society caused him to increasingly use or manipulate religion to legitimate his state socialism and broaden his popular support. His need to counter and control an Islamic opposition as well as to resist Saudi Arabia's increasing assertion of transnational Islamic leadership moved Nasser to use Islam carefully in his foreign policy. The Saudis had become progressively more leery of Nasser's aggressive, expansionist assertion of Pan-Arab leadership. They were also threatened by Arab socialism's populist critique of the "feudalism" of conservative Arab monarchies and its support for their overthrow. The Saudis countered the threat

of Arab nationalism by espousing a Pan-Islamic ideology and leadership
and by condemning Nasser's un-Islamic "socialism." They used their
Islamic claims as keepers of Islam's sacred cities of Mecca and Medina
and protectors of the pilgrimage, and their oil wealth, to promote themselves as patrons of Islam and to encourage Muslim solidarity. They created international Islamic organizations such as the World Muslim League
(1966) and the Organization of the Islamic Conference (1969), through
which they distributed funds for the promotion and preservation of Islam
(the building of mosques, schools, hospitals, and the printing and distribution of religious literature) and organized Muslim countries and institutions.

Nasser countered by employing religious symbols, leaders, and institutions to legitimate and win support for his Arab socialist ideology and
policies. His government controlled or coopted the religious establishment.
It nationalized al-Azhar University, the oldest seat of Islamic learning and
religious authority, and controlled salaries and funding for many mosques
and religious personnel. Nasser used both the religious scholars of al-
Azhar and a state magazine, *The Pulpit of Islam*, to legitimate Arab socialism and its policies of state ownership and nationalization. He identified Islam with Arab socialism and its principles of anti-imperialism, social
justice, and equality. At a meeting of the Arab–Islamic conference on
liberation organizations, Nasser emphasized that the Arab and Islamic
worlds were facing one enemy–imperialism. Egypt sponsored international
meetings such as the Afro-Asian Conferences in 1964 and 1965, which
explored Islam's relevance to the struggle against imperialism.[30]

However, at its core Nasser's Arab nationalism, like that of the Baath,
remained primarily secular in orientation. Nowhere was this clearer than
in the 1967 Arab–Israeli war, which was fought under the banner and
slogans of Arab nationalism/socialism. The disastrous defeat of Arab
forces stood as an indictment of Arab nationalism, further inflamed Arab
and Muslim passions against Israel and American neoimperialism, and
became a major catalyst for the Islamic resurgence.

The first half of the twentieth century witnessed both the end of European
colonialism and the emergence of modern Muslim nation-states. Both experiences were heavily dependent upon or influenced by the West. The
breakup of the Ottoman empire and the creation by Britain and France of
mandate countries created a legacy which has contributed to the instability
of regimes and leaders down to the present. It enhanced the image of a
militant imperialist West and created modern states whose artificially
drawn boundaries and mandate-appointed or approved rulers possessed
questionable political legitimacy.

Throughout the turbulent politics of the postcolonial, postindependence period, the roller-coaster relationship between the West and the Muslim world continued. On the one hand, Europe and America represented the example par excellence of modernization and development, of what it meant to live fully in the modern world, from architecture and medicine to education and technology. On the other hand, in the eyes of many, the Muslim world's relative backwardness and Sisyphean battle to build strong, stable societies were attributed to the bitter harvest of European colonialism. The creation of Israel, the Suez crisis, and the politics of the Cold War were regarded as aspects of post–World War II neocolonialism, a hegemonic chess game between the United States and the Soviet Union which threatened the identity and integrity of the Muslim world.

While Arab nationalism/socialism had swept aside the failures of liberal nationalism, the heady visions of unity and power symbolized by Gamal Abdel Nasser in the sixties were shattered by the inescapable realities of the 1967 Arab–Israeli war. Arab nationalism/socialism had proved a grand bust, a shattered myth—in the eyes of others, a setback from which it still has not recovered. Ideologically, it failed to produce Pan-Arab unity and solidarity: Pan-Arabism proved incapable of transcending the diverse and often competing interests of Arab leaders and societies. Socioeconomically, Arab socialism with its nationalization and land reform did not usher in the promised egalitarian Arab order or significantly alter the plight of the masses. As the Six-Day War demonstrated, diplomatically and militarily the Arab governments had proved impotent in the international arena. Parliamentary democracy had proven incapable of controlling ruling elites and the military. Despite several decades of independence, imported ideologies and development schemes seemed to have failed. Old issues of identity, national ideology, political legitimacy, socioeconomic reform, and Western domination persisted. The failures of governments and national ideologies (liberal nationalism and Arab socialism), epitomized by the humiliation of 1967, precipitated a deepening sense of disillusionment and crisis in many Muslim societies and contributed to the political and social resurgence of Islam.

4

Islam and the State:
Dynamics of the Resurgence

In the minds of most Westerners, for whom the history of Islam and the West are at best a vague notion, knowledge of and attitudes toward Islam and the Muslim world have been shaped by contemporary images and experiences encapsulated in terms such as *Islamic fundamentalism* and *terrorism*. The phrase ''Muslim fundamentalist'' has become a convenient, if misleading, way for the media and Western governments to identify a wide-ranging array of groups in the Muslim world, as well as a ready ''bogey'' for Muslim regimes wishing to discredit and disparage their opposition. For many, ''fundamentalism'' conjures up images of mobs shouting death to America, embassies in flames, assassins and hijackers threatening innocent lives, hands lopped off, and women oppressed. The contemporary revival of Islam in Muslim politics is far more multifaceted and significant than these images and slogans communicate. Its presence in and impact upon Muslim societies is more pervasive and nuanced as both a political and a social phenomenon. What is the diversity of political Islam as revealed in the recent experiences of Muslim states? How have governments used Islam, and how has the implementation of Islam affected the dynamics and development of Muslim politics? How has the West misinterpreted, and developed policies that have reinforced, Muslim stereotypes of an anti-Islamic neocolonialism and thus contributed to further alienation and resentment?

Islam and the Modern State

By the midtwentieth century most of the Muslim world had achieved political independence. The influence and continued attraction of the West

74

was evident in the more secular path chosen by most rulers and modern elites. Even in those countries where Islam had played an important role in nationalist movements, the new generation that came to power opted for a more secular orientation. As one looked across the Muslim world, three orientations or models for the relationship of religion to the state could be distinguished: Islamic, secular, and Muslim. Saudi Arabia was a self-declared Islamic state. The monarchy of the house of Saud based its legitimacy on Islam, claiming to govern and be governed by the Quran and Islamic law. The house of Saud had established a close relationship with the *ulama*, who continued to enjoy a privileged position as advisers to the government and officials in the legal and educational systems. The Saudi government used Islam both to legitimate domestic policies and to conduct foreign policy.

At the other end of the spectrum Turkey, the only remnant of the Ottoman empire, had opted for a secular state with religion severely restricted to personal life. Turkey, under the leadership of Kemal Ataturk (president, 1923–38), embarked upon a comprehensive process of Turkification and Westernization, and a secularization that transformed language and history as well as religion and politics. Western script replaced Arabic script, and history was rewritten, suppressing its Arabic component and glorifying (and at times fabricating) its Turkic heritage. Ataturk autocratically oversaw a series of reforms which deposed the sultan, abolished the caliphate, disestablished Islam, closed seminaries, proscribed the wearing of clerical garb, and replaced traditional institutions (law, education, government) with modern, Western-inspired alternatives.

The majority of countries in the Muslim world, however, fall into a middle position. They are Muslim states, in that the majority of the population and its heritage are Muslim, yet they have pursued a moderated secular path of development. While most looked to the West for the basis of their systems of modern constitutional government, law, and education, they have also injected Islamic provisions into their constitutions, requiring that the head of state be a Muslim or that Islamic law be recognized as a source of law (even when this was not the case in reality). These governments sought to control religion by incorporating religious institutions within the bureaucracy—within ministries of law, education, and religious affairs. With few exceptions the general trend, expectation, and goal of governments and their Western-educated elites was to create modern states modeled upon Western paradigms.

Ideologically the prevailing tendency, following Western models, was to foster secular forms of national identity and solidarity and to limit religion to private rather than public life. Local (Egyptian, Syrian, Libyan) or regional/linguistic (Arab or Baath) forms of nationalism or socialism prevailed. This secular trend began to change almost imperceptibly in the sixties, however, and the change became more pronounced in the seventies and eighties. As examples from the Sudan, Egypt, Libya, and Iran illustrate, the usage and manifestations of Islam varied significantly. Differences in sociopolitical environments, leadership, and economic conditions determined how Islam was defined and implemented. Similarly, Islam proved to be both a challenge and a threat—a source of stability and instability, of legitimacy and revolt, utilized by pro-Western and anti-Western governments alike. Military (and ex-military) rulers like Libya's Muammar Qaddafi, the Sudan's Gaafar Muhammad Nimeiri, Egypt's Anwar Sadat, and Pakistan's Zulfikar Ali Bhutto and Gen. Zia ul-Haq appealed to Islam to strengthen their legitimacy, mobilize popular support, and justify government policies. By contrast, Tunisia's Habib Bourguiba and the Shah of Iran pursued more overtly secular paths.

Sadat, Qaddafi, and Nimeiri shared a common link with Egypt's charismatic leader, Gamal Abdel Nasser. Qaddafi and Nimeiri seized power in 1969, patterned their revolutions on Nasser's 1952 July Revolution, and aligned themselves with Nasser's brand of Arab nationalism/socialism with its vision of Arab unity. In 1970 Qaddafi, Nasser, and Nimeiri concluded the Tripoli Pact, which aimed at the complete merger of Libya, Egypt, and the Sudan. A similar pact was concluded with Nasser's successor, Anwar Sadat, but it ultimately failed to be implemented.

In the wake of the 1967 Arab defeat and its discrediting of Arab nationalism, the revolutionary nationalist/socialist governments of Libya, the Sudan, and Egypt turned to Islam to buttress their faltering nationalist ideologies.

Libya

> O you people, tear to shreds all imported books which do not set forth [the values of] the Arab heritage and of Islam, of socialism and of progress.
>
> —MUAMMAR QADDAFI

With these striking words, Muammar Qaddafi announced his wide-ranging cultural revolution, an indigenous socialist vision rooted in Libya's Arab heritage and Islamic faith.[1] Few leaders in the Muslim world have captured the attention of the West and symbolized "Islamic radicalism and terrorism" in the seventies and eighties more stridently than Qaddafi. Long before the Islamic revolutionary slogans of Khomeini's Iran, billboards in Libya, referring to Qaddafi's seizure of power on the first (Al Fateh) of September, declared: "Al Fateh is an Islamic Revolution."[2]

Libya's modern development has been profoundly affected by two events. In 1959 oil was discovered there, and so this poor nation of one million inhabitants, which had been economically dependent upon Britain and America, became a leading oil producer within a decade. In 1969 a dramatic coup d'état brought Qaddafi to power. As with similar revolutionary movements in the Arab world that came to power in Egypt, Syria, Iraq, and Algeria during the late fifties and early sixties, the rationale for the Libyan coup was socioeconomic reform necessitated by the failure of a Western-influenced monarchy. Under Qaddafi three interrelated ideas were woven into Libya's ideological identity: Pan-Arabism, socialism, and Islam.

Qaddafi's appeals to Islam were influenced by his personal piety and the sociopolitical realities of his country. "Islam has been and remains the basic glue of Libyan society. As the primary unit of loyalty and identity, religion has been 'a political symbol of crucial importance in controlling and mobilizing the masses.' "[3] Shortly after coming to power in September 1969, Qaddafi turned to Islam so as to enhance his legitimacy and that of Libya's socialist revolution as well as to spread his influence in the Arab and Muslim world.[4]

Qaddafi deposed the conservative monarchy of King Idris, whose right to rule had been Islamically legitimated by his descent from the nineteenth-century Islamic revivalist leader Muhammad ibn al-Sanusi (1787–1859), who had established an Islamic state in Libya. Thus it was not surprising that Qaddafi and the clique of young officers who had overthrown the king found it useful, if not necessary, to justify their actions Islamically. Qaddafi's early statements placed his new government on an Islamically legitimated Arab socialist path: "a socialism emanating from the true religion of Islam and the Noble Book."[5]

During the seventies Qaddafi introduced a series of reforms which reasserted Libya's Arab–Islamic heritage and thus employed Islam to buttress its national ideology and Arab nationalism/socialism. This emphasis combined his fundamental belief in both Arab nationalism and Islam, in both Arab and Muslim unity. Signs of Libya's European (Italian, British, and American) Christian colonial past were suppressed or replaced. Churches were closed; missionary activities were banned, British and American military bases were closed. Arabic was reintroduced as the official language; Arabic names and street signs replaced their Western counterparts. Islamic laws forbade alcohol consumption, nightclubs, and gambling; the Islamic Call Society was established for the propagation of Islam at home and abroad. Islamic criminal penalties (the *huddad*, "limits" of God) were reinstated: amputation for theft, stoning for fornication and adultery. However, if closely examined, despite much fanfare by the Libyan government

and the Western press, Islamic law has in fact remained relatively periph-
eral to Libyan society.

During the latter part of the seventies, Qaddafi issued his master plan,
a utopian vision of society, *The Green Book*. Its title was deliberately
suggestive in its Islamic and universal claims. Muslims believe that their
book, the Quran, is the literal word of God and source of guidance for
Muslim society. They acknowledge that Jews and Christians as People of
the Book (i.e., recipients of God's revelation). The Chinese had their *Red
Book*, Mao Tse-tung's ideological guide for Third World revolution. Since
the color green is associated with the Prophet Muhammad, the title of *The
Green Book* could be understood as both an Islamic alternative and an
option for the Third World as well. Similarly, just as China had its Red
Guard, Qaddafi also created a Green Revolutionary Guard to implement
his cultural revolution.

The Green Book is a series of three small volumes: *The Solution to the
Problem of Democracy* (1975), *Solution of the Economic Problem: Socialism* (1977), and *Social Basis of the Third International Theory* (1979).
It was taught in the schools, became required reading for all Libyan citizens, and was propagated through the innumerable wall posters which
seemed to dominate the Libyan landscape. Qaddafi's assessment of the
Arab world's plight was cast in the categories of traditional Islamic revivalism. *The Green Book* championed many of the themes common to
Arab nationalism and contemporary Islamic thought: anticolonialism and
anti-imperialism; dependence on the West as the source of Muslim weakness and loss of identity; social injustice characterized by exploitation and
corruption; the return to Islam to restore Arab/Muslim power and great-
ness; and Qaddafi's own brand of Islamic socialism or social justice. Qaddafi called for return to an Islam that provided a comprehensive guide for
humanity: "We must take the Quran as the focal point in our journey in
life because the Quran is perfect; it is light and in it are solutions to the
problems of man . . . from personal status to . . . international problems."[6]

The Green Book heralded a universal, revolutionary ideology, Qaddafi's
Third International Theory, for the creation of a new political and social
order—a third alternative to the two great modern options of capitalism
and Marxism. Despite the initial Islamic ideological basis for *The Green
Book*, the last two installments omitted any reference to Islam. Qaddafi's
ambitions were far broader. First, *The Green Book* was to serve as the
blueprint for Libyan society, which would then serve as a model for the
Third World. Second, his revolutionary goal was to create a new populist
socialist world order with *The Green Book* as its guide: "*The Green Book*
is the guide to the emancipation of man. *The Green Book* is the gospel.
The new gospel. The gospel of the new era, the era of the masses."[7]

Qaddafi's new gospel for the world was but an extension of his earlier decision to implement his own version of a socialism distinct from the prevailing foreign ideologies and erected on the twin pillars of Arabism and Islam:

> Our socialism is both Arab and Islamic. We stand midway between social-
> ism and communism and socialism and capitalism. Our socialism springs
> directly from the needs and requirements of the Arab world, its heritage,
> and the needs of society. It consists of a social justice which means suffi-
> ciency in production and just distribution. These principles are to be found
> in the Islamic religion, and particularly in the law of *zakat* [alms].[8]

Qaddafi implemented his vision for society during the midseventies, creating a populist socialist state of the masses (*jamahiriya*). Libya's new
populist identity and ideology were institutionalized in March 1977 when
the General People's Congress, which replaced Qaddafi's ruling Revolutionary Command Council, changed Libya's name from the Libyan Arab
Republic to the Socialist People's Libyan Arab Jamahiriya. Qaddafi resigned as president to become the philosopher/ideologue of the revolution.
Mixing populist ideological statements with political, social, and economic
experimentation, Qaddafi undertook a cultural revolution. However, it was
based not on the divine guidance of the Quran or the example of the
Prophet, but on the iconoclastic thought of Qaddafi.

Libya's Al-Jamahiriya (state of the masses) was to be a people's state.
Libya became a decentralized, participatory government of people's committees which controlled government offices, schools, the media, and
many corporations. Qaddafi encouraged people's committees to take over
Libya's embassies and mosques.

The economic policy of *The Green Book* included the abolition of private land ownership, wages, and rent in favor of worker control and participation in the means of production. Implementation of the new socialist
experiment began in 1978. Libyans were limited to ownership of one home
or apartment, so as to meet Libya's housing crisis. Private retail trade was
all but abolished. Factory workers were encouraged to seize their factories,
and self-management programs spread throughout Libya's public companies as workers overnight became partners in this workers' revolution.[9]

"Qaddafi's Islam"

While the Western media found it attractive to speak of Libya's Islamic
fundamentalist state and to label much of what Qaddafi did or threatened
to do as Islamic—Islamic laws, Islamic bombs, Islamic terrorism—many

Muslims were increasingly incensed by Qaddafi. Qaddafi subordinated Islam to his interests and revolutionary ideology, used Islam to export his influence in the Muslim world, and earned the condemnation of Muslims inside and outside Libya for his unorthodox interpretation of Islam. Qaddafi, not the *ulama*, defined Islam. Though he used Islam to legitimate Arab socialism and his radical populist state, he did not tolerate alternative Islamic voices and visions. He denounced the *ulama* as "reactionaries," rejected their authoritative role as guardians of Islam, and sought to reform their centuries-old interpretation of Islam: "As the Muslims have strayed from Islam, a review is demanded. The [Libyan revolution] is a revolution rectifying Islam, presenting Islam correctly, purifying Islam of the reactionary practices which dressed it in retrograde clothing not its own."[10]

Qaddafi maintained the right of all learned Muslims (not just the traditional religious leadership) to interpret Islam. This provided the rationale for Qaddafi to freely and idiosyncratically reinterpret Islamic belief and practice. He produced what his critics regarded as a radical Islam that rejected key aspects of Islamic tradition to support Libya's populist state and his Third International Theory.

Contrary to stereotypes, Qaddafi's Libya was not an Islamic fundamentalist state tied to an inflexible literalist return to Islam. Qaddafi's brand of Islam was highly innovative and, for many Muslims, a radical revisionism tantamount to heresy. The major example of Qaddafi's innovative interpretation of Islam concerned the place of Islamic law, the Sharia, in the state. Traditionally, the accepted criterion for an Islamic state was a Muslim ruler's official acknowledgment of the Sharia. But Qaddafi set Islamic law aside. *The Green Book* replaced the traditional, comprehensive role of the Sharia. The Quran and *The Green Book*, which Qaddafi maintained was rooted in the Quran, became the ideological foundation of Libyan society. However, the Quran was restricted to private life (religious observances such as prayer, fasting, almsgiving) while Qaddafi's *Green Book*, not Islamic law, governed politics and society.

Qaddafi also boldly denied the authenticity and binding force of many prophetic traditions (Muhammad's exemplary practice), changed the dating of the Muslim calendar, declared that the pilgrimage to Mecca was not obligatory, equated the alms tithe (*zakat*) with social security and, contrary to tradition, maintained that this tithe could be a variable rate rather than a fixed (2.5 percent) tax.[11]

Qaddafi's usurpation of religious authority and his interpretation of Islam set him on a collision course with religious leaders who resented his attack on their authority and interests as well as his reinterpretation of Islamic doctrine. The *ulama* condemned Qaddafi's "innovative" interpretations—his rejection of the binding force of prophetic traditions, his substitution of *The Green Book* for Sharia governance, and his abolition of private property—for their deviation from Islamic tradition. Qaddafi justified his autocratic rule as a religiopolitical leader/ideologue and his rejection of traditional religious leaders in the name of the people's authority and Islamic social justice. People's popular committees were "instructed to 'seize the mosques' to rid them of 'paganist tendencies' and of *imams* [religious leaders] accused of 'propagating heretical tales elaborated over centuries of decadence and which distort the Islamic religion.' ''[12]

Qaddafi's authority and legitimacy have also been challenged by Islamic movements such as the Muslim Brotherhood and the Islamic Liberation Organization (ILO). In a country where organized dissent is extremely dangerous, a regime which has used Islam to enhance its legitimacy has faced opposition in the name of Islam not only from the religious establishment but from Islamic movements. These activists share Qaddafi's criticism of the religious establishment as obstacles to change, but regard Qaddafi as a military opportunist who has manipulated and distorted Islam for his own ends. Qaddafi in return regards the Brotherhood, a strong religiopolitical movement in Egypt and the neighboring Sudan, as a political organization whose ideology, goal, and organization (antisocialist, Pan-Islamic, hierarchical) are a direct threat to his populist, socialist, Arab nationalist vision. The ILO, active in Jordan, Tunisia, and Egypt as well as Libya, infiltrated the military and was implicated in attempted coups in 1983 and in 1984.[13] Reports of militant Islamic opposition have persisted in the late eighties and nineties. Members of groups referred to as al-Jihad and Hizbullah were executed in 1987. Muslim student activism became more noticeable in 1989 with greater numbers of women wearing head scarves on campus, student demonstrations at Tripoli's al-Fatah University which were attributed to the Muslim Brotherhood, and a resumption of political discussions at mosques.[14] In the fall of 1989, Islamic militants participated in bloody confrontations with security forces and were denounced by Qaddafi as a "cancer, the black death and AIDS."[15] One observer has concluded: "The Islamic movement in Libya may well form the best articulated and potentially most powerful opposition in the *Jamahiriyah.*"[16]

Foreign Policy

Since Qaddafi envisioned himself as the major revolutionary leader in the Muslim world, Islam served as an important element in Libya's export of its cultural revolution. Like Saudi Arabia, Libya under Qaddafi combined appeals to Islamic solidarity with oil wealth to promote its role as a leader in the Islamic world. Islam was never the only factor but one of many in

Libya's foreign policy, joined with Arabism, Africanism, and a broader Third Worldism. Moreover, separating rhetoric from reality often proves difficult, given Qaddafi's pragmatism, his penchant for exaggerated rhetoric, and the Western media and the United States' bestowal on him of a larger-than-life image as a major source of worldwide terrorism.

Qaddafi's foreign adventurism grew out of his desire to fill the shoes of his hero Gamal Abdel Nasser as the leader of the Arab world and to be acknowledged as a leader and hero in Africa and the Third World. His militant universal vision drew its early inspiration from his interpretation of Islam, its expansionist universal message and mission, and its relevance to world liberation. He also learned from the example and methods of Egypt's Nasser and King Faisal of Saudi Arabia, who both had used Islamic rhetoric and organizations in the late sixties to compete for international leadership in the Muslim world. As a result, where feasible, Qaddafi combined missionary activity and propaganda with revolutionary politics. His radical politics proceeded from a worldview which demonized the West, especially the United States, and blamed the ills of the Arab and Muslim worlds (as indeed of the entire Third World) on European colonialism, American neocolonialism, and the state of Israel. Qaddafi rejected communism (Marxist atheism and its values) as an ideology, but had no difficulty aligning Libya with the Soviet Union and Eastern Europe.

For Qaddafi, the goal in a world dominated by the West was retribution and the struggle for national liberation.[17] He employed ideological appeals to Pan-Arabism, Pan-Islam, and Third World liberation. Libya funded governments, Islamic organizations, and extremist movements of many stripes around the world. Libya donated schools, mosques, and hospitals, and funded economic development projects as well as kidnappings, bombings, and murder. Qaddafi called for the destruction of Israel as easily as he advocated the overthrow of Saudi Arabia or Egypt. He supported, claimed to support, or was claimed to have supported tyrants like Idi Amin of Uganda and Jean-Bédel Bokassa of the Central African Republic, Muslim minority liberation movements in the Philippines and southern Thailand, Islamic extremist movements from Egypt to Indonesia, Abu Nidal's radical Palestinian group, and the Irish Republican Army (IRA).

Because of the early identification of Libya as a "fundamentalist Islamic state," owing to its implementation of Islamic laws and criminal punishments, Libyan state-sponsored terrorism, regardless of its motives, came to be indiscriminately associated with Islam whether the actors were the Irish Republican Army, Arab or Palestinian organizations, Maoists, or Islamic extremists. Regardless of the orientation or authenticity of a movement, to be associated with Libya was often tantamount to admission of violent radicalism. Indeed, many governments in the Muslim world often found in Libya a ready-made ostensible cause for discrediting opposition movements.

The primary organizational example of Libyan use of Islam to promote its activities in the Muslim world is the Islamic Call Society. Within the post-1967 context of the Muslim world, with its renewed emphasis upon Islamic identity and solidarity domestically and internationally, Libya's Revolutionary Command Council established the Society in 1972 as a major vehicle of Libya's foreign policy. Its goal was not simply the preaching and promotion of Islam at home but its spread abroad as an integral part of Libyan diplomatic and political objectives. Mass media, religious publications, missionary activities, mosque building as well as medical and social welfare services were among the main tools for the spread of Libyan political influence. Recalling Libyan influence in Africa, a former Gambian diplomat noted:

> Those of us who have served as diplomats from Africa in these parts of the world know that significant amounts have been spent on these kinds of ventures. There is no Muslim country or country with a significant number of Muslims that has not received some financial support from the Libyans to build a mosque of some size.[18]

Combining diplomacy with the activities of the Islamic Call Society, Libya in the seventies and early eighties competed with Saudi Arabia in its use of Islam, employing its petrodollars to extend its influence from Muslim student groups to liberation movements. Thus for example, in the early seventies Libya was one of the first and the strongest supporters of the separatist Moro National Liberation Front (MNLF) in the southern Philippines, giving sanctuary to its leaders and extending aid for religious activities and refugees as well as military and diplomatic support.[19] Both Saudi Arabia and Libya were prime movers in bringing the Marcos government and the MNLF together for the ill-fated Tripoli Agreement.

The fixation of the Reagan administration on Qaddafi and Libya, and the attention that the media lavished on them, often elevated Qaddafi and his relatively small African state to a global significance which far exceeded his resources and capabilities and overshadowed the more pervasive terrorist activities of the Soviet Union and Syria. In addition, Libya's reputation as an Islamic fundamentalist state led to the identification of Qaddafi and terrorism with Islam, and the equation of all Islamic activists with radicalism and extremism. By the mideighties governments in the Middle East, Africa, and Southeast Asia as well as the United States and Europe were wary if not condemnatory of Libyan foreign intervention and violence. Libya's reputation as a radical regime that promoted revolution and terrorism was firmly established. For the Reagan administration, Qaddafi and Khomeini became symbols of worldwide terrorism, as menacing as the "evil empire." Many governments in Africa, a major area of Libyan activity, no longer regarded its presence and that of the Islamic Call Society as a welcome source of development funds and greater Islamic solidarity. In their eyes, Libya's political support for militant Islamic activists and revolutionary groups constituted a threat to their security far outweighing its aid.[20] Libya's influence and its effective export of Islam waned in the eighties in many parts of the world, as many governments and Islamic organizations became leery of Libya's tactics and as its oil revenues dried up and its relations with the Soviet Union cooled.

The Sudan

On September 8, 1983, Gaafar Muhammad Nimeiri declared an "Islamic revolution" that would impact Sudanese politics, law, and society. The Sudan, Africa's largest country, was henceforth to be an Islamic republic governed by Islamic law. Like Muammar Qaddafi, Nimieri had come to power in a military coup in 1969. When the Free Officers, led by Colonel Nimeiri, seized power in their May revolution, three important ideological forces were at work in the Sudan: Islam, Gamal Abdel Nasser's Arab socialism, and communism. A failed communist coup in 1971, led by his former leftist allies, transformed Nimeiri into a committed anticommunist and, as a result, a close ally of the United States and Egypt's Anwar Sadat. The link to Sadat was so strong that the Sudan was the only major Arab country that did not break off diplomatic relations with Egypt after Sadat signed the Camp David Accords.

Personal as well as political factors influenced Nimeiri's espousal of an Islamic direction in his life and government. By 1977 domestic politics and the broader Islamic revivalist currents in the Arab world had come to serve as catalysts for the intensification of Islam's role in Sudanese politics. The appeal to Islam offered Nimeiri a new way out of a deteriorating situation. A series of events during the seventies had progressively narrowed his political options. After the abortive coup in 1971 in which he narrowly escaped death, he reportedly became more religiously observant, abstaining from alcohol and gambling, as well as resolutely antileftist. However, Nimeiri's own brand of Arab socialism had failed as a national ideology, proving unable to garner popular domestic support in the face of a collapsing economy, nor could it unify the disparate religious and ethnic–tribal interests. The Sudan's national debt spiraled out of control. Responding to pressures from the World Bank and the International Monetary Fund, the Sudan had lifted government subsidies on staples such as bread and sugar, causing popular antigovernment demonstrations and food riots in 1979 and again in 1982. Insurrection grew in the predominantly non-Muslim South. Nimeiri continued to be challenged by the National Front, an alliance of national Islamic organizations. He countered and preempted his Islamic critics in the National Front by himself harnessing religion to enhance his legitimacy. His public statements emphasized a holistic understanding of Islam, similar to that espoused by Islamic organizations that had opposed his rule, the Ansar or followers of the Mahdi and the Muslim Brotherhood. He even wrote a book, *Why the Islamic Way?*, about his increased emphasis upon Islam, advocating the application of Islamic law in the Sudan.[21] Nimeiri's appeal to Islam had continuity with the Islamic character of Sudanese political history and social culture, and thus, he believed, had the potential to consolidate popular support among Sudan's 70-percent Muslim population even if it threatened to alienate the Christian and animist southern third of the country.

Nimeiri struck a deal with the National Front in 1978 by signing the National Reconciliation Pact, which enabled his Islamic opposition to return to public life. Islamic political parties were able to compete successfully for parliamentary seats in national elections. The Muslim Brotherhood, an Islamic activist organization with a wide following among university graduates and professionals in urban areas, became closely associated with the government. Nimeiri appointed Dr. Hassan al-Turabi, the Sorbonne-educated leader of the Brotherhood and former dean of the University of Khartoum Law School, to the post of attorney general. Muslim Brothers were to be found in the cabinet and in important positions in key institutions. Islam increasingly became a rallying point as well as a source of division and opposition in Sudanese politics.

Nimeiri's "Islamic" laws of September 1983 marked the formal institutionalization of Sudan's Islamic path. Traditional Islamic legal punishments such as flogging for alcohol consumption, amputation for theft, and death for apostasy were implemented. In contrast to Libya and Pakistan, where Islamic punishments were legalized but seldom carried out, amputations for theft became common in the Sudan. The Sudan's Islamization program was very much "Nimeiri's Islam." New "Islamic" laws were decreed on a weekly basis to suit his needs and whims. Islamic regulations and policies were hastily formulated in a piecemeal and ad hoc fashion, without consultation with the attorney general or chief justice. They were issued by presidential decree, not by legislative action. Nimeiri circumvented the Sudan's duly established judiciary by creating special "decisive justice courts." Thousands were arrested and brought before government-appointed judges, whose courts often functioned more like military tribunals, employing "Islamic" punishments such as flogging quite liberally for a variety of crimes. Government officials and military leaders were required to take a pledge of allegiance to Nimeiri as a Muslim ruler (a requirement imposed by the early caliphs of Islam). Nimeiri even attempted unsuccessfully to take the title Imam, that is, religiopolitical leader of the Muslim community.

In 1983–84 Nimeiri used flamboyant public acts to dramatize his new Islamic order. He released thirteen thousand prisoners to give them a "second chance" under Islamic law; poured eleven million dollars' worth of alcohol into the Nile in a media event that gained both national and international attention; and in May 1984 banned European-style dancing and subjected a nightclub owner to twenty-five lashes for permitting mixed (heterosexual) dancing.[22]

In the socioeconomic sphere, new guidelines were enacted for taxation and banking. The Zakat Tax Act of 1984 replaced much of the state's taxation system with Islam's alms tax. The Sudan now joined a number of self-styled Islamic governments, like Pakistan and Iran, in passing legislation that empowered the state to levy, collect, and distribute what had been a voluntary alms tithe. Nimeiri's stated intention to convert all of the Sudan's banks into interest-free institutions was especially controversial. The move to an Islamic banking system in the Sudan, as in Pakistan and Iran, was to be the first step in basing the entire economy on Islamic principles. These policies greatly disturbed many in the Sudan as well as foreign interests, in particular the U.S.-based multinational companies operating there.

Nimeiri's Islamization program fragmented more than unified the Sudan, generating opposition among many sectors of society who regarded him as little more than an Islamic dictator. Initially, Islamization had proven popular in the Muslim North, where many felt that, as a result, crime and corruption were on the decrease; public floggings and amputations drew large supportive crowds. However, Nimeiri's use of Islam to expand his power and justify an increasingly repressive regime, erratic decisions by "decisive justice courts," the indiscriminate use of flogging, and the imposition of Islamic law on non-Muslims undermined his image at home and abroad. Sadiq al-Mahdi, a former prime minister and the Oxford-educated great-grandson of the Sudanese Mahdi, the Islamic revivalist reformer who had driven out the British and established an Islamic state in the Sudan in the 1880s, dismissed Nimeiri's "Islamic" September laws as opportunism. He argued that the imposition of Islamic law was premature and unjust, requiring first the creation of a more socially just society. For this, Sadiq was eventually imprisoned. Nimeiri's Islamization of society disrupted the fragile peace treaty achieved in the early seventies with the non-Muslim South and led to a new civil war, led by John Garang's Sudan People's Liberation Army (SPLA), the military wing of the Sudan People's Liberation Movement (SPLM).

Internationally, conservative Muslim states like Saudi Arabia, to whom Nimeiri looked for financial aid, became concerned about a negative image of Islam and Islamic justice in the Sudan, as the international media reported on a seemingly endless series of floggings and amputations. The United States and international organizations expressed concern over the violation of human rights caused by the imposition of Islamic law on non-Muslims. The U.S. Congress threatened to cut aid to the Sudan. A host of American officials and diplomats traveled to Khartoum to communicate U.S. concerns. The United States froze $114 million in economic aid in December 1984, siding with the IMF in pressing the Sudan to introduce economic reforms in order to control its soaring deficit of $9 billion.

At first, it seemed as though Nimeiri's "Islamic authoritarianism" was tempered. He responded to his international critics with a series of reforms which moderated his Islamization program. He discontinued the floggings and amputations in the North, backed away from his plan to divide the South, and gave assurances that Islamic law would not be implemented there. As he moderated his push for Islamization, talk of an imminent introduction of an interest-free Islamic economy also subsided.

However in 1985, amid growing domestic criticism of his Islamization program, Nimeiri desperately sought to silence his critics, rally popular Muslim support, and find a scapegoat for the failures of his regime. In January, masking authoritarianism in the guise of protecting Islamic orthodoxy, on grounds of apostasy he arrested, tried, and executed the seventy-six-year-old founder and leader of the Republican Brothers, Mahmud Muhammad Taha. Many Muslims, including followers of Sadiq al-Mahdi, the Muslim Brotherhood, and the local Sufi leaders, had long regarded Taha's religious claims and his modernist reinterpretation of Islam as not simply liberal reformism but heresy. Taha had earned Nimeiri's wrath because of his opposition to Nimeiri's sectarian politics and attempts to implement Islamic law. Nimeiri's action seemed the move of a desperate man; his actions were seen by many not only as contradicting the Sudan's long tradition of political tolerance, but also as "a violation of Islamic law—as determined by an appeals court *ex-post-facto*."[23]

In March 1985 Nimeiri continued his attempt to salvage his tottering regime, answer his critics, and redirect blame for the Sudan's ills away from himself. He moved to eliminate the Muslim Brotherhood as a political force, making it a scapegoat for the failures of his regime. In a statement that seemed to be meant more for his American allies than the Sudanese people, Nimeiri claimed to have thwarted a coup by the Muslim

Brotherhood, who, he charged, were armed by Iran in order to overthrow his pro-American government. Nimeiri dismissed all members of the Muslim Brotherhood from the government and ordered the arrest of two hundred of its leaders, including Hassan Turabi.

The removal of Brotherhood leaders from key positions and new government "reforms" were a response to the United States, Egypt, and Saudi Arabia as much as to his domestic critics. Indeed, he took these steps immediately after the visit of Vice President George Bush and a U.S. delegation. The timing was such that, both within the Sudan and throughout the Arab world, rumors circulated that the four conditions Bush presented for lifting the freeze on American economic aid included discontinuation of Islamic criminal punishments (*hudud*) and dismissal of Islamic activists from the government and its institutions. The other two alleged points were halting contacts with Libya and accepting the economic reforms demanded by the IMF. The fact that Bush ended his visit by announcing resumption of U.S. aid, and that a team from the World Bank left for the Sudan the following day, appeared to confirm U.S. responsibility for Nimeiri's new initiatives. This perception was reinforced in late March when the Sudan's government, yielding to IMF and U.S. pressures, lifted subsidies on staples, an act which proved to be the undoing of the regime. As a result, Islamic activists in the Sudan and the broader Muslim world were convinced that a bias against Islam was behind U.S. policies—specifically, opposition to the implementation of Islamic law and the involvement of activists in government. The State Department did little to counter these assertions. If government officials seemed worried about militant Islam, Islamic activists were convinced they were victims of the sons of the Crusades, a Christian West that still sought to dominate. However much both proceeded from stereotypes, their fears were grounded in their experience. For the United States, Islamic activists in government meant Islamic law and punishments, civil war, and infringement on minority rights. For activists, anti-Islamic America continued to intervene, to dictate policy and control the course of their lives from Washington. Each side regarded the other as a threat to its interests.

Critics of American policy accused the United States of hypocrisy in its concern about human rights in the Sudan. Many believed that, despite its democratic principles, the United States had been willing to tolerate autocratic rulers and dictators in the Sudan as in other Third World countries, making its support contingent solely upon a ruler's strong anticommunist position. Yet when Islam was involved, new criteria and the question of human rights were invoked to justify U.S. intervention in the policies of a sovereign country despite U.S. principles of self-determination. Anger at such intervention in the economic and political life of the Sudan became evident in the days leading up to the fall of Nimeiri, as anti-Americanism surfaced in antigovernment demonstrations and marches. Perhaps fittingly, it was during Nimeiri's visit to the United States that his government fell from power.

Islam, Democracy, and the Return to Military Rule

Nimeiri was overthrown on April 5, 1985, by a military coup. Democracy was restored by the interim military government in 1986, when a civilian government was elected with Sadiq al-Mahdi as prime minister, and parliament was reconstituted. The role of Islam and the Sharia continued to be an issue in Sudanese politics. While Sadiq distanced himself from the excesses of Nimeiri's Islamization program, he was never able to resolve the issue of Islamic law, which remained a bone of contention between the rebels in the South and the government in the North. Moreover, Sadiq al-Mahdi took a more independent position toward the United States, holding meetings with Iran and Libya. After three years of democracy, his ineffectual government was replaced by the military regime of Gen. Omar al-Bashir, who seized power in June 1989.

In the immediate aftermath of this coup, Bashir's military government suspended parliament and all political parties; imprisoned leaders of the major religiopolitical parties, including Sadiq al-Mahdi and Hassan Turabi; and pledged itself to restore political stability, eliminate sectarian politics, and freeze the implementation of Islamic law. However, the issue of Islamic law again proved an insurmountable obstacle. The SPLM rejected Bashir's decision to resolve the question of implementation of Islamic law through a national referendum, believing that the northern (Muslim) majority would thus be put in the position of seeming to vote against Islam.[24] An attempt by former president Jimmy Carter in late 1989 to negotiate a settlement between the Bashir government and the SPLM also failed in large part over the issue of Islamic law.

Despite initial disclaimers, the regime proved to be heavily influenced by the National Islamic Front, a successor to the Muslim Brotherhood led by Hassan Turabi. NIF members and sympathizers filled important positions in government both at home and at key embassies overseas. Despite SPLM insistence on a secular state, Bashir promised to implement Islamic law, and Turabi called for the Islamization of Africa. Although Turabi initially declined direct participation in government, as head of the NIF, he undeniably exerted ideological and political influence. The policies adopted by the NIF- and Turabi-supported regime contradicted Turabi's early liberal reformist positions and support for democracy, which had

split the movement in the sixties and caused some militant Islamists outside Sudan to regard his views as heretical.[27]

Turabi had supported democratic elections and the NIF had used the
ballot box in its attempt to come to power in 1986, when, given the
opportunity to exercise power, however, it rationalized a different approach. Maintaining that Sudan's political development had failed because
of its sectarian-based politics, which resulted in people voting uncritically
for members of their own religious sect or group, the NIF-backed regime
advocated a federal system with consultative regional and provincial councils, a nonsectarian, non-multiparty-based Islamic government. Although
Bashir maintained that most Sudanese were Muslim and would vote for
an Islamic state, many would also argue that the same majority would
nevertheless not have voted for the NIF, nor would secularist and non-
Muslim citizens and supporters of the SPLA. Sudan's Islamic state clashed
directly with its advocacy of a "secular democratic" state and thus constituted a primary obstacle to any negotiated settlement between the government and the SPLA.[28] However, it is equally true that in open elections,
an overwhelming number of Sudanese would not vote for John Garang's
SPLA.

The central government in Khartoum remained fully in control on most
important policies and silenced other religious interest groups, the Khat-
miyya and Ansar, as well as secular and non-Muslim citizens who objected
to policies they deemed detrimental to their political and/or religious interests. In 1993, the Revolutionary Command Council (RCC) was formally
dissolved (most became members of the cabinet) and Bashir became president of a "no-party" Transitional National Assembly. NIF appointments
dominated most of the states in the new federal form of government. In
1996 Sudan held "no-party" elections in which Bashir was elected president and Turabi, after his election to a seat in the National Assembly,
was elected Speaker, the constitutional successor in the event of the president's death.[29]

Sudan was identified by many of its neighbors in Africa and the Middle
East and by the United States and European powers as a haven and training ground for terrorists: Afghan veterans, Hamas and the PLO, and Islamic Jihad from Egypt. Although generally denying such charges, in 1994
Sudan extradited Carlos "the Jackal" to France. Egypt charged that the
Sudan was behind a 1995 attempt to assassinate Hosni Mubarak on his
visit to Ethiopia. The United States placed Sudan on its list of terrorist
states and imposed economic sanctions. Despite charges that Sudan provided a shelter for terrorists, however, there were no documented cases
proving direct government involvement in major acts of terrorism.

The Khartoum regime purged the bureaucracy, military, professional associations, trade unions, and university faculty and suppressed student campus opposition. Christian organizations have been restricted in their activities and at times suppressed. The pope and the archbishop of Canterbury have been critical of the regime's treatment of Christian churches. Prominent Muslim religious organizations and families have been suppressed, their properties confiscated, and their political parties banned. A longtime expert on the Sudan reflected the seriousness of the crisis:

> The situation in the Sudan is one of multiple crises. The heritage of ineffective rule, both civilian and military, is frightening. The issue may in fact have changed from who will rule Sudan to whether or not Sudan will be able to survive in any meaningful fashion. . . . The military leaders of Sudan will have to be more flexible so that Sudan will not repeat the old cycle again or descend into anarchy.[30]

Sudanese political leaders achieved their goal of replacing Sudan's sectarian politics with a nonsectarian Islamic political system. However, they failed to establish an inclusive system that would have a place for and attract the support of Sudanese secularists and non-Muslims. Despite its periods of military intervention and rule, Sudan's political legacy has also included democratically elected governments in which Islamic parties have fully participated. However, the current Islamist government, despite its introduction of a federal system with promises of broader political participation and representation, still retains control of the bulk of government power and policy. It has not offered a successful solution to Sudan's sectarian and tribal political problems; nor has it responded effectively to issues of political and religious pluralism. Islamization governments under Nimeiri and Bashir, though different, have used religion to legitimate military and civilian Islamist authoritarian rule and stifle political dissent. Their "Islamic" policies have exacerbated the civil war with southern opponents, particularly John Garang's SPLA, which has continued to demand a secular state, something unacceptable to most Sudanese Muslims (non-Islamist as well as Islamist). Garang has enjoyed support from African and Western countries that see the current government as a radical Islamic "fundamentalist" threat not only within Sudan but regionally. Hassan Turabi's call for the Islamization of Africa has been seen as a call for militancy, not evangelism. His 1991 creation of the Popular Islamic and Arabic Conference in Khartoum as a pan-Islamic movement to spread political Islam reinforced these fears. Despite outside support, Garang has not been able to lead a united southern front. Southern rebels have them-

selves been divided and factionalized along ethnic lines; some are little
more than local warlords. The Khartoum government has effectively exploited these divisions. Southern rebels also divided in disagreement over
policy toward Khartoum. Seven southern Sudanese rebel leaders signed a
peace agreement in April 1996. The agreement ratified a multiparty system
and, for the first time in Sudan's history, allowed a self-determination
referendum to determine whether the South would remain part of a united
Sudan or would eventually secede.[31]

The continuation of Sudan's civil war is less about the failure of both
Bashir and Garang to provide viable ideological alternatives than the continued belief on both sides that the war was winnable. In reality, neither
Khartoum nor its southern opponents have had the ability or the resources
to defeat the other. Failure to negotiate has resulted in a fifteen-year-old
war in which the welfare of the masses has been held hostage to the
political ambitions of northern and southern leaders. The result has been
famine, death, mass migration of populations, and widespread displacement and breakup of families and tribes. Some have charged that neither
the United States nor Western Europe has shown a real desire to see an
end to the war. In an East Africa in which one-party authoritarian rule is
not unique to Khartoum, U.S. policy (as in other parts of the world) has
been less concerned with reining in authoritarian governments than with
its own strategic interests. In December 1997, while peace talks were
taking place in Nairobi, Secretary of State Albright met with rebel leaders
and openly expressed moral support for their struggle.[32] An unstable and
weakened Sudan, distracted by its war in the South, is less likely to
threaten the stability of Egypt, a strong American ally: ''Peace does not
necessarily suit American interests, aid officials said. American foreign
policy in the region hinges on protecting the secular Government in Egypt,
the largest recipient of United States aid, and containing Islamic fundamentalism.''[33]

The differing relationships of Sudan's Islamization governments with
the West reveals the extent to which politics, not religion, determines the
nature of states as well as their perceived threat to the West. Nimeiri and
Bashir differed significantly in their relations with the West, particularly
the United States (as well as with its neighbor, Egypt). Nimeiri was for
many years a U.S. ally (one of the few Arab or Muslim governments to
support Camp David and maintain relations with Sadat's Egypt), whereas
the Bashir government has been labeled a ''radical fundamentalist'' government and officially declared a terrorist or rogue state by the United
States.

Egypt

> I am Khalid Islambuli, I have killed Pharaoh and I do not fear death.
>   —Lt. Khalid Islambuli

Such were the words of the assassin who had shot and killed Pres. Anwar Sadat in an act which stunned the world and, in the wake of the Iranian Revolution, dramatically drew world attention to radical Islam in Egypt. Like Iran, Egypt had long been regarded as among the most modern Muslim countries, a leader in the Arab world politically, militarily, culturally, and religiously. It had offered a barometer for modernization which was predominantly Western and secular in orientation. The seemingly sudden eruption of militant Islam contrasted sharply with modern expectations and values. Today Egypt provides a remarkable example of the diverse and complex impact of Islam on sociopolitical development. For several decades Islam has been part of the political scene in Egypt, used by both the government and its opposition. Egypt has been a cradle of both Arab nationalism and Islamic revivalism under its last three rulers: Gamal Abdel Nasser, Anwar Sadat, and Hosni Mubarak.

Sadat's Islamic Path

Gamal Abdel Nasser's death in 1970 shocked Egypt and the Arab world. Millions of Egyptians poured into the streets of Cairo for his funeral. Although the pride fostered by Nasser and the credibility of Arab socialism had been shattered by the catastrophic Arab defeat in 1967, the death of the charismatic Nasser left a void that few men could have filled. Anwar Sadat, Nasser's successor, had been completely eclipsed by Nasser. Sadat, who was neither a charismatic nor a popular leader, lacked political legitimacy. Tellingly, in the early days of his rule, Sadat's picture was always seen alongside that of Nasser. Struggling to be regarded as a leader in his own right and to enhance his political legitimacy, he turned to and relied heavily upon Islam. Sadat appropriated the title "The Believer President," had the mass media cover his praying at the mosque, increased Islamic programming in the media and Islamic courses in schools, built mosques, and employed Islamic rhetoric in his public statements. Sufi brotherhoods and the Muslim Brotherhood, suppressed by Nasser, were permitted to function publicly. The creation and growth of Islamic student organizations on campuses was promoted to counter the opposition of Nasserites and leftists who opposed Sadat's pro-Western political and economic policies. Sadat used Islam to legitimate key government actions and policies such as the 1973 Egyptian–Israeli war, the Camp David Accords, and Muslim family-law reforms, and to denounce as extremism the increasing challenges to the regime by Islamic activists during the late seventies.

By 1977, Islamic organizations such as the Muslim Brotherhood and student groups were securely established. They became more independent and critical of Sadat's policies: his support for the Shah of Iran and condemnation of the Iranian revolution as a "crime against Islam,"[34] the Camp David Accords, pro-Western economic and political ties, and the failure of his government to implement Islamic law. More ominously, a new crop of secret revolutionary groups, some founded by radicalized former Muslim Brothers imprisoned under Nasser, began to challenge what they regarded as Sadat's hypocritical manipulation of Islam and to reject the moderate posture of the Muslim Brotherhood. Militant groups like Muhammad's Youth, the Army of God, and the Islamic Society resorted to acts of violence in an attempt to overthrow the government.

Sadat was seen by his critics as a prime example of Egypt's Westernized elite in both his personal and his political life. His penchant for imported suits and pipes as well as the high public image and international profile of his half-British wife Jehan, which sharply contrasted with the more reserved public image of wives of Egyptian rulers and politicians, offended his Islamic critics. Many activists, moderate as well as radical, rejected Sadat's reform of Muslim family law (the law governing marriage, divorce, and inheritance) as "Jehan's law," meaning that it was influenced by her Westernized outlook. His open-door economic policy—resulting in the higher profile of America's presence, as symbolized by a towering new embassy and an influx of U.S. businessmen—along with his support for the Shah and criticism of Khomeini, and the Camp David Accords, were all regarded as evidence of Sadat's capitulation to the West. These critics condemned his political and military dependence on the West and the more pernicious threat, Western cultural penetration and acculturation, a theme which struck a responsive chord among many: "Culturally, fathers have seen their sons and daughters influenced by what they consider to be immoral Western behavior and believe them to be neglecting their traditional values. Thus now, as in the 1930's, there is an outcry against the cinema, theater, magazines, books, clubs, and all associations that popularize modern concepts such as individualism and the lack of concern with family problems and wishes of parents and older brothers."[35] Attacks against bars, nightclubs, cinemas, Western tourist hotels, and government institutions and personnel signaled their grievances. The militants believed that the liberation of Egyptian society required that all true Muslims undertake an armed struggle or holy war against a regime which they regarded as oppressive, anti-Islamic, and a puppet of the West.

Criticism and condemnation of Sadat seemed confirmed by his responses to his growing opposition. In February 1979 he called for the separation of religion and politics, a position seen as un-Islamic by Muslim organizations calling for an Islamic state and the implementation of Islamic law. Organizations of Islamic university students were banned. Sadat used government control of nationalized mosques and religious institutions, and the dependence of the religious establishment on the government for its salaries, to dictate and control sermons and mosque activities. At the same time he attempted to extend state control to Egypt's more numerous private mosques, whose preachers were far more independent and increasingly critical of the regime. In April 1980 Sadat moved to blunt his critics with a highly publicized amendment to the constitution declaring that "Islam is the religion of the state" and that the Sharia was "the main source of legislation." Yet for radicals, this was mere window dressing: Sadat's track record, his failure to actually implement Islamic law, and his pro-Western policies rendered him an apostate who merited the death penalty. Sadat's growing authoritarianism and suppression of dissent, whether secular or religious, reached its apogee in 1981, when he imprisoned more than fifteen hundred people—Islamic activists, lawyers, doctors, journalists, university professors, political opponents, and ex-government ministers.

On October 6, 1981, Sadat was assassinated by members of the Organization for Holy War (Jamaat al-Jihad) as he reviewed a parade commemorating the 1973 war. Lt. Khalid Islambuli, the leader of the assassins, cried out: "I am Khalid Islambuli, I have killed Pharaoh and I do not fear death." Sadat's popularity in the West and his international image as an enlightened leader stood in sharp contrast to his growing unpopularity at home, where both secular and religious opposition referred to him as "Pharaoh." For many in Egypt, "Khalid therefore appeared as a sort of 'right arm' of the popular will, and not merely as a militant exponent of an Islamicist group."[36] Al-Jihad had been formed by remnants of another militant group, Muhammad's Youth or the Islamic Liberation Organization (ILO). ILO leaders had been executed for their 1974 attempt to seize the Technical Military Academy in Cairo as part of a foiled coup d'état.

The leadership and members of al-Jihad were drawn from a cross section of society: civilian, military, and religious. They included members of the presidential guard, military intelligence, civil servants, radio and television workers, and university students and professors. The rationale for their actions was articulated in a tract entitled *The Neglected Obliga-*

tion. Written by their ideologue, an electrician named Muhammad al-Farag, it maintained that jihad was the sixth pillar of Islam and that armed struggle or revolt was an imperative for all true Muslims so as to rectify the ills of a decadent society: "[W]e have to establish the Rule of God's Religion in our own country first, and to make the Word of God supreme. . . . There is no doubt that the first battlefield for jihad is the extermination of these infidel leaders and to replace them by a complete Islamic Order. From here we should start."[37]

For Sadat, as for Nasser, Islam was an instrument of foreign policy which did not determine but was determined by other political and economic priorities. He emphasized both Arabism and Islam and at times seemed to equate the two. However, reflecting his pro-Western policies, Sadat, unlike Nasser, did not emphasize anti-imperialism. Instead he increasingly emphasized the Islamic community (*ummah*) and the common interests of Muslim states, as well as "the commonality of interests between the Islamic states and the West; oil in exchange for technology and the common interest against the Soviet threat."[38] However, as previously noted, his pro-Western orientation and policies—economic reforms, the Camp David Accords, and support for the Shah of Iran—undermined his credibility with many Egyptians and alienated Islamic groups.

Hosni Mubarak and the Institutionalization of Islamic Revivalism

The style of both the Egyptian presidency and Islamic revivalism changed in the eighties after the death of Sadat. While Islamic revivalism in Egypt seemed to degenerate into confrontation and violence during the seventies, the eighties witnessed the growth of a broader-based, quiet revolution, overshadowed or eclipsed at times by the violence of a more vocal and militant minority.

In contrast to his predecessor, Hosni Mubarak pursued a path of greater political liberalization and tolerance, while at the same time responding firmly to those who resorted to violence to challenge the authority of the government. He distinguished more carefully between religious and political dissent and direct threats to the state. He crushed outbursts and riots fomented by Islamic militants, intervened in clashes between Muslims and Coptic Christians, and tried and executed the assassins of Sadat. At the same time he surprised many when he released more than 174 defendants in the Sadat trials acquitted by the courts. Unlike Sadat, Mubarak permitted religious critics public outlets for their opposition: they could compete in parliamentary elections, publish newspapers, voice criticism in the media. The government sponsored television debates between Islamic militants and representatives of the religious establishment, religious scholars from al-Azhar University. Government-run television and newspapers regularly featured religious programs and columns which were often independent in their tone and criticisms. At the same time, however, the government used members of the state-supported religious establishment to debate and dismiss militants as deficient in their knowledge of Islam and misguided, if not heretical, in their beliefs.

However, by the mid-eighties Mubarak's flexible response to Islamic activism had failed to coopt or silence his Islamic opposition. Political liberalization opened up new opportunities for the Muslim Brotherhood. The Brotherhood had become more of a major political, social, and economic force; it emerged as the chief political opposition in parliamentary elections and an effective social and economic actor through its publishing, banking, and social services. Muslim Brothers and other activists were dominant voices in professional organizations and syndicates of lawyers, doctors, engineers, and journalists. Increasingly, moderate activists such as the Muslim Brotherhood presented their criticisms and demands within the context of a call for greater democratization, political representation, and respect for human rights.

Mubarak's attempt to discredit and isolate religious extremists infuriated Islamic radicals. Radical groups became more assertive in Cairo, Alexandria, Asyut, and Minya. Muslim militants attacked Coptic Christian churches and destroyed their shops and property. Bars, nightclubs, cinemas, and video stores, symbols of Western influence and immorality, were burned or bombed in major cities and towns. Street demonstrations and protests were organized to demand the imposition of Islamic law. Popular militant clerics like Shaykh Hafiz Salaama led public demonstrations. In an attempt to control the spread of radicalism, in July 1985 the Mubarak government placed all private mosques under the Ministry of Religious Endowments, arrested Salaama, who had led demonstrations calling for the implementation of Islamic law, and closed down his mosque, a center of dissent.

The degree of discontent and polarization between the government and moderate opposition groups was reflected in the failure of opposition leaders to distance themselves completely from extremist acts. When a disturbed border policeman killed several Israeli tourists in the Sinai in December 1985, Muslim Brotherhood leaders, joined by opposition newspapers and political parties, described the killings as an act against the "enemies of the nation." Their ire was directed at both Israel and the United States. Ibrahim Shukry, leader of the Socialist Labor Party, reflected the mood of many: "This young man who has removed the shame from Egypt after Israel has bombarded the P.L.O. headquarters in Tunisia and after the Americans have hijacked the Egyptian plane [referring to the *Achille Lauro* incident]."[39]

The military also continued to prove vulnerable to infiltration by Islamic militants. In December 1986 thirty-three activists—including four military officers allegedly connected to al-Jihad, Sadat's assassins—were arrested and charged with plotting to wage a holy war in order to overthrow the government. The government continued quietly to purge those suspected of being "fundamentalists." Clandestine groups kept on growing and sporadically confronted the government, which increasingly struck back, sometimes indiscriminately. In 1989 as many as ten thousand Islamic militants were arrested. Thousands were held without charge; the Arab Human Rights Organization accused the government of routine torture.[40]

Mubarak's lackluster image, his failure to provide dynamic and creative political leadership, and a weak economy, worsened by the loss of jobs and foreign revenue from millions of expatriate Egyptian workers in the Gulf, led to a more diffident political liberalization program. At the same time it made his government more vulnerable to its Islamic critics, who countered that less economic and political dependence on the West, a rejection of the Camp David Accords, and the implementation of Islamic law offered the only solution.

Throughout the 1990s, the Egyptian government identified "Islamic terrorism" as the major threat to state and regional security. In the post-Gulf War period, Egypt projected an image abroad of a close U.S. ally playing a supportive and constructive role in the Middle East peace process and at home of a moderate government beset by religious revolutionaries.

Violent extremists, quieter in the early Mubarak period, boldly and directly challenged the regime in Asyut, Minya, Cairo, and Alexandria, calling for immediate implementation of Islamic law, separation of the sexes, and the banning of Western music and concerts. The chief militant Islamic challenge to the Mubarak government came from the Gamaa Islamiyya (Jamaat Islamiyya, or Islamic Group) and Jamaat al-Jihad, who were locked in a deadly battle with security forces and police.[41]

The Gamaa Islamiyya had evolved from a student group active on university campuses and in politics in the Sadat era into an umbrella organization of clandestine groups active in Cairo, Alexandria, Asyut, Minya, and Fayyum. In contrast to the urban, university-based Gamaa of the Sadat period, many activists were high-school aged. Active in small villages and towns as well as in urban areas, they were less educated, living in more desperate conditions of poverty and unemployment, more radical ideologically, and more random in their use of violence.

Bent upon destabilizing the state and the Egyptian economy and thus the regime, extremists attacked and murdered Coptic Christians, government officials, and foreign tourists, the most important source of Egypt's foreign revenues, providing income for millions of Egyptians. They bombed and burned banks and government buildings, as well as cinemas, theaters, video stores, and bookstores that popularized Western culture. Bombings—of churches, homes, and shops—beatings, and murders increased not only in large cities but also in small towns (Biba, Sennouris, and Qena) and villages. Coptic Christians, caught in the battle between militants and the government, charged that the number and significance of such incidents were downplayed by officals, who often attributed them to personal conflicts and vendettas instead of identifying them as religiously motivated attacks. Prominent critics such as columnist Farag Foda (d. 1992), who had been outspoken in his denunciation of fundamentalism, were assassinated or injured (Egypt's elderly Nobel laureate, Naguib Mahfouz, was stabbed). Others required twenty-four-hour security.

The Egyptian Organization for Human Rights (EOHR) put the blame squarely on the shoulders of the Islamic Group. They condemned the "actions of the organization known as Gamaa Islamiyya, which has persisted in its recourse to violence, in its advocacy of the hatred of citizens of the Christian faith, in its incitement to various forms of discrimination against them and in actively taking part in such acts of discrimination."[42] The EOHR charged that, outstripping the government's own use of indiscriminate firepower, killings, and arbitrary arrests, militant Islamists were in fact responsible for the bulk of human rights abuses (including the deaths of Christians, police, and a foreign tourist) in Upper Egypt.[43]

The Mubarak government mounted a formidable response to the threat of religious extremism and terrorism, utilizing its military and security forces as well as special military courts. Extremists and the government became locked in a "holy war" in which the government's police and security forces, like the religious extremists, at times appeared to have their own hit list for murder and assassination rather than arrest and prosecution. An Amnesty International report noted that security forces "appear to have been given a license to kill with impunity."[44] Special military courts, which do not grant a right of appeal to those convicted, were created to try civilians accused of terrorism quickly and secretly. The number of prisoners executed vastly exceeded those executed for politically motivated crimes in the past, such as the attempt to kill Nasser or the assassination of Sadat. The U.S. State Department's human rights report on Egypt noted that the government "perpetrated many abuses, including the arbitrary arrest and torture of hundreds of detainees, the use of military courts to try accused terrorists, the failure to punish officials responsible for torture."[45] Officials of international nongovernmental human rights organizations warned, "This poor human rights record has yielded resentment, the narrowing of civil society, religious intolerance and erosion of the rule of law in Egypt—and fertile ground for the growth of extremist alternatives."[46]

At the same time, Islamic political and social activism in the nineties continued to root itself more deeply and pervasively in Egyptian society, growing among the lower and middle classes, educated and uneducated, professionals, students and laborers, young and old, women and men. Islamists gained cultural legitimacy, becoming a more visible and effective part of mainstream Muslim life and society. State institutions were complemented or challenged by Islamically oriented counterparts. The Muslim Brotherhood and other activists became dominant voices in professional organizations and syndicates of lawyers, doctors, engineers, and journalists. They presented their criticisms and demands within the context of a call for greater democratization, political representation, and respect for human rights.

The Mubarak government's aggressive response to Islamic radicalism in the nineties attempted not only to eradicate violent extremism but also to counter and control the legal institutionalization of Islamic activism socially (social welfare, professional associations, schools, and mosques) in Egyptian society. In its war against "terrorism," a broad government crackdown and massive arrests of suspected terrorists included not only the extremists but also moderate Islamists in an attempt to silence any and all Islamic opposition. Thousands were held without charge; the Arab Human Rights Organization accused the government of the routine use of torture.[47] By June 1994, the Mubarak government's war against the terrorism of the Gamaa Islamiyya and also against its strongest legal opposition, the Muslim Brotherhood, had become, in the words of one commentator, an attempt "to curtail not only those movements that have carried out violent attacks, but also one that has come to dominate many municipalities, professional and labor associations, and university faculties."[48]

The government moved to silence the sources of criticism and opposition (focusing on professional syndicates, mosques, and the media) and maintain its tight control over elections. Professional syndicates—democratic and voluntary associations of teachers, lawyers, physicians, engineers, and journalists—had been a pillar of Egyptian civil society:

> Denied access to the political arena, they [the Brotherhood] have made professional syndicates perhaps the most vibrant institutions of Egyptian civil society. . . . Islamists have worked to extend medical insurance to syndicate members and their families, establish social and recreational clubs

(and not just in large cities), increase the stock of housing available to members at lower prices, and assist the families of those members arrested or otherwise detained by the regime.[49]

The government-controlled People's Assembly in 1993 passed legislation that placed stringent quorum requirements on syndicate elections, which, if not met, enabled the government to appoint syndicate board members. Attempts to intimidate and silence syndicate opposition led the head of the 70,000 member Cairo branch of the Lawyers Syndicate, Abdel Aziz Mohammed (himself not an Islamist but a lawyer who defended a Cairo University professor accused by Islamists of apostasy), to charge that the government's real aim was "to weaken the syndicate as an institution of civil society in the guise of waging a fight against militancy."[50]

When members of the Brotherhood continued to win syndicate board elections, the state in 1995 and 1996 closed the lawyers' and engineers' syndicates, placing them under state "guardianship." State appointees were put in charge, financial assets frozen, and most activities curtailed.

The Mubarak government also moved to control mosques and preachers, which it regarded as a major breeding ground of radicalism. The vast majority of Egypt's mosques were private rather than state-controlled (and thus independent of government supervision or control of preachers, sermons, and activities). Attempts by Sadat and later Mubarak (in 1985) to take control of private mosques, given the enormous number of mosques and limited government resources, produced limited results. The ministry of religious affairs announced that all sermons at state-controlled mosques would be subject to approval by government-appointed officials, all private mosques would be brought under the control of the ministry, and the building of private mosques would be curtailed.

The Egyptian government continued to be "the president's state." In 1995 presidential elections, Hosni Mubarak won by 94 percent of the vote with no opposition candidate. Both the Independent Commission of Election review and "rulings from the highest courts in the land . . . declared that serious fraud and irregularities had taken place in more than half of the 222 voting districts."[51] The People's Assembly and the bureaucracy continued to be dominated by the government's National Democratic Party; the government maintained absolute control over the creation and continued existence of political parties. In the period from December 1995 to December 1996 the applications of five would-be political parties were rejected by the government's Political Parties Committee. In 1997, it could be said that it had refused all applications to form new parties.[52]

On November 23, 1995, Egypt's Higher Military Court convicted 54 (acquitting 27) members of the Brotherhood, including Dr. Essam al-Din Aryan, the second highest officer in the Doctors' Syndicate, who received a five-year sentence. They were found guilty of "directing an illegal organization with plans to impede the law and the constitution." State security officers had cited a strategy meeting at which participants (54 of the defendants denied having attended this legal conference) discussed increasing the Brotherhood's representation in legal institutions like parliament and the syndicates. The court rejected the attempt to link the Brotherhood with armed insurgent groups, acquitting the accused of financing terrorist activity. Amnesty International described the jailed Brothers as "prisoners of conscience" convicted in a trial that "outraged both international and domestic observers."[53] Some noted that the government curiously did not arrest the senior elderly leaders of the Brotherhood but rather its more dynamic midlevel leadership, including officers in the professional syndicates, in a move designed to cripple its more effective younger leadership. Moreover, the verdict had come less than a week before the November 29 parliamentary elections, in which fifty-one of the defendants were candidates. Their detention (as well as that of thirty additional Brothers arrested in October) and trial had made their active participation in the elections impossible.

In the lead-up to parliamentary elections, the government also used a controversial press law (Law 93) to protect government officials and members of the government's ruling National Democratic Party and their families who were accused in government and opposition press reports of corruption. This move drew widespread criticism from many sectors of society. Editors and reporters of leading newspapers were arrested, tried, and convicted.

In the wake of the 1995 elections, former Muslim Brothers, representing a younger generation looking for change, joined with others (leftists, Nasserites, Christians, women) to create a new political party, Hizb al-Wasat (the Party of the Center), aimed at bridging the divide between Arab nationalists and Islamists. Wasat advocated the democratization of the political order, the joint role of Muslims and Christians in Egyptian society, and implementation of the Sharia, which it described as the "touchstone of [Egyptian] civilization," according to modern legal thinking.[54] The government responded by refusing to register it as a political party. Several of its founders and members were arrested and tried before a military court for "joining an illegal and secret group which aims to overthrow the ruling regime and to circumvent legitimacy by forming Al-Wasat party to act as the voice of the banned Muslim Brothers group." Seven were sentenced to prison. Egypt's Center for Human Rights and Legal Aid (CHRLA) warned that "the Egyptian authorities' use of military courts as a tool to block peaceful and open political activities will only lead to more violence, terrorism, and outlawed activities, which in turn will threaten the situation of human rights and civil liberties in Egypt.''[55]

If the balance of power seemed to be in the hands of extremists in the early nineties, by the mid-nineties most believed that the government had won, eliminating the extremists or greatly reducing their numbers. However, a spate of incidents were a stark reminder of the ever present threat of terrorist attacks. Several plots to assassinate Mubarak, including an attack in Addis Ababa in June 1995, were uncovered. Seventeen Greek pilgrims and an Egyptian were killed outside the Europa hotel in Cairo in September 1996. (The Gamaa apologized, saying they had been mistaken for Israeli tourists.) A string of attacks in October and in spring 1997 (on February 12, 1997, fifteen Coptic Christians were murdered inside a church in Abu Qurqa, a small town in southern Egypt) took the lives of many Coptic Christians and police in Upper Egypt. On November 17, 1997, sixty-eight tourists and three Egyptians were massacred at Luxor, an act attributed to the Battalions of Havoc, a wing of the Gamaa.

The government blamed domestic groups—their exiled leaders and members in Europe, America, Iran, and Sudan—for the renewed terrorist onslaught. Many called for even tougher government measures to eradicate extremism. Others, although agreeing on the need to identify and punish terrorists, insisted that political and economic reforms, not indiscriminate repression, were the ultimate solution. They charged that a series of government actions had contributed to a climate that fostered violence and terrorism instead of strengthening civil society: the failure to restrain police and security force brutality; the government's refusal to respond to a call for a cease-fire from senior Gamaa leaders in July 1997; the expansion of state power and curtailment of civil liberties (indiscriminate mass arrests and imprisonment without trial of some 20,000 suspected terrorists); the banning of union and other ''unofficial'' gatherings; the passing of controversial legislation by the government-dominated parliament enabling the jailing of editors and reporters for defaming government officials and government takeovers of syndicates and mosques; and the manipulation of elections.

One observer noted that ''the future development of the Islamic movement depends on how it is treated (or mistreated) by those in power and not on any inherent conflict between Islam and freedom. . . . Egypt's rulers can expect to see an Islam that faithfully reflects the skill or folly of their own statecraft.''[56]

Islamic activists, whether moderate or radical, failed to offer a specific concrete alternative program and were content simply to criticize the failures of the incumbent government. Both the nature and diverse agendas of these movements as well as the realities of Egyptian politics were causes. Many Islamic activists and organizations chose to emphasize the creation of a more Islamically oriented society through sociomoral rather than political reform. These activists focused on religiosocial programs and issues, rather than defining the nature of an Islamic state and its institutions. Even the Muslim Brotherhood emphasized building its base of support through educational and socioeconomic programs. In oppositional politics it was content to seek the implementation of Islamic law rather than directly challenging the head of state. For its part, the government criticized the Brotherhood's lack of specificity and maintained that, if it came to power, it would lack specific programs and so be doomed to failure. Yet the government, like most Muslim governments, has chosen not to test its conviction. It has neither allowed the Brotherhood to become a political party nor fostered political reforms which would allow a real electoral challenge. Indeed, by the late 1990s, the government sought to coopt, control, or suppress the Brotherhood and any viable opposition.

The most important characteristic of Islamic revivalism in Egypt in the nineties is the extent to which revivalism has become part and parcel of moderate mainstream life and society, rather than a marginal phenomenon limited to small groups or organizations. No longer restricted to the lower or lower middle class, renewed awareness and concern about leading a more Islamically informed way of life can also be found among the middle and upper class, educated and uneducated, peasants and professionals, young and old, women and men. They are active in Quran study groups (run by both women and men), Sufi gatherings, mosques, and private associations. As a result, Islamic identity is expressed not only in formal religious practices but also in the social services offered by psychiatric and drug rehabilitation centers, dental clinics, day-care centers, legal-aid societies, and organizations which provide subsidized housing and food distribution or run banks and investment houses.

The *ulama* and the mosques have also taken on a more prominent role. The popularity of preachers such as Shaykh Muhammad Mitwali al-Shaarawi and Abd al-Hamid Kishk, an outspoken critic of both Nasser and Sadat, made them religious media stars. They appear regularly on television and have newspaper columns. Their audiocassettes, pamphlets, and books are sold not in specialty shops but in ordinary bookstores, at airports and hotels, and by street vendors. The popularity of these preachers extends beyond Egypt to much of the Arab world. Thus their voices are heard not only in mosques or religious gatherings but also on cassettes played in taxicabs, on the streets, in shops, and in the homes of the poor and middle class alike. Wherever one finds magazines, audio tapes, or books being sold, there, amid the coverage of politicians and movie stars, will also be popular religious materials. Private, nongovernment mosques and their imams have for some time been a source of independent criticism and opposition to the government. While the laity (non-*ulama*), through modern Islamic organizations such as the Muslim Brotherhood, have exercised leadership in relating Islam to the demands and needs of modern society, more and more mosques and their religious officials have also become increasingly involved in providing much-needed social services. As a result Islamic revolutionaries, though active from time to time, have become more and more marginalized and limited in their appeal.

The Islamic Republic of Iran

> The cry that comes from the heart of the believer overcomes everything, even the White House. . . . This wave has already spread throughout the world, and the world is now liberating itself from the oppression to which it has been subjected.
>
> —AYATOLLAH KHOMEINI

For more than a decade Iran represented the embodiment of the Islamic threat, and the Ayatollah Khomeini served as the living symbol of revolutionary Islam. If Khomeini denounced the West—and the United States in particular—as the great Satan, for many in the West he represented a medieval cleric, a menace to the Middle East and the West. From presidential statements to popular music and billboards, Khomeini soon became the man many Americans loved to hate.

For a West convinced of the stability of the Shah of Iran, the fall of the Shah was unthinkable, a shock intensified by the victors, the mullahs of Iran. Muhammad Reza Pahlavi had ruled for more than thirty years (1941–79). Like Anwar Sadat, he had come to be viewed in the West as an enlightened ally, the head of a modern state. The Pahlavis, like the Sadats, spoke English, dressed in well-tailored Western clothes, and appeared on American television, interviewed by the likes of Barbara Walters. (They were like ''us.'') Yet in 1971 the world witnessed Iran's celebration of the twenty-five-hundredth anniversary of Persian monarchy. Before an audience of the world's leaders, including the vice president of the United States, the Shah crowned himself emperor of Iran. Under the Shah, oil revenues had been utilized in an ambitious modernization program, the White Revolution, whose goal was the modern transformation of Iran by the twenty-first century. Iran possessed the best-equipped military in the Middle East and enjoyed close relations with the United States and Europe. That such a shah would be overthrown was unthinkable; that the Pahlavi dynasty would come crashing down at the hands of a revolution led by a bearded, exiled ayatollah and conducted in the name of Islam was incomprehensible.

Islam, Nationalism, and the State

Despite the popular Western image of Shii Islam as a religion of revolution and martyrdom, its relationship to the state in Iran throughout Islamic history has been diverse and multifaceted. Islam in Iran incorporates a variety of outlooks and orientations. It has been capable of multiple levels of discourse and interpretation. Indeed, once the 1978–79 revolution had dethroned the Shah and the smoke had cleared, the diversity within Iran's Shii community would surface in contention and conflict.

Religion and the state had been intertwined in Iran ever since the establishment of the Safavid dynasty (1501–1732), when Shii Islam was declared Iran's state religion. Iran's shahs claimed to rule in the absence of the Twelfth Imam, who had disappeared in 874 and whom devout Shii believed would return in a future age to end tyranny and usher in a new age of justice. The clergy often proved far from revolutionary. They accepted the necessity of temporal rule in fact, if not in theory or doctrine. The relationship of the *ulama* to the state in Iranian history varied from royal patronage to opposition, depending on the sociopolitical context. Their authority was often subordinated to and limited by rulers. At other times they led or participated in opposition movements. While the Safavids controlled the clergy, their successors, the less powerful Qajar dynasty (1794–1925), faced a more independent and assertive religious establishment who were not afraid to take to the streets in opposition.

On two more recent occasions—the Tobacco Protest of 1891–92 and the Constitutional Revolution of 1905–11—Islam and the clergy played an important oppositional role in the emergence of modern Iranian nationalism. Having previously thwarted attempts by the government to sell concessions to Europeans for the development of banking, railroads, and mining, religious and secular leaders joined together in protest movements first to protect Iranian national interests and then to constitutionally limit the Shah's power. The Tobacco Protest was a response to Nasir al-Din Shah's attempt to sell the tobacco concession to a British company (and thus create a monopoly). A religious proclamation (*fatwa*) legitimated a nationwide boycott led by religious leaders and merchants. The Constitutional Revolution utilized religious symbols, clergy, and mosques, which served as centers of political organization, to mount a popular protest movement through which Iranian nationalists sought to curb or constitutionally limit the absolutism and abuses of the monarchy.

Under Pahlavi rule (1925–78), religion was carefully controlled and the *ulama* remained relatively quiescent and apolitical. Both Reza Shah Pahlavi (1925–41) and his son, Muhammad Reza Shah Pahlavi (1941–78), controlled religion, combining cooptation with coercion of the religious establishment. For their part, Iran's religious leaders preferred quietism to political action, order to the threat of civil disorder, limited patronage to persecution. The creation of a modern secular school system and Western-based legal codes, as well as the control of many Islamic institutions by government ministries, sharply curtailed the power of the *ulama*. Their replacement by modern-educated judges, lawyers, and civil servants eroded the sources of their status and revenue.

The broader social impact of Muhammad Reza Shah Pahlavi's modernization programs, the White Revolution, which like his educational and legal reforms were influenced by the West, proved a mixed blessing. Despite accomplishments in education, health, and agricultural reform, the benefits of modern reforms went disproportionately to a small and growing group of modern, urban elites. The lights and glitter of modernized cities obscured the actual conditions of the urban poor and of the masses in the villages of Iran. While a minority prospered, a once agriculturally self-sufficient country was spending more than one billion dollars on imports. Those who poured into the cities from the villages expecting a better life, lacking requisite job skills, became unemployed inhabitants of overcrowded, congested urban slums: "For these millions, most of whom had been forced out of the villages into new shantytowns, the oil boom did not end poverty; it merely modernized it."[57]

Both the traditional merchant classes (*bazaari*) and the religious classes suffered as a result of the Western-oriented Pahlavi modernization program, which affected their lives from dress, education, and law to land reform and commerce. The *bazaari*, like the *ulama*, found Iran's tilt toward and dependence upon the West a threat to their status, economic interest, and religiocultural values. Reza Shah's dress codes in the twenties and thirties, which had mandated Western dress for men, banned the veil, and restricted the wearing of clerical attire, were now followed by the seeming Westernization of Iran's modern elites and many of its urban centers under his son. The merchants' wealth and power were threatened by the influx of Western banks and corporations and the new entrepreneurial class that emerged and prospered with state support.

Iran and the West

The West had long been a challenge and a threat to Iran. Although Iran had never been directly ruled by colonial powers, the Soviet Union in the north and Britain in the south had vied for influence. The danger of foreign intervention and dependence, symbolized by events provoking the Tobacco Protest, was realized in 1941, when Britain and the Soviet Union forced Reza Shah to abdicate in favor of his son. It was even more evident in 1953, when the Shah was driven into exile by a nationalist movement headed by Prime Minister Muhammad Mossadegh, whose nationalization of Iran's oil threatened the interests of Western oil companies. The Shah's return from Rome to Teheran, aboard an American military plane with the head of the CIA at his side, was orchestrated by the United States with British support. Iran's political, military, and economic ties with the West, and with the United States in particular, increased significantly. The United States, Britain, and France benefited from lucrative arms sales and helped train Iran's military and secret police (SAVAK). At a time when the United States was heavily committed in Vietnam and Britain was withdrawing its forces from the Persian Gulf, the Shah's Iran represented policies and interests that coincided with those of the United States, from the Shah's rejection of Nasserism and pragmatic relations with Israel, and his nation's stable presence in the Gulf, to its oil wealth and market for American products. American and European bankers and businessmen along with diplomats and military advisers enjoyed a high-profile presence in Iran. By the late sixties "pro-Pahlavi policy and support came to dominate the very highest levels of the American foreign policy establishment."[58]

Dissent began to grow and spread to a broader social base during the early seventies. Concern about foreign intervention and dependence on the West was not restricted to the traditional classes but included a generation of modern-educated, politically sophisticated, and socially minded Iranians. Middle-class nationalists and intellectuals joined merchants and clergy to voice their concerns for Iran's national identity and independence. Calls for social and political reforms increased amid complaints about concentration of wealth, corruption, growing political repression, and excessive dependence upon the West.

Repression and Dissent

By the seventies the Shah was no longer an inexperienced youth placed on the peacock throne by foreign powers, but an entrenched, increasingly autocratic ruler. As James Bill has commented, his policy of "cooptation with coercion, repression with reform," gave way to "increasing megalomania."[59] The October 1971 celebration of the twenty-five-hundredth anniversary of Persian monarchy was a symbolic turning point, marking at once the acme and the incipient decline of Pahlavi fortunes. More than two hundred million dollars was spent to gather dignitaries from around the world at Persepolis, the uninhabited pre-Islamic capital of Persia, where the Shahanshah (Shah of Shahs) aligned himself with the ancient Persian king, Cyrus the Great, the King of Kings. The week-long celebration, featuring a feast catered by Maxim's of Paris that included twenty-five thousand bottles of wine, epitomized the Shah's insensitivity to his critics and to Iran's Islamic identity and traditions. Royal extravagance and excess were combined with a Western-style celebration at a pre-Islamic site. Thereafter, the bloody suppression of student demonstrations prefigured a new policy which tolerated little dissent and "resulted in a reign of terror."[60]

Iranian reformers, the government's opposition, represented a cross section of society: nationalists and leftists, secularists and religious, traditional elites (merchants and clergy) and modern elites. Critics of Iran's military, economic, and political dependence on the West also feared the cultural alienation that would result from the progressive Westernization of Iranian education and society. Issues of national identity, Western influence, social justice, and political participation cut across social and ideological boundaries, and were articulated by lay and clerical critics alike. Among the most influential were Jalal-e-Ahmad, Mehdi Bazargan, Dr. Ali Shariati, and the Ayatollah Khomeini. Their ideas and leadership influenced a generation of students, intellectuals, and professionals (scientists, engineers, journalists) drawn from both the traditional and the modern middle class. Islamically oriented students and professionals would join with the clergy, seminarians, and *bazaari* in the broad-based opposition movement that toppled the Shah.

Jalal-e-Ahmad (1923–69) a secularist and socialist, gave voice to the fears of many that modern educational and social reforms were resulting in a seductive process of cultural assimilation, "Weststruckness," which threatened to rob Iran and particularly the younger generation of its sense of national identity: "We're like a nation alienated from itself, in our clothing and in our homes, our food and our literature, our publications, and most dangerously of all, our education. We effect Western training, we effect Western thinking, and we follow Western procedures to solve every problem."[61]

Jalal-e-Ahmad did not see a simplistic world of monolithic, stereotypical choices, either a path of modernization/Westernization of society or a retreat to the past. He opted for a third alternative, a return to Irano-Islamic culture as a source of national identity, unity, history, and values. His secular intellectual indictment of Westernization, with the call for continuity of modern Iran's identity and culture with its past, was a pri-

mary agenda for others as well, religiously oriented lay and clerical ide-
ologists, laymen like Mehdi Bazargan and Ali Shariati and clerics like the
Ayatollah Khomeini.

In 1962, the year when Jalal-e-Ahmad's *Gharbzadegi*, a criticism of
"Weststruckness," was published, Mehdi Bazargan (b. 1907) delivered a
lecture entitled "The Boundary Between Religion and Social Affairs" on
the relationship of religion to politics. Bazargan, a French-trained engineer
with a strong Islamic commitment, had been jailed in 1939 for his opposition to Reza Shah and again from 1962 to 1969 for his opposition to
Muhammad Reza Shah. He had been active in Prime Minister Mossadegh's National Front and cofounded the Liberation Movement of Iran to
bridge the gap between modern secular and traditional religious Iranians
and work toward a more Islamic state and society. In 1979, with Khomeini's approval he would become the provisional prime minister of the
Islamic Republic of Iran.

Bazargan's political activism was inspired and shaped by his Islamic
orientation. He combined a traditional religious outlook and vocabulary
with modern concerns. Thus he was effective with modern professionals
and also, because he spoke their language, with the *ulama*. He had long
argued that because of the interrelatedness of religion and politics in Islam,
the *ulama* should move away from their political neutrality and become
actively involved in politics to bring about the renewal of Islamic society
in Iran.

The socialist inclinations of Jalal-e-Ahmad and the Islamic reformist
spirit of Bazargan were combined in Dr. Ali Shariati (1933–77), whose
revolutionary populist Islam was at once appealing to secularists and leftists, and in particular to university students, who often found the traditionalism of their religious leaders unconvincing and the Western secular
outlook of many professors disorienting. Shariati incorporated many of the
reformist currents of his times: opposition to the Shah, rejection of Westernization, religious revivalism, and social reform.

The son of a progressive preacher-scholar, Shariati had earned a doctorate from the Sorbonne. After his return to Iran in 1965, Shariati was
the subject of both controversy and adulation. Initially imprisoned for his
opposition to the Shah during his student days in Paris, he proved an
enormously attractive and successful lecturer in Teheran, drawing
thousands of admiring students, and developed a wide following among
students, intellectuals, and the Left. More than one hundred thousand copies of his lectures and writings were published and distributed.[62] Regarding
Shariati increasingly as a threat, the government denounced him as an
"Islamic Marxist," imprisoned him in 1973, and finally permitted him to
leave Iran. Dying shortly after his arrival in England of an apparent heart

attack (his supporters suspected SAVAK of foul play), Shariati became even more influential in death than in life. His talks were collected, printed, and distributed widely. He became a hero and ideologue of the revolution in Iran, and after that revolution his writings and ideas would spread throughout much of the Muslim world, finding attentive audiences from Cairo to Jakarta.

Shariati preached what may be described as an Islamic theology of Third World liberation, an indigenous populist Shii ideology for sociopolitical reform. It combined a reinterpretation of Islamic belief that incorporated modern sociological language (Emile Durkheim and Max Weber) with the Third World socialist outlook of Frantz Fanon and Che Guevara, whom he had come to admire during his student days in Paris, which had coincided with the Algerian and Cuban revolutions. However, in contrast to Fanon's rejection of traditional religions, Shariati, like Jalal-e-Ahmad, insisted that the defeat of Western imperialism required the reclamation of Iran's Islamic roots, its national, religious, and cultural identity. Shariati emphasized the dynamic, progressive, scientific nature of Islam and the need for a thoroughgoing reinterpretation of Islam to reclaim this forgotten heritage, reverse the retrogressive state of Islam, and revitalize the Muslim community. An innovative Islamic reformer, he was often at odds with both the religious traditionalism and political quietism of many *ulama* and the Westernized, secular outlook of many university professors. Both the political and the religious establishments were wary of him.

Like Jalal-e-Ahmad, Shariati denounced the evils of "Weststruckness": "Come, friends, let us abandon Europe; let us cease this nauseating, apish imitation of Europe. Let us leave behind this Europe that always speaks of humanity, but destroys human beings wherever it finds them."[63] Shariati combined denunciation of Western imperialism with an Islamic brand of socialism. The goal was national identity and unity and socioeconomic justice for a politically subjugated and economically exploited Iran, caught in the grips of "world imperialism, including multinational corporations and cultural imperialism, racism, class exploitation, class oppression, class inequality, and *gharbzadegi* [Weststruckness]."[64]

The decline of Muslim society was due not only to Western imperialism but to a religious establishment which had allowed the dynamic, revolutionary ideology of "original" Shiism to become an establishment religion. Like numerous contemporary Islamic reformers, Shariati blamed the *ulama* for many of the ills of Muslim society. In the hands of the religious establishment, Shii Islam had become scholastic, institutionalized, and historically coopted by Iran's rulers, eclipsing the true, dynamic, pristine revolutionary religiosocial message of its early years. Traditional Islam

under the *ulama* had become mired in a fossilized past of scholastic man-
uals, the popular, fatalistic opiate of the masses. It had ceased to be a
social force, effectively addressing the changing realities of society. Shariati's "return to Islam" was not a retreat to the medieval Islamic worldview of conservative *ulama*, but a revolutionary vision of early Shii Islam
which provided the inspirational basis for a modern reinterpretation of
Islam. This would require men of vision—not the *ulama* but a religiously
minded lay intelligentsia, Islamically oriented but with a knowledge and
command of modern thought and methods.

For Shariati, true Islamic society was to be classless, a haven for the
disinherited who were "plundered, tortured, hungry, oppressed and discriminated against." His was a populist message of a God who "had
promised the wretched masses they would become leaders of mankind;
He had promised the disinherited they would inherit the earth from the
mighty. . . . [T]his universal Revolution and final victory is the conclusion
of the one great continual justice-seeking movement of revolt against oppression."[65] It remained for the Ayatollah Khomeini to lead that revolt to
its triumphant if not successful conclusion.

If Shariati was the ideologue of the Iranian Revolution, the Ayatollah
Khomeini (1902–89) was its living symbol and architect. Although he was
a junior ayatollah, Khomeini's maverick politics, his charismatic persona,
and a series of circumstances would catapult him into the leadership of
the revolution and, subsequently, of the Islamic Republic of Iran. While
the majority of Iran's *ulama* had remained apolitical, Ruhollah Khomeini
had become a strident voice for reform. He had vigorously spoken out
against the Shah's policies during 1963–65, been arrested and imprisoned
several times, and then exiled to Turkey, to Iraq, and finally at the very
end to France. Throughout his exile Khomeini continued to criticize the
Shah. Copies of his writings and speeches as well as tape cassettes were
smuggled into Iran and circulated through the mosque network.

Khomeini shared with other Islamic ideologues, such as Mawlana Mawdudi of the Jamaat-i-Islami and Hassan al-Banna of the Muslim Brotherhood, a comprehensive vision of Islam:

> Islam has a system and program for all the different affairs of society: the
> form of government and administration, the regulation of peoples' dealings
> with each other, the relations of state and people, relations with foreign
> states and all of the political and economic matters. . . . The mosque has
> always been a center of leadership and command, of examination and anal-
> ysis of social problems.[66]

He also shared a polarized view of the world, a world torn between
East and West, and an Islamic world facing a crusading West. For Kho-

meini, the world was divided into two groups: oppressors (the United States and the West in general, as well as the Soviet Union) and oppressed (Muslims and the Third World).[67] The majority of governments in the Muslim world and the Third World in general were seen as client states, lackeys of the West and the East, hence the revolution's slogan, "Neither East nor West, only Islam." Khomeini's view of the world was particularly colored by his hatred of Western colonialism and imperialism: "the foul claws of imperialism have clutched at the heart of the lands of the people of the Quran, with our national wealth and resources being devoured by imperialism . . . with the poisonous culture of imperialism penetrating to the depths of towns and villages throughout the Muslim world, displacing the culture of the Quran." Iran's relations with Israel, which he regarded as an American colonial outpost, came under blistering attack:

> The sinister influence of imperialism is especially evident in Iran. Israel, the universally recognized enemy of Islam and the Muslims, at war with the Muslim peoples for years, has, with the assistance of the despicable government of Iran, penetrated all the economic, military, and political affairs of the country; it must be said that Iran has become a military base for Israel which means, by extension, for America.[68]

By the seventies Khomeini's original demand for reform was transformed into a revolutionary call for jihad. He denounced Iran's monarchy as illegitimate and anti-Islamic and called for a government guided, if not ruled, by the clergy. In a series of lectures collectively entitled *Islamic Government* which did not become widely known at the time, Khomeini rejected monarchy as un-Islamic, maintained that the Islamic character of a government is determined by Sharia rule, and called for its reimplementation in place of the man-made foreign codes which Iran had adopted. Given the centrality of Islamic law, Khomeini argued, the *ulama* played a necessary advisory and supervisory role for temporal rulers. He even hinted at the possibility of direct clerical rule.

Khomeini's views on Islamic government were not widely known or understood and would have remained academic, had the political situation in Iran not deteriorated so rapidly. The Shah's repressive policies crushing any and all forms of dissent and leading to the indiscriminate arrest, imprisonment, torture, and death of many at the hands of the secret police, created martyrs, set in motion a cycle of regime and antiregime violence, and provoked the rapid growth of a broadly based resistance movement. In the midst of a widespread suppression of intellectuals, journalists, politicians, liberal nationalists, socialists, and Marxists, Khomeini, with his vitriolic condemnation of the Shah and call for a new political order which would include a constitutional government and socioeconomic reform, became the symbol and center of opposition.

Iran's "Islamic" Revolution

As opposition mounted within Iran, Iran's Shii heritage offered a common set of symbols, a historic identity, and a value system—an indigenous, non-Western alternative, an ideological framework within which a variety of factions could function. The mullah–mosque network served as the leadership and organizational backbone for opposition to the government. Iran's thousands of mosques, scattered throughout every city and village, provided a natural, informal nationwide communications network. As in the Tobacco Protest and the Constitutional Revolution, mosques served as centers for dissent, political organization, agitation, and sanctuary. The government could ban and limit political meetings and gatherings, but it could not close the mosques or ban prayer. The clergy and their students represented a vast reservoir of grass-roots leadership; at the weekly Friday communal prayer, mosque and sermon were transformed into a religio-political event and platform, attracting thousands and often resulting in political demonstrations as the faithful left the mosques to return home. The influence of the clergy was joined to that of Islamic lay reformers like Shariati and Bazargan, who enjoyed the respect of many, especially of an increasingly alienated and militant younger generation.

Historically, Shii Islam had been both revolutionary and quietest. In the early centuries of Islamic history, Shii movements had threatened the stability of the caliphate and been a catalyst in the fall of the Umayyads. However, much of Shiism had settled later into a more apolitical quietism reinforced by a messianic belief in the eventual return of the Twelfth Imam. Thus Shii Islam, like all religious traditions, was capable of multiple interpretations. In Iran in the seventies, Shiism moved from quietism to revolutionary activism.

The defeat of Shii forces and the martyrdom of Husain at Karbala by the army of the caliph Yazid in 680 C.E., the paradigmatic event in Shii history, took on special significance, providing the inspirational model for the Iranian Revolution. Husain's martyrdom symbolized the role of Shii Islam as a protest movement in which a small righteous party struggled against the overwhelming forces of evil; it symbolized the battle between good and evil, the forces of God and of Satan, the oppressed and the oppressor, and the revolt of the disinherited. For many Shii, the Shah and his overwhelming military army, like Yazid's army, represented the evils of corruption and social injustice. Like Husain and his forces, the righteous had a religious right and duty to revolt against this modern-day Yazid and undertake a holy war to restore God's law and social justice. Self-sacrifice and even death in God's path (for God and country!) were to be freely accepted, for to die in God's struggle was to become a martyr and win eternal reward.

One Iran or Many Irans?: Diversity and Difference

Heterogeneous groups in the political spectrum, from secularists to Islamic activists, from liberal democrats to Marxists, joined together under the umbrella of Islam. However, beneath the seeming unity of purpose—opposition to the Shah and the desire for a more indigenously rooted modernity—lay a variety of religious and political outlooks and competing agendas. The political opposition ranged from those for whom an Irano-Islamic alternative simply meant Iran's cultural heritage and values, to those who wished to see the establishment of an Islamic state and society. Similar differences existed among the Islamically committed. Clergy as well as laity differed sharply in their Islamic ideologies, their views of the nature of the new political order and its leadership. Nowhere was this clearer than in the juxtaposition of the Ayatollah Khomeini and Dr. Ali Shariati—Khomeini who embodied clerical authority and power; Shariati and other Islamic modernists who represented a far more nonclerical, innovative, creative reformist approach. These differences would emerge in the aftermath of the revolution.

As public political protests and demonstrations mounted in 1978, so did the repressive measures of the state. Events came to a head in Teheran on Black Friday, September 8. Unable to break up a demonstration, the military and police fired upon the crowd of seventy-five thousand from helicopter gunships and tanks which, many would not forget, were purchased from the West and manned by the Western-trained Iranian military. Black Friday was a turning point in the revolution: white- and blue-collar workers, traditional and modern middle classes, city dwellers and rural peasants swelled the ranks of the opposition and engaged in political action. Women who had worn modern attire now joined their more traditional sisters in donning the veil as a symbol of protest against a monarch whose modernization program had once attempted to ban it.

In December, during the sacred month of Muharram which commemorates Husain's martyrdom, Islamic symbol and ritual were fused with contemporary political realities as religious processions became protest demonstrations. In Teheran almost two million people called for the overthrow and death of the Shah, the creation of an Islamic government, and the return and leadership of Khomeini. On January 6, 1979, the Shah, buffeted by widespread dissent and violence, unable to count on a military whose soldiers were defecting, and finding his American patrons wavering in their support, left Iran.

From Monarchy to Islamic Republic

The euphoria of victory and the sense of revolutionary solidarity proved fleeting. Few Iranians were prepared for what unfolded during the early years of Iran's Islamic Republic. These were revolutionary times. For historical and cultural reasons, Islam had emerged as the most effective means for political mobilization. With the fall of the Shah, deep differences in worldviews and interests quickly came to the fore. Few were prepared for the power struggle that would ensue. Those who expected that the mullahs would quietly go back to their mosques or settle into an advisory role to the new government were in for a rude awakening.

Khomeini's criticisms and denunciation of the Shah and his call for a new and just political and social order had been framed in religiocultural categories not unlike those of many other critics of the Shah, and thus masked the deep differences in outlook and agenda which existed. Furthermore, his advisers in Paris and in the early days after his return to Teheran included modern laymen influenced by the outlook of Ali Shariati. Although the opposition had a common enemy (the Shah, Pahlavi despotism, foreign control) and a common purpose (a more just and egalitarian government), there had been no agreement upon the particular form of government or even its leadership.

Few were familiar with Khomeini's writings on the nature of Islamic government. In particular, his belief in direct clerical rule, guardianship or government by a jurist or expert in Islamic law (*vilayat-i-faqih*), was neither a prominent Shii doctrine nor one which had enjoyed widespread support among Iran's religious establishment. Thus few foresaw the control which he and the *ulama* would exert in their creation of a clergy-dominated Islamic government. The implications of this doctrine were only to be realized during the post-1979 period, when Khomeini asserted his role as overseer of Iran's government.

From its inception in February 1979, the provisional government of the new Islamic Republic of Iran witnessed a struggle between moderates and militants. The authoritarianism of the Shah and his modern secular elites was replaced by that of the Imam as Guardian and his clerical cohorts. The coalition which had brought about the revolution disintegrated under the swift and often harsh judgments of a new authoritarianism. Not only Pahlavi officials and supporters but all who differed with the new "clerical autocracy"—secular and religiously oriented, lay and clerical, women and religious minorities—felt the swift arm of Islamic justice, meted out by revolutionary guards and courts. Prisons were again filled, and summary trials and executions got so out of hand that the Ayatollah Khomeini himself intervened and warned against such excesses. The Islamic Republic's first prime minister, Mehdi Bazargan, resigned in disgust; Bani-Sadr, its first elected president, fled to exile in France; Sadeq Gobtzadeh, who had held a number of government posts, was executed for his participation in an alleged plot to assassinate Khomeini. All had been protégés of Khomeini. Those religious leaders who did not accept Khomeini's doctrine of "rule by the jurist" were hounded and harassed by fellow clerics. The Ayatollah Shariatmadari, a senior ayatollah revered for his learning and piety, was himself "defrocked" in the spring of 1982.

The *ulama* and/or their supporters consolidated their control of the government, parliament, the judiciary, the media, and education. Iran's revolution was successfully institutionalized. Government purges of political organizations, the military, the judiciary, educational institutions, and government bureaus), control of the media, and intimidation of dissident clergy severely restricted the opposition. Similarly, the cultural revolution was promoted and institutionalized in the schools and the media, while alternative viewpoints were restricted or suppressed. Just as the Shah had tried to mandate Western dress, so Islamic dress codes were now enforced on the streets, in government offices, and in the universities.

Clerical and lay voices of dissent were offset by a critical mass of committed clergy and laity. The militant clergy were supported by the "lay stratum of the Islamic republic," who accepted clerical rule, served in the government, and filled many key positions in the bureaucracy.[69] Most shared a common social status (lower middle class and *bazaari* families) and educational background (first-generation university graduates in the sciences and medicine).[70] Thus the Islamic republic was based upon a clerical–lay alliance committed to the Imam and the revolution, though with differences of vision and policy.

The Islamic Threat: Iran's Export of the Revolution

Institutionalization of the revolution was accompanied by a twin goal, export of Islamic revolution. Fear of its export dominated much of Middle Eastern politics for more than a decade.[71] It had a significant impact on both the Muslim world and the West:

> For some, it has been a source of inspiration and motivation; for others, revolutionary Iran has symbolized an ominous threat to the stability of the

export 3 repercussions

Middle East and the security of the West because it has been associated with terrorism, hostage-taking, attacks on embassies, and the promotion of revolutionary activities. Indeed, for the Reagan administration, Iran often seemed synonymous with worldwide terrorism and revolution.[72]

Amid the hysteria of the postrevolutionary period, assessing the Iranian threat, separating fact from fiction, proved difficult if not impossible for the West and its allies. The shock of a revolution which had made the unthinkable a reality resulted in an overcompensation that saw both Iranian domestic politics and foreign policy through the lenses of Islamic radicalism and extremism. Intolerant Islamization at home was complemented by the threat of the spread of worldwide terrorism. Fear of other Irans and of a fundamentalist attempt to spread revolution not only in the Muslim world but also throughout the Third World were fed by the public rhetoric and propaganda of Khomeini's Islamic Republic, the outrage of an "America Held Hostage" (the seizure and captivity of the American embassy and its staff), Shii disturbances in the Gulf, and warnings from both Western and Muslim governments of the dangers of radical fundamentalism. The initial euphoria among many in the Muslim world, especially other Islamic movements, merely solidified the image of an expansionist Islamic revolution poised to menace the world. At times there seemed little exaggeration in saying that—for differing reasons—when Khomeini spoke, the whole world listened.

Export of a revolutionary Islam sprang from the Ayatollah Khomeini's ideological worldview, an interpretation of Islam which combined a religiously rooted brand of Iranian nationalism with a belief in the transnational character and global mission of Muslims to spread Islam through preaching and example as well as armed revolution. The promotion and spread of Islam was a primary foreign-policy objective, reflected in the exhortation, in the constitution of the Islamic Republic of Iran, "to perpetuate the revolution both at home and abroad."[73] Khomeini advocated peaceful means like preaching and propaganda, as well as confrontation and armed struggle: "We want Islam to spread everywhere . . . but this does not mean that we intend to export it by the bayonet. . . . If governments submit and behave in accordance with Islamic tenets, support them; if not, fight them without fear of anyone."[74]

The Ministry of Religious Guidance was charged with providing preachers and publications, conducting conferences for *ulama* from overseas, and distributing propaganda abroad. At the same time the Ayatollah Khomeini and broadcasts of Iran's Voice of the Islamic Revolution called upon Muslims of the Gulf and throughout the world to rise up against their governments. He denounced the monarchies of the Gulf and many other Muslim governments both because monarchy was un-Islamic and because they had ties with the United States, an influence which he sarcastically dismissed as "American Islam."

Iran's revolutionary impact on other Muslim countries varied significantly. In two countries—Lebanon and Bahrain—its intervention was direct, tangible, and significant. In many others its influence was more indirect, inspirational, and motivational, encouraging and confirming preexisting Islamic political tendencies and stimulating political thinking from Egypt to the southern Philippines. Though more often than not indirect, Iranian influence was often exaggerated both by disproportionate media coverage and by the tendency of Muslim governments (Egypt, the Sudan, Indonesia, Tunisia, Iraq) to use the Iranian threat as a pretext to discredit or suppress domestic Islamic opposition and as a means to encourage aid from Western governments.

Divisions Within the Government

Criticism of the Shah's Western-inspired modernization program and calls for redressing the oppression of the poor had provided a common ground for opposition, but postrevolutionary attempts to implement an Islamic order revealed substantial ideological and policy differences. Islam was used to justify both state control of the economy and private-sector freedom. While all accepted the authority of Islamic law, competing "Islamic" policies resulted from differences in religiolegal interpretation and conflicting class interests. Some insisted that answers must be found in or based upon explicit texts in traditional Islamic jurisprudence, i.e., past legal interpretations or regulations. Others argued that new problems required new interpretations of God's revelation. Confusion and indecision characterized much of the attempt to institute substantive social reform. A majority in parliament attempted to implement a social revolution. Laws were passed to control prices and markets; to nationalize many industries, banks, and foreign trade; to expropriate urban land for use by the poor and homeless; and to undertake a major redistribution of agricultural lands. However merchants, who had been a major source of financial support for the revolution, and landowners including clerical leaders strongly lobbied politicians and senior clerics against such measures. The Council of Guardians (a committee of clerical experts in Islamic law who determined whether or not parliamentary laws were Islamically acceptable) vetoed much of the reform legislation.

Sharp political differences arose in 1988 in the aftermath of the Iran–Iraq war. That war, while devastating in its human and economic tolls, had provided an excuse for Iran's serious economic problems, minimized criticism of the government, and mobilized support for the regime. Disillusion with the failure to achieve victory, exhaustion of the economy by the war, a general deterioration in the quality of life, and growing public disaffection—all were exacerbated by ideological differences within the government over strategies for national reconstruction and export of the revolution.

The pragmatist camp espoused a policy of national reconstruction and normalization of relations with the West, though the United States remained a special problem. Iran's export of the revolution was to be through example only, rather than political intervention. Radicals or revolutionary purists repudiated any talk of normalization with the West and any retreat from international revolutionary political activism as once again opening the door to dependency on the West.

The tide abruptly turned in February 1989 with the Ayatollah Khomeini's call for the execution of Salman Rushdie, author of *Satanic Verses*. The Rushdie affair provided the radical camp with an issue to counter the ascendancy of the pragmatists; enabled Khomeini to reassert his Islamic leadership internationally, mobilizing militant fervor for the defense of Islam; and distracted attention from Iran's pressing socioeconomic problems and growing social discontent.

Despite their differences, the death of the Ayatollah Khomeini in June 1989 did not precipitate a catastrophic power struggle between pragmatists and radicals. They closed ranks to assure a smooth transition that would foil the hopes of their enemies. Hashemi Rafsanjani and the Ayatollah Khamenei emerged as the key players. Rafsanjani was elected the new president of Iran, and the Assembly of Experts elected former President Khamenei Iran's "guardian" jurist. Iran's new leadership steered a more flexible course, working together for economic reconstruction and normalization of diplomatic and economic ties with the international community. Rafsanjani cut back on Iran's support for more radical Shii factions in Lebanon, sought the release of American hostages in Lebanon, and pursued diplomatic and economic relations with the West.

The development of the Islamic Republic in the 1990s has been dominated by three men: Hashemi Rafsanjani, Ayatollah Khamenei, and Mohammed Khatami. Although each has an individual leadership style, together they represent the primary political actors in Teheran's collective clerical leadership. Plagued by factionalism, shifting alliances, and contention, Iran's domestic politics and foreign affairs have been subject to the ebb and flow of rivalries based upon differences of ideology, class, and self-interest.[75] Faced with a faltering economy, growing popular discontent, and demands for more freedom and more openness in society, government politics and policies vacillated between authoritarianism and increased political participation, repression and freedom to dissent, new

initiatives for rapproachment with Arab neighbors and better relations with
the West, and militant denunciation of the dangers of foreign intervention.

Iran was accused of supporting radical religious regimes (e.g., Sudan)
that harbored and trained terrorists and militant organizations such as Hizbullah in Lebanon and Hamas in Palestine/Israel, and of assassinating Iranians abroad. In the United States the Clinton administration denounced
Iran for promoting terrorism, maintaining a clandestine nuclear weapons
program, violating human rights, and opposing the Middle East peace
process. Viewing Iran and Iraq as destabilizing forces in the Middle East—
a threat to the Gulf oil-producing states and to Israel—the Clinton administration crafted a policy of dual containment that included economic
sanctions to isolate Iran and Iraq politically and economically. The
Republican-dominated Congress passed legislation to support the desta-
bilization of Iran's Islamic government.

Iran's Islamic foreign policy was more pragmatic than ideological,
driven more by national interest than religious ideology. Although it maintained close ties with the Islamic Republic of Sudan, it distanced itself
from the Islamic Republic of Afghanistan. The Taliban of Afghanistan,
the Islamic student (*taliban*) militia group that had captured more than
two-thirds of the country, had harshly enforced an extreme brand of Islamic public standards and had declared Afghanistan's Shii community to
be unbelievers. In 1997 Iran denounced the Taliban for its un-Islamic
behavior. Although supporting Islamic activists' struggle to create an Islamic state in Algeria, Iran condemned mindless acts of violence by the
Armed Islamic Group, charging that its wanton killing of fellow Muslims
was anti-Islamic and could undermine the struggle of Islamic groups. Iran
undertook new initiatives to reclaim or strengthen its position in the Gulf
and broader Muslim world, in particular to mend fences with the OIC
(Organization of the Islamic Conference) and the Gulf Cooperation Council (GCC). Calling for Islamic unity, Iran sought to strengthen its ties with
the OIC and with Saudi Arabia and other GCC neighbors.

Political Liberalization

The late 1990s saw a significant expansion of political participation and
dissent. Both Rafsanjani's more moderate policies and the space created
by rival factions and centers of power offered conditions that tolerated
differences and dynamic change within the limits of Iran's Islamic ideology. Though the process of candidate selection was controlled, presidential and parliamentary elections continued to occur without interruption
and often with relative independence. Parliamentarians engaged in heated
debates over government policies and proposals, feeling free to criticize

the government, reject presidential appointments, and oppose the regime's legislative initiatives. Intellectual life and debate, as well as the publication of independent newspapers, magazines, and journals, increased significantly.

Iran often displayed a degree of political diversity and popular participation that contrasted sharply with many of its Arab neighbors. Despite limitations on their freedom in public life, Iranian women enjoyed more freedoms than many of their sisters in the Gulf, ranging from education and employment to voting, holding political office, and driving cars. Public discussion and debate between conservative and more liberal or feminist voices (religious and secular) occurred regularly in magazines and books.

Nevertheless, conservatives continued to dominate some key government positions (and support Iran's "supreme guide," the Ayatollah Khamenei) and the parliament. Thus reformers remained vulnerable to attack by militants who disrupted classes at the university and attempted to silence liberal professors and intellectuals like Abdul Karim Soroush, who has challenged the clergy's role in government. Through his university lectures and publications he has advocated a liberal reformist theology. Offensive books, videos, and shops have been destroyed.

Perhaps the most stunning example of the diverse currents in Iran—its increasing, though limited, moderation and pluralism—was offered by the presidential elections of 1997. Given the conservative domination of the parliament and the role of the Ayatollah Khamenei, most observers expected Ali Akbar Nateq-Nuri, Speaker of the parliament, to win handily. Nateq-Nuri, former interior minister and standard-bearer of the conservative clergy, had allied himself with Rafsanjani against the hard-liners in the elections of 1992. Once elected, however, he distanced himself from Rafsanjani in the conservative-controlled parliament. Nominated for president by influential clerics in Qom, close to Khamenei, Nateq-Nuri had criticized liberal reforms, called for greater Islamization of the universities and of society, and criticized the West vigorously.

Cleric Muhammad Khatami had strong revolutionary credentials as an early supporter of Iran's revolution. The son of one of Iran's most revered ayatollahs and a sayyid (descendant of the Prophet Muhammad), he also had a record of political moderation. His liberal views as minister of Islamic culture and guidance and his criticism of the failures and excesses of the regime had led to his being forced out of office. Khatami's emphasis on greater individual and collective freedoms, the rule of law, political tolerance, and respect for the people's will rankled conservatives, who saw this as a threat to the authority of the supreme guide, or faqih (Ayatollah Khamenei), who was above the constitution, law, and popular will.

Many did not expect Khatami even to be approved as a candidate, since it was generally known that Nateq-Nuri was favored by Khamenei. In a stunning victory on May 23, 1997, Khatami won with 69 percent of the votes cast by 67 percent of eligible voters. His victory demonstrated a broad-based appeal, since he won support from the higher middle and upper classes, Iranian youth and women, intellectuals, professionals, and artists who preferred the moderately liberal message of Khatami over the conservatism of Nateq-Nuri. However diverse their backgrounds and motivations, voters shared one thing in common—a desire for greater liberalization and change and a demand for more political and cultural space in society.

During his first year in office, Khatami initiated a national dialogue on the themes of civil society and civilizational dialogue. Public discussion and debate on issues such as the compatibility of Islam and democracy, the relationship of religion to politics, political liberalization, the rule of law, pluralism, and women's status and rights occurred openly in conferences and the media in major cities like Teheran and Qom. Cultural and intellectual exchanges between Iran and the United States were pursued by both sides.

However, the tension between the more progressive vision symbolized by Khatami and the more conservative hard-line followers of Khamenei persisted. The powers of the presidency remained limited by the supreme leader or guardian's paramount power, and his authority over the armed forces, Revolutionary Guard, and judiciary. The more open space created by Khatami encouraged the expression of many diverse viewpoints but was perceived as a threat by the more conservative, hard-line clerical establishment. If Khatami and his protégés saw a need to transform and relegitimate the Islamic Republic, believing that public discontent could otherwise rise to dangerous levels, others saw this as a challenge to the authority of the faqih, Ayatollah Khamenei. Khamenei's qualification to be the supreme leader was questioned by Ayatollah Montazeri, a senior cleric once designated (the designation was later withdrawn) by Khomeini to succeed him as faqih, and others. In public conferences and meetings in Teheran and in Qom, the compatibility of Islam and democracy was discussed, as well as the compatibility of governance by the faqih with democratization and civil society. Some questioned whether the doctrine did not need to be redefined.

Although Khatami and Khamenei consulted often and outwardly were mutually supportive, Khamenei's more conservative followers occasionally tried to undercut reformers. The conservative majority in parliament reelected Ali Akbar Nateq-Nuri as Speaker by a vote of 165 to 84. The parliament forced the resignation of the interior minister, whom Khatami then appointed a vice president. More significantly, in a heavily publicized case, the popular and effective mayor of Teheran, Gholamreza Karbaschi, a protégé of Rafsanjani and of Khatami, was indicted for corruption (taking bribes). In a verdict that stunned many, he was sentenced in July 1998 to five years in jail, banned from politics for twenty years, and condemned to receive sixty lashes.

In one of the clearest examples of the Khatami government's new direction, on September 24, 1998, Iran's foreign minister, Kamal Karrazi, announced the lifting of the death threat against Salman Rushdie, after almost nine years. Speaking to a press conference at the United Nations, Karrazi stated, "The Government of the Islamic Republic of Iran has no intention, nor is it going to take any action whatsoever to threaten the life of the author of *Satanic Verses* or anybody associated with his work, nor will it encourage or assist anybody to do so." While noting that many Iranians still found the book offensive, Karrazi declared that Iran "dissociates itself from any reward that has been offered in this regard and does not support it."[76] The announcement occurred during a visit to the United States by President Khatami in which he addressed the U.N. General Assembly. Khatami's decision, seen by many as part of his emphasis on civilizational dialogue as a means to strengthen Iran's role as a member of the international community, was welcomed by Great Britain, which immediately announced the restoration of full diplomatic relations with Iran. However, the Khatami decision proved more complicated, again revealing the tug-of-war between conservatives and progressives. Almost immediately three senior religious leaders, among them Grand Ayatollah Mohammed Fazel Lankarani, issued separate death threats (*fatwas*) stating that Rushdie's condemnation to death was irrevocable and that it was the duty of all Muslims to carry it out. Their actions were signs of a conservative backlash in the ongoing struggle between supporters of President Khatami and Iran's supreme religious leader, or faqih, Ayatollah Khamenei.

In the wake of Iran's elections, the United States set preconditions for normalization of relations. Iran must halt its support of terrorism, cease the development of nuclear weapons, and drop its opposition to the Middle East peace process. Iran countered that groups like Hamas and Hizbullah (which the United States regards as terrorist but Iran supports) were guerilla movements fighting Israel's illegal occupation of Muslim lands (Palestine and southern Lebanon). It demanded that the United States make the first goodwill gesture by releasing the billions of dollars in Iranian assets that have been frozen since the 1979 revolution. The movement toward restoration of relations between Iran and the United States was opposed not only by forces within Iran but also by many in the U.S.

Congress. The legacy of twenty years of mutual satanization proved a potent obstacle to change. Yet, in a major interview for CNN, Khatami, although not denying Iran's historic grievances, took the occasion to acknowledge the religious roots and values of the United States, warn of the dangers in a clash of civilizations, and call for a dialogue of civilizations and religions.

Although Iran's leadership remained united in its commitment to the survival of the Islamic Republic, individuals differed significantly in their visions for its survival. For some, the revolution remained seamlessly intact, with Khomeini succeeded by his designated successor, Khamenei. For many others, postrevolutionary Iran was now in its third revolutionary phase: Khomeini, Rafsanjani, and Khatami. Given the failures and shortcomings of the republic, from the Iran–Iraq war to Iran's economy, the election of Khatami represented a last chance to relegitimate the Islamic Republic. It was also an opportunity to ask forcefully: Who is to run the country, an unelected clerical hierarchy or an elected government?

When Iran was nearing the celebration of the tenth anniversary of its Islamic revolution in the late eighties, many saw the country as stabilizing and moderating. The Salman Rushdie affair, which was fomented by hardline ideologues who believed the spirit of the revolution was slipping away, dealt a stunning blow to the moderating trend. A decade later, in the aftermath of Khatami's election, as Iran approached the twentieth anniversary of the revolution, the struggle between contending ideologies continued to perpetuate a fluid and potentially unstable political climate whose final resolution remained unclear.

For almost two decades Islam has reemerged as a source of government legitimacy and national development. The pervasive belief that nation building required a clear secular path and orientation has been challenged across the Muslim world. As we have seen, governments have appealed to Islam to enhance their authority, buttress nationalism, legitimate policies and programs, and increase popular support. However, a review of contemporary Islamic politics at the state level challenges perceptions of a monolithic Islamic threat. State implementation of Islam has varied markedly in terms of its forms of government, domestic programs, and foreign policies. Monarchs, military rulers, presidents, and clergy have ruled governments as diverse as Saudi Arabia's conservative monarchy, Libya's populist socialist state, Iran's clerical republic, and the Sudan and Pakistan's military regimes. Within specific countries, contending voices and groups have vied for power in the name of Islam. Moreover, the appeal to Islam has also served as a double-edged sword. Those who wield it run the risk of being judged by that very Islamic yardstick, challenged or toppled. While state use or manipulation of Islam can broaden a ruler's base of support, it also draws Islamic as well as secular critics. Sadat and Qaddafi's appeals to Islam increasingly set them on a collision path with Islamic organizations.

Internationally, the Islamic state has not necessarily led to the strengthening of bonds of unity or to a Pan-Islamic threat. Sadat, the "believer-president," had no qualms about supporting the Shah and denouncing the Ayatollah Khomeini as a madman. Egypt's turn to Islam did not prevent the Organization of the Islamic Conference or the Arab League and most Arab and Muslim governments from breaking diplomatic relations after Egypt signed the Camp David Accords. Qaddafi's Islamic period paralleled his cool relations both with Sadat's Egypt and Nimeiri's Sudan. A lesson to be learned is that while Islam can influence a Muslim nation's attitude toward greater cooperation or foreign aid, in most cases the overriding determinant will be national interest. This also accounts for the diversity of relationships that have existed between Islamically oriented governments and the West. Sadat's Egypt, Nimeiri's Sudan, Zia ul-Haq's Pakistan, and King Fahd's Saudi Arabia all enjoyed close ties with the United States, while Qaddafi's Libya and Iran have more often than not been among its severest critics. The extent to which specific leaders and circumstances rather than Islam affect policy can be seen in the Sudan and Pakistan. In the Sudan, Islamic governments have been introduced by Gaafar Nimeiri and more recently by Omar al-Bashir. The former enjoyed close relations with the United States, while under the latter relations have deteriorated markedly.

The imposition of Islam from above has raised many questions: Whose Islam? What Islam? Why a negative Islam? In answer to the first question, Islam—like all ideologies, secular and religious alike—can be a positive social force. It can also be manipulated by dictators and demagogues and, as will also be seen in the next chapter, by Islamic movements. Is the nature and implementation of Islam simply to be left to rulers or to a parliamentary process? More often than not, rulers and governments have used Islam, as they have used other ideologies, to solidify power rather than to promote political participation. Heads of state (kings, generals, former military officers) have found it a useful tool. At the same time many of the clergy, who see themselves as the protectors of Islam, and contemporary Islamic organizations have sought their turn in power. However, increasingly in the Muslim world there is a demand for greater political participation, for governance not simply by strong rulers but through elected parliamentary bodies.

To respond to the second question, "What Islam?," the call for more Islamically oriented societies and the experiments undertaken thus far also raise questions about the nature and direction of Islamic renewal and re-form. Is the implementation of Islam in state and society to be a restoration or a reformation, the resurrection of past doctrines and laws or the recon-struction of new models rooted in faith but appropriate to the changed circumstances of life today? The issue is clear when we look at the ques-tion of Islamic law. For many, the Islamic character of the state is deter-mined by the implementation of Islamic law. However, differences of interpretation abound. For some Muslims, this simply means the wholesale reapplication of classical or medieval laws. Others argue that, just as the laws delineated in the early Islamic centuries were the product of reve-lation and human interpretation, conditioned by historical and sociopoli-tical contexts, so too today Muslims must distinguish between that which is immutable and a vast body of legal regulations that are subject to re-interpretation and reform. The battle between traditionalists and modern reformers is one which all faiths have witnessed, made more acute when its results are to be applied not only to personal but also to public life.

Finally, the significance of the questions "Whose Islam?" and "What Islam?" are highlighted by that of "Why a negative Islam?" For many observers within and without the Muslim world, the implementation of Islam politically has too often seemed less a process of inspiration, re-newal, and unity than a means for political and social manipulation and control. Restrictive laws, summary courts, and Islamic punishments and taxes, rather than social and political reform and greater emphasis on hu-man rights, have prevailed. Both rulers who would implement Islam from above, and populist movements that wish to do so from below, are in-creasingly challenged by those in their societies who ask how an Islami-cally oriented state and society will be more effective than secular regimes in issues of political liberalization and participation, socioeconomic reform and cultural authenticity. Or, to put it bluntly, is the choice simply between secular and Islamic autocracy?

5

Islamic Organizations:
Soldiers of God

Modern Islamic organizations have been the driving force behind the dynamic spread of the Islamic resurgence. They have also been the focal point or embodiment of the Islamic threat in the eyes of Western governments as well as many governments in the Muslim world. For some, Islamic movements represent an authentic alternative to corrupt, exhausted, and ineffectual regimes. For many others, they are a destabilizing force—demagogues who will employ any tactic to gain power. The violence and terrorism perpetrated by groups with names like the Party of God, Holy War, Army of God, and Salvation from Hell conjure up images of religious fanatics with a thirst for vengeance and a penchant for violence who will stop at little. The assassination of Anwar Sadat, the taking of hostages in Lebanon, and the hijacking of planes embody a "Sacred Rage" that has become all too familiar.[1] Yet again the reality is far more complex than its popular image. The majority of Islamic organizations would claim that, where permitted, they work within the political system and seek change from below through a gradual process of reform. Many Islamic organizations today espouse political liberalization and democratization. Their members participate in elections and serve in legislatures and cabinets.

Given the pivotal role that Islamic movements have played and continue to play both in the politics of the Muslim world and in the plans, calculations, and responses of Western governments, understanding their nature, goals, and activities becomes critical in assessing Islamic movements and the Islamic threat.

While Islamic revivalism and Islamic movements are integral to Islamic history and in some sense may be seen as part of a recurrent revivalist cycle in history, most movements today differ from those of earlier centuries in that they are modern, not traditional, in their leadership, ideology, and organization. If we speak of fundamentalism as a return to the foundations of Islam, the Quran, and the example of the Prophet in order to renew the community, then these movements are neofundamentalist or neorevivalist, for they look to the sources of Islam not simply to replicate the past but to respond to a new age.

The Muslim Brotherhood and the Jamaat-i-Islami

In trying to understand the origins and nature of modern Islamic movements, two organizations in particular dominate the landscape of the Muslim world in the twentieth century. Contemporary Islamic activism is particularly indebted to the ideology and organizational example of the Muslim Brotherhood and the Jamaat-i-Islami (Islamic Society or Group). Their founders and ideologues, Hassan al-Banna and Sayyid Qutb of the Brotherhood and Mawlana Abul Ala Mawdudi of the Jamaat, have had an incalculable impact on the development of Islamic movements throughout the Muslim world. They are indeed the trailblazers or architects of contemporary Islamic revivalism, men whose ideas and methods have been studied and emulated from the Sudan to Indonesia.

Hassan al-Banna (1906–49), a schoolteacher and former disciple of the Islamic modernist Rashid Rida, established the Muslim Brotherhood (Ikhwan al-Muslimin) in Egypt in 1928, while Mawlana Abul Ala Mawdudi (1903–79), a journalist, organized the Jamaat-i-Islami in India in 1941.[2] Both movements arose and initially grew in the thirties and forties at a time when their communities were in crisis. Both blamed European imperialism and a Westernized Muslim leadership for many of the current problems.

In Egypt the Brotherhood's critique of Western imperialism and the ills of Egyptian society in time found a receptive audience among the religiously inclined as well as the more Western, secular-oriented elites. Initial faith in liberal nationalism had been shaken by the defeat of the Arabs in Palestine, the creation of the state of Israel with British and American support, Egypt's continued inability to shake off British occupation, and massive unemployment, poverty, and corruption. Muslim Brothers greatly enhanced their credentials as patriotic sons of Egypt and Arab nationalists in their significant participation in the 1948 Palestine war and again in the 1951 Suez crisis.

In South Asia Mawlana Mawdudi had witnessed the collapse of the Ottoman empire and the failure of the Caliphate Movement to save that empire from being dismembered by Britain and France for its support of Germany during World War I. Growing Hindu assertiveness in the Indian Freedom (Independence) Movement in South Asia contributed to Mawdudi's perception of the continued deterioration of Muslim power and the threat to Islam and the Muslim community. Mawdudi blamed European colonialism and the emergence of modern nationalism, a foreign and Western ideology which divided rather than united peoples, replacing the universal or Pan-Islamic ideal and solidarity with a more tenuous and divisive identity based upon language, tribe, or ethnicity.

Hassan al-Banna and Mawlana Mawdudi, who were contemporaries, were pious, educated men with traditional Islamic backgrounds and knowledge of modern Western thought. Both saw their societies as being dependent on the West, politically weak, and culturally adrift. Each in his early years had been an anticolonial nationalist who turned to religious revivalism to restore the Muslim community at home and universally. These founders and ideologues of their organizations drew on the example and concerns both of eighteenth-century Islamic revivalist movements like the Wahhabi of Saudi Arabia and nineteenth- and twentieth-century Islamic modernist predecessors for their critique of Muslim society, their revivalist and reformist worldview emphasis on organization, and their sociopolitical activism. They did not simply retreat to the past but instead provided Islamic responses, ideological and organizational, to modern society.[3] Hassan al-Banna and Mawlana Mawdudi appropriated and reapplied the vision and logic of the revivalist tradition in Islam to the sociohistorical conditions of twentieth-century Muslim society. In a very real sense they modernized Islam by providing a modern interpretation or reformulation of Islam to revitalize the community religiously and sociopolitically. However, they did this not by purifying Islam of cultural accretions or un-Islamic beliefs and values or by restoring early practices of the community, however authentic. They self-consciously reapplied Islamic sources and beliefs, reinterpreting them to address modern realities. Yet they distinguished their method from that of Islamic modernism, which they equated with the Westernization of Islam. If Islamic modernists legitimated the adoption of Western ideas and institutions by maintaining their compatibility with Islam, al-Banna and Mawdudi sought to produce a new synthesis which began with Islamic sources and found either Islamic equivalents or Islamic sources for notions of government accountability, legal change, popular participation, and educational reform.

Hassan al-Banna and Mawlana Mawdudi shared a common anti-imperialist view of the West, which they believed was not only a political and economic but also a cultural threat to Muslim societies. Westernization threatened the very identity, independence, and way of life of Muslims. Indeed, they regarded the religiocultural penetration of the West (education, law, customs, values) as far more pernicious in the long run than political intervention, since it threatened the very identity and survival of the Muslim community. Imitation of or dependence on the West was to be avoided at all cost. The Brotherhood and the Jamaat proclaimed Islam as a self-sufficient, all-encompassing way of life, an ideological alternative to Western capitalism and Marxism. They joined thought to action, creating organizations that engaged in political and social activism.

Though hostile to Westernization, they were not against modernization. Both Hassan al-Banna and Mawlana Mawdudi engaged in modern organization and institution building, provided educational and social welfare services, and used modern technology and mass communications to spread their message and to mobilize popular support. Their message itself, though rooted in Islamic revelation and sources, was clearly written for a twentieth-century audience. It addressed the problems of modernity, analyzing the relationship of Islam to nationalism, democracy, capitalism, Marxism, modern banking, education, law, women and work, Zionism, and international relations. Mawdudi far more than al-Banna wrote extensively and systematically, attempting to demonstrate the comprehensive relevance of Islam to all aspects of life. The range of his topics reflected his holistic vision: Islam and the state, economics, education, revolution, women.

Despite differences, al-Banna's and Mawdudi's reinterpretations of Islamic history and tradition produced a common ideological worldview which has inspired and guided many modern Islamically oriented sociomoral reform movements. This worldview not only governed their organizations but also informed Islamic movements that sprang up throughout the Muslim world in subsequent decades.

Among the primary principles of al-Banna's and Mawdudi's ideological worldview were the following:

1. Islam constitutes an all-embracing ideology for individual and corporate life, for state and society.

2. The Quran, God's revelation, and the example (Sunnah) of the Prophet Muhammad are the foundations of Muslim life.

3. Islamic law (the Sharia, the "path" of God), based upon the Quran and the Prophet's model behavior, is the sacred blueprint for Muslim life.

4. Faithfulness to the Muslim's vocation to reestablish God's sovereignty through implementation of God's law will bring success, power, and wealth to the Islamic community (ummah) in this life as well as eternal reward in the next.

[handwritten: Banna = everyone]
[handwritten: Maududi = elite]

5. The weakness and subservience of Muslim societies must be due to the faithlessness of Muslims, who have strayed from God's divinely revealed path and instead followed the secular, materialistic ideologies and values of the West or of the East—capitalism or Marxism.

6. Restoration of Muslim pride, power, and rule (the past glory of Islamic empires and civilization) requires a return to Islam, the reimplementation of God's law and guidance for state and society.

7. Science and technology must be harnessed and used within an Islamically oriented and guided context in order to avoid the Westernization and secularization of Muslim society.

Both the Brotherhood and the Jamaat saw but two choices, darkness or light, Satan or God, ignorance (that which is un-Islamic) or Islam. At the heart of the message of the Brotherhood and the Jamaat was the conviction that Islam provided a divinely revealed and prescribed third alternative to Western capitalism and Soviet Marxism.

Scripture and tradition were appealed to and reinterpreted by the founders of these modern religious societies. The inspiration and continuity of the past were coupled with a response to the demands of modernity. This combination of past and present are demonstrated not only by their reinterpretation of Islam but also by their organization and activities. Organizationally, the Brotherhood and the Jamaat followed the example of the Prophet Muhammad (also emulated by seventeenth- and eighteenth-century revivalist movements) in gathering together believers committed to establishing societies governed by God's law. They were to be a vanguard, a righteous community within the broader community—the dynamic nucleus for true Islamic reformation or revolution, returning society to the straight path of Islam.

Both organizations recruited followers from mosques, schools, and universities: students, workers, merchants, and young professionals. They were primarily urban, based among the lower middle and middle classes, with whom they were especially successful. The goal was to produce a new generation of modern-educated but Islamically oriented leaders prepared to take their place in every sector of society. However, while al-Banna worked to develop a broad-based populist movement, Mawdudi's Jamaat was more of an elite religious organization whose primary goal was to train leaders who would come to power. An Islamic revolution was ultimately necessary to introduce an Islamic state and society. However, this Islamic revolution was to be first and foremost a social rather than a violent political one. The establishment of an Islamic state first required the Islamization of society through a gradual process of social change. Both organizations espoused an ''Islamic alternative'' to conservative religious leaders and modern, secular, Western-oriented elites. The *ulama* were generally regarded as passé, a religious class whose fossilized Islam and cooption by governments were major causes of the backwardness of the Islamic community. Modernists were seen as having traded away the very soul of Muslim society out of blind admiration for the West.

Though these organizations were quick to denounce the evils of imperialism and the cultural threat of the West, both the Brotherhood and the Jamaat nevertheless realized that the Muslim predicament was first and foremost a Muslim problem, caused by Muslims who had failed to be sufficiently Islamically observant. Its rectification was the primary task of Muslims. Rebuilding the community and redressing the balance of power between Islam and the West must begin with a call or invitation (*dawa*) to all Muslims to return to and reappropriate their faith in its fullness— to be born again in the straight path of God. Both the Brotherhood and the Jamaat reemphasized and interpreted the concept of *dawa*. The call to Islam has two aspects: an invitation to non-Muslims to convert to Islam, and the calling of those who were born Muslim to be better Muslims. Both organizations focused on the latter, the transformation (Islamization) of the individual and society. The reversal of the fortunes of Islam and of the Muslim community was to be accomplished through a social revolution. Religious commitment, modern learning and technology, and activism were combined as the Brotherhood and the Jamaat disseminated their interpretation of Islam through schools, publications, preaching, social services, and student organizations.

Neorevivalism and the West

Like secular and Islamic modernists, al-Banna and Mawdudi acknowledged the weakness of Muslim societies, the need for change, and the value of science and technology. However, they criticized both secular and Islamic modernists for excessive dependence on the West, the cause of the continued impotence of Muslim societies. On the one hand, secularists separated religion from society and took the West as the model for development: "Until recently, writers, intellectuals, scholars and governments glorified the principles of European civilization . . . adopted Western style and manner."[4] Despite their anticolonial politics, secular Muslim leaders were in effect regarded as indigenous Western cultural colonizers. On the other hand, Islamic modernists were also criticized: in their zeal to demonstrate the compatibility of Islam with modernity, they employed or relied upon Western values, producing a Westernized Islam.

All these people in their misinformed and misguided zeal to serve what they hold to be the cause of Islam, are always at great pains to prove that Islam contains within itself the elements of all types of contemporary social and political thought and action. . . . [T]his attitude emerges from an inferiority complex, from the belief that we as Muslims can earn no honour or respect unless we are able to show our religion resembles modern creeds and is in agreement with most of the contemporary ideologies.[5]

In contrast to Islamic modernists, these neorevivalists were more sweeping in their indictment of the West and their assertion of the total self-sufficiency of Islam. They maintained that Muslims should not look to Western capitalism or communism (white or red imperialism) but solely to Islam, the divinely revealed foundation of state and society. The Brotherhood charged that faith in the West was misplaced. Western democracy had not merely failed to check but contributed to authoritarianism (the manipulation of the masses by modern elites), economic exploitation, corruption, and social injustice. Western secularism and materialism undermined religion and morality, society and the family. The inherent fallacy of Western secularism, separation of religion and the state, would be responsible for the West's moral decline and ultimate downfall. Finally, the Brotherhood maintained that, despite Arab subservience to the West, the West had betrayed the Arabs in its support for the Israeli occupation of Palestine: "The Palestine question became the starting-point for attacks on the United States . . . [and resulted in] the full identification of Zionism with crusading Western imperialism."[6] In contrast to Islamic modernists, the goal of the Brotherhood and the Jamaat was not to render Islam compatible with Western culture, but to create a more indigenously rooted, authentic Islamic state and society through a process of renewal or Islamization based upon "a return to the principles of Islam . . . [and] the reconciliation of modern life with these principles, as a prelude to a final Islamization (of society)."[7]

Denunciation of the West did not mean wholesale rejection of modernization. Both al-Banna and Mawdudi distinguished between Westernization and modernization, between Western values and modern ideas and institutions. Thus the best of science and technology as well as political ideals could be appropriated, though selectively and carefully, if separated from Western values contrary to Islam and informed instead by Islamic values. In the final analysis, the renaissance or reformation of Islam would not come from reason and secularism but revelation. As Mawdudi noted:

We aspire for Islamic renaissance on the basis of the Quran. To us the Quranic spirit and Islamic tenets are immutable; but the application of this spirit in the realm of practical life must always vary with the change of conditions and increase of knowledge. . . . Our way is quite different both from the Muslim scholar of recent past and modern Europeanized stock. On the one hand we have to imbibe exactly the Quranic spirit and identify our outlook with the Islamic tenets while, on the other, we have to assess thoroughly the developments in the field of knowledge and changes in conditions of life that have been brought during the last eight hundred years; and third, we have to arrange these ideas and laws of life on genuine Islamic lines so that Islam should once again become a dynamic force; the leader of the world rather than its follower.[8]

Mawdudi's attitude toward democracy provides an excellent example of his method. Since Islam's worldview was God-centered rather than human-centered, a parliamentary democracy based upon popular sovereignty rather than divine sovereignty was unacceptable. Mawdudi rejected democracy—that is, Western democracy, which in the name of majority rule permitted practices such as alcohol consumption and sexual promiscuity that were contrary to God's law. However, parliamentary political participation or consultative assemblies subordinated to Islamic law, God's law, were permissible. Here both al-Banna and Mawdudi reinterpreted and utilized the Islamic concept of consultation (*shura*) to provide Islamic justification. Mawdudi preferred to speak of the Islamic system as a "theo-democracy," as distinct from a theocracy or clerical state, in which the popular will was subordinated to and limited by God's law. Mawdudi did not shrink from those who ridiculed him for "religious authoritarianism." Indeed, Mawdudi did not envision submission to God's absolute authority as a deprivation of man's liberty, but rather as a condition of it. Thus he had no problem characterizing an Islamic government or theodemocracy as "Islamic totalitarianism."

Radical Islam: Sayyid Qutb, Martyr

Just as the ideological worldviews of Hassan al-Banna and Mawlana Mawdudi had been shaped by their social context, so too the ideology of Islamic revivalism in Egypt became more militant and combative in the late fifties and sixties as a result of the Muslim Brotherhood's confrontation with the Egyptian state. One man stands out as the architect of radical Islam, Sayyid Qutb (1906–66). By the sixties Qutb, increasingly radicalized by Nasser's suppression of the Brotherhood, transformed the ideological beliefs of al-Banna and Mawdudi into a rejectionist revolutionary call to arms. Like al-Banna, Qutb would come to be remembered as a martyr of the Islamic revival.

Also like al-Banna, Qutb studied at the Dar al-Ulum, a modern college established by reformers to train teachers in modern subjects. It was here that he became familiar with Western literature and, like many young intellectuals of the time, grew up to be an admirer of the West. After graduation he worked as an official in the Ministry of Public Instruction.

He was an active participant in the literary and social debates of his times and soon became a prolific writer, publishing works of poetry and literary criticism. Qutb was also a devout Muslim who had memorized the Quran as a child and in the post–World War I period wrote increasingly on Islam and the state of Egyptian society. In 1948 he published *Social Justice in Islam*, in which he maintained that, in contrast to Christianity and communism, Islam possessed its own distinctive social teachings or path, Islamic socialism, which avoided the pitfalls of separation of religion and society on the one hand and atheism on the other.

> Christianity looks at man only from the standpoint of his spiritual desires and seeks to crush down the human instincts in order to encourage those desires. On the other hand, Communism looks at man only from the standpoint of his material needs; it looks not only at human nature, but also at the world and at life from a purely material point of view. But Islam looks at man as forming a unity whose spiritual desires cannot be separated from his bodily appetites, and whose moral needs cannot be divorced from his material needs. It looks at the world and at life with this all-embracing view which permits of no separation or division. In this fact lies the main divergence between Communism, Christianity, and Islam.[9]

In 1949 Sayyid Qutb traveled to the United States to study educational organization. This experience proved to be a turning point in his life. After this visit he became a severe critic of the West and, shortly after his return to Egypt in 1951, he joined the Muslim Brotherhood. Although he came to the United States out of admiration, Qutb experienced a strong dose of culture shock which drove him to become more religiously observant and convinced of the moral decadence of Western civilization and its anti-Arab bias. He was disgusted by what he judged to be racial prejudice toward Arabs, reflected both in how he and other Arabs were treated and by U.S. government and media support for Israel.[10] He was scandalized by the sexual permissiveness and promiscuity of American society, the free use of alcohol, and free mingling of men and women in public. In his writings

> [h]e describes Americans as being violent by nature and as having little respect for human life. . . . American churches were not places of worship as much as entertainment centers and playgrounds for the sexes. Americans, according to Qutb, were primitive in their sexual life, as illustrated in the words of an American female college student who told him that the sexual issue was not ethical, but merely biological.[11]

During the fifties Qutb emerged as a major voice of the Muslim Brotherhood and its most influential ideologue. His commitment, intelligence, militancy, and literary style made him especially effective within the con-

why Qutb advocated jihad?

text of a growing confrontation between a repressive regime and the Brotherhood. Government harassment of the Brotherhood and Qutb's imprisonment and torture in 1954 for alleged involvement in an attempt to assassinate Nasser only increased his radicalization and confrontational worldview. During ten years of imprisonment in the equivalent of a concentration camp, he wrote prolifically, completing *In the Shade of the Quran*, a Quranic commentary, as well as his most influential Islamic ideological tract, *Maalim fil Tariq* (*Signposts* or *Milestones*). His thought now reflected a new revolutionary vision born of his extended imprisonment and torture. He carried the ideas of Hassan al-Banna and especially Mawlana Mawdudi to their literalist, radical conclusions.

For Qutb, Islamic movements existed in a world of repressive, anti-Islamic governments and societies. Society was divided into two camps, the party of God and the party of Satan, those committed to the rule of God and those opposed. There was no middle ground. Strongly influenced by Mawdudi, Qutb emphasized the development of a vanguard, a group (*jamaa*) of true Muslims within the broader corrupted and faithless society. The Islamic movement (*haraka*) was a righteous minority adrift in a sea of ignorance and unbelief (*jahiliyya*). He dismissed Muslim governments and societies as un-Islamic (*jahili*), being in effect atheist or pagan. Thus the classical historical designation of pre-Islamic Arabia as a society of ignorance (*jahiliyya*) was appropriated to condemn modern societies as un-Islamic or anti-Islamic. For Qutb, the cause was the displacement of Islam's God-centered universe by a human-centered world.

Qutb maintained that the creation of an Islamic system of government was a divine commandment, and therefore not just an alternative but an imperative.[12] Given the political realities of authoritarian, un-Islamic regimes, Qutb concluded that attempts to bring about change from within the existing repressive Muslim political systems were futile, and that jihad was the only way to implement a new Islamic order. Jihad as armed struggle in the defense of Islam against injustice became the prescribed path for all true believers in the current crisis. Islam stood on the brink of disaster, threatened by repressive anti-Islamic governments and the neocolonialism of the West and the East. Those Muslims who refused to participate or wavered were to be counted among the enemies of God. Qutb's formulation became the starting point for many radical groups.[13] The two options—evolution, a process which emphasizes revolutionary change from below, and revolution, the violent overthrow of established (un-Islamic) systems of government—have remained the twin paths of contemporary Islamic movements.

For Qutb, as for al-Banna and Mawdudi, the West is the historic and pervasive enemy of Islam and Muslim societies, both a political and a religiocultural threat. Its clear and present danger comes not only from its political, military, and economic power, but also from its hold on Muslim elites who govern and guide by alien standards which threaten the identity and soul of their societies. However, Qutb went beyond his predecessors when he declared Muslim elites and governments to be atheists against whom all true believers should wage holy war.

In 1965 the Muslim Brotherhood, blamed for an attempt on Nasser's life, was massively and ruthlessly suppressed by the government. Qutb and several other leaders were arrested and executed, and thousands of Brothers were arrested and tortured, while others went underground or fled the country.

Political Action

The political lives of the Muslim Brotherhood and the Jamaat-i-Islami tell us much about the nature of Islamic movements and their development both in the past and today. In particular, their diverse paths underscore the influence of sociopolitical contexts on the ideologies and politics of movements, their degree of militancy, and their use of violence. Though the Muslim Brotherhood and the Jamaat began as sociomoral reform organizations, they both became heavily involved in politics, convinced that a more Islamic state and society ultimately required the cooperation and support of the state in implementing Islamic law. The Brotherhood of Hassan al-Banna during the rule of King Farouk, and later in the time of Sayyid Qutb under Nasser's regime, were drawn into confrontation with governments that resisted their demands. Both al Banna and Qutb came to be remembered as martyrs of Islamic revivalism. Hassan al-Banna was killed reportedly by secret police in retaliation for the Brotherhood's reputed involvement in the assassination of an official in King Farouk's government. Similarly, Sayyid Qutb was hanged as the ringleader of an alleged massive Brotherhood conspiracy against the government.

Though ostensibly one organization, the Muslim Brothers had in fact split internally into several factions. After al-Banna's death, no single leader enjoyed his authority. While Qutb's radical rhetoric appealed to a more militant wing, especially disaffected youth, many other Brothers, including their leader or Supreme Guide, were wary of a direct confrontation with the regime. The political strategy of the Brotherhood remained unresolved, with two competing models, evolution and revolution. While some Brothers may have conspired to overthrow the government, many of the older guard, fully aware of the power of the state, preferred to pursue change through preaching and social activism. Since they were divided, they were no real threat to Nasser. However, they did provide a convenient means for Nasser to deflect attention from his domestic and international problems: "The 'new conspiracy of the Muslim Brotherhood' offered an ideal scapegoat that would enable the leader to reunite the people behind him."[14] As we shall see, despite the Brotherhood's suppression in 1954 and its apparent extinction in 1965, it would reemerge in Egypt in the seventies.

Mawlana Mawdudi and the Jamaat have always been embroiled in Pakistani politics; though militant, they have participated within the political system. Although initially objecting to the creation of Pakistan, after independence Mawdudi and the Jamaat became leading voices in the Islamic Republic of Pakistan, functioning as a political party and pressing their demands for an Islamic state. Although Mawdudi and Jamaat leaders confronted the government from time to time and were imprisoned for their activities, on the whole they were prominent in parliamentary politics. The Jamaat has never been able to score impressive victories in electoral politics but has nonetheless had a significant impact, especially during the rule of Gen. Zia ul-Haq (1977–88). Internationally, Jamaat organizations exist and have been politically active in Pakistan, Bangladesh, India, Afghanistan, and Kashmir. Mawdudi's writings have been disseminated throughout the Muslim world and have influenced Islamic activists from Sayyid Qutb to the current generation ranging from Tunisia to Indonesia.

It is difficult to overestimate the impact of al-Banna, Qutb, and Mawdudi. The ideas and strategies of these modern pioneers continue to be major ideological influences on the worldview and development of Islamic organizations today. Combining religiopolitical activism with social protest or reform, contemporary Islamic movements represent a spectrum of positions from moderation and gradualism to radicalism and revolutionary violence, from criticism of the West to rejection of and attack upon all that is associated with it.

Contemporary Islamic Movements in Egypt: Evolution or Revolution?

Within five years after the death of Sayyid Qutb and the suppression of the Muslim Brotherhood, those who had pronounced its demise were stunned to see the phoenix rise from its ashes. Astonishingly, Anwar Sadat, Nasser's vice president and protégé who had sat on military tribunals that condemned Muslim Brothers, and who had succeeded Nasser as president in 1970, became the patron of Egypt's Islamic resurgence, rehabilitating the Brotherhood and fostering Islamic student organizations. However, Islam proved to be a two-edged sword, for Sadat was subsequently assassinated by religious extremists in its name. The fractured and factionalized legacy of the Muslim Brotherhood and the confrontation of its extremist offshoots with the state have set the pattern for Islamic politics for more than a decade. The majority of Muslim organizations, epitomized by the Muslim Brotherhood, pursue an evolutionary path of preaching and sociopolitical action, while a minority of extremists with names like Holy War and Salvation from Hell directly threaten the authority of the state.

The Muslim Brotherhood, 1970–1991

From 1970 to 1991 the Muslim Brotherhood rebuilt its organization, self-consciously espousing a policy of moderate reformism under both Anwar Sadat and his successor, Hosni Mubarak. Initially many dismissed them as a weakened remnant of defeated and cowed old men. This judgment seemed true in the early Sadat years. The government established a working relationship with the Supreme Guide of the Brotherhood, Omar Tilmassani, whom Sadat had freed from prison. Radical groups charged that the Brotherhood's leadership had been broken by their prison experience and coopted by the government. In fact, the moderate faction of the Brotherhood had prevailed while younger members, radicalized by their prison experiences and inspired by a literal and militant interpretation of Sayyid Qutb, formed secret underground groups bent upon the violent overthrow of the regime.

The Brotherhood worked out a modus vivendi with the Sadat government. While still not recognized as a political party, it was once again able to function openly, preaching its message, publishing magazines, establishing social welfare and financial institutions. Muslim Brothers long underground and those in exile now returned to work again with their colleagues who had been released from prison. They continued to draw their members from the middle and lower middle classes: businessmen, bureaucrats, doctors, engineers, lawyers. Revenue poured in from Brothers working in the oil-rich countries of the Gulf and Iraq and from patrons like Saudi Arabia. While the Brotherhood was not silent, during the early Sadat years it attenuated its criticism of the government, emphasizing cooperation. The leadership of the Brotherhood consistently eschewed violence and confrontation and was critical of the Islamic radical groups' use of force. If the period 1945–65 had been marked by sporadic confrontation and antiregime violence, the post-1970 Brotherhood, under its third Supreme Guide, Tilmassani, underwent an unambiguous transformation. It clearly opted for sociopolitical change through a policy of moderation and gradualism which accepted political pluralism and parliamentary democracy, entering into political alliances with secular political parties and organizations as well as acknowledging the rights of Coptic Christians. Even in the late seventies, when it felt the wrath of Sadat for its growing independence (rejection of the Camp David Accords and Muslim Family Reforms, bitter denunciation of the United States and Israel), it nevertheless continued to pursue the path of critic and pressure group. Though sympathetic to many of the concerns of extremist groups, it remained steadfast in its rejection of violence and terrorism and stayed scrupulously within the limits of Egyptian law.

Although the radical groups that challenged and eventually assassinated Sadat received the most attention during the late Sadat period, by the eighties the Brotherhood once again proved to be a significant dynamic force in Egyptian society, possessing both wealth and power. Under Hosni Mubarak's more open political system, Islamic revivalism emerged as part of mainstream Islam. No longer could it simply be dismissed as religious extremism, a radical fringe of alienated, marginalized Egyptians. The revivalist spirit, increased religious consciousness and observance, was evident throughout much of society and had become normalized and institutionalized, as witnessed in personal religious observances, the growth of Sufi mysticism, and the proliferation of Islamic banks and investment houses, social welfare services (schools, day-care centers, hospitals, and clinics), publishing houses, and media. Though many Islamic associations are apolitical, these organizations and activities carry an implicit political critique of the Egyptian government's failure to meet the needs of society. The Egyptian sociologist Saad Eddin Ibrahim has commented:

> This strand of Islamic activism has therefore set about establishing concrete Islamic alternatives to the socio-economic institutions of the state and the capitalist sector. Islamic social welfare institutions are better run than their state–public counterparts, less bureaucratic and impersonal. . . . They are definitely more grass roots oriented, far less expensive and far less opulent than the institutions created under Sadat's *infitah* (open-door policy), institutions which mushroomed in the 1970's and which have been providing an exclusive service to the top 5% of the country's population. Apolitical Islamic activism has thus developed a substantial socio-economic muscle through which it has managed to baffle the state and other secular forces in Egypt.[15]

The Muslim Brothers reemerged in the eighties during Mubarak's rule as the largest and strongest Islamic organization, relying on both social and political activism. They ran an extensive network of banks, investment companies, schools, medical and legal services, factories, agribusinesses, and mass communications organizations. The Brotherhood was a major force in professional organizations and syndicates (lawyers, engineers, journalists, doctors) and in the universities. Prevented from participating in elections as a political party, the Brotherhood joined with the Wafd party in the 1984 elections and subsequently formed a new coalition, the Islamic Alliance, with the Labor party in the 1987 elections. Campaigning with the slogan "Islam is the solution" and calling for the implementation of Islamic law, they won 17 percent of the vote, emerging as the chief political opposition of Mubarak's government.

Islamic Revolutionary Groups in Egypt

Throughout both the Sadat and Mubarak years, secret Islamic revolutionary groups waged jihad to disrupt society and challenge the authority and legitimacy of the state. Weapons, bombs, armed confrontation, kidnapping, and assassination have been an integral part of their action. Among the major groups were the Islamic Liberation Organization (also known as Shabab Muhammad, or Muhammad's Youth), Jamaat al Muslimin (Society of Muslims) or, as it was more popularly known, Takfir wal-Hijra (Excommunication and Emigration); Jamaat al-Jihad (Holy War Society); and Salvation from Hell.

The Islamic Liberation Organization and Takfir wal-Hijra sprang up after the 1967 Arab–Israeli war. The humiliating Egyptian defeat and the loss of Jerusalem were taken as clear signs of a politically impotent, inept, and corrupt system of government. While the Muslim Brothers moderated their voices during the early Sadat years, this new generation of Islamic militants, some of whom had been among the younger members of the Brotherhood imprisoned and tortured during the Nasser years, espoused a violent antigovernment strategy. The Islamic Liberation Organization attempted a coup d'état in April 1974. Although it seized Cairo's Technical Military Academy, government forces foiled its attempt to assassinate Anwar Sadat and declare an Islamic republic. In July 1977 Takfir wal-Hijra kidnapped Husayn al-Dhahabi, a teacher at al-Azhar University and former minister of religious endowments, who had been a strong critic of extremists. They subsequently killed him when their demands were not met. In retaliation, the leaders of both Muhammad's Youth and the Takfir were executed by the government, and many of their members were tried before military courts and imprisoned.[16] Although suppressed, many militants again went underground and became active in other radical groups such as the Jund Allah (Army of God) and Jamaat al-Jihad (Holy War Society).

Jamaat al-Jihad, which assassinated Anwar Sadat on October 6, 1981, developed from the survivors of the abortive coup staged by Muhammad's Youth in 1974. Separate groups grew up around local leaders in Upper Egypt (Asyut, Minya, Fayyum) as well as in Cairo and Giza.[17] Members were drawn from the presidential guard, military intelligence, civil servants, radio and television workers, and university students and professors. In 1980 the different groups were brought together in a loosely organized movement governed by a consultative council. All were united in their belief that the establishment of an Islamic society required the restoration of the caliphate. All Muslim rulers were regarded as apostates: "The Rulers of this age are in apostasy from Islam. They were raised at the tables of imperialism, be it Crusaderism, or Communism, or Zionism."[18] Thus holy war against Egypt's "atheist" ruler and state was considered both necessary and justified.

Jihad: The Forgotten Obligation

The group al-Jihad's ideology was set forth in a brief tract by Muhammad al-Farag. *The Neglected Obligation* (*Absent Commandment*, i.e., jihad) articulated the obligation of jihad, drawing heavily on the ideological worldview of al-Banna, Mawdudi, and Qutb. Farag took their thoughts on Islamic revolution literally and, following Qutb, pushed them to their logical conclusion. At the heart of al-Jihad's message and mission was the call to true believers to wage holy war against Egypt's un-Islamic state and its leader, Anwar Sadat. It maintained that jihad was the sixth pillar of Islam, a fact often forgotten or obscured by the *ulama* and most Muslims.

> Jihad . . . for God's cause, in spite of its extreme importance for the future of religion, has been neglected by the *ulama* . . . of this age. They have feigned ignorance of it, but they know that it is the only way to the return and the establishment of the glory of Islam anew. . . . There is no doubt that the idols of this world can only disappear through the power of the sword.[19]

The goal was the creation of an Islamic state, the eradication of Western law, and the imposition of Islamic law. Al-Jihad believed that radical surgery was required; power must be seized. "We have to establish the Rule of God's Religion in our own country first, and to make the Word of God supreme. . . . There is no doubt that the first battlefield for jihad is the extermination of these infidel leaders and to replace them by a complete Islamic Order. From here we should start."[20]

Despite the imprisonment and execution of al-Jihad leaders for the murder of Sadat, a small group called Salvation from Hell, an offshoot of al-Jihad, resurfaced. Salvation from Hell rejected anyone associated with the "atheist" regime of Mubarak. They declared a holy war against Egypt's "infidel" rulers and society and sought to create an Islamic state.[21] In September 1989 members of Salvation from Hell were sentenced for the attempted assassination of two former cabinet ministers and a journalist who had written articles condemning religious extremists.

The Ideological Worldview of Islamic Militants

The radical confrontational worldview of Islamic militants incorporated the polarized anti-Western perception of the world preached by Sayyid Qutb in the last years of his life. The Westernization of Muslim society was blamed for political corruption, economic decline, social injustice, and spiritual malaise in Egyptian society. Following Qutb, they likened the condition of Egyptian society to the ignorance, paganism, and barbarism prior to Islam. The West's Crusader mentality and neocolonialism and the power of Zionism were believed to be behind a Judaeo-Christian conspiracy which pitted the West against the Islamic world.

Since the legitimacy of Muslim governments is based on Islamic law, militants believed that Egypt's failure to implement the law rendered their country an "atheist state" against which all true Muslims were duty-bound to wage jihad. Jihad against all unbelievers is a religious duty; militants reinterpreted Islamic beliefs, maintaining that true believers are obliged to fight those Muslims who do not share their total commitment and that non-Muslim "People of the Book" were also to be regarded as infidels.

Militants were equally harsh in their denunciation of the religious establishment and their government-supported and regulated mosques. The official *ulama* were regarded as puppets of the government. Their quiescent interpretation of jihad, which downplayed armed struggle and limited jihad to the pursuit of virtue, compromised the true revolutionary meaning of Islam by preaching subservience to the state. Moreover, the officials of al-Azhar could be counted on to support government policies from Camp David and the denunciation of the Ayatollah Khomeini to the condemnation of militant Egyptian groups. Thus Shaykh Abdul Halim Mahmud, rector of al-Azhar, had declared that young activists had been "seized by the devil," and that "the religious and political authorities had to defend the world of Islam against such heresies."[22] Militants told their members to shun state-supported and controlled mosques as places of unbelief, since God's will and the Prophet's teachings were not upheld there. The Muslim Brotherhood was also rejected. Their moderate tone and agenda, their advocacy of a gradual Islamization of Egyptian society, were seen as unrealistic and as a capitulation to the government. Compromise was regarded as collaboration with the enemies of God.

Leadership and Organization

The leadership and organization of Egypt's radical Islamic organizations have reflected the temperament and styles of their leaders. Shukri Mustafa ran the Takfir as a highly disciplined organization, controlled and guided by its Amir. Like Muhammad's Youth, Takfir viewed contemporary Egyptian society as un-Islamic, a domain of unbelievers. Emulating the Prophet Muhammad who, when faced with the unbelief of Mecca, had emigrated to Medina, Takfir set up its own "rightly guided" (i.e., faithful to God's word) communities working, studying, and praying together. Its goal was the establishment of a separate community of true believers in Egypt. As in the Muslim Brotherhood and Pakistan's Jamaat-i-Islami, there were gradations of membership. Full members were expected to devote themselves totally to the work of the community, leaving their jobs, family, and former friends behind. The ideal was martyrdom: a willingness to give up even one's life in the struggle for Islam. The Amir or leader demanded unquestioning obedience. Errant members might be excommunicated and/or punished.

While members of Muhammad's Youth were equally militant, well organized, and disciplined, they were governed more democratically by an executive council which relied on consultation rather than one-man rule. Thus the council had decided to seize the Military Academy and assassinate Sadat despite their leader's personal belief that such action was premature.

But who are these militants? Contrary to many stereotypes and expectations, they have not been uneducated peasants ignorant of the modern world, rejecting modernization in order to bury themselves in the past. The leadership of Muhammad's Youth and Takfir wal-Hijra combined an early traditional religious upbringing with a modern education. Dr. Salih Siriya, founder of Muhammad's Youth, had earned a doctorate in science education. Born in Palestine, he had been a member of the Islamic Liberation Organization (ILO), founded in Jordan by a former follower of Hassan al-Banna. The ILO is an international Islamic organization with a network of clandestine cells in many Muslim countries. It is very secretive, strongly anti-Western, particularly interested in recruiting members from the military, and dedicated to the restoration of the caliphate (a universal Islamic state) and the creation of a unified worldwide Islamic movement. Shukri Mustafa, founder of Takfir wal-Hijra, held a bachelor's degree in agricultural science. Both Mustafa and Siriya had been members of the Muslim Brotherhood and as a result had been imprisoned. Mustafa had in fact been imprisoned in Nasser's suppression of the Brotherhood in 1965 and was among those released in 1971 by Sadat. Though Siriya and Mustafa honored the memory of Hassan al-Banna and Sayyid Qutb, they believed that the Brotherhood had drifted from its early commitment, that its members were broken, mellowed, or burned out. Therefore each had begun to develop his own organization during the late sixties and early seventies.

The key leaders of Jamaat al-Jihad have been Muhammad al-Farag, Col. Abbud al-Zumur, Lt. Khalid Islambuli, and Shaykh Umar Abd al-Rahman, reflecting a civilian, military, and religious alliance. Farag, an electrician, was the chief ideologist of al-Jihad. Like the founders of other militant organizations, he was a former Muslim Brother who had become disaffected by its moderate posture. Col. al-Zumur and Lt. Islambuli were primarily responsible for Sadat's assassination.[23] Shaykh Abd al-Rahman, the religious adviser for al-Jihad, issued decrees which religiously justified al-Jihad's actions.

Profile of Membership

Activist organizations recruited members from local mosques, schools, and universities and were organized into secret cells. Many members were modern-educated, highly motivated individuals from the lower middle and middle class. The majority had university degrees in modern scientific and technical professions like engineering, medicine, science, and law rather than in religion or the humanities. Most had migrated from villages and towns to Cairo, Alexandria, and Asyut. One Egyptian expert concluded:

> The typical social profile of members of militant Islamic groups could be summarized as being young (early twenties), of rural or small-town background, from middle and lower middle class, with high achievement motivation, upwardly mobile, with science or engineering education, and from a normally cohesive family. It is sometimes assumed in social science that recruits of "radical movements" must be somehow alienated, marginal, anomic, or otherwise abnormal. Most of those we investigated would be considered model young Egyptians.[24]

However, these young Egyptians encountered vividly the "new ways" of city life. The wealth and ostentatious life-styles of the rich contrasted starkly with the poverty and massive unemployment of overcrowded ghettos, and the clash between Western and traditional Islamic values in dress and social (especially sexual) mores on the streets and in the media was a further source of scandal and outrage. While the freedom and delights of city life proved seductive for some, for many Islamically minded young Egyptians modern Egyptian life produced a sense of isolation and alienation.

Independent private mosques, freed from government control, have proven especially important in the development of Islamic movements, providing a center for organization and recruitment. They provide natural meeting places and organizational centers for Islamic militants. During the seventies the number of private mosques doubled from approximately twenty to forty thousand. Out of forty-six thousand mosques in Egypt, only six thousand were controlled by the Ministry of Religious Endowments. Private mosques and their preachers, in contrast to state-supported mosques, were financially and politically independent. The religious establishment and the government-controlled media were often seriously undermined by fiery sermons in private mosques delivered by charismatic preachers.

Groups like al-Jihad extended their influence through a network of educational and social welfare societies, including Quran study groups for the faithful and social centers which offered food, clothing, and assistance in obtaining housing to the poor in crowded urban areas. Student organizations at universities assisted with free books, clothes (including "Islamic dress" for women), tutoring, and housing. In the membership, Egypt's younger generation was heavily represented. Islamic organizations offered a new sense of community, a society organized into cells called families (*usrah*). More important, their community was based upon an Islamic ideology which provided a sense of identity and continuity as well as a critique of society and an agenda for radical change.

The educational and religious backgrounds of many militants remind us that, however repugnant the acts of extremists might be, they were not mindless or irrational. Specific causes motivated their actions: food riots in January 1977 in Cairo, unemployment, acute housing shortages, poverty, Sadat's open door (*al-infitah*) economic program, the Camp David Accords with Israel. Sadat's religious and secular critics charged the the open-door policy simply meant greater Western (especially American) economic involvement and dependence which lined the pockets of multinational companies and Egyptian elites but failed to address the basic economic and social problems of the majority of Egyptians. Camp David was viewed by many Egyptians and by most Arab and Muslim governments, which broke diplomatic ties with Egypt, as abandonment of the Palestinians displaced or living under Israeli occupation, and a unilateral capitulation to Israel and, by extension, to its American patron.

Egyptian Islamic Movements in the Nineties

Despite sporadic eruptions of violence and continued confrontation between the government and Islamic militants, in general a quiet rather than a violent revolution occurred in Egypt. The impact of the Islamic resurgence was evident across the religious, political, and socioeconomic spectrum of society—in the continued strength of conservative establishment Islam, the new vitality of Sufi mysticism, and the proliferation of moderate Islamically oriented organizations and voluntary social welfare associations.[25] The desire to lead a more Islamically informed way of life can be found among the middle and upper class, uneducated and educated, peasants and professionals, young and old, women and men. Mosques abound, built both by the government and by private individuals. They include not only formal buildings but thousands of structures and rooms added onto hotels, hospitals, and private dwellings. Religious programming and literature is not only more evident in the government-controlled media and in newspapers, but also in bookshops and scattered among the popular secular magazines and books of street vendors.

Egypt's militant groups remain fragmented and small. They do not enjoy broad popular support, though at times their critique of society has won admiration or support in a society often on the brink of economic disaster. However, social discontent has not always translated into membership. Thus they remain a distinct minority voice in society. The Muslim Brotherhood and a host of smaller Islamic societies and organizations have enjoyed more support, and they function as effective voices for social and political change. Some are political, while others remain apolitical religious and social activists. While the Muslim Brotherhood has grown and become a major voice in Egyptian life, again one must remember that its message is not the dominant one but that of a significant, well-organized, vocal minority.

Lebanon's AMAL and Hizbullah

Just as Iran and the Ayatollah Khomeini became household names during the eighties, so too Lebanon's AMAL and Hizbullah became part and parcel of the evening news headlines. As in Iran, Shii Islam in Lebanon became the basis for the political mobilization of Shii Muslims into protest and revolutionary movements. Lebanon often seemed another example of radical fundamentalism and of "Americans held hostage." As many in the West were stunned by the overthrow of the Shah of Iran and the rampant anti-Americanism in what had long been regarded as a strong Western ally, so too the disintegration of Lebanon—the "Switzerland of the Middle East," where Europeans and Gulf shayks invested their money and built summer palaces—was impossible to fathom. That both Western-oriented Iran and Lebanon would become hotbeds of Shii radicalism seemed irrational. Both Iranian and Lebanese leaders and those of the Western world appeared to have been caught completely off guard. As with other Islamic movements, however, the rise of Shii political activism in Lebanon must be seen within the context of Lebanese politics and society.

For much of Lebanon's modern history, Christians were the dominant political and economic power.[26] Muslims regarded themselves as second-class citizens, and Shii Muslims in particular were at the bottom of the ladder of privilege. But in the seventies and eighties the status quo was challenged as Shii political organizations and militias sprang up to vie with Christian, Israeli, and Palestinian military forces. As in Iran, the emergence of Islam in Lebanese politics was the product of sociopolitical factors combined with a charismatic leadership that skillfully used religious symbols to organize popular support. However, in contrast to Iran, Shii Islamic movements grew in a soil in which the Shii community was a distinct religious minority, predominantly rural, poor, disorganized, and lacking an effective clerical leadership.

Lebanon has often been viewed as another modern, Western-oriented casualty of militant Islam. Lebanon's modern, Westernized capital of Beirut had been a banking, financial, educational, and cultural center of the Middle East. Its beaches and mountain resorts attracted great waves of tourists from Europe and the Middle East. Foreign presence and influence could be found everywhere in its restaurants, stores, boutiques, nightclubs, schools and universities, fashions, cinema, books, and high-tech products from the United States, Europe and Asia. However, this prosperous country, an ally of the West, would be torn apart by a fifteen-year civil war. Lebanon became a land of death and unimaginable destruction, a country without a representative government, a fertile ground for the development of militant Shii politics and Iranian influence, a battleground of Muslim and Christian militias, Israeli and Palestinian forces, a land of hijackings, kidnappings, and attacks on Western embassies and personnel.

Lebanon is an example of colonialism's mixed legacy. U.S. and European influence could be seen in its history. Once under Ottoman rule, Lebanon had become a French protectorate during the mandate period. The modern state of Lebanon, which includes what was formerly Greater Syria, is a nation whose geographic boundaries were artificially determined by the French. Long regarded as patrons and protectors of the Christian (especially Maronite) communities, the French assured a Christian-dominated state. Beirut became a center of American and European influence, symbolized by large foreign diplomatic and business communities, American-, French-, and British-run schools and banks, and a Western-educated, trilingual (Arabic, French, and English) elite class. Indeed, to have obtained the best education meant that, whether Christian or Muslim, a Lebanese had attended American or European primary and secondary schools often run by Christian missionaries and then studied at the American University of Beirut (formerly the Syrian Protestant College) or the French Jesuit University of Saint-Joseph.

Lebanon's multiconfessional government, like the geographic boundaries of the state, reflected the politics of French colonialism and the realities of religious communalism. The state had been created in such a way as to assure Christian dominance under French protection. Religion has played a real though at times amorphous role in Lebanese society. Augustus Richard Norton has observed: "Religion is an ascriptive fact in Lebanon. The Lebanese is born into a religion, which conditions his cultural realm and that decisively defines his social and political identity. Thus, religion as a label is an inescapable fact, both because of Lebanon's natural history and her political system that only takes account of citizens as members of one religion or another."[27]

Based upon a French-conducted census in 1932, a National Pact or Covenant was drawn up in 1943, assigning political power and representation on a proportional basis to the major religious/confessional communities: Maronite Christian, Sunni Muslim, Shii Muslim, and Druze.[28] Thus the president was a Christian, the prime minister a Sunni Muslim, and the speaker of the Chamber of Deputies a Shii Muslim. Key positions in the cabinet, parliament, bureaucracy, and military were distributed proportionally among the confessional groups.

The Shii (Shia) of Lebanon were politically disorganized and the most economically disadvantaged of the communities. Two imams (religious leaders) from Iran—Imam Musa Sadr and Imam Khomeini—and the establishment of the two organizations that they inspired, AMAL and the Hizbullah, reversed that situation.

The Revolt of the Dispossessed: Musa Sadr and AMAL

If the Shii of Lebanon had been leaderless and disorganized, by the eighties they possessed a broadly based political organization and militia. Much of the resurrection of the Shii community is due to the charismatic leadership of Musa Sadr, the founder of AMAL. Musa Sadr came from a prominent clerical family. Of Lebanese ancestry, he was born in Iran and educated in Najaf, Iraq, a major center of Islamic learning. Many of Shii Islam's leading ayatollahs and scholars were based in Najaf. While most were apolitical, Najaf would also come to be remembered for two militant voices, Muhammad Baqir al-Sadr, Musa Sadr's cousin, who was executed by Saddam Hussein, and the Ayatollah Khomeini, who taught there during part of his thirteen-year (1965–78) exile.

There had been centuries of close religious and cultural ties between the Shii of Lebanon and those of Iran and Iraq. The latter countries were centers of clerical training and pilgrimage, containing the shrines and tombs of the family of Ali and many great Shii leaders. Musa Sadr's family reflected this connection. It had originally come from Lebanon, so he accepted an invitation to "return" to lead the Shii community in Tyre in southern Lebanon. With the exception of a few wealthy and powerful Shii feudal families, the Shii of Lebanon, who were concentrated in the south, Beirut, and the Bika valley, trailed the other communities politically and socioeconomically. But within little more than a decade, Musa Sadr asserted his role as a major Shii leader and brought organization and a sense of communal identity and purpose to the Shii of Lebanon. He became leader of the Supreme Islamic Shii Council, a group of prominent Shii religious leaders, and founder of the Movement for the Dispossessed, a religiosocial movement whose goal was parity and social justice.

Although Lebanon's demographics had changed and Muslims (Sunni and Shii) were now a majority, Maronites continued to dominate the government. The Shii, who had grown from 18 percent of the total population in 1932 to 30 percent in 1968, by the nineties constituted more than one third of Lebanon's population (one million out of a total population of two and one half to three million). Despite changes in demography which made them Lebanon's largest community, however, the Shii remained a distant third in political and economic power. In the midst of the wealth and conspicuous consumption of a prosperous Beirut, sprawling Shii slums expanded. Moreover, "the Shiis constituted the highest percentage (twenty-two percent) of families earning less than 1,500 Lebanese pounds. According to every indicator, the Shiis were at the very bottom of the socio-economic ladder."[29]

The Movement for the Dispossessed provided Musa Sadr with a platform and vehicle to mobilize Lebanese Shii and to pressure the government for socioeconomic reforms. As in Iran, Shii history and belief were interpreted to provide an ideology of protest against social injustice and to champion the rights of the disinherited and oppressed. Early Shii suffering at the hands of Sunni rulers, in particular the martyrdom of the revered Shii Imam Husain by the army of the caliph Yazid at the battle of Karbala in 680, were equated with the discrimination and exploitation suffered by Shii under the Christian-dominated confessional system. At times Sadr's words and images could belie his chosen role as a reformer rather than a violent revolutionary:

> This revolution did not die in the sands of Karbala, it flowed into the life-stream of the Islamic world and passed from generation to generation, even to our day. . . . It is a deposit placed in our hand that we may profit from it

as from a source of new reform, a new position, a new movement, a new revolution to repel the darkness, to stop tyranny, and to pulverize evil. Brothers, line up in the row of your choice: that of tyranny or that of Hussein [Husain]. I am certain that you will not choose anything but the row of revolution and martyrdom for the realization of justice and the destruction of tyranny.[30]

Mass demonstrations, strikes, and marches were organized to press Shii demands for a more equitable reapportionment of political representation and economic power, as well as improved housing, hospitals, roads, irrigation projects, and educational opportunities. Sadr found ready recruits. The Shii, unlike the Christians, Sunni, and Druze, had no political parties. An emerging new Shii middle class of merchants and young professionals who had taken advantage of rapid modernization, along with university students, had become politicized and involved in multiconfessional leftist and communist groups. They now found a Shii alternative for social protest under a dynamic and charismatic leader.

In 1975, with civil war impending, Musa Sadr created the militia AMAL to protect Shii rights and interests. AMAL is an acronym for the Lebanese Resistance Battalions (Afwaj al-Muqawimah al-Lubnaniyah) which also means "hope." In a land of militias, the Shii had been the only major community without one. Although initially AMAL was a militia or military wing of the Movement for the Dispossessed, it absorbed the sociopolitical movement within it. Socioeconomic disparities along with several major events contributed to the growth of AMAL and the radicalization of Shii in Lebanon: the Lebanese civil war of 1975–76, the disappearance of Musa Sadr in 1978, the Iranian Revolution of 1979, and Israeli invasions and occupation of Lebanon in 1978 and 1982.

The outbreak of Lebanese civil war in 1975 exacerbated communal differences, divided communities, undermined interconfessional alliances, and drove most Lebanese to fall back upon their sectarian/confessional community for protection. Despite the war, the Maronite-dominated government refused to address the new demographic realities. Shii grievances and demands for a redistribution of power went unheeded, contributing to further radicalization and the belief that the Lebanese system was no longer a representative government but simply Christian minority rule.

Next, Shii in southern Lebanon were caught in the crossfire as their lands became a battleground between entrenched PLO forces and Israeli commandos. The Israeli invasion of southern Lebanon in 1978 realized the worst Shii fears with "an active campaign of air attacks, raids, kidnappings and house bombings."[31]

The mysterious disappearance of Musa Sadr in 1978, while on a visit to Libya to meet with Muammar Qaddafi, marked a turning point in the history of AMAL, profoundly affecting its growth and leadership. AMAL now had its martyr and Imam. However, his influence encompassed all the disparate elements within the Shii community of Lebanon.

> In Shia Lebanon, in the slums of Greater Beirut, in the villages of the Bekaa Valley, and in the south, posters bearing Imam al Sadr's picture were everywhere. He was claimed by sly politicians, by starry-eyed young boys, pushed out of the villages of the south into the anarchy and confusion of Beirut. . . . The Shia were to swing all the way from quietism to martyrology. Men needed "saints," and in Sayyid Musa they found the elements out of which militant sainthood could be constructed. His aura hovered over the ruined world of the Shia in Lebanon, and its politics became, in many ways, a fight over the realm of a vanished Imam.[32]

Eclipsed by the civil war, AMAL now took on new life. Although many believed that Musa Sadr died in Libya, his disappearance was easily associated with Shii doctrines of martyrdom and of the occultation or seclusion of the "Hidden Imam" (i.e., the last Shii Imam who disappeared in the ninth century and whose return is awaited).[33] Like the Ayatollah Khomeini, Musa Sadr had cultivated a religious persona, often identifying his role with the spiritual leadership of the great early Imams, Ali and Husain. Nor did he discourage those who called him "Imam," a title which, strictly speaking, only belongs to the successor of Muhammad, through Ali, as religiopolitical leader of Islam. Like Khomeini, he became a symbol of Shii political activism—in death, even more of a cult hero, the symbol of martyrdom and messianic hope.

The Iranian Revolution, in Lebanon as in much of the Muslim world, was a source of inspiration and awe. The discrediting of Qaddafi caused by the disappearance of Musa Sadr, coupled with Iran's "Islamic" revolution, attracted many Shii businessmen and professionals away from Arab nationalism and the Left and toward AMAL. Ironically, it also led to the transformation of its leadership from clerical to a more secular orientation as Nabih Berri, a lawyer and representative of the new Shii professional class, gained control of AMAL. By 1982 Berri was at the head of an AMAL that was clearly the largest Shii political organization or militia and a formidable political force in Lebanese politics. However, despite ties with Iran, Berri steered AMAL on a nationalist path. AMAL's primary identity was as a Shii nationalist organization. It sought political and economic parity for the Shii community, working within the multiconfessional political system; thus its goal was reform, not revolution. In contrast to Iran and to Hizbullah, it did not seek to establish an Islamic state.

The Rise of Hizbullah

The impact of the Iranian revolution, the Israeli invasion of Lebanon in 1982, Israel's subsequent occupation of the south (1982–85), and the massacre of Palestinians and Lebanese in the Shatila and Sabra refugee camps by Christian Phalangists with Israeli complicity, contributed to the formation of extremist revolutionary Islamic organizations, in particular Hizbullah (Party of God) and al-Jihad, whose goals were to emulate Iran. Following Iran's example, they were against the United States and Israel and sought to violently overthrow the Lebanese government and impose an Islamic state. Hizbullah's pro-Iranian orientation was clearly set forth in its manifesto:

> We, the sons of Hizbullah's nation, whose vanguard God has given victory in Iran and which has established the nucleus of the world's central Islamic state, abide by the orders of a single wise and just command currently embodied in the supreme Ayatollah Khumaini. . . . We have opted for religion, freedom and dignity over humiliation and constant submission to America and its allies and Zionism and their [Christian] Phalangist allies. We have risen to liberate our country, to drive the imperialists and the invaders out of it and to take our fate in our hands.[34]

The U.S. relationship with Lebanon had spanned decades, involving an educational, missionary, commercial, and diplomatic presence; in 1958 President Eisenhower had sent Marines to protect Lebanon's president. Yet the United States had supplied Israel with aircraft and arms and failed to condemn Israel's 1982 invasion and occupation of Lebanon in the United Nations. Many Lebanese regarded the United States as a tacit partner in Israel's sweep through Lebanon, and it had continued to support Lebanon's (Maronite) Pres. Amin Gemayel, whose regime radical Shii regarded as unrepresentative and illegitimate. Thus for many in 1958 the multinational force was seen as part of the problem and not the solution—as protecting the Gemayel government and Israeli interests.

The year 1982 proved to be a turning point in Shii politics. In addition to the Israeli invasion, it witnessed a schism in AMAL, the radicalization of Shii populist movements and politics, and with it a major challenge to AMAL's dominance of Shii political activism. When Nabih Berri agreed to participate in the National Salvation Committee, an alliance with other confessional groups, shortly after the Israeli invasion of 1982, Hussein Musawi, a former teacher and member of AMAL's Command Council, challenged his leadership. Musawi accused Berri of collaboration with Israel and rejected his secular nationalist goal of a multiconfessional state. He broke away and withdrew to Baalbek in the Bika Valley where he formed Islamic AMAL, a militant organization strongly influenced by Khomeini's Iran and committed to the creation of an Islamic republic in Lebanon. Baalbek was already a center of Iranian and militant Shii activity. Iran had sent fifteen hundred Revolutionary Guards (Pasdaran) to Lebanon in 1982 shortly after the Israeli invasion, to assist in the resistance. There they provided training and support for Hizbullah, an Iranian-inspired radical Shii organization which had emerged in the wake of the Iranian revolution, but which came to prominence only as a response to the 1982 Israeli invasion.[35]

In contrast to AMAL and Islamic AMAL, Hizbullah's leadership was clerical and mosque-based. Young pro-Iranian Lebanese Shii clerics led groups of young people and professionals in a network of loosely organized militias. Many of these clerics had been educated in Najaf, Iraq, during the sixties and seventies, when it was a center not only of Islamic learning but also of militant Islamic thought. Among its leading Iraqi ayatollahs were Muhsin al-Hakim and Baqir al-Sadr, who were joined in 1965 by the Ayatollah Khomeini. It was here that Lebanese students, sitting beside their colleagues who had come from all over the Shii Muslim world to study at Najaf's seminary, imbibed an ideological worldview that countered the inroads of the West and posited Islam as an alternative to nationalism and communism. Senior clerics lectured and wrote on such topics as Islamic government, law, economics, and revolution. It was in Najaf in 1970 that the Ayatollah Khomeini delivered his lectures on the nature of Islamic government and clerical rule. Though they received little recognition at the time, by 1979 an idea had been transformed into a reality in postrevolutionary Iran and become a source of inspiration and guidance for many Shii in Lebanon.

For the young Lebanese Shii clerics and their followers, Khomeini and Iran became spiritual and financial godfathers. Posters and pictures of the Ayatollah Khomeini were to be found in homes and mosques, on public walls, and at marches and rallies. His speeches and writings were the source of sermons and political speeches. As Musa Sadr's picture came to dominate the AMAL newspaper's masthead, so the visage of Khomeini graced the masthead of Hizbullah's *Covenant*. Much as in Iran, women wore the *hijab* (head scarf) and men sprouted beards, considered a sign of Islamic identity, in emulation of the Prophet. Hizbullah leaders traveled regularly to Iran, as did Iranian officials to Lebanon. The Iranian embassy in Damascus (Syria was one of the few Arab countries that was an ally of Iran) became a center for organizing and coordinating Iranian support (training, money, and weapons) for political violence. Iran provided training and financial support for Hizbullah's military operations and social services. By 1987, estimates of Iranian aid were as high as ten million dollars per month. Iranian materials were used to train and indoctrinate a new generation of holy warriors. At the same time Hizbullah won the hearts and minds of new supporters and retained the loyalty of others through an impressive program of social assistance which included housing, schools, hospitals, clinics, cooperative supermarkets, and financial assistance and educational scholarships for the victims of war. Some reports estimated that Hizbullah provided scholarships for some forty thousand students.[36]

Organization and Leadership of Hizbullah

Organizationally, Hizbullah was more of a loosely organized ideological movement than a political party. In contrast to AMAL's political organization, identification with a single leader, and fixed membership, Hizbullah was a confederation of like-minded groups and militias spread out in the neighborhoods, villages, and towns of Beirut, the Bika Valley, and southern Lebanon. By the mideighties Hizbullah encompassed a number of revolutionary groups: Islamic AMAL, Jund Allah (Army of God), the Hussein Death Squad, the Revolutionary Justice Organization, and al-Jihad. All shared a common outlook and agenda: the dismantling of the Lebanese state and the creation in its place of an Islamic state; the acceptance of Khomeini and Iran as the model to be emulated; a consensus that its enemies were the Lebanese government, other confessional groups, the United States, and France, as well as pro-Western Arab governments such as Saudi Arabia and Kuwait; and belief that it was a religious duty to destroy the "enemies of God" through jihad, martyrdom, and self-sacrifice. There were many leaders, rather than one. While they cooperated in joint ventures, they also felt free to act on their own. Hizbullah became more structured, with a Supreme Consultative Council of clergy and militia leaders as well as regional councils and committees. However, it remained more of an umbrella group than a tightly knit movement.

> Much ink has been spilt on the issue of who leads Hizbullah, but the fact is that—at best—we are dealing with a collegial leadership which subsumes many factions and cliques. Even Iran must cajole rather than direct and order in such an environment. In other words, despite their links to Iran, it would be erroneous to assert that the cliques within Hizbullah lack a considerable freedom of action.[37]

Over the years a number of senior leaders have emerged, in particular shaykhs Abbas al-Musawi (killed in 1992), Subhi al-Tufayli, Raghib Harb, and especially Muhammad Husayn Fadlallah. Shaykh Fadlallah (b. 1935) is perhaps the most prominent Shii cleric in Lebanon, a religious scholar whose reputation and following extend beyond Lebanon. Although he has resolutely maintained that he is not the leader or even a member of Hizbullah, he is widely regarded as its spiritual guide.[38] Born and educated in Najaf, in 1966 he returned to Lebanon, his parents' homeland, where he quickly established his reputation as a leading religious authority. A gifted preacher, he draws large crowds to his mosque in Beirut. Although he is primarily a religious scholar, the experience of the Lebanese civil war and the Iranian revolution influenced his espousal of political activism.[39] Like the Ayatollah Khomeini, Musa Sadr, and other Shii activist leaders, Fadlallah combines traditional religious scholarship with a powerful reinterpretation of Islamic history and belief that emphasizes political activism and social reform: "As Moslems we consider politics to be part of our whole life, because the Koran emphasizes the establishment of justice as a divine mission. . . . In this sense, the politics of the faithful is a kind of prayer."[40] Thus while he has written a multivolume commentary on the Quran, he has also authored *Islam and the Logic of Force* and *The Islamic Resistance*. His message rejects quietism in the face of the oppressed status of Shii life and advocates struggle against social injustice: "Muslims are to embark on an 'Islamic revolution' . . . under the guidance of religious officials, the 'ulama,' whose knowledge and integrity guarantee the ultimate triumph of Islam over the Satanic forces of disbelief."[41]

Fadlallah is an activist but denies any formal political role: "I am a servant of the community, working for Moslems and non-Moslems. I even have supporters among the Sunnis because I speak about Islam as a movement to establish freedom and justice."[42] His counsel is sought, although not always followed, and he often speaks out in defense of Hizbullah and related groups. Where contradictions or discrepancies exist between what Fadlallah says and what Hizbullah does, it is difficult to know how much this is due to genuine differences as opposed to Fadlallah's disingenuousness.

Ideologically, Hizbullah's Islamic revolutionary orientation differs from the more reformist, nationalist stance of AMAL. While Hizbullah demands an Islamic state, AMAL has continued to respect the integrity of the Lebanese state and worked toward a multiconfessional state with a more equitable distribution of power. Hizbullah's clerical leadership, high Islamic profile, close Iranian ties, and near cult of the "path of the Imam Khomeini" contrasts with AMAL's nonclerical, more Westernized and moderate image. While Hizbullah assumes a more universal, international, and self-consciously Islamic orientation, AMAL is content to focus almost solely on national interests. Hizbullah's name, the Party of God, indicates its transnational identity as a movement of all Muslims that extends beyond Lebanon. Like Khomeini's movement in Iran, it sees itself as part of a worldwide Islamic revolution and champions Pan-Islamic causes such as the liberation of Palestine.[43] In contrasting Hizbullah's and AMAL's relations with the Palestinians, Shaykh Fadlallah's comments reveal the difference between Hizbullah's more worldwide or Pan-Islamic concerns and AMAL's narrower nationalist commitment: "Hizbullah's strategy is a strategy of jihad that insists the presence of Israel in Palestine is illegal . . . as for AMAL, it may consider the liberation of the south [of Lebanon] as its sole task."[44]

Conflict Between Hizbullah and AMAL

Like activists in Iran, Hizbullah also employed Shii doctrines of self-sacrifice and martyrdom in the service of a jihad against oppression and injustice. This at times took the startling form of suicide and car bomb attacks against Western and Israeli targets. A series of suicide bombings were aimed at the American embassy, French and American military compounds, and businesses during 1983–84. More than 250 U.S. Marines were killed in the October 1983 bombing of their barracks on the outskirts of Beirut. Israeli forces were similarly targeted from 1983 to 1985. The withdrawal of the Multinational Force from Beirut and the retreat of Israeli forces to their security zone in southern Lebanon enhanced Hizbullah's image as the most effective defender of Shii rights and interests.

Hizbullah's use of force and its successes constantly put pressure on AMAL, with whom it increasingly competed for the minds and hearts of Shii, to forsake moderation and prove its militancy and effectiveness. The split in AMAL in 1982 and the growing prominence of radical organizations like Hizbullah eroded AMAL's primacy as defender of Shii interests. The two groups' ideological and political differences led to confrontations and armed conflict as they often fought each other rather than a common enemy.

AMAL differed with Hizbullah and related groups in its attitude toward the West and Israel. Berri traveled regularly to the United States, where he held a green card as a resident alien and his ex-wife and children resided. AMAL's policy was more focused in its concerns about U.S. policy and Israeli intervention, which contrasted sharply with Hizbullah's unrestrained anti-Americanism and militant cries of "Death to America." AMAL clashed with Islamic radicals over the TWA 847 hijacking in 1985, kidnapping, and hostage taking, and especially the kidnapping and execution of Col. William R. Higgins of the U.N. peace-keeping force (UN-IFIL) in Lebanon in 1989. Berri had worked for the release of the TWA passengers. In contrast to Hizbullah, which viewed the U.N. presence as another form of foreign (American and Israeli) intervention, AMAL saw it as necessary to restore stability in southern Lebanon and sought to guarantee its security. Higgins's abduction triggered a fierce battle between AMAL and Hizbullah militias for control of West Beirut and southern Lebanon. Though Syria was an ally of Iran, it increasingly backed AMAL because Hizbullah's call for an Islamic state threatened Syrian preeminence in Lebanon.

The differences between AMAL and Hizbullah continued right up to the very end of the Lebanese civil war. Whereas AMAL joined with other confessional groups in accepting the Saudi-brokered Taif Accords, which provided a more equitable distribution of power (while retaining a Maronite president), Hizbullah remained adamant in its rejection of the accords. Hizbullah's strength was dramatically affected by the restoration of peace in Lebanon and a change in its relationship with Iran. With the Ayatollah Khomeini's death and the end of the Iran–Iraq war, Iran's government altered its priorities, emphasizing domestic development and international trade. Iran's new president, Hashemi Rafsanjani, pursued a more pragmatic and less militant foreign policy, halting support for the violent export of its revolution, and denounced the taking of hostages. Hizbullah's aid from Iran was cut dramatically and its isolation increased. At the same time Syria pressured Hizbullah to release its hostages. With the end of the Cold War and the loss of Soviet patronage, Syria sought to shed its terrorist image and improve its relations with the West.

As in Egypt, sociopolitical realities had spawned a number of Islamic movements in Lebanon. Among the Shii the disparities between rich and poor, and the marginalization of the Shii masses, proved fertile ground for both reformist and revolutionary movements. Ironically, Iranians influenced the formation of both AMAL and Hizbullah. The former owed its origins and inspiration to Musa Sadr and the latter was ideologically and financially indebted to the Ayatollah Khomeini. Yet despite their common soil, AMAL pursued a path of reform within the established state while Hizbullah rejected the past and sought to impose its vision of an Islamic order. While AMAL, though not adverse to armed conflict, was careful to foster relations with the West, Hizbullah rejected the "Great Satan" and boldly pressed its claims through violence and terrorism.

Islamic Politics in the Maghreb

For much of the eighties, while world attention was riveted on Iran and Libya, Khomeini and Qaddafi, few studies of Islamic revivalism took North Africa seriously. Indeed, many would have observed, "It may have occurred in the Middle East but never in francophone, if not Francophile,

North Africa: Algeria, Tunisia, and Morocco.'' Their authoritarian regimes banned Islamic parties and political organizations. While it acknowledged Islam in its constitution, Algeria was basically regarded as a hard-line socialist state, firmly controlled by a secular-oriented leadership. Tunisia under Habib Bourguiba was modern and Western-oriented. In his pursuit of modernization, Bourguiba had publicly broken the fast of Ramadan and outlawed (rather than simply restricted) polygamy. Morocco's leader, King Hassan, appeared to be successful in combining a religious dimension to his political legitimacy with a strong Western orientation and tight control over any and all opposition.

By the end of the eighties, however, electoral politics indicated that the leading political opposition in Tunisia and Algeria was Islamic: the Islamic Tendency Movement (MTI) or Renaissance Party (Ennahda) in Tunisia and the Islamic Salvation Front in Algeria. Though prevented from running as a political party, members of MTI won 17 percent, and in some urban areas as much as 40 percent, of the vote in government-controlled national elections in Tunisia in April 1989. Algeria and, indeed, much of the Muslim world seemed traumatized as the Islamic Salvation Front, within the space of only a year, went from being an outlawed party to scoring a stunning upset and sweeping the municipal elections in 1990 and then subsequently the parliamentary elections in 1991.

Islamic movements in the Maghreb, as in most of the Muslim world, have developed a new or modern Islamic form of organization. In contrast to traditional religious organizations, Sufi mystical brotherhoods (*tariqah*) and *ulama* associations active in the nationalist struggle, modern Islamic activist organizations have a lay rather than clerical leadership, are urban-based, and thrive primarily among students and educated professionals while also attracting members of traditional occupations (merchants, traders, craftsmen). In their formative stage, most of these organizations have been particularly influenced by the trailblazers of contemporary Islamic activism: Mawlana Mawdudi, Hassan al-Banna, and Sayyid Qutb. In addition they draw on early Islamic reformers like ibn-Hazm and ibn-Taymiyya as well as twentieth-century Muslim activists and nationalist leaders in the Maghreb such as Malek Bennabi and Ben Badis. Like their counterparts in other parts of the Muslim world, in recent years, where governments permit, Islamic activists have moved from the periphery to the center and now participate in electoral politics and mainstream society. Most advocate working within the system rather than using violence to come to power.

The Maghreb also offers an excellent example of the evolution of many Islamic movements. From relatively small apolitical Quran or religio-cultural reform societies, Islamic movements there have come to function as modern social movements and participatory political parties or organizations that espouse populist causes like political liberalization, jobs, better services, integrity in government, human rights, more equitable distribution of wealth, and greater emphasis on Arab–Islamic cultural identity. They now include both a first and a second generation of members who are educated and middle-class, organizationally and intellectually sophisticated. At the same time both leadership and rank and file include a diversity of religious, political, and educational orientations—conservative and reformist, moderate and militant. The case of Tunisia's Islamic Tendency Movement shows the nature of Islamic movements in the Maghreb and the dangers of radicalization.

Tunisia and the Islamic Movement

For most of Tunisia's history from its independence in 1956 to 1987, it had but one ruler. Habib Bourguiba, the "Great Combatant" of Tunisia's nationalist struggle, ruled a unified, one-party political state for more than thirty years. More than any other Muslim ruler except Turkey's Ataturk, who established a totally secular state, Bourguiba set Tunisia upon a path of modernization which was decidedly pro-Western and secular, becoming a valued friend of both France and the United States. Tunisia's Arab–Islamic heritage was overshadowed by an official and elite Francophile culture. French rather than Arabic was the official language of government, higher education, and elite culture and society. Bourguiba carefully circumscribed the presence and influence of Islam. Shortly after independence, Tunisia passed a Personal Status Law (1957) which went further than any other Muslim country except secular Turkey in banning rather than simply restricting polygamy. Even more symbolic of Bourguiba's approach to religion and modernization and his wholehearted acceptance of Western values, was the abolition of Sharia courts, the ban on the wearing of the *hijab* (head scarf) by women, and his attempt to get workers to ignore the fast of Ramadan, during which he drank a glass of orange juice on national television. He decried the deleterious effects of fasting during daylight hours, claiming that it affected national productivity and economic development. The Zaytouna, a famed center of Islamic learning in North Africa and the Muslim world, was closed. The *ulama* were debilitated rather than, as in many Muslim countries, coopted by the government. For Bourguiba, Islam represented the past; the West was Tunisia's only hope for a modern future. No wonder, then, that experts concluded: "Historically the most open and Mediterranean of the Arab countries, Tunisia is an improbable site for an Islamist upsurge."[45]

The development of Islamic movements as a reaction to personal lives, social conditions, and government policies and actions can be seen quite clearly at every stage in the development (from its formation through its major transformations) of Tunisia's major Islamic organization, the Islamic Tendency Movement or, as it is known today, the Renaissance Party (Hizb al-Nahda or Ennahda).

The life of its paramount leader, Rashid Ghannoushi, follows the pattern of many activists of his generation:

1. Traditional and then modern education, but with a clear emphasis on Arabic rather than French.
2. Youthful enthusiasm and participation in the Arab nationalist movement of Gamal Abdel Nasser.
3. Subsequent disillusionment and an identity crisis when Arab nationalism was discredited by the bitter Arab defeat in the 1967 war.
4. A turn away from Arab nationalism and return to Islam, in particular an ideological revivalist worldview indebted to Hassan al-Banna, Sayyid Qutb, and Mawlana Mawdudi.
5. A strongly negative reaction to his direct encounter with Western culture and values, and a deeper reappropriation of his Arab–Islamic heritage after studying in France.
6. Assumption of the dual leadership role as teacher–activist, a path similar to that of many other activists like al-Banna and Qutb in Egypt, Mawdudi in Pakistan, and modern-day leaders such as Abdesallem Yassin in Morocco, Abbasi Madani in Algeria, and Hassan Turabi in the Sudan.
7. Subsequent realization of the limited relevance of outside activists, whose outlook and strategies were conditioned by their local experiences, and thus the need to contextualize the Islamic message and ideology.
8. A resulting transition from an Egyptian Muslim Brotherhood orientation to a more Tunisian-centered movement, and from a militant Qutb-inspired activism to more pragmatic, moderate, accommodationist activism.

Ghannoushi's development and that of the Islamic movement in Tunisia were shaped by events in the early seventies. The causes or influences were many: fallout from the defeat of 1967 and the discrediting of Arab nationalist ideas; high unemployment and food shortages resulting from the failure of the government's planned socialist economic development program (in particular the collectivization of agricultural lands from 1962 to 1970); the national strikes and food riots of 1978; the reemergence of Islam and of Islamic organizations such as the Egyptian Muslim Brotherhood and the Jamaat-i-Islami of Pakistan in Muslim politics; the use of oil revenues by Saudi Arabia and Libya to promote their influence in the Muslim world; and the Iranian Revolution.

The Tunisian government, anxious to distance itself from the failures of its socialist policies of the sixties, embarked upon a policy of political and economic liberalization in the seventies and also showed greater interest in the revivification of Tunisia's Arab–Islamic identity and heritage. The reassertion of this identity was reflected in the establishment of cultural societies, in particular the Quran Preservation Society at Tunisia's venerable Zaytouna mosque, and in the growth of Islamically oriented student groups at the universities and secondary schools, which contributed to the growth of Islamic revivalism. The reaffirmation of Islamic identity was also strongly influenced ideologically by Egypt's Muslim Brotherhood. The writings of Muslim Brothers such as Hassan al-Banna, Sayyid Qutb, Muhammad Qutb, and Muhammad al-Ghazzali were readily available and had a powerful influence on the nascent Islamic movement in Tunisia.

Rashid Ghannoushi proved a popular preacher, teacher, and youth leader. He drew large crowds from among the poor working class to his sermons as he moved from one mosque to another and attracted students from his school to the weekly discussions conducted at the Quran Preservation Society. The Society was dedicated to the promotion of Tunisia's Arab–Islamic heritage and enjoyed government sponsorship. To the extent that it remained an apolitical cultural society, Bourguiba found it useful as a foil against his leftist critics.

For Ghannoushi, teaching, preaching, and participation in the Society were interrelated aspects of his mission to restore Tunisia's Arab–Islamic roots and civilization. His experience and that of many others not from the elite classes reflected Tunisia's deep-seated identity crisis and the source of its weakness: "I remember we used to feel like strangers in our own country. We had been educated as Muslims and Arabs, while we could see that the country had been totally molded in the French cultural identity. For us the doors to any further education were closed since the university was completely Westernized. At that time, those wanting to continue their studies in Arabic had to go to the Middle East."[46]

Ghannoushi's preaching and writing drew heavily upon the interpretations and ideological worldview of Muslim scholar-activists such as Mawlana Mawdudi, Hassan al-Banna, Sayyid Qutb and his brother Muhammad Qutb, Malek Bennabi, and Muhammad Iqbal. The message was one condemning the political, social, economic, and cultural backwardness of Tunisian society, its loss of identity and morals owing to dependence upon a morally bankrupt and crisis-ridden Western society, and the need for a return to Islam. The culprits were the West, the Bourguiba government, and Tunisia's Westernized elites as well as the traditional religious establishment, which, coopted by the government, preached a stagnant rather than a dynamic Islam. Ghannoushi believed that the only hope for Tunisia, the Muslim world, and indeed the Third World was Islam. However, during the period 1970–78 the Islamic movement and its message remained primarily concerned with religiocultural change in society. Ghannoushi and a small group of colleagues, among them Abdelfattah Mourou, a lawyer and activist, pursued their goals within the context of the Quran Preservation Society. As an officially apolitical religiocultural movement, it posed little direct threat to the government. The official discussions and activities of the Society obscured the political consciousness and intellectual politicization that were also taking place among Ghannoushi and his colleagues.

The late seventies saw a progressive politicization of the Islamic movement in response to the internal situation in Tunisia and events in Iran. As in much of the Muslim world, the period 1978–79 proved to be a political turning point in the history of Tunisia's Islamic movement. Bourguiba's use of the military to brutally crush protest demonstrations in January 1978 and the subsequent victory of Iran's Islamic Revolution in 1979 underscored the failures of Tunisian Westernized secular society and fired the enthusiasm of many for a return to Islam. The confrontation between the government and the General Union of Tunisian Workers (UGTT) culminated in a general strike on January 26, 1978, in which many were killed or injured by government forces. Tunisia's trade union movement was considered by some to be the strongest in Africa and the Arab world, but Ghannoushi and the Islamic movement had avoided any involvement in it because they were leery of unionism, and because the UGTT was controlled first by the government's Destour Party and then by Marxists: "The social confrontation between rich and poor is a Marxist formula that did not correspond to our understanding of life. Later on, we realized that Islam also has a say in the confrontation, and that, as Muslims, we could not stay indifferent to it. Islam gives support to the oppressed."[47] The Islamists found themselves forced to rethink their ideas and strategy. In the words of one MTI leader, they struggled with the question, "How could we be that much out of touch with what was actually going on within our own society so that we did not play any role in society?"[48]

The response of Ghannoushi and other senior leaders in the wake of the labor unrest of January 1978 also underscored the tension within the Islamic movement between the older generation and its student followers, a tension over strategy and methods which would resurface at critical points in its history. While a communiqué was issued which supported the workers' demands, it also deplored the violence, a stance which contrasted sharply with the more militant position of the movement's student supporters.[49]

Deteriorating conditions in Tunisia and the Islamic movement's position outside the political arena convinced Ghannoushi and the movement of the need to move beyond broad ideological statements and relate Islam directly and specifically to the real, everyday political, economic, and social problems of the people. Islam must be seen as a source not only of identity but also of true liberation—of the whole person and society. This new direction placed the Islamists on a collision course with the apolitical stance of the Quran Preservation Society: in 1978 they were expelled, denounced as inflexible reactionaries.[50] The transformation of this relatively small group from a religiocultural force into a sociopolitical movement was formalized with the establishment of the Islamic Association (Jamaah al-Islamiyya) in 1979, one year after the 1978 riots and in the wake of Iran's revolution. Ideologically and organizationally, the Islamists were influenced by the example of the Egyptian and Sudanese Muslim Brotherhoods. Thus a hitherto informal group of like-minded people, run by its founders and key leaders and centered around group meetings and discussions, became a more structured, participatory, activist organization with rules, guidelines, and a commitment to social action.

The Islamic Association was set up as a national organization guided by its Amir (leader), Ghannoushi, and an elected consultative council (*majlis al-shura*). Like many other Islamic activist organizations, the organization had both a public and a secret private profile. The transformation of the Islamic movement into a sociopolitical organization directly involved in Tunisian political and economic affairs enhanced its popularity but also invited government pressure. The realities of functioning under an increasingly hostile regime required that its cells be secret and that much of its activities be underground. Ghannoushi preached his message of a holistic Islam relevant to issues of political and economic rights in the mosques of Tunisia. He correctly identified the mind and pragmatic concerns of Tunisian youth:

> What concerns the young people of today? . . . The position of the Mutazilites [an early theological school or movement] on the attributes of God . . . whether the Quran is pre-existent or created? Was Islam revealed for this kind of useless, sterile argument? I wonder how our students feel studying "Islamic philosophy" when it offers them a bunch of dead issues having nothing to do with the problems of today. . . . I propose that these shrouds be returned to their graves, that these false problems be buried and that we deal with our problems—economics, politics, sexual license.[51]

Tunisia's mosques hosted gatherings and provided platforms from which the struggle for Islam could be equated with the needs and grievances of the poor and oppressed. The movement also addressed these problems in communiqués, conferences, and the movement's publication *al-Marifa*, established in 1973, which provided religious legitimacy for the movement's sociopolitical message. Students and workers in particular were drawn to the new organization as either members or sympathizers. Ghannoushi and the Islamic Association spoke directly to current issues—workers' rights, jobs, wages, poverty, Westernization versus a more authentic national and cultural identity, political participation—presenting a living Islam rather than the "museum Islam" which Ghannoushi had encountered as a student.

Ghannoushi now combined his earlier role in France as a Muslim missionary and social activist among poor workers with that of a youth leader. The movement attracted most of its membership from the urban and rural working and lower middle classes. His message of political freedom and social activism in defense of the rights of the poor and the oppressed enabled the Islamic Association to align itself with the General Union of Tunisian Workers (UGTT) and win support within its ranks. At the same time it targeted universities and schools. Islamic student organizations grew and proliferated on campuses, attracting young men and women from the science and engineering faculties in particular. Although they clashed with secular nationalists and leftist students, Islamic student organizations eventually dominated student politics.

In April 1981, when the Bourguiba government briefly liberalized Tunisia's one-party political system, the Islamic Association was transformed into a political party, called the Islamic Tendency Movement (MTI), indicating that it was one of a number of trends (Islamic, secular, leftist, etc.) in Tunisian society. The phrase "Islamic Trend or Tendency" was already in use by Islamic university student groups, who had borrowed it from their Sudanese counterparts.

Although Bourguiba refused to issue a license legalizing the party, MTI continued to challenge the secular state. Its agenda included reassertion of Tunisia's Islamic–Arabic way of life and values, restriction of Tunisia's Westernized (Francophile) profile, and promotion of democracy, political pluralism, and economic and social justice. The brutality of Bourguiba's response to any and all opposition and the restrictive policies of his government alienated many Tunisians, spawning a religious and secular opposition which shared grievances and had both been equally repressed. MTI proved effective in attracting many of the disaffected, not only students, workers, and union members but also middle-class professionals, professors, teachers, engineers, lawyers, scientists, and doctors.

The politicization of the Islamic movement drew the wrath of Habib Bourguiba, who regarded it as a threat to his government. He had tolerated Islamic organizations as long as they remained apolitical, so as to counter the charges of his Islamic critics and the leftists. However, a political opposition was quite another matter. MTI's sociopolitical platform was a double challenge, for it echoed the criticisms of other (secular) opposition groups with whom it was willing to work and, even more threateningly, did so in the name of Islam. This challenge occurred at a time when much of the Muslim world was experiencing a resurgence of Islam and when many Muslim governments were nervous about the "Iranian threat"— Iran's declared intention to export its Islamic revolution.

In 1981 the Bourguiba government, which some experts had come to describe as a "modern administrative dictatorship,"[52] cracked down on MTI, arresting and imprisoning Ghannoushi and many of its leaders. Many were tortured in prison; those who escaped went underground or into self-imposed exile abroad. Despite the government's attempt to paint MTI as retrogressive, fundamentalist fanatics and a violent Iranian-backed revolutionary movement, Ghannoushi had distanced the movement from the excesses of the revolution and advocated a Tunisian rather than an Iranian solution. Ghannoushi denounced the use of violence and instead chose to work within the system, emphasizing a gradual process of social transformation and political participation as the means to realize MTI's long-range goal of establishing an Islamic state. He had been careful to talk about institutional reform rather than violent revolution, about change from below rather than the imposition of an Islamic system from above, about Islamic reform rather than implementation of medieval formulations of Islamic law.[53]

During this period more than ever before, MTI came to realize the limitations of the Muslim Brotherhood's ideology, which was conditioned by its Egyptian origins and experience. There was a growing conviction about the need to address the particular conditions of Tunisia by developing an ideology, program, and solutions more suited to the Tunisian experience.

The imprisonment of many of its leaders spawned new leadership and initiated a process of reevaluation. Students were recruited from the mosques and schools. They were invited (*dawa*) to Islam and were taught about it. At the same time that they were exposed to Western ideas in science and technology, these students of Tunisia's postindependence generation were required to read books on Islam and also on communism, in order to confront the communists. Looking for new solutions, many adapted well both to new Western scientific ideas and to an Islamic orientation. Thus they provided an alternative to the communists and the nationalists on campus.

Like Anwar Sadat and the Shah of Iran, Bourguiba refused to rein in his authoritarian tendencies. In later life he had exiled his wife, son, and prime minister. Moreover, an Islamic opposition proved doubly distasteful, representing for him an anachronistic retreat to the past which flew in the face of all that he had tried to represent, and a potentially potent popular force as well. Many rulers had become accustomed to branding their opposition Marxist as a smoke screen for their repression and to curry favor and support from the West. Bourguiba now joined those who in the eighties found a new global threat, the danger of "radical fundamentalism," in particular that of Iran, behind any challenge to their authority. However, "despite attempts to link the Islamist movement with Iranian extremism, [the Tunisian government] had not been able to eradicate what Bourghiba routinely and contemptuously described as the vestiges of an outdated religious traditionalism."[54] The image of Tunisia as a shining example of enlightened development, like that of Lebanon before it, seemed to crack if not shatter as the Bourguiba government attempted to stave off further popular strikes and riots and clashed with Islamic activists and professional syndicates.

Bread riots in 1984 forced Bourguiba to release Ghannoushi and other political prisoners after three years of imprisonment, as part of his attempt to ease tensions. However, government pressure on MTI continued.

> The 1984 amnesty did not end harassment. . . . The government banned civil servants from praying during work hours and closed mosques it had opened previously to buffer "leftist extremism." Public institutions were ordered not to hire back Islamists who had lost their jobs during the 1981–84 incarceration. Women wearing the veil were barred from the universities and workplaces. Islamist university students were expelled and drafted into the military. Taxi drivers caught wearing neatly trimmed beards—the mark par excellence of the Islamist—or listening to Islamist cassettes had their beards cut and their licenses revoked.[55]

Ghannoushi, although freed, was forbidden to speak in mosques or other public gathering places, nor was he allowed to teach, publish his writings, or travel abroad. In response to the prison experience of 1984–87, MTI was restructured with emphasis on its secret as well as public dimensions and a decentralized leadership. Along with a greater emphasis on clandestine cells, Ghannoushi's leadership role as the primary ideologue, though not the sole leader, was reinforced by the creation of a cadre of leaders across the country. Security measures which assured that no single individual would hold all the power or knowledge of MTI membership and activities were instituted.

Within three years after Ghannoushi's emergence from prison in 1984, Bourguiba once again moved against MTI. In March 1987 he arrested Ghannoushi and set off street battles and clashes between Islamic activist students and leftists in the universities. When the French government arrested six expatriate Tunisians for possession of arms, Bourguiba took the occasion to move once more against MTI, charging it with an Iranian-inspired plot to overthrow the government, although France had established no MTI connection and in fact claimed the six were members of the pro-Iranian Islamic Jihad and Hizbullah. More than three thousand MTI members were arrested. When Islamic Jihad subsequently claimed responsibility for a series of hotel bombings, ten members of MTI, not Islamic Jihad, were charged, despite the fact that the majority had already been imprisoned at the time of the alleged crime. Although the Bourguiba government tried to discredit MTI as "Khomeinists," Dirk Vanderwalle observed:

> The Islamic Tendency Movement . . . posed no threat to the country's rulers or its political system. But the movement's criticism of personal power, economic mismanagement, corruption, and moral laxity allowed it to become a symbol—perceived especially by the younger, educated generation as an alternative in a country void of political alternatives.[56]

Bourguiba was so intent upon eradicating his "Islamic threat" that when the courts sentenced Ghannoushi to life imprisonment at hard labor but not death, he ordered a new trial.

The 1981 and 1987 repression of MTI put severe strains upon the leadership and its moderate stance and exacerbated differences within the movement. As rumors spread that Bourguiba was intent upon Ghannoushi's execution and the eradication of MTI, MTI's members divided over the proper strategy; voices were increasingly raised advocating a tough response to government oppression. In November 1987, as the debate raged and a popular uprising seemed likely, Zeine Abedin Ben Ali, Bourguiba's prime minister, seized power from the aging dictator.

Ben Ali moved quickly to legitimate his rule and counter the government's Islamic opposition. He promised political liberalization, democratization, and a multiparty political system, precisely what all the opposition parties had been clamoring for. Moreover Ben Ali, reminiscent of Egypt's Anwar Sadat, the Sudan's Gaafar Nimeiri, and Pakistan's Zulfikar Ali Bhutto, sought to enhance his legitimacy, broaden his base of popular support, diffuse criticism, and thus lessen the appeal of Islamic activists through an appeal to Tunisia's Arab–Islamic heritage. Ben Ali went on a much-publicized pilgrimage to Mecca; his speeches incorporated Islamic formulae; television and radio broadcast the call to prayer; the theological faculty at the Zaytouna mosque was reopened; the fast of Ramadan was officially observed; and Ben Ali promised to allow MTI to again publish its own newspaper or journal.

MTI responded to the promised political liberalization and movement toward democracy by offering to work with the new leader and participate in his call for a National Pact, in exchange for official recognition as a political party. Although Ben Ali, as Bourguiba's minister of internal affairs, had overseen the attempt to crush MTI, MTI's leadership took the risk. Most observers anticipated government recognition of the Renaissance Party, but in December 1989 Ben Ali categorically ruled out any political recognition for it, claiming that this decision "emanates from our firm belief in the need not to mix religion and politics, as experience has shown that anarchy emerges and the rule of law and institutions is undermined when such a mixing takes place."[57]

Two events in particular influenced Ben Ali's change of heart. The impressive performance of MTI candidates in national elections in 1988 demonstrated the party's political potential and validated its claim to be Tunisia's leading opposition group. This was followed by the Algerian government's movement toward political liberalization in the wake of riots and its recognition of Islamic political parties. The victory of the Islamic Salvation Front in the 1989 municipal elections realized the worst fears of Ben Ali and many Muslim rulers (and of many Western governments), who saw in political Islam not simply the threat of liberalization or democratization of their regimes but that of a "fundamentalist" victory.

Though the Renaissance Party (formerly MTI) avoided confrontational politics in the early years of Ben Ali's rule, the government's decision not to recognize it as a legal party, and its growing use of force and violation of human rights to intimidate its members, led the Renaissance Party to denounce the government for authoritarianism and the undue influence of the "secular left."[58] The confrontation between the government and the Renaissance Party escalated. Student demonstrations and strikes were crushed; Renaissance Party leaders were imprisoned or harassed. The deterioration of Tunisia's human rights record drew criticisms from human rights organizations. Ben Ali's political liberalization program proved far from democratic. As *The Economist* observed, "His party, the Constitutional Democratic Rally, rigged the poll in the 1989 general election and took every seat in parliament. Far from legalizing the leading opposition group, the Islamic party, Ennahda [Renaissance Party], the president has sought to crush it. . . . There is no real democracy and no press freedom."[59]

The Gulf War marked a turning point, as Ben Ali moved against the Renaissance Party in a "transparent effort to discredit it."[60] The war ushered in a period which would intensify the clash between the government and the Renaissance Party, a reputed coup attempt, and a split in its leadership with the defection of Abdelfattah Mourou. In May 1991, shortly after security forces had killed several students at a university demonstration, the Ben Ali government charged that it had uncovered a Renaissance

Party plot, which included members of the Tunisian military, to seize power and establish a theocratic state. More than one third of those arrested were members of the Tunisian military reputed to be members of the Renaissance Party's secret military wing. Ben Ali called for unity in the face of a fundamentalist threat.[61]

Tunisia's Renaissance Party provides an example of the radicalization of movements in response to government manipulation of the political system, suppression, or violence. Increased government repression intimidates, factionalizes, and radicalizes. The result has been an escalation of confrontation and violence. Bent on decapitating the movement, the government embarked on a systematic effort to repress Ennahda (the Renaissance Party), arresting and imprisoning its leaders and members, intimidating their families, and employing military tribunals noteworthy for their swift sentences rather than justice. Rashid Ghannoushi received asylum in London while those Ennahda leaders who were not arrested fled to France or went underground. The "fundamentalist threat" became an excuse for Ben Ali to back away from Tunisia's political liberalization, allowing the government to suppress Ennahda and tighten its grip on the country. In national elections in 1993, he was elected with 99.91 percent of the vote, in what (as we shall see in chapter 6, p. 277) was widely regarded as a predetermined result.

Algeria

While many witnessed the reassertion of Islam in contemporary Muslim politics in Iran and elsewhere, the consensus in the first half of the eighties was that it could never happen in Francophile and Francophone North Africa. Governments were controlled by strong rulers (Bourguiba in Tunisia and King Hassan in Morocco) and in Algeria by a single party, the FLN (Front de Libération Nationale, National Liberation Front), that had dominated the political scene. In the late eighties both failing economies and the wave of political liberalization that accompanied the fall of the Soviet Union ushered in new realities in many countries. However, it was Algeria that stunned governments, policymakers, and experts alike in the Muslim world and the West. The Islamic Salvation Front (FIS) swept municipal and later national parliamentary elections. The unthinkable now seemed on the horizon, an Islamic movement would come to power not through bullets but through ballots. Early 1992 witnessed in Algeria a military coup, repression of the FIS, and the beginning of a civil war that so far has claimed more than thirty thousand lives.

Islam and Algerian Nationalism

Islam had played an important role in the political development of Algeria.
It is not only the faith of the vast majority of Algerians, but also, as in
much of the Muslim world, has historically provided a sense of national
solidarity and unity. This was particularly true during the French occupation (1830–1962). Islam was an integral component of the independence
and nationalist movement, providing a refuge and a battle cry, a sense of
inspiration and organization: "From the moment of the French intrusion
in the 1830's, Islam provided a refuge of collective identity for Algerians,
and Islamic sentiment was a constant source of anti-colonial resistance."[62]
Islamic reformers like Abd al-Hamid Ibn Badis (1889–1940) founded in
1931 the Association of Algerian Ulama (AAU), whose motto was "Islam
is my religion; Arabic is my language; Algeria is my Fatherland." The
AAU combined Islamic reformism and nationalism and disseminated its
message through a network of mosques and schools.

The Algerian revolution of the fifties and sixties was particularly informed by Islam. Islamic ideology, symbolism, rhetoric, and institutions
were central to the struggle, antidotes to the identity crisis triggered by
the political, military, economic, and cultural threat of French imperialism.
The slogan of the revolution was "Algérie Musulmane" not simply "Algérie Arabe." The struggle was declared a jihad: its fighters were called
mujahidin (holy warriors) and its journal El Moudjahid (The Holy War-
rior). The leaders of the revolution, secular as well as religious, "took up
Algeria and reintroduced it as a strategic weapon . . . in order to rally Algerians against the French. People were told not to drink, not to smoke,
not to eat during Ramadan. Religious rules were made compulsory for
political purposes. A puritan, violent Islam was used against the spineless,
the unconvinced and the unfaithful. Algerian and Muslim were made synonymous. Revolutionary chiefs frequently made use of threats and repri-
sals in the name of Islam. There were moments when a 'religious terror'
was put in force. Algerians responded to it though they did not all agree
with it."[63]

Islam and the Postindependence State

In 1962 more than a century of French occupation was brought to an end
after a particularly bloody eight-year revolution. After independence, the
Islamic reformism which had been one of the components of the nationalist movement receded in political life. The FLN, which had led the war
of independence, consolidated its power and "until the 1980's, a sturdy
triple alliance of army, state, and a single party controlled Algerian poli-

tics."[64] Though called the Democratic and Popular Republic of Algeria, Algeria emerged as a populist-authoritarian state. It was ruled by successive autocratic FLN governments, first by President Ahmad Ben Bella, who was overthrown by Houari Boumediène in a June 1965 military coup. Upon his death in 1978, Boumediène was succeeded by Chadli Benjedid (ruling until 1992), a former senior member of the military, in a state in which the military remained a dominant force.

Algeria's Arab socialist state was legitimated constitutionally by a thin veneer of Islam. The National Charter of the Algerian Popular Democratic Republic of 1976 identified Islam with Algeria's socialist revolution: "The Algerian people is a Muslim people. Islam is the state religion. . . . The Muslim world has only one way out of its predicament to regeneration: it must go beyond reformism and commit itself to the path of social revolution."[65]

The state monopolized religion as it did power, nationalizing religious schools, institutions, and officials in the name of a national, socialist Islam. In fact, the FLN, in the guise of Islamic socialism, pursued an essentially secular path of political and economic development implemented by a Western-oriented ruling elite. However, in the social sphere tensions existed due to a bifurcation in society between the Francophone secular elite and the more Arabized masses for whom Arabic language and culture were primary components of Algerian identity. After independence, the interconnectedness of language, religion, national identity, and authenticity continued to be an issue.

The Islamic Movement

The first Islamist student movements grew out of this cultural clash. During the late sixties and early seventies, individuals and organizations like al-Qiyam (Values) emerged. Their writings and thought were eclectic, reflecting the influence of transnational Islam. They drew on the Islamic modernism of Afghani, Abduh, and Muhammad Iqbal, as well as Hasan al-Banna and Sayyid Qutb of the Muslim Brotherhood and Mawlana Mawdudi of the Jamaat-i-Islami. In contrast to the conservative *ulama* who tended to simply reject Western culture and thought, these reformers spoke French and had mastered modern science. Like the Islamic modernist movement in Egypt and South Asia, their knowledge of modernity both empowered them and provided them with a vantage point from which to critique the West. Such an attitude was exemplified by the French-educated Malek Bennabi, an admirer of modern science and engineering, who reasserted the central importance of Algeria's Arab–Islamic heritage. Like Iqbal he called for a reconstruction of Islam.

By the late seventies and throughout the eighties a transition from issues of culture and ritual to a more comprehensive Islamism took place. Small groups congregated and shared ideas at mosques: "These were no longer lessons dealing with how to pray or perform a fast . . . we touched on all the problems which the Algerian nation was confronting. We spoke about everything . . . the economy . . . of all aspects of life."[66] Discussion and debate spilled over into the universities and the street. The conflict between Arabophone and Francophone students became acute. Realization that Arabophone education was generally not as helpful as Francophone education in obtaining the best jobs exacerbated the polarization. The Arabic-educated tended to dismiss the French-educated as secularists or Marxists and from time to time clashes occurred. The cultural lines, Arab–Islamic versus French, were further drawn over the family law reforms debate that raged from 1975–84 as students and women's organizations demonstrated and clashed.

Failure of the State

Algeria's state-run economy and socialist programs, which took responsibility for education, employment, housing, and social services, had greatly benefited from its ample hydrocarbon resources, which supported material and social development or modernization. However, in the mid-eighties, Algeria (whose oil and gas revenues accounted for more than 90 percent of its exports) joined many countries in suffering the impact of a world economic crisis precipitating an oil glut and fall in energy prices. Algeria's demographics, with its large population of unemployed youth, exacerbated social tensions between the ruling elite and the majority of the population, who felt the full impact of imposed austerity measures and were increasingly critical of government failures.

In October 1988 Algeria was rocked by massive street protests and so-called food riots. A wave of public demonstrations swept across the country, precipitated by the dramatic fall in living standards (high unemployment, severe housing and food shortages, corruption, and inefficient government). Beginning in Algiers, the riots quickly spread to many other major cities, including Oran and Constantine. It was in this context of social crisis that the Islamic Salvation Front (FIS), a coalition of groups, emerged as a political actor, gaining legitimacy and credibility. FIS activists were among the most visible and organized leaders, seen by some as the instigators of the popular revolt as well as among the chief victims of the military's brutal suppression, which resulted in an estimated five hundred civilian deaths.[67]

The message of Algeria echoed that, as in other parts of the Arab world, the "ruling bargain" had failed:

> Under this arrangement, the ruled traded their rights to independence political activity in return for the rulers' guarantee of social welfare and job security. To provide these benefits, the state relied on oil revenues, foreign remittances, tourist spending, and foreign aid to finance huge government bureaucracies and inefficient state-run enterprises, institutions whose primary mission was to provide guaranteed employment and a minimum level of social equity rather than efficient capital accumulation and production.[68]

It is against this background of nationwide political, economic, and cultural unrest that the rise of Islamic movements in Algeria and the subsequent "war" must be understood.

The Road to Reform, the Path to Destruction

In the late eighties, the Benjedid government, like many of the states in the region, promised greater political liberalization and democracy to counter public discontent. Benjedid's political reforms included a national referendum and revision of the Constitution in 1989 which retreated from Algeria's socialist tradition. It ended the FLN's monopoly of the power, transforming Algeria's one-party state into a competitive multiparty political system. While liberals called for greater political and economic freedoms, it was the Islamists who emerged as self-proclaimed voices of the oppressed masses. Thirty years of one-party rule and the absence of opposition parties made the FIS the only formidable challenge to the authoritarianism and legitimacy of the government. The growth of "street mosques, and prayer rooms in factories, schools and government offices threatened the power and secularism of a faltering state."[69]

The FIS, drawing its support from the poor and middle class, denounced the failure and corruption of the regime, called for greater Arabization and Islamization of society, and effectively penetrated state institutions, especially the schools and universities. Its proclamation of Islam's message of social justice, in particular its condemnation of societal failures in education, housing, and employment as well as of government corruption, proved especially popular among Algeria's unemployed youth and rural–urban migrants. With more than 60 percent of the population under twenty-five years of age and a high percentage of them unemployed, young people proved ready recruits, exchanging idleness and boredom for a sense of direction and hope as they swelled the crowds at mosques and engaged in political action.

The network of independent mosques (freed from government control) and social welfare agencies became increasingly important as state institutions faltered in the late eighties. Given the historic role of Islam in the nationalist movement and revolution, its roots in popular culture and the nonelite sectors of society, Islamists offered an attractive populist message. They proclaimed an Islamic alternative of the failures of the government and of Algeria's Westernized secular elite. Their social services were an implicit critique of the government's failures. When Algeria was hit by an earthquake in 1989, the Islamists were the first to respond and did so effectively. They, rather than the government, supplied blankets and medicine, and thus scored further points while the government reinforced its image of ineffectiveness.

When the Algerian government, like others in the area, opened up its political system in 1989, it promised elections and a multiparty system. In contrast to Tunisia and Egypt, which continued to ban Islamic political parties and thus forced candidates to run as independents or in coalition with recognized political parties, Algeria permitted Islamic political parties. Among the almost sixty opposition parties that quickly sprouted in response to the government's opening were several Islamic parties or associations, among them Hamas (Mouvement de la Société Musulmane), Ennahda (Renaissance Party), and the Islamic Salvation Front (Al-Jabhatu al-Islamiyyatu Lil'inqadh, whose French acronym was FIS, for le Front Islamique du Salut). The FIS was an umbrella organization or coalition established in 1989 under the leadership of Shaykh Ali Abbasi Madani (b. 1931), a moderate religiously and Western-educated professor at Algiers University, and Ali Belhadj, a younger, more radical preacher.

Abassi Madani was born in southeastern Algeria, the son of a religious leader and imam. He emphasized Arabic and Islamic studies and thus possessed both nationalist and Islamist credentials. A political activist in the early fifties, he joined the National Liberation Front and was imprisoned by the French during the occupation for eight years and later four years by Benjedid. Like many Islamists in the Arab world, disillusionment with the failures of Arab nationalism had led to his turn to an Islamic alternative. In 1963 he joined the Values (al-Qiyam) Society, which advocated a reassertion of Algeria's Arab–Islamic heritage. He took part in demonstrations in 1966 against the execution of Sayyid Qutb, the ideologue of the Egyptian Muslim Brotherhood. Disillusioned by the Arab defeat in the 1967 Arab–Israeli Six-Day War and increasingly critical of the FLN's socialist policy, he returned to school, earning degrees in psychology and philosophy. In 1978, he received a British doctorate in education and taught at the University of Algiers.

The Islamic Salvation Front

In 1982, Madani became embroiled in campus and national politics during clashes between students and government forces at the University of Algiers. Islamic political activism became more visible in the early eighties on the campuses and in urban neighborhoods. Student activists and Islamic pamphlets called for political, educational, and social reforms, from abrogation of the National Charter and the establishment of an Islamic government to curriculum reform, separation of the sexes on campus, and prohibition of alcohol. As the government's economic programs had failed, so too its religious policy proved impotent and incapable of controlling the spread of populist Islam. As a front, the FIS was able to attract and include a cluster of orientations and constituencies under its umbrella. The organization of the FIS proved both a strength and a weakness. On the one hand, it was broad enough to include a wide diversity of individuals and perspectives; on the other hand, it lacked a unity of leadership and vision on critical issues.

Nowhere was this tension clearer than in the differences between its two most prominent leaders, Madani and Belhadj. While both were critical of the system and called for substantive Islamic reforms, Madani projected the image of reason, moderate in his discourse, publicly supportive of democratic elections and pluralism. Ali Belhadj, on the other hand, was more combative in his rhetoric. Belhadj, who was born in Tunisia in 1956, lost both his parents in Algeria's war of independence. Unlike Madani, he is the product of a totally Arab–Islamic religious education. He became a secondary school teacher of Arabic and an imam, a mosque preacher. He was imprisoned from 1982 to 1987 during a crackdown against Islamists. In contrast to Madani and many modern Islamist activist leaders in other Muslim countries, Belhadj had no exposure to the West or to the world outside Algeria. As a result, he tended to be dogmatic. His more militant style, his call for immediate imposition of the Sharia, and his denunciation of the Algerian government and of the West proved popular among many young Algerians.[70] In contrast to Madani, Belhadj was dismissive of democracy, which he saw as but another tool of the West.

FIS Ideology

Abbasi Madani is the FIS's primary leader and chief ideologue. While the FIS leadership represents a variety of positions, Madani's intellectual vision and worldview represents its thrust and general orientation. He describes the FIS as a popular front and political party. As a contrast to capitalism and communism, the FIS espouses an Islamic solution, based upon the belief that Islam offers a comprehensive ideology for state and society. While advocating participatory democracy, Madani believes that justice, freedom, equality, and moral political principles can be best realized in an Islamic democracy, one based upon Islamic principles, which, in contrast to Western democracy, is less pragmatic and more socially just:

> Democracy in Algeria cannot be given the same philosophical and political interpretation as that of pragmatic philosophers like Adam Smith, Kant, and Dewey, who define it as the right to exercise capital freedom, even if it exceeds the needs of other classes of society, i.e., the working class or the poor. Democracy in the U.S., in a liberal and pragmatic sense, has given the individual more rights to personal freedoms at the expense of the group. It has given more rights to the powerful and less to the weak. This is freedom at the expense of social and economic justice. . . . Liberal democracy is not free of contradictions, nor is socialist democracy free of oppression and injustice. Democracy in the socialist and communist sense is nothing but emptiness and historical marginalism.[71]

Madani identifies the FIS's brand of democracy with Islam. The Islamic model of democracy precedes modern forms ("new thought") and is a system in which individual and social freedoms do not oppose each other; they are "two faces of a single coin."[72] Islam provides a complete and just political system in which individuals are free to vote, compete for elective office, and govern. The Sharia is the cornerstone of justice and freedom, the means of achieving a system which balances the rights and duties of the individual with those of society. Thus, Madani maintains, the Islamic model is more perfect than liberal and socialist democracy; it is the best model to confront the ideological crises of civilization.[73]

At the heart of Madani's interpretation of Islam is an emphasis on Islam as the religion of the people and the source of social justice, capable of producing and guiding a just political and social order. His populist Islam gives political and economic primacy to the people over individual self-interest. Although he accepts a multiparty system and power sharing, in which the rights of the minority are to be affirmed and safeguarded, Madani dismisses Algeria's political parties as failures. Just as he accuses the West of fostering individual rights at the expense of the community, so too does he see Algeria's political parties as narrow, elite organizations, driven more by self-interest and partisanship than by the needs of the people. A former member of the FLN, he charged that it had departed from its noble principles and become a party dominated by presidential personalities and elite interests which produced a system that was "politically and morally bankrupt." Despite the fact that other political parties such as the Movement for Democracy and the Front for Social Forces called for democracy, Madani also charged that they were "founded for selfish or partisan reasons and not for ... guaranteeing the self-determination of the people. ... They are like museums and are not able to face the historical crisis confronting us."[74]

Madani often presents an Islamic ideal in which the world is one of white and black, right and wrong, self-interest and altruism. It is a world of transcendent principles and "shoulds." The FIS presumptively embodies this ideal, an ideal that is used to discredit and judge its rivals. Thus the FIS views itself as the party of the people, of self-determination, of all Algerians. All other parties are seen as flawed, driven primarily by narrow self-interest and power. While a multiparty system and power sharing are affirmed, it is not always clear whether those who are judged "misguided and elite" will be permitted to participate. The place for religious, ideological, political, and social differences is not clear. The assertion of an ideal or a mythic unity of the Muslim community seems at times to counter an affirmation of diversity and pluralism. Despite the fact that the electoral success of the FIS did not enjoy universal acceptance, Madani generalized about Algerians' "current lack of doubt about the capabilities of Islam in solving their problems and their readiness to apply Islamic solutions."[75]

As in politics so too in economics; the FIS agenda attempted to balance individual and societal interests as it sought to address both Algeria's chronic unemployment and the maldistribution of wealth. The FIS did not offer a blueprint for economic reform. It did, however, reject the discredited socialist system of the past and advocate a free enterprise system: "The Islamic Salvation Front has proposed programs of free investments and private enterprise in agriculture, industry, commerce and banking. ... It is proposing an economic model based on justice which provides assurances for the investment of capital and the creation of a climate for the human resources to flourish by the investment of technological skills and expertise."[76] Madani attributed Algeria's stagnant economy to government monopoly and restrictions: "While the liberal motto of 'laissez faire' has moved the liberal economy, in socialist Algeria we find that the motto 'don't do' has hindered the economy."[77]

The FIS advocated economic reforms that would preserve Algeria's oil reserves and exploit instead its other resources. The failures of Algeria are attributed not only to the FLN and its bureaucracy but also more broadly to a Western neocolonialism and imperialism that has dominated the oil market and adversely affected the economies of developing nations like Algeria. Madani accused the FLN of mortgaging Algeria's future for its present by making Algeria dependent on an oil market controlled by the West: "The neo-colonialist imperialist policy that is controlling the oil market and other major markets, has forced our countries to sell the more expensive commodities at a low price and buy the cheaper commodities at a higher price—and that's the way to poverty. . . . We are buying expensive eggs and selling cheap oil."[78]

The FIS and the West

As with most Islamic movements, and for that matter Third World populist movements, European colonialism and Western neocolonialism loom large as the reputed sources of failure and oppression. America in particular in its role as a superpower is seen as a political and economic threat. Its oil policy, which makes it dependent on outside sources, results in a strategy that "does not exploit its oil reserves but adds to its oil stock from the world oil supply. . . . The oppression of America . . . puts its interest at the expense of others and wants to get richer while we get poorer."[79] For Madani, America's economic and political oppression go hand-in-hand. Its domination of the world market, and its "neo-colonial greediness" coupled with a "cowboy" foreign policy, deepened the plight of the oppressed in the Islamic world. Madani believed that the Gulf War and American attitudes toward the Middle East were due to Zionist influence, the media, and a "colonial crusade," reminiscent of the Crusades, a regression to the Middle Ages and religious warfare.

Like most Islamists the world over, Madani regards secularism and related ideologies as a major cause for Muslim decline and impotence. It is a foreign import imposed first by colonial powers and then by the state and Western-oriented Muslim elites through state institutions and media. The conflict between Islam and secularism is not one initiated by Islam. Thus Algerian secularism, which dismisses Islamists and fundamentalists, has waged an ideological war that Madani characterizes as attempting to pressure the Algerian people to "abandon their Islamic identity and moral values."[80] Although critical of the United States, Madani maintains that he desires a constructive cooperative relationship based upon recognition of Algeria's autonomy, that is, its right and that of the Muslim world to determine its destiny. Madani maintains that the FIS economic programs "open the doors for American investors. They will be given an equal opportunity to participate in Algeria as long as their presence is not of a neo-colonial nature. . . . [However,] the American incursion in the Gulf makes some of us have reservations about dealing with U.S. companies or U.S. backed development programs."[81]

From Opposition to Electoral Politics

On June 12, 1990, Algeria had its first multiparty elections since independence. Municipal and regional elections tested both the government's new direction and the strength of Islamists. In contrast to Egypt, Morocco, and Tunisia (where Islamic political parties were banned and Islamists had to run as independent candidates), the Benjedid government permitted the FIS to participate as a political party. Given the FLN's control of the political process, the power of the ruling elite, and opposition from Algeria's feminist movement, the question seemed not to be whether the FLN would win but how well in defeat the Islamists would do. The clear expectation of government officials, experts, and the media in Algeria and internationally was that the combination of secular forces and Algeria's long association with the West, politically and culturally, would limit the performance of the FIS. The government and Western-educated critics warned of the fundamentalist threat to Algeria's secular orientation, to democracy, pluralism, women's rights. Thus, few were prepared for the outcome. With 65 percent of the electorate voting, the FIS swept the elections, controlling 55 percent (853 of 1,551) of the municipal councils and two thirds (thirty-two) of the forty-eight regional assemblies, in contrast to the dismal showing of the FLN, which won only 32 percent of the municipal and 29 percent of the regional elections. The FIS won a majority in all the major cities: 64.18 percent in Algiers, 70.50 percent in Oran, and 72 percent in Constantine.[82] Algeria, North Africa, and the West stood stunned; the unthinkable had happened.

This was not an Iranian-styled Islamic revolution but an overwhelming victory at the ballot box which defied the secular presuppositions of modernization theory and the vision of Algeria as a modern state. For Islamists, the electoral victory was part of a broader ongoing ideological battle between Islam and Westernization: "The secularists are not the only ones to be sad over an Islamic victory. There are also the Western planners and enemies of Islam. This victory is a rejection of Western and secular values, which were implanted in the heart of the Muslim Arab country and reinforced by colonial masters and their stooges [a minority secular Muslim elite who perpetuated the legacy of French occupation]."[83] Rulers' fears of its international impact and implications were fed by Islamists who declared:

> Algeria stepped forward to usher in a new era. . . . This situation will soon
> become a common denominator in the entire Arab homeland, incessant
> demonstrations, rebellion and protests by hundreds of thousands of people
> everyday will become a real problem for Arab governments, regardless of

their ideology. The importance of Algeria as a pioneering and leading case in this universal Arab economic and political transformation lies in the experience it will provide other peoples and other countries.[84]

The FIS victory was due to a discredited FLN, its European models of development, and its failure to permit a strong secular opposition to develop, coupled with actual support for the FIS. While public apathy kept some voters away from the polls, many others turned out. In many ways, the elections were a repudiation of a failed system, ideologically and materially, by a popular movement which brought together disparate groups in opposition to the government. The FIS provided the core and backbone of the movement, attracting a broad base of support across the country, but particularly in urban areas. They brought a level of organization and ideological commitment, lacking in other sectors of society, as well as an impressive record of social responsibility and welfare. The FIS network of medical clinics and charitable associations served the poorest and most crowded urban neighborhoods, providing free tutoring in mosques, housing, creating shops and jobs, cleaning up neighborhoods.[85] Standing in the void created by the abysmal failures of the government and the FLN, corruption, and growing gap between rich and poor, the FIS offered an indigenous alternative. The FIS possessed an agenda with broad appeal: denunciation of the failures of the regime and its Western models of development; reassertion of Algeria's Arab–Islamic identity, heritage, and values; championing of popular political participation and economic reform (jobs and housing); effective delivery of social services; denunciation of political and moral corruption; espousal of the rights of the economically oppressed and promise of a more equitable redistribution of wealth; and reemphasis on family values. At the same time, the lack of any other viable alternatives meant that the FIS also benefited from those who abstained and, more importantly, from those who cast their vote for the FIS less out of support for their party than as a protest vote against the FLN, reflecting the high level of frustration and outrage with the prevailing political and social order.

Government Counterattack

In the aftermath of the elections, the government moved aggressively to cut off funds to the municipalities, thus hindering elected FIS officials' ability to provide adequate services. Despite charges that the FIS would bring radical change and Iranian-style government, local councils proved more interested in local governance and improvements as well as in "small-scale symbolic issues such as dress, alcohol consumption and gambling than radical changes in state, society and economy."[86] Moreover, with few exceptions, the FIS did not impose the veil, ban public bathing, close bars, or prevent women from voting or working. They did pass more conservative regulations in areas that were amenable to such measures.[87]

As the rescheduled June 1991 multiparty elections drew near, the government introduced a new election law which gerrymandered or redrew voter districts to weaken the performance of the FIS and favor the FLN in the upcoming national elections. The FIS responded with demonstrations in opposition to the government's attempt to introduce new electoral laws. When the FIS leadership called for a nationwide general strike in May 1991, the government responded with force. The president declared a state of siege and called in the army to restore order. Madani and Belhadj, as well as some five thousand of their supporters, were arrested on June 30 and elections were postponed. The two leaders were tried before a military court, charged with conspiracy against the state, and sentenced to twelve years in prison.

If some charged that the FIS was challenging the system and undermining state security, others noted that "the FIS demonstrations in June were not an attempt to 'obstruct' the democratic process but were calling for the abrogation of an undemocratic law implemented by the government. Virtually in uninterrupted fashion since its legalization in 1989, the Islamic Salvation Front has adhered to democratic procedures if not principles, the same principles which those in and out of government vigorously defend."[88]

Moves against the FIS, in addition to providing a breathing space for the government and secular forces to regroup, gave other Islamic organizations the opportunity to come to the fore in what some hoped would produce a more divided Islamic front. Shaykh Mahfoud Nahnah, whose Movement for Reform and Guidance (also called Hamas), like the Association of Algerian Ulama, had avoided direct involvement in politics, then founded the Islamic Alliance, a coalition of religious and social organizations. Nahnah had originally opposed religious organizations like the FIS becoming political parties. Many Algerian secularists and Western observers saw Nahnah and the Alliance as a liberal alternative to the FIS which would severely hamper FIS electoral fortunes.[89]

On December 26, 1991, Algeria held the first multiparty parliamentary elections in its thirty-year history. Despite the advantages that the government and the FLN enjoyed, from gerrymandered voter districts and control of state institutions and the media to the continued imprisonment of Madani and Belhadj, with 59 percent of Algeria's registered voters casting ballots, the FIS won 47.54 percent of the vote and 188 of the 231 seats, 28 short of a majority, in the first round.[90] Its closest rival, the Socialist Forces Front, managed only 26. The FLN was routed, finishing third with just 16 seats. The remainder of the seats in a parliament that totaled 430 were to be determined in a runoff election on January 16, 1992.

The FIS and Democracy

The euphoria of the FIS and the exhilaration that swept across Islamic movements throughout the Islamic world were matched by the disbelief and apprehension of many Muslim rulers and Western governments. While Islamists saw the FIS victory as a vindication of the representative nature of their movements and the extent to which they had successfully become institutionalized and part of the mainstream socially and now politically, their opponents charged that the FIS had "hijacked democracy." The FIS denied this accusation and claimed to recognize the importance of the electoral process. Critics maintained that the FIS was simply using the democratic process to come to power and then in turn impose an Islamic system of government with little tolerance of political pluralism and the rights of women. The statements of FIS leaders did not effectively counter these charges.

However much the FIS might be united in slogans like "Islam Is the Solution," differences abounded. As we have seen, as a front or coalition, the FIS included leaders and followers with diverse orientations and attitudes regarding Algeria's future and democratization. The statements of FIS leaders were often vague or contradictory. For some, political participation did not translate into a democratic political process. Abbasi Madani, while ostensibly supporting the democratic process, nevertheless seemed to equivocate and respond tactically when he stated: "Yes, the way is the elections; it is the way for all those who wish to yield to the will of the people. There is no other way at the present moment. All other ways have been obstructed by Allah. Therefore, the way to power is elections which are decided through the popular will of the people."[91] A similar note of pragmatic accommodation could be heard in a statement by another prominent FIS leader, Abdelkader Hachani, a petrochemical engineer: "We say to you Algeria [Algeria's new rulers], Our constitution is the Koran and the Traditions, but we will go down the path of your constitution, not because we believe in it, but because we would give you a pretext [to crack down if we disregarded it].[92] Hachani seemed to accept a multiparty system: "Within the framework of our values and our own civilization, several parties will be allowed to exist. Politics will be enriched by this."[93] On the other hand, Ali Belhadj categorically rejected democracy as an un-Islamic concept, and Imam Abdelkader Moghni declared, "Islam is light. Why do you fear it? It is in democracy that darkness lies. . . . Individual liberties will be respected in the general interest, but liberty must not be confused with permissiveness.''[94] The range of statements made by FIS leaders and their seeming equivocation about democracy and equal rights for women left them vulnerable to criticism and skepticism regarding the true nature of their ultimate agenda.

Military Intervention: Democracy Aborted

On January 12 the Algerian military, disregarding the majority of voters, intervened in what was a de facto coup to prevent the FIS from enjoying the fruits of their democratically elected and earned power. In many ways, Algeria and its neighbors had laid the ground for rationalizing intervention when several months earlier North African governments met and established a task force to combat "radical Islam." As one expert has noted:

> Their message, aimed in part at the West, was unmistakable and could be encapsulated as follows: "the governments in power are worth preserving. For no matter what their shortcomings, ranging from political exclusion to severe human rights violations, they form the only barrier against fanatics who want to confront the West." According to this interpretation, local forms of authoritarianism are regrettable, but they are the only road toward western-style political pluralism.[95]

In the name of preserving state security and stability, the military acted just days before the second round of parliamentary elections in which it appeared that the FIS was poised for another electoral victory that would give them a two-thirds to 80 percent majority in the parliament.[96] The military forced President Benjedid, whom it feared had accepted the FIS electoral victory and intended to enter into a power-sharing agreement with them, to resign. A ruling coalition, a figurehead Council of State or High Security Council, was appointed by the military to govern. Algeria's democratic experiment was suppressed and a process of massive repression of the FIS initiated.

On February 9, 1992, the Council replaced the budding democratic process with a state of siege. It declared a state of emergency, annulled the results of the December elections, canceled the second round of parliamentary elections, and postponed all elections indefinitely. Journalists (non-Islamist and Islamist) were arrested and several newspapers were closed. The government moved to dismantle the FIS. In March 1992, the FIS was banned, and subsequently leaders, members, and those suspected of membership or sympathy with the FIS were arrested, imprisoned, and in some cases tortured. More than ten thousand Islamists were detained in desert concentration camps in the Sahara; the FIS's mosques and social welfare centers were closed and their assets seized. Imams sympathetic to the FIS were replaced by state-approved clergy while others were arrested "for using the pulpit for political purposes."[97] One international magazine commented: "Now it seems to be official. Torture has made a comeback in Algeria."[98] John Entelis, a leading expert on Algeria, wrote:

> The military's cancellation of the elections in January represents nothing less than a political coup and, most likely, the end of Algeria's democratic experiment for the immediate future. Despite government contentions to the contrary, the stability of the state was not in danger. The stability of the regime, to the extent that it was a regime to the army's liking, is a different matter.[99]

The military's swift move to crush the FIS raised serious questions about the nature of Algeria's democratic path. They denied the FIS the power they had earned through participation in the political system, purportedly to safeguard the security of the state. At the same time, the FIS became an example of the difficulty most regimes in the Muslim world have in defining and tolerating opposition. The initial response of FIS leaders was to call for moderation and avoid violence. Abdelkader Hachani reminded FIS members that as a result of the elections, the FIS "had achieved a legitimacy that nothing and no one can take away from it."[100] However, the military's attempt to decapitate the movement and provoke confrontation, coupled with the arrest of moderate FIS leaders like Hachani, set in motion a spiral of violence which would eventually lead to virtual civil war.

While the cancellation of elections was applauded by members of the ruling secular elite, other secular opposition politicians such as Hocine Ait Ahmed, leader of the Socialist Forces Front, an opponent of the FIS, observed that Algeria was experiencing a coup "if not in form, then certainly in fact. . . . They won't make anyone believe that stopping the electoral process is a democratic advance."[101] It also led to international human rights organizations' criticism of "mounting human rights abuses" and their call for the release of Abdelkader Hachani and Rabah Kebir, FIS leaders, "arrested . . . for acts of peaceful expression, as well as all those who have been arrested for offenses involving nonviolent speech or association."[102] The gains that had been made from 1989 to 1991 with an opening of the political system—the introduction of a multiparty system, release of political prisoners, lifting of press censorship, termination of arbitrary arrests and torture—were reversed. While the FIS was the primary target of the government's repression, its secular opposition (intellectuals, politicians, and journalists) was also silenced.

From Legal Opposition to Guerrilla Warfare

Arrests and confrontations between the government and the FIS escalated. Having functioned first as a legitimate opposition, contesting elections and winning handily both in the municipal and parliamentary elections, the FIS had been denied its democratically earned place in the government. The military's crackdown drove the FIS from a legal opposition to a combative, and for some segments, revolutionary movement. With many of its leaders in prison or exile, the coalition fractured. Government repression transformed the FIS from a reform to a revolutionary movement. An organization that had challenged the regime from within the system became a polarized movement whose more disaffected followers, responding to state repression and violence, moved from a defensive to an offensive position and thus became a militant threat.

In a scenario somewhat reminiscent of Egypt's Muslim Brotherhood during the rule of Gamal Abdel Nasser in the sixties, the FIS split into moderate and more militant factions. Repression and torture spawned extremist guerrilla groups. Drawn from radicalized elements of Algeria's Islamist movement, they reject participation in the political process and espouse armed struggle (jihad) and terrorism, bent upon the violent overthrow of what they deem a corrupt, anti-Islamic government and the imposition of an Islamic state. Armed paramilitary and clandestine groups, former FIS members radicalized by the military coup and government repression, other Islamists, the "Afghans," Algerians who fought in Afghanistan during the Soviet occupation, like Hizbullah and the Armed Islamic Group (GIA), inaugurated their own reign of violence and terror with bombings, ambushes, attacks on army barracks, police stations, and prisons. The GIA explicitly condemned the FIS for its moderation, rejected any compromise or reconciliation, and pressed for an all-out jihad against the government and its supporters, Algerians, foreigners, and foreign powers. The FIS also spawned an unofficial military wing, the Islamic Salvation Army (AIS), which in the absence of dialogue pursued an armed struggle against the regime.

As the insurgency spread, the situation deteriorated into virtual civil war, what some American officials called "low-intensity warfare." The military and armed Islamists became locked in mortal combat. Extremists attacked and killed not only government officials, military, and police, but also civilians, leading secular intellectuals, journalists, entertainers, "unveiled" women, and schoolgirls. If security forces saw the beard and head scarf as symbols of fundamentalist terrorism, militants now targeted women in Western dress and secular intellectuals as symbols of a Western-oriented state despotism and repression. Algiers became an armed camp "with 15,000 troops brought in to fight the (invisible) enemy."[103] By late 1993 and early 1994, many outlying areas were controlled by militants who seemed able to strike at will. As both the military and radical Islamists ruthlessly engaged in a no-holds-barred war with innocent civilians caught in the middle, some moderate elements of the FIS attempted to distance themselves from the terrorist actions of groups like the Armed Islamic Group. When the Algerian military killed a leader of the GIA, known as Gjafar al-Afghani, although FIS leaders denounced the action, it was reported that he had been betrayed by another group loyal to the FIS. At the same time, rumors flew that the government, having in the past steadfastly refused to include the FIS in any national dialogue, was in conversation with Abbasi Madani and Ali Belhadj.[104]

Attacks on civilians also reflected an underlying cultural and class conflict. The FIS and other Islamists, who drew heavily from the unemployed Arabophone, urban lower class, should they come to power would be a direct threat to the power and privilege of the Westernized, Francophone, educated urban elite. The military crackdown and attempt to crush the FIS was seen and experienced by many in the FIS as tied to the preservation of the interests and life-style of Algeria's secular, Western-oriented elite, who generally supported military intervention. The conflict was transformed into a jihad between secularism and Islam, Westernization and Islamization. However, these generalizations about the profile of contending social forces should not obscure the diversity of Algerian responses, from secularists (French and Arabic speaking, elite and nonelite) who deplored military rule to FIS support not only from unemployed youth but also from modern educated professionals: doctors, engineers, teachers, and even elements in the military.

The spiral of violence deepened the polarization in society. The government and the army, reflecting the broader society, split into two tendencies: those convinced of the need for dialogue and national reconciliation (les réconciliateurs) and entrenched hard-liners (les éradicateurs the eradicators), who continued to support the total suppression of the FIS. The latter were comprised of many elites who were motivated as much by self-interest as ideology: "many with much to lose, hold out against real negotiations for the basest of reasons—greed."[105] In addition, anti-Islamic death squads, like the Organization of Free Young Algerians and the Organisation Secrète de Sauvegarde de la République de l'Algérie, emerged. Believed to be composed of members or former members of the security and armed forces, their goal is to counter "fundamentalist terrorism," and they have claimed responsibility for attacks and the murder of Islamists.[106]

The power and threat of political Islam exacerbated ethnic tensions and the army found itself increasingly caught between two flanks, Islamists and Berbers. The Berbers predated the coming of Islam to North Africa, and although they converted to Islam they have remained independent and fiercely loyal to their language and culture. Antigovernment and even more antifundamentalist, more militant Berber leaders like Dr. Said Saadi of the Assembly for Culture and Democracy (RCD) denounced the government and called for armed resistance against what he charged was fundamentalist genocide against fellow Algerians.[107]

From Reconciliation to Eradication

Nineteen ninety-four saw a dramatic increase in the level of violence and terrorism as well as signs of behind-the-scenes contact between the government and the imprisoned FIS leadership. In September 1994, the government released reveal FIS leaders and transferred Madani and Belhadj from Blida prison to house arrest in what looked like a first step toward a negotiated settlement. However, Madani refused to participate in a national dialogue until certain conditions were met: "the installation of a 'neutral' government until a 'legitimate' government was elected; the relegitimization of the FIS; the lifting of the state of emergency; proclamation of a general amnesty; the cessation of all judicial proceedings against Islamists; and the army's return to its barracks."[108] President Liamine Zeroual flatly rejected the request. In December 1994 and January 1995, FIS representatives joined with other Algerian opposition parties (including the FLN) in a summit sponsored by the Sant Egidio Catholic community in Rome.

The fourteen-point agreement, signed by Algeria's major secular, non-Islamist, and Islamist leaders and parties, included a call for civil liberty, an end to military intervention in politics, lifting of the ban on the FIS, multiparty democracy, a unilaterally declared cease-fire by all armed opposition, the release of all political prisoners, termination of Algeria's state of emergency, and the convening of a national conference that would lead to free and pluralistic elections. The United States praised the agreement and France, a supporter of the Algerian regime, also responded positively. The Algerian government, imposed and backed by the military, refused to recognize or attend the meeting, regarding it as a nonevent. Portraying it in the media as a resumption of the Christian Crusades, the government denounced the agreement's proposal as a capitulation to the Islamists. Madani and Belhadj, who had been released and placed under house arrest, were returned to prison and the government pressed on with its war to eradicate the Islamists.

Although those who had signed the Sant Egidio agreements "represented 82 percent of Algeria's citizens who voted in the first round of the parliamentary elections of 1991, their voices have in effect been drowned out by the increasingly violent solutions on both sides."[109]

The spiral of violence continued as the bulk of Algerians were caught between religious and secular extremists, principally the GIA and death squads associated with factions in the military. It also deepened the culture war between militant secularists and Islamists, contributing to a growing polarization in society in which the bulk of the civilian population was caught in the middle. The government persistently blocked access to Algeria by the international community (media, human rights organizations, and government delegations). Representatives of Algeria's media faced the threat of assassination from radical Islamist groups like the GIA and a "similar doom from various factions of the security forces."[110] Both the international press and human rights organizations like Amnesty International in its 1997 report, *Algeria: Civilian Population Caught in a Spiral of Violence*, increasingly identified two major polar sources of violence and terrorism—the armed (Islamist) opposition and factions within the military and security forces. Amnesty noted, in a charge not disputed by the Algerian authorities, that although most of the massacres occurred near the capital, "on no occasion have the army or security forces intervened to stop or prevent the massacres or to arrest those responsible."[111] Despite the fact that many of the largest massacres (such as the slaughter of 300 men, women, and children in Sidi Rais in August 28, 1997) occurred in areas with army barracks and police posts nearby, none intervened. Nor, as in other cases, were there any subsequent arrests or prosecutions.

On June 5, 1997, Algeria held parliamentary elections (with the FIS excluded from participation) and elected its first multiparty assembly since gaining independence in 1962. Amid criticisms from U.N. observers and charges of "massive fraud" from losing parties, an Islamic movement, Mahfoud Nahnah's Movement of Society for Peace (MSP), formerly HAMAS, earned the second highest number of votes. (Ennahda, another Islamic party, won 34 seats.) Positioning itself as a modern, moderate, nonviolent Islamic alternative, the MSP appealed to those who were tired both of violence and economic hardship (unemployment stood at 28 percent of the working population) and wanted an alternative to the military-backed regime of President (formerly General) Liamine Zeroual. The MSP won 69 seats (as compared to the 156 of President Zeroual's National Democratic Rally) of the 380 legislative seats and were given four (of 30) cabinet and three secretary of state posts in the new government.

Despite the elections, the violence and killings continued and spread from urban to rural areas, becoming more random. The groups perpetrating the violence and terrorism expanded beyond the armed Islamist opposition and the military and security forces, as new groups and militias engaged in acts motivated by local politics, and tribal and family conflicts. In a series of remarkable revelations, reports emerged of government investigations and arrests of local officials. Those arrested included mayors, policemen, and self-defense groups known as "patriots," who were accused of killings, rape, theft, corruption, and summary and extrajudicial executions (some in police stations).

Both the Islamist opposition and the government splintered and became more factionalized. In contrast to the GIA, which remained committed to an all-out war to achieve its goals, the FIS and its armed wing, the AIS, and other Islamist groups, some of which had broken with the GIA, declared a cease-fire and a desire to pursue a dialogue with the army. Both this decision and the lack of any tangible results deepened their divisions. At the same time, President Liamine Zeroual and the army chief of staff were themselves engaged in a power struggle. The army remained divided between officers open to dialogue and eradicators ("éradicateurs"), extremist factions in the military who opposed any form of national reconciliation. Believing that national stability required total eradication of all Islamist opposition, they (like their radical Islamist opposition) employed murder and terrorism as a means to achieve their goal.

Turkey: The Military and the Defense of Secularism: Radical Secularism or Radical Islam?

For much of the seventies and eighties, Turkey provided the secular paradigm for those who viewed the Islamic resurgence with alarm. Whatever seemed to be happening in other parts of the world, pundits agreed that Turkish secularism was immune from the "threat" of political Islam. With the breakup of the Soviet Union, many, fearing the Islamic influence of Iran, Saudi Arabia, and Pakistan, and the dangers of Islamic activism in the newly independent Central Asian states, advocated the Turkish secular model, sometimes referred to as "Muslim secularism" or "secular Islam." Two factors seemed to preclude Turkey's being swept up by the Islamic wave that seemed to be moving across much of the Middle East and broader Muslim world: (1) the revered memory and legacy of Ataturk (1881–1938) with its strong secular (laic) tradition and institutions and (2) the self-proclaimed role of the army as the "guardian of the secular republic," defenders of secular ideology and state stability. By 1996, however, secular Turkey had its first Islamist prime minister, Necmettin Erbakan, and more than twenty-eight cities had elected Islamist mayors in elections in which the Welfare (Refah) Party, an Islamic party, garnered up to 21 percent of the vote. By 1997, Erbakan had been forced out of office by the Turkish military. As in other parts of the Muslim world, change in Turkish politics and society has been the product of both political economy and political culture.

Secularism, Islam, and the Turkish State

Modern Turkey was created as a secular state. Ataturk disestablished religion, abolishing the sultanate and caliphate, replacing the Sharia with a Western-inspired secular legal system and closing many religious institutions. The caliphate was replaced by a republic whose secularism was enshrined in the 1924 Constitution, a single ruling party (Ataturk's Republican Peoples Party, RPP), and a powerful military. The introduction of multiparty politics and democracy in 1945 gave more space to religion. Mosques were built and repaired, the Islamic faculty at Ankara University was reopened, the ban on religious broadcasts was lifted, and religion classes were reintroduced in schools. Sufi brotherhoods were permitted to function, and the muezzin once more called the faithful to prayer in Arabic (the universal practice in Islam) rather than Turkish. Limitations on the pilgrimage were lifted. By 1982 Turkey sent the third largest number of pilgrims to Mecca.

Secularism had been imposed from above by Ataturk and by an urban-based minority ruling elite (civil servants, military, intellectuals). Realization of the gap between Turkey's Kemalist secular elite and the Turkish masses, for whom religion remained a potent force, was reflected in the absence of any strong commitment to democracy. The principle of democracy was secondary to that of state secularism, a radical secularism imposed by a one-party political system. As Nilufer Gole has observed, "It [democracy] was absent from the six founding principles [republicansim, nationalism, populism, statism, secularism, and revolutionism/reform] of Turkish republicanism. This ordering was a consequence of the suspicions of the ruling elite that the sovereignty of people would end up in the sovereignty of Islam."[112]

Political and economic factors in the fifties and sixties brought new patterns of development and fostered a climate in which Islam became a more visible presence in society. The political liberalization of the fifties, introduced by the Democratic Party (DP) after its defeat of the RPP in 1950, had signaled the failure of Kemalism to take root in society: "Only the cities and large towns benefited under Kemalism and developed a small class committed to it. The countryside remained virtually untouched by the benefits of modern education, and literacy grew only slowly."[113] The

DP, which drew its support from the villages and rural populations, incorporated its living Islamic culture into mainstream politics. However, the greater visibility of Islam in public life was primarily a religious-cultural and not a political phenomenon, consisting of individuals and groups (intellectuals, Sufi mystics, and cultural organizations) who sought to bring about a religious and moral renewal of society. Most were apolitical, from Sufi brotherhoods (the Naqshbandi, the Qadaris, and the Tijaniyya) to the followers of Said Nursi, a religious intellectual who built a nationwide organization with international branches. However different from each other, all were critical of Turkish secularism and reaffirmed the centrality of Islam. Turkey's new economic development also produced a new group of managers and technocrats. In contrast to the established militant secularism of the military-bureaucratic elite (although they too had received modern educations), these managers retained Islam as a formative influence in their lives. By the sixties, rapid industrialization, international economic development, social dislocation and left-wing politics, and increased fears of a communist threat all contributed to the politicization of Islam.

The Islamist response in the sixties took the form of a more pronounced political activism. The most prominent example was a movement initiated in 1970 by Necmettin Erbakan (1926–) in Konya. An engineer who had studied at Istanbul Technical University and had earned a doctorate at Aachen Technical University in Germany, Erbakan combined careers in academia, business, and politics. He became a full professor at Istanbul Technical University in 1965 and established and directed an engine factory. He also served briefly as director general of the Turkish Union of Chambers of Commerce and Industry in 1969 before entering politics full-time.

Erbakan represented an emerging new alternative to the old elite. He came from a well-to-do, conservative Muslim family in Anatolia. Having a modern education and an Islamic orientation, he was committed to a Turkish nationalism based on Ottoman-Islamic traditions, a Turkey economically and culturally independent of the West, which he associated with decadence and immorality. It was, he maintained, blind dependence on the West that had robbed Turkey of its identity and strength. As some of his advisers noted:

> Thus the European, by making us copy him blindly and without any understanding, trapped us in this monkey's cage and, as a result, forced us to abandon our personality and nobility. That is to say, he was successful in this because he used agents recruited from within, who felt [inferior and] disgusted with themselves, bringing to his knees the Turk who for centuries could not be defeated by the crusades and external blows.[114]

Politically active in the sixties, Erbakan was elected to the National Assembly in 1969 and created the National Order Party (NOP) in 1970. The NOP program emphasized technological innovation, rapid industrialization, and a spiritual and moral renewal of society. It preached material as well as spiritual salvation to those Turks (small businessmen, laborers, young provincial professionals and intellectuals) who had become the victims of rapid development, import substitution companies, mass migration to the cities, and the cultural schizophrenia precipitated by modern, urban, secular society. Erbakan criticized the social imbalance and injustice of Turkish society: "The economic mechanism works in favour of the merchants of the big cities and the merchants of Anatolia are simply their step-children. The lion's share of import quotas is saved for the merchants of three or four cities."[115] Erbakan's commitment to industrial, economic, and technological development, rooted in Turkey's Islamic culture and values, was combined with a call for democratization at a time when many experienced the repression of military rule. Some have questioned whether that commitment to democracy was simply political and pragmatic.[116] Throughout the years, however, Erbakan and the Islamic parties that he founded would continue to reiterate their desire to create a modern, democratic, industrialized, and socially just Turkey.

Banned in 1971 by the military, the NOP was reorganized eighteen months later as the National Salvation Party (NSP), again based on a platform that combined rapid industrialization and religious/moral reform. Blaming foreign cultural influences for the decline of the Ottoman empire, the NSP criticized Turkey's mainstream political parties, "members of the Western club," for falling into the same trap. Infatuated with a Western civilization devoid of faith and morality, they were incapable of charting the course for a rapid industrial development that must be based on authentic, indigenous cultural sources. The NSP did not directly challenge the legitimacy of the Kemalist state or seek to overthrow it but called for a space for religion within state secularism—for Turkish nationalism and society to reaffirm and appropriate its Islamic faith and values. Thus Erbakan and NSP ideology were based on a strong sense of Turkish nationalism, Islamic identity, anticommunism, and anti-Western dependency.

The NSP electoral performance was far from impressive, winning only 11.8 percent of the vote in 1973 and 8.6 percent in 1977. However, by the mid-seventies, Erbakan controlled enough seats in parliament to participate in three coalition governments; he served as deputy prime minister in all three governments.[117] Between 1973 and 1980, NSP members and sympathizers found their way into parliament, government offices, education, and business. The military seized power in a coup d'état in September 1980, disbanding parliament and all political parties. Erbakan and the NSP leadership (in contrast to other party leaders) were not only arrested but also tried by military courts. As it would in all its interventions, the military claimed to be defending Ataturk's secularism. Thus one justification given for the coup was the "threat of radical Islam as embodied by Erbakan's National Salvation Party."[118] Charged with subverting the secular tenets of the Turkish republic, NSP leaders were finally acquitted. Erbakan, however, was detained in military barracks for almost three years.

In 1983, which saw a return to civilian and multiparty politics, Erbakan founded a successor to the banned NSP, the Welfare or Prosperity (Refah Partisi) Party (WP). Its name reflects its mission to create a more socially just society by increasing the country's wealth and assuring a more equitable distribution of resources. The WP would become a modern mass party, the only truly grassroots party Turkey had had. Its members, 4 million strong, were to be found in major cities as well as the provinces. Under the strong and single leadership of Necmettin Erbakan, WP was far from monolithic. It included professionals as well as laborers, faculty and students, corporate leaders as well as factory workers, men and women, progressive and conservative Islamic orientations. Its support came from lower-middle and middle classes having modern educations while maintaining conservative religious provincial backgrounds.[119] The majority were not from sheltered, uneducated rural backgrounds but from state secular schools where they had been trained in the sciences, technology, and Western thought. Financial support came not only from members but from overseas workers and supporters.

Islam in the Political Process

Other forces in society also contributed to the increased profile of Islam in Turkish society. Ironically it was the self-described defenders of secularism—the military and an elected head of state, Turgut Ozal, a former member of the NSP—who were responsible for the new openings. During the three years (1980–83) after their coup the military employed religion as part of its liberalization program and foreign policy. Among their concessions were the introduction of religious education in state schools and a reemphasis on Turkey's Muslim identity in foreign policy. Although the presence of religion was expanded, the state could hope to control the teaching of religion (teachers and the curriculum) and thus the "brand" of Islam (antifundamentalist or nonfundamentalist) that was taught, use religion to strengthen the moral fabric of society, counter the influence of the Left (communist and Marxists), and enhance its efforts to strengthen its "Islamic foreign policy," that is, economic ties and markets in Muslim countries.

The election of Turgut Ozal and his Motherland Party in May 1983 reinforced the pursuit of a liberalization policy that included a free market economy as well as a greater emphasis on Turkey's religious culture and values. Like Erbakan, Ozal (1927–93) was a practicing Muslim, a graduate of the Istanbul Technical University, and, for a time in the seventies, had been a member of the National Salvation Party. Like Erbakan, he believed that Islam remained an essential part of Turkish culture and identity. In contrast to Erbakan, however, he favored closer political and economic links with Europe and the West, emphasizing that Anatolia shared the roots of European history and civilization (a "Judeo-Christian-Islamic civilization") and affirming Turkey's role as a bridge between Europe and Asia, between the Christian and Muslim worlds.[120] Turkey was a staunch member of both NATO and of the Organization of the Islamic Conference (OIC). Ozal also asserted and worked hard for Turkey's right to be a member in the European Union.

After the election of the Motherland Party in 1983, the military, General Kenan Evren, and Prime Minister Ozal stressed the importance of religious values. Evren attended the 1984 meeting of the OIC as president of Turkey. However, it was the policies of Turgut Ozal that contributed most toward the legitimizing of political Islam. Espousing a synthesis of Turkish nationalism and Islam, Ozal reasserted the importance of Turkey's Islamic heritage as a primary source of Turkish identity, unity, and society as well as a counterweight to the influence of the Left within the limits of its secular state: "What holds together, or rather brings together, our unity and our cohesiveness is the fact that we are all citizens of the Turkish Republic. . . . Our state is secular. But what holds our nation together, what serves in a most powerful way in our national cohesiveness and what plays the essential role is Islam."[121] Religion was made a compulsory subject in primary and secondary schools. The imam-hatip schools (schools for the training of prayer leaders and religious teachers) were recognized as high schools, thus enabling their graduates to qualify for admission to university and for jobs in the government and private sector. As a result, many found their way into government, serving in the bureaucracy and in ministries of education and culture. Ozal permitted the introduction of Islamic banks and other Islamic financial institutions. Islam was increasingly visible in publications, institutions, and ritual. The Diyanet, which oversees religious publications, mosques, and Quran schools, reported an increase from 2 million copies of thirty religious publications in 1979 to 5,702,000 copies of fifty-three books in 1982; the number of Quran schools increased from 2,610 in 1979–80 to 4,715 in 1988–89 and their students increased from 68,486 to 155,403; the number of Turks making the hajj increased from 10,805 in 1979 to 92,006 in 1988.[122]

A variety of Islamically oriented groups, many nonpolitical, became more visible in promoting a religious renewal of society. Sufi orders like the Naqshbandi and Nurcu groups played a particularly important role. Spread across Turkey (and indeed international in scope), the Naqshbandi and Nurcu created a vast network active in business, mass media, education, and social welfare services. Their offshoots, such as Fethullah Gulen's group, the Fethullahci, became a major religious and social force.[123] Fethullah Gulen, an intellectual and a disciple of Said Nursi, represents a nationalist Islamic but more apolitical movement.[124] In Turkey's increasingly politicized context, his group attempted to steer a course between militant secularists and Islamists like the WP. It sought to distinguish itself from the "fundamentalists." It has been inclusive rather than exclusive, attempting to balance multiple identities and interests. Emphasizing both religion and secular nationalism, modern and religious education, science and technology, West and East, Islam and other religions, Gulen and his followers walked a fine line, carefully acknowledging the significance of Ataturk, expressing respect for the military, and warning of the dangers of politicized religion. The group's message has been effectively communicated through its widely circulated newspaper, *Zaman,* a major television station, and publishing houses. Throughout the eighties, Nurcu groups like the Fethullahci and WP significantly expanded their presence in the economic sector through large holding companies, banks, investment houses, insurance companies, and chain stores. The class structure of these Islamic organizations changed considerably as their membership came to constitute a counterelite (over against the entrenched Westernized secular elite) in business, government, and education, as well as among the working poor. Their educational projects (building schools and universities and dormitories for tens of thousands of students, publishing and distributing books, sponsoring tutorials, and providing financial aid) have been major attractions, drawing members and volunteers and powerfully influencing the next generation of professionals. They often combine religious, educational, and business interests in Turkey and abroad. With the financial help of members from the corporate community, they have created an extensive network of schools throughout Turkey and have founded more than five hundred high schools in Central Asia, the Balkans, and the Caucasus.[125]

Although many came to see Gulen as representing a "moderate Islam," his religious and mystical claims, his politics, and his open criticism of WP politicization of Islam drew criticism from WP leaders on religious

as well as political grounds. Many of the more militant secularists (in the
military and intelligentsia) also remained wary and suspicious, often lump-
ing Gulen's group with the WP and other more politicized groups and
referring to them as Islamists.

Turgut Ozal's use of Islam in the eighties and the more open climate
that enabled Sufi and other Islamically oriented organizations to thrive
contributed to the growing politicization of Islam. This was reflected in
the fortunes of the Welfare Party. Although Welfare garnered only 7.2
percent of the vote in 1987, by 1991 its fortunes had begun to change as
it won 17.2 percent in national elections.

Welfare's Path to Power

The sudden death of Ozal in 1993 was followed by a period of transition
in which the Welfare Party profited from the failures of the state, the
internecine battles of Turkey's political leadership, and Welfare's dedicated membership. The opening of the economy brought economic
growth, as well as inflation rates of 60 to 100 percent and a rising national
debt. As Jenny White has noted,

> The costs of the new policies have reached many, the benefits few. As in
> other countries, the introduction of an open market economy has been ac-
> companied by growing socioeconomic inequality. The contrast is especially
> apparent in the cities, which the rich share with masses of migrants from
> the countryside. . . . The stark economic inequality gives impetus to Islamic
> groups that preach social justice and an end to favoritism and corruption.[126]

Welfare was able to engage effectively in opposition politics, criticizing
the failure of previous Motherland and True Party governments to solve
Turkey's economic and social problems or to stem the tide of corruption
and economic incompetence—a charge that many outside the ranks of
Welfare agreed with. As one commentator noted in 1996, "The RP can
be perceived as fruit from the performance failure of the Turkish right,
which had been in power most of the time during the multiparty period.
With a broadening power base, which includes the protest vote of those
having suffered under competitive market conditions since 1980, the RP
is the most serious competitor of all the parties on the right."[127]

The WP was a credible and effective agent for change, a model of
effective organization and efficiency, a bold critic of ineffective, insensi-
tive, and corrupt Turkish governments and political parties, while being
responsive to the socioeconomic needs of the urban poor. It benefited from
the inability of national political leaders to rise above bitter petty politics
and engage in coalition building, a system marked by inefficiency and

corruption at the highest levels of government. Welfare was the only party that offered an alternative with a track record of responding effectively to the needs of society. Its holistic approach—a comprehensive understanding of Islam—resulted in a critique of Turkish politics and society. Its message was as much about government corruption, economic development, schools, poverty, jobs, housing, and the environment as about religious belief and practice. Incorporating the religious culture and values of the masses, Refah provided a sense of shared identity and community in the new and often alienating environments of large cities. Party volunteers worked tirelessly in reaching out to others with assistance, recruiting votes with promises of a more socially just society and a better future.[128] Welfare created a dynamic system of social welfare and patronage, of mutual assistance and obligation, assisting urban immigrants from small towns and rural areas find jobs, food, apartments, medical care, and educational opportunities.

Women were a part of Refah's organization and activity (as they were in many other Islamic groups), often identifiable by their choice of "Islamic" or "Muslim" dress over Western fashions. Kemalism had imposed its own singular definition of modernity; this included defining the model of a modern Turkish woman. More traditional women found it difficult to retain their own distinctive, religiously informed identity and dress while modernizing. As in other Muslim countries, women's dress has become a contentious symbol in the struggle to defend or redefine national identity. In Turkey, it bears witness to their faith and symbolizes the alternative moral/social order that Islamists seek within a modern secular society. It is not seen so much as a choice between Islam and modernity or Islam and secularism as an effort to define an alternative, Islamically informed model for being a modern Turkish woman, "to build an Islamic way of life in a secular order, and hence render Islam a living social practice."[129] Many Islamically oriented women embody their own brand of "feminism," wishing to liberate women from the constraints of patriarchal society and redefine the role of women in a way that combines their central role in the family with the right to education, employment, and political activism. They publish magazines like *Woman and the Family* (*Kadin ve Aile*) and *Letter* (*Mektep*), which root reforms within an Islamic framework. Thus the status and role of Muslim women is not merely a religious question but a political and social issue.

The growth of Islamism and the increasing presence and electoral power of Welfare were made more visible by women donning new forms of Islamic dress. What began as a curiosity became increasingly more common in urban areas and on university campuses as Islamist women and their dress became more fashionable, with shops, boutiques, and magazines to match. Welfare provided assistance to those who wished to dress Islamically and established dormitories near universities for like-minded Muslim women who wished to live together. Women volunteers played an essential role in grassroots organizing and in providing social services, holding conferences and organizing socials to meet, assist, and introduce others to the party and its platform. Despite the centrality of their partic-ipation, however, women tended to be noticeably absent from the party ticket.

Ideologically, Welfare members ranged from those who sought a greater space for Islam within Turkey's secular state to those who ultimately de-sired an Islamic state. The religious conservatism of some was matched by the progressive technocrat mentality and reformism of many others. Although most sought accommodation, others flirted with and at times engaged in confrontation. Erbakan attempted to incorporate and balance both tendencies within Welfare. In the nineties, Erbakan increasingly com-bined the rhetoric of anti-imperialism with the rhetoric of traditional Islam. He criticized Western capitalism and the influence of international Zion-ism, and he called for regional Muslim cooperation. He assumed an anti-NATO, anti-Zionist, anti-Western posture. Believing that Turkey belonged to a Muslim Commonwealth, Erbakan advocated a NATO-style defense pact and an EU-style economic compact for the Middle East. The WP was about politics and patronage as much as identity and values. It drew strength and support for its responses to socioeconomic as well as spiritual needs. Like many other Islamic movements, Welfare was well organized, highly motivated, and responsive to the plight of the working class. The party emphasized and instilled a sense of Muslim community both locally and internationally that was visible in working-class neighborhoods among the poor and lower-middle classes as well as in schools and on university campuses.

Welfare used democracy as a yardstick by which to judge the failure of Turkish secularism to be truly pluralistic and to respect the rights of all citizens, including their freedom of conscience or right to live accord-ing to their religious beliefs. Erbakan had maintained that true secularism (separation of religion from the state) should not only mean state auton-omy but religious autonomy. That is, religion also has its autonomy, which is respected by the state and is free from state interference. The state should not intervene in the religious sphere by attempting to regulate dress (the right of women to wear a headscarf or, for that matter, men to wear a beard) or religious practice. The WP wished to add a new amendment to the constitution regarding the definition of secularism to guarantee the right of all people to live in accordance with their religious beliefs. Tur-key's radical secularists regarded this as a direct threat: "The radical secularists, comprising the majority of the intelligentsia, including a number of leading journalists, believe this stand on the part of RP is a challenge to the secular premises of the state. They think that the RP is concealing its long-term intention to establish an Islamic state in Turkey."[130]

In 1994 Welfare emerged as the leading political party in municipal elections, winning 24.1 percent of the vote, scoring especially well in working-class areas, and electing mayors in twenty-eight municipalities, including Istanbul and Ankara, Turkey's capital city. Welfare Party successes were attributable to many factors, including the failures of previous governments, which created a crossover protest vote from disgruntled voters who would normally support other parties. The vote was as much, if not more, about politics and economics (double- and triple-digit inflation, urban poverty, inadequate social services and health care, pollution, congestion, high unemployment, inadequate housing, crime, corruption) as about religion. Indeed, a 1994 survey found that only one-third of those voting for the WP did so primarily because it was an Islamic party.[131] Welfare's focus on issues like employment, pensions, health care, housing, and environment, as well as its indictment of the failures of society reflected in WP slogans of "clean politics" and a "just order," proved effective.

Welfare also benefited from what Eric Rouleau has called the " 're-Islamization' of the Turkish state." The reintroduction of religious instruction in the public schools in the eighties and "government funding of 450 imam-hatep religious schools where more than 470,000 adolescents, many future state functionaries, are imbued with Islam; and taxpayer support for the construction of hundreds of new mosques have contributed to the rise of political Islam."[132] In addition, Turkey in the nineties adopted a foreign policy that when convenient, emphasized Islamic solidarity as it attempted to extend its influence in the Central Asian Muslim republics of the former Soviet Union, the Caucasus, and the Balkans.

The reason for the successes of Welfare mayors in many municipalities such as Istanbul and Ankara was widely acknowledged: "Refah Party mayors have offered better services than their predecessors and worked hard to improve public services. They have reduced corruption and nepotism in the municipalities and acted more professionally than other parties of the left and right."[133] The combined track record of many Welfare municipal governments and of the WP workers in neighborhoods brought effective social change and made for a formidable force in electoral politics. At the same time, its support for private enterprise and economic liberalization drew support from small businessmen who had benefited from Ozal's economic policies and resented the state's continued ownership of as much as 60 percent of the financial and manufacturing sector, its failure to curb the powers of big industrialists, and its dependence on European imports. Welfare enjoyed the support of MUSIAD, a Muslim business association founded in 1990 that advocates full liberalization and privatization of the economy. Both WP and MUSIAD support the growth of small to medium-sized businesses informed by Islamic values, strengthening political and economic ties with Muslim countries, and a more independent stance vis à vis the West. Emerging Anatolian businessmen favor an ideology that is socially Islamic but economically liberal. The products of an Islam-centered provincial culture, they found Islamic symbols useful in criticizing an economy long dominated by the state (state ownership) and big industrialists. They were the beneficiaries of economic expansion that resulted from the economic liberalization introduced by Ozal and advocated by Erbakan and Welfare. MUSIAD, like Welfare, opposed entrance into the European Union, feared that unification would favor state intervention and big business, blamed the West (Europe, the United States, and the IMF) for many of its economic problems, and favored instead the creation of an Islamic Common Market.

On December 24, 1995, Welfare won 21 percent of the vote, tripling its performance in 1987, and 150 seats in parliament. It attracted more votes than any other party. Despite their common desire to keep WP out of government, Turkey's secular political leaders (Motherland's Mesut Yilmaz, True Path Party's Tansu Ciller, and Bulen Ecevit) failed to transcend their personal rivalries and animosities and were unable to form a coalition government. Erbakan and the Welfare Party, whose 150 seats constituted the largest party in the 550 National Assembly, came to power in a coalition with former Prime Minister Tansu Ciller's secular, right-wing, True Path Party. Cynics noted the irony of such a political marriage. Ciller had previously warned that if Welfare came to power it would not only drive Turkey back into the Dark Ages but would create an Islamic wave that would sweep across Europe. Popular belief was that Erbakan had won Ciller's support in exchange for a promise not to pursue a parliamentary investigation of corruption charges that had been lodged against her. With Erbakan and the WP coming to power, many secular Turks and many in the West warned of another Iran, Sudan, or Afghanistan. The most secular of Muslim states had its first Islamist prime minister.

Many in Turkey who revered Necmettin Erbakan called him ''hodja,'' a term reserved for honored teachers. Others vilified him as a deceptive, radical Islamic fundamentalist, a wolf in sheep's clothing. A western reporter observed that the new prime minister was ''the most interesting politician to have emerged from the Muslim world in many years. He is cultivated and worldly, a master of subtle political maneuver, yet has slashed his way through the jungle of Turkish politics with fiery oratory about Zionist conspiracies, the decadence of the West and the superiority of Muslim law and culture. He favors elegantly tailored suits and imported silk neckties and prays five times a day."[134]

During Erbakan's brief tenure as prime minister, Welfare encouraged the expanded role of religion in society, increasing the number of schools, religious foundations, businesses, banks, social services, and media. Both secular Muslims and religious minorities such as Turkey's Alevi Muslim minority (perhaps 20 percent of its 98 percent Muslim population), despite the public assurances, were skeptical about the Welfare Party's commitment to pluralism. They questioned whether its redefinition of the state would affect its ability to respect the rights of others, including other (non-Welfare) Muslims, nonbelievers, and religious minorities. Cynics charged that the WP, like the FIS in Algeria, was using the democratic system to come to power in order to dismantle Turkey's democratic and secular state. Indeed, opponents saw little distinction between Welfare and violent groups of religious extremists who struck in the nineties. Secular elites like Ugur Mumcu, an outspoken advocate of secularism and a critic of Islamists, were assassinated. In July 1993, Islamic extremists set fire to a hotel, killing thirty-seven liberal secular writers, journalists, and intellectuals who were attending a conference. Among the conference participants was Aziz Nesin, who had recently been denounced for translating sections of Salman Rushdie's *Satanic Verses*.

In power, Erbakan proved more pragmatic than some had expected. His moderation and flexibility won praise from some but were seen as disingenuous pragmatic accommodations by others. Despite his longtime anti-Western, anti-Zionist rhetoric and his threat to pull out of NATO and wage a jihad for Jerusalem, Erbakan did not pull Turkey out of NATO but did turn to the International Monetary Fund for assistance in addressing Turkey's economic problems. Moreover, at the Welfare Party's first postelection convention, Erbakan declared his friendship for the United States and Europe and described Welfare as "the guarantor of secular rule."[135] Although he did promote greater Islamic solidarity, drawing criticism from secularists and Western powers for his visits to Libya and Iran (visits that his predecessor Tansu Ciller had also made with no public outcry) and for his desire to improve relations with Iraq, Erbakan also honored Turkey's agreements with Israel for military and economic relations despite his anti-Zionist position. As a result, Israeli prime minister Benjamin Netanyahu stated that "today we are very pleased with Mr. Erbakan's government."[136]

Like many other Muslims, secular and Islamist alike, Erbakan remained convinced that the West's relations with the Muslim world were imperialist. He charged that they proceeded from a prejudice that was visible in the foreign policies of the United States and Europe, as witnessed in Bosnia, Kashmir, and Chechnya, where political repression and violation of human rights had been tolerated to a degree that would never have been acceptable in the Christian West. Similarly, he noted that despite Turkey's centuries-long presence in Europe and its forty-year membership in NATO, the European Union has resisted its entry. Former prime minister Ozal had assessed the situation bluntly: "Why are we not in the European Community? . . . The answer is simple. You are Christians and we are Muslims."[137] (Both overlooked additional factors such as EUs criticisms of Turkey's human rights record and the Kurdish conflict.)

Predictably, Erbakan's biggest obstacle proved to be the military. Turkey's military has a long history of influence and intervention in domestic politics. As I have previously noted, the military left its "barracks" to seize power in 1960–61, 1971–73 and 1980–83. Staunch secularists (some might say militant secularists) with a low opinion of Turkey's politicians, they have consistently defended Kemalism and have reacted allergically to any form of religion in public life, from the right of female students to wear a headscarf (hejab) to Islamist politics. Among the justifications for previous coups was the charge that the government had betrayed Ataturk's principle of secularism. The military took every occasion to signal concern about any compromise of Turkey's secular principles. They instituted a new purge of officers suspected of being Islamists. (Grounds could be the fact that an officer's wife wore a headscarf or that he prayed at a mosque.) When the Iranian ambassador called for implementation of the Sharia in Turkey, tanks were sent through the streets of the city, Sincan, a suburb of Ankara and a Welfare Party stronghold, where the statement was made. The military kept up its pressure. In spring 1997, it presented the Erbakan government with a set of eighteen demands that were designed to stem an Islamist threat to the secular state. These included restrictions on wearing Islamic dress, measures to prevent Islamists from entering the military or government administration, and a mandate to close the imam-hatep religious schools, which it believed taught religious propaganda and served as a training ground for Islamists. At the same time, the military demanded that compulsory secular education be increased from five to eight years. These concerns seemed ironic, since the schools were established and funded by the government and were subject to state regulation and inspection. In April, General Cevik Bir publicly declared that the military's top priority, more important than its ten-year battle with Kurdish separatism, was the struggle against antisecular Islamists.[138]

Erbakan and the Welfare Party's brief government proved to be a lightening rod for militant secularists, contributing to the polarization of society. Erbakan moderated his rhetoric and previous positions and accommodated the military to the extent that many in his party believed his compromises had undermined the identity, message, and credibility of Welfare. This mattered little to Turkey's radical secularists (much of the military, civil service, and intelligentsia), whose secularism was not simply based on a belief in the separation of religion and the state but rather on an antireligious secular ideology or belief system that was as rigid, militant, and intolerant as it believed "Islamic fundamentalism" to be. The fears and charges of radical secularists led some to observe that "there is a neurotic edge to the way many secularists talk about the awkward, rather earnest, just-up-from-the-country sort of people who make up most of Mr. Erbakan's following."[139] As in Algeria, the secularist establishment was willing to compromise Turkey's commitment to democracy in order to prevent Islamists from participating in politics and society. They would rather preserve their power, privilege, and life-style than allow voters to choose through free and open elections. They were unwilling to take the risk that democracy always involves, a risk that some leading Turkish secularists had believed was necessary if democracy was to prevail:

> A marriage between Islam and democracy in Turkey can be consummated if the radical secularists stop trying to impose their preferred life-style and set of values upon the Islamists, and if the latter do not attempt to undermine by word or deed the basic tenets of the secular democratic state in Turkey. A critical mediating role can be played by moderate secularists whose numbers are on the increase.[140]

In many ways, the military and radical secularist intellectuals remained true to an earlier pattern. As Adnan Adiver noted in the early fifties, "The domination of Western thought, or rather of the positivism of the West, was at times so intense that one can hardly call it thought. It should be termed the 'official dogma of irreligion.'"[141] More recently, Ayse Kadiogl commented that the Republican elite, the political offspring and disciples of Ataturk, were moved by a "disgust" toward religion even if they sometimes resorted to religious symbols, paying lip service to religion.[142] Sherif Mardin's comparison of this Kemalist attitude to Voltaire's hatred of the church goes a long way toward illuminating the source and living legacy of militant secularism in Turkey.[143]

Erbakan and the Welfare Party had to contend with increased pressure from the military, no-confidence votes in parliament, and in May 1997 a petition to the Constitutional Court by Turkey's chief prosecutor to ban Welfare for violating the Turkish constitution's articles on secularism and pushing the country towards civil war. The military intensified its campaign in June, conducting briefings for judges, attorneys, and the media on the Islamist threat to the Turkish state. The Erbakan-Ciller coalition finally collapsed when it lost its parliamentary majority as several of Ciller's DYP members resigned. Erbakan submitted his resignation on June 18, 1997. President Demirel asked Mesut Yimaz of the Motherland Party to form a new government. On February 28, 1998, Turkey's Constitutional Court issued an order that banned Welfare. Welfare's assets were seized, and Erbakan was expelled from parliament and barred from participating in the political process for five years. He and a number of other leaders were tried for sedition. In February 1998 a new law was passed requiring that children complete eight years of secular education before being permitted to take Quran classes. Weekend and summer Quran courses were banned. Female students and teachers in Islamic schools were barred from wearing the hejab, extending a ban that already existed in all other areas of education and in government departments.

In 1998, former Welfare Party members and supporters regrouped and formed the Virtue (Fazilet) Party (VP), the unofficial successor to Welfare. Erbakan was banned from politics, but he managed to have his old friend Recai Kutan named head of the party, thus preventing younger reformists led by Tayyip Erdogan, the popular and effective mayor of Istanbul, from taking charge. The new party emphasized that it was not simply a clone of Welfare. Virtue was to be a more open party (in terms of membership and ideology) which was demonstrated in several ways. It sought to soften its Islamist image and not appear as simply an Islamist party, emphasizing instead that it was a political party that respected Turkey's Islamic traditions and culture. In this spirit it named three women (two of whom do not wear the hejab and are not known to be Islamist) to Virtue's executive board. Nazli Ilicak, a journalist and board member, stated that she did not believe that Virtue had an Islamist agenda; rather, it was a conservative party that respected the religious beliefs of the Turkish people. Abdullah Gul, who had served as state minister in the Welfare government, signaled a departure from Welfare's foreign policy, declaring that the Virtue Party favored full integration with the West to assure democracy and civilian rule.

Ataturk created and shaped modern Turkey as a secular state, the only totally secular state in the Middle East. After Ataturk died, political realities produced a more fluid situation in which Islam and Muslim identity became more visible in Turkish politics and were used at various times by the military and the government to counter communism or to reinforce morality. At the same time, Islam remained strong in nonurban areas (the majority of the country) and in popular piety. In the past two decades, Turkey has witnessed the progressive growth and impact of political Islam, culminating in the electoral successes of the Welfare Party. The emergence of Welfare as a key political player precipitated a cultural and a political crisis pitting secular elites against Islamists. As Hakan Yavuz has observed, "Because secularism did not separate religion and politics, but rather subordinated religion to the political realm, it promoted the politicization of Islam and struggle between secularists and Muslims for control of the state."[144] During Welfare's brief period in power, the thrust of its agenda was not political but socioeconomic. It imposed not an Islamic state but a "just order" that was understood to include the creation of a more just and equitable society, and an end to blatant corruption and nepotism. For this reason the Welfare Party was able to attract voters who did not have a high degree of Islamic orientation. Welfare, like many other Islamic organizations, sought a more pluralistic state. It sought to create a space alongside the Kemalist Westernized secular model in which people could live their lives in accordance with their Islamic culture and values within the Turkish secular state. For many in the establishment, such a course endangered Turkish secularism. Given their militant secularism rooted in a nineteenth-century rationalism, they viewed the recourse to religion as retrogressive and antimodern, a retreat to the Dark Ages and a threat to their power and life-style.

The suppression of the Welfare Party and attempts to restrict other religious organizations and activities threatened to further polarize Turkish society and ended, at least temporarily, an experiment that had broader implications. Many had hoped that if "Erbakan can peacefully safely steer moderate, democratic Turkey onto a fundamentalist path, he could, in effect, make the rest of the Muslim world safe for fundamentalism."[145]

Conclusion

The varieties of Islamic activist groups and experiences are a testimony to the flexibility of Islam, and political Islam in particular. They illustrate the extent to which specific contexts, differences of political economy, Islam's capability of multiple and varied interpretations, and the distinctive personalities and ambitions of its leaders or ideologues shape the ideology and strategy of Islamic movements. This diversity underscores the problem of terminology, the extent to which facile labels can become an obstacle to understanding. How does one encompass in one term (revivalism, fundamentalism, militant Islam) the meanings and usages of Islam by rulers (Qaddafi, Khomeini, Zia ul-Haq, Nimeiri) and Islamic organizations, their differing attitudes toward and relationships with the West, as well as the diversity of strategies and goals employed by mainstream activists versus violent radical revolutionaries? Islamic politics must be viewed within specific country contexts: far from being a monolithic reality, it manifests a rich diversity of leaders and forms.

A second obstacle in assessing the future impact of Islamic movements—including the extent to which they will be a challenge or a threat—is their lack of a well-developed political agenda. Theoretical or ideological statements are often not accompanied by specific models for change. Islamic movements tend to be more specific about what they are against than what they are for. While all may speak of an Islamic order or state, of implementation of the Sharia, of a society grounded more firmly on Islamic values, the details are often vague. This has been true for older movements such as Egypt's Muslim Brotherhood as well as for more recent groups. After the electoral victory of Algeria's FIS (Islamic Salvation Front), when Abbasi Madani was questioned about his program, he described it as broad. When pressed for its practical steps, he replied, "Our practical program is also broad." Similar experiences are true for other Islamic movements. Though many speak of Islamic government, they differ in their understanding of its nature, speaking about a variety of forms—a caliphate, consultative government and a strong executive, or a multiparty system—but do not go beyond this. Most activist leaders admit that, should they gain power, they would lack personnel, paradigms or models (political, economic, legal), and experience. Realizing their current unpreparedness to govern, some are more comfortable in the opposition or in parliament. Their critics—Muslim governments and Western policymakers—often seize upon this failure to be specific. Ironically, many critics argue that the extent to which movements represent only a minority of the population and have no real program dooms them to failure. Yet none seems willing to provide them with the opportunity to discredit themselves. Instead, despite fits of democratic rhetoric, political liberalization and democratization have been placed on hold or subverted, while Western governments are generally content to look the other way.

At the micro level, Islamic organizations have been successful in responding concretely to people's problems. Their Islamic ideologies offer a framework for meaning and purpose that responds to issues of identity, faith, and authenticity. As social movements they respond to the needs of many by providing educational and social welfare services. Islamic movements may at times be antiforeign, but seldom antimodern. Social gains have been accompanied by successes in the political arena as well. The Islamic movement has bridged the mythical divide between religion and secular modernization in the cities and towns of the more advanced countries of the Muslim world: Iran, Egypt, Lebanon, and Tunisia.

Islamic organizations often enjoy an impact disproportionate to their actual size and numbers. They have features that few political parties are able to match. They are well organized, disciplined, and highly motivated. While some advocate violence and engage in terrorism, many today, if given the opportunity, participate within the political system. Many exemplify a high degree of integrity and self-sacrifice, have a clear sense of purpose and commitment, foster a sense of certitude and God-ordained mission. Activist organizations prove especially attractive because they offer an indigenously based and religiously legitimated alternative. They exude a strong sense of self-confidence and identity to those who are dissatisfied and disillusioned, who experience their governments and society as inadequate, corrupt, and incapable of responding to their people's political and socioeconomic needs. Islamic organizations and parties have proven especially successful where failed economics, unemployed and disaffected youth, and repressive governments make them effective critics of regimes. Their voices for political liberalization and social change often represent the only credible alternative to the government. The electoral record of Islamic organizations and their emergence as the major opposition in Egypt, Algeria, Tunisia, and Jordan illustrate this reality.

Despite stereotypes of activists as fanatics who wish to retreat to the past, the vast majority share a common call for the transformation of society not through a blind return to seventh-century Medina but a response to the present. They do not seek to reproduce the past but to reconstruct society through a process of Islamic reform in which the principles of Islam are applied to contemporary needs. Each speaks of a comprehensive reformation or revolution, the creation of an Islamic order and state, since they regard Islam as comprehensive in scope, a faith-informed way of life.

The modern nation-state is seen as in collapse; modern society is often described as in disorder (*fitna*). Why? Both the West and the traditional religious establishment (coopted preachers of a static Islam) are denounced as the culprits. They especially blame Western models of development and Westernized ruling elites—what Rashid Ghannoushi has called the "dictatorship of the ruling elite minority." A tyranny of the few over the many has led to political and economic dependence on the West and loss of cultural identity. All activist movements advocate a process of resocialization or re-Islamization of the individual (greater religious education and awareness) and mobilization of the community's political, economic, and administrative systems. The process is one of *dawa* and jihad, the call to be more self-consciously Islamic and the struggle to implement Islam in personal life and in state and society.

Despite their critique of the nation-state, most Islamic movements today, like most Muslims, accept its reality, but within the broader context of Islamic universalism they look toward the *ummah*. Like early Islamic modernists such as Abduh and Iqbal, they believe national reform is not contrary to, but a necessary step in and part of, the reconstitution of Islamic universalism. All advocate independence from the West and the East politically, economically, and culturally. However, they vary in their posture toward the West. Some, such as Hizbullah and many of the followers of the Ayatollah Khomeini, have totally rejected the West. Others like Egypt's Muslim Brotherhood, AMAL, and the Renaissance Party do not preclude relations with or selective borrowing from the West.

Most movements have increasingly taken great care to identify themselves with the disinherited or oppressed (*mustadhafin*) and emphasize issues of social justice. The socioeconomic situations in their own countries as well as the Iranian example have been formative influences. The plight of the poor, the condemnation of corruption, disparities of class and wealth, and the failure of the economy in general, whether it be capitalism or state socialism, are important to their populist messages.

In recent years most Islamic movements have moved toward a populist, participatory, pluralistic political stance, championing democratization, human rights, and economic reform. While many were critical of "democracy" in the past, they claim that this was a response to the secularism of the modern state as well as the autocratic nature of Muslim regimes. To varying degrees in recent years, most Islamic movements have emphasized change not through violence (which many now view as counterproductive) but through the political and social transformation of society. They speak of the need to prepare people for an Islamic order rather than to impose it. They seek recognition of political rights and participation in the electoral process. Yet there are differences within. Abdessalem Yassine and Algeria's Abbasi Madani have been slower than Ghannoushi to recognize multiparty politics and the democratic process. Moreover, the history of Islamic movements in Egypt, Algeria, and Tunisia has shown that, where regimes deny political participation or suppress movements, state violence often begets violence. As the recent examples of the Renaissance Party and FIS demonstrate, there are diverse tendencies within Islamic movements, state repression and violence—suppression of demonstrations, denial of free and fair elections, arrests, imprisonment, torture—exacerbate differences, threaten to divide organizations, and often result in violent responses in what is regarded as legitimate self-defense against state oppression.

Just as the political economies and national experiences (from policies of cooptation and accommodation to violence and repression) of Muslim countries vary, determining the differing relations between governments and Islamic organizations, so too differences in ideological orientation and strategy exist within Islamic movements. All major Islamic leaders or ideologues and movements have emphasized and been influenced by belief in the need to construct their own solutions to their specific contexts and local problems. There are many such organizations; equally important, within each movement—the Renaissance Party and FIS, for example—there are different currents of thought. Madani's comment, "There is diversity in FIS but it is united," has been echoed by Ghannoushi. This diversity extends to attitudes toward modernization, militancy, the West, democratization and pluralism, the role of women, and most recently, the Gulf War and the use of force in domestic politics. Just as MTI experienced the defection of the Progressivists in the past, so too Ghannoushi and many other party members differed regarding support for Iraq during the Gulf War. Ghannoushi and some other Renaissance Party leaders, in particular Abdelfattah Mourou, split over tactics (in particular the use of violence) in responding to government repressions. In Algeria's FIS, Madani and Ali Benhadj differed sharply in their public statements about democracy. Moreover, Madani's statement—"There is no other way at present . . . the way to power is elections which are decided through the popular will of the people"[110]—does not answer those who wonder whether the espousal of democracy by Islamic movements is a pragmatic, tactical accommodation or a principled position. Of course the same could be said as well for many incumbent Muslim governments and secular elites that advocate political liberalization and democracy.

6

Islam and the West: A Clash of Civilizations?

> Islam and Christian Europe have sporadically been at war since the time of the Crusades . . . There are people (on our side and on theirs) who want to turn this into a holy war between two civilizations—as if that could produce anything but death, or lasting misery, for millions.[1]
>
> —WILLIAM PFAFF

Fear often issues in the demonization of an enemy or threat. For decades, international relations were conducted within the context of a superpower rivalry, between East and West, the Soviet Union and the United States. In the post–Cold War period, many who seek new demons warn of an Islamic threat to Western civilization or of an impending clash of civilizations. Increasingly, voices in America and Europe proclaim, "The Muslims are coming, the Muslims are coming!"[2] not only as a political but also as a demographic threat. Similar attitudes lay behind the initial response of those experts who saw the Oklahoma bombing as the handiwork of Middle East terrorists or Islamic fundamentalists. What is the source of such fears? Writing in the early eighties, Edward Said observed:

> For the general public in America and Europe today, Islam is "news" of a particularly unpleasant sort. The media, the government, the geopolitical strategists, and—although they are marginal to the culture at large—the academic experts on Islam are all in concert: Islam is a threat to western civilization. Now this is by no means the same as saying that only derogatory or racist caricatures of Islam are to be found in the West. . . . What I am saying is that negative images of Islam are very much more prevalent

212

than any others, and that such images correspond not with what Islam "is" ... but to what prominent sectors of a particular society take it to be: Islam and the West: A Clash of Civilizations? Those sectors have the power and the will to propagate that particular image of Islam, and this image therefore becomes more prevalent, more present, than all others.[3]

Political events in the Muslim world and the West, as well as statements by government leaders and prominent opinion and policymakers, continued in the eighties to perpetuate notions of an Islamic threat and a clash of civilizations. During the Bush administration, the vice president of the United States (Dan Quayle) spoke of the danger of radical Islamic fundamentalism, associating it with Nazism and communism. Magazines and newspaper editorials spoke of Islam's war with the West and its incompatibility with democracy; a respected national newspaper ran a series on Islam whose general tenor was captured by the title of its introductory piece, "The Sword of Islam." It was often difficult to know where reality ended and mythmaking began.[4]

The problem persists in the nineties. Fears of radical Islam, its threat to the Middle East and to the West, loom large: that the Islamic republics of Iran and Sudan collaborate as major exporters of terrorism and revolution, that Islamists are out to "hijack democracy" through participation in elections in countries like Algeria, and that fundamentalist terrorism has been exported to new battlegrounds, America and Europe. In an effort to counter a reputed international fundamentalist network, the Clinton administration announced a freeze on all U.S. assets belonging to some thirty organizations and individuals believed to have ties to Islamic militants overseas. Newt Gingrich, Speaker of the House of Representatives, declared: "There is a worldwide phenomenon of Islamic totalitarianism funded and largely directed by the state of Iran."[5]

The bombing of New York's World Trade Center in March 1993 rekindled fears of a global "fundamentalist" holy war now exported to America. For the first time, the wrath of the Islamic threat had been brought to the shores of the "Great Satan." Charges flew that radical Muslim fundamentalists, with bases in the United States and Europe and international support from Iran and Sudan, were linked to Shaykh Umar Abd Al-Rahman, a blind Egyptian cleric who had been tried but acquitted for alleged involvement in the assassination fo Anwar Sadat. The hijacking of an Air France jetliner (December 24, 1994) by Algerian extremists and the report that they planned to blow it up over Paris reinforced fears of a domestic Islamic threat, poised to overrun Europe.

Belief in an impending clash between the Muslim world and the West was reflected in America and Europe by headlines such as "A Holy War

Heads Our Way," "Jihad in America," "Focus: Islamic Terror: Global Suicide Squad," "I Believe in Islamaphobia," "Algerians in London Fund Islamic Terrorism," and "France Back on the Rack," in which the author observed in the wake of the Air France hijacking:

> Nowhere more than there [Algeria] does political Islam now appear, in Western eyes, as the new villain, successor to communism and the evil empire; nowhere more than there do Islamists themselves, or their extreme factions, deem themselves so viscerally, so genetically, at war with another civilization—that of the unbeliever, the Crusader, the Jew. . . . Yet it only dramatizes what is already known, that the deepening Algerian crisis is likely to spill over into Europe, and France first of all, more disruptively than Palestine ever has, and that it poses a moral and political dilemma of an excruciating, all-but-insoluble, kind.[6]

There are lessons to be learned from the Cold War. Celebration of the unraveling of communism and the victory of democracy has been tempered by questions that go to the heart of our ability to understand, analyze, and formulate policy. Delight at the triumph of democracy was accompanied by a growing realization of the extent to which fear and the demonization of the enemy blinded many to the true condition and extent of the Soviet threat. Viewing the Soviet Union through the prism of the "evil empire" was ideologically reassuring and emotionally satisfying, justifying the expenditure of enormous resources and the support of a vast military-industrial complex. However, our easy stereotypes of the enemy and the monolithic nature of the communist threat also proved costly in other respects. Despite an enormous amount of intelligence and analysis, few seemed to know until the end that the emperor had no clothes. Neither government agencies nor academic think tanks predicted the extent and speed of the disintegration of the Soviet empire. The exaggerated fears and static vision that drove us to take Herculean steps against a monolithic enemy blinded us to the diversity within the Soviet Union and the profound changes that were taking place.

In understanding and responding to events in the Muslim world, we are again challenged to resist easy stereotypes and solutions. There is an easy path and a hard path. The easy path is to view Islam and Islamic revivalism as a threat—to posit a global Pan-Islamic threat, monolithic in nature, a historic enemy whose faith and agenda are diametrically opposed to that of the West. This attitude leads to support for secular regimes at almost any cost (regardless of how repressive) rather than risk an Islamically oriented government's coming to power.

The more difficult path is to move beyond facile stereotypes and ready-made images and answers. Just as perceiving the Soviet Union and Eastern Europe through the prism of the "evil empire" had its costs, so too does the tendency of governments and the media to equate Islam and Islamic fundamentalism with radicalism, terrorism, and anti-Westernism seriously hamper our understanding and condition our responses. As Patrick Bannerman, a former diplomat and analyst for the British Foreign Office, observed in his *Islam in Perspective*, "How non-Muslims think of Islam conditions the manner in which they deal with Muslims, which in turn conditions how Muslims think of and deal with non-Muslims."[7] The challenge today is to appreciate the diversity of Islamic actors and movements, to ascertain the causes or reasons behind confrontations and conflicts, and thus to respond to specific events and situations with informed, reasoned responses rather than predetermined presumptions and reactions.

In the post-Gulf War period, the effort to articulate a New World Order has come up against an inability to move beyond the stereotypes and biases of the past. Exhilaration over the prospect of democratization in Eastern Europe contrasted sharply with the fear or at best silence of many in the West at the prospect of similar demands by Islamic populist movements in the Arab and broader Muslim world. The failure to speak out forcefully for political participation and democratization in the Middle East and to condemn indiscriminate government repression against Islamic movements in Egypt, Algeria, Turkey, and Tunisia in effect denies Islamic activists the same rights to political participation and human rights accorded to other citizens and raises serious questions about such a selective approach to democratization. At the heart of this selective approach is the tendency to define stability in Muslim countries in terms of support for the status quo, however much it may contradict democratic values of self-determination, political participation, and human rights.

The easy excuse for looking the other way and continuing to support autocratic Middle Eastern regimes is the claim that Islam is antidemocratic or that Islam or Arab culture is not conducive to democratization and modernity.[8] Ironically, a similar concern and policy were not adapted with regard to the Soviet Union and Eastern Europe. Is it because the peoples of Eastern Europe and the Soviet Union, steeped in decades of communist rule and socialization, are somehow less prone to authoritarianism? Or because we believe that a shared Judeo-Christian cultural tradition, with the West provided a more accommodating ideological soil, is inherently more democratic? Are we still being held back by the baggage of the past? A combination of ignorance and stereotyping, history and experience as well as religiocultural chauvinism often blind even the best intentioned when dealing with the Arab and Muslim world. Of course, the same could be said about the monolithic approach of many Muslims to the West and a tendency to blame all their problems on Europe or America. The result is a mutual tendency to regard each other as a threat; belief in an impending confrontation or clash of civilizations can be found among many in the Muslim world as well as in the West.

As we have seen, though Islam is the second largest of the world's religions and the Judeo-Christian tradition has strong historic and theological links with Islam, the history of Jewish-Christian-Muslim relations has been more one of competition and combat than dialogue and mutual understanding, driven by competing theological claims and political interests. The confrontations and conflicts have spanned the ages and have reinforced images of a historic and global militant Islamic threat: the early Muslim expansion and conquests; the Crusades and the fall of Jerusalem; Ottoman Muslim hegemony over Eastern Europe, and with the siege of Vienna, its threat to overrun the West; the great jihads against European colonial rule; the Arab-Israeli wars, the economic threat of oil embargoes; Iran's humiliation of an "America held hostage" and its threat to export its revolution; media images of despots (Qaddafi, Khomeini, and Saddam Hussein) wielding an Islamic sword and calling upon frenzied faithful to rise up against the West; and the specter of radical revolutionary groups seizing Western hostages, hijacking planes, and inaugurating a reign of wanton terrorism. Death threats against author Salman Rushdie, the attempted assassination of Egypt's Nobel laureate, Naguib Mahfouz, and the killing of intellectuals by extremists in Algeria reinforce images of an intolerant and dangerous Islam.[9]

Saddam Hussein's call for the world's Muslims to rise up and wage holy war against Western Crusaders during the Gulf War of 1990–91 was a chilling reminder of the Ayatollah Khomeini's threat to export Iran's Islamic Revolution. It confirmed fears of a militant, confrontational Islamic threat or war against the West. The support that Saddam enjoyed from leaders of Islamic movements in Algeria, Tunisia, the Sudan, and Pakistan reinforced the arguments of those who view Islam and the Muslim world as on a collision path with Western priorities and interests.[10]

Despite predictions by some experts that the political phenomenon identified as "Islamic fundamentalism" was a spent force,[11] the continued vitality of Islamic revivalism/activism could be seen in the streets and in the polling booths from North Africa to Southeast Asia. This vision can reinforce the understanding of Islam's political challenge as a threat. In the aftermath of the triumph of the Islamic Salvation Front in Algeria's municipal elections (and its subsequent sweep of national parliamentary elections), similar fears surfaced in other North African countries and Europe:

> Across North Africa and especially in Tunisia and Morocco, leaders are anxiously waiting for further shock waves in the politicization of Islam, where banned fundamentalist movements threaten the status quo. There are

similar fears in France, Belgium, Italy and Spain which have over 2 million Algerians. Meanwhile the victory of the fundamentalists is alienating foreign investors, who equate Islam with political and economic risk.[12]

The West (the media in particular) equates Islam with danger or threat when it views the Islamic world through slogans or epithets like "militant Islam," "Islamic fundamentalism," "Islamic terrorism," and "Islamic Bomb." At the same time, our selective memory blocks our ability to appreciate the other side of the equation—the sources of Muslim images of the West itself as the "real" threat to them. Many in the Arab and Muslim world see the history of Islam and the Muslim world's dealings with the West as one of victimization and oppression at the hands of an expansive imperial power. They counter that "militant Christianity" and "militant Judaism" are the root causes of failed Muslim societies and instability: the aggression and intolerance of the Christian-initiated Crusades and Inquisition; European colonialism; the breakup of the Ottoman empire and artificial creation of modern states in Iraq, Lebanon, Syria, Transjordan, Palestine; the establishment of Israel; Israel's occupation of the West Bank and Gaza and its invasion and occupation of Lebanon; the role played by oil interests in maintaining support for autocratic regimes.

The realities of colonialism and imperialism, forgotten or conveniently overlooked by many in the West, are part of the living legacy, firmly implanted in the memory (however exaggerated at times) of many in the Muslim world. As the Iranian Revolution demonstrated, several decades did not erase the memories and humiliation of imperial intervention: the willingness of the Soviet Union to invade a "neutral" Iran in 1941; the British and Soviets forcing Reza Shah to abdicate in favor of his son, Muhammad Reza Shah; and U.S. intervention in Iranian politics in the early fifties. The democratically elected government of Prime Minister Mossadegh was removed after a media campaign that depicted him as procommunist, and the Shah was returned from exile in Italy to Teheran, an action that served Britain's imperial interests. In recent years the memories of centuries of Western hegemony, followed by continued dependence upon the West, have left deep scars and resentments that become both easy excuses for societal failures and combustible materials in Muslim politics. If there is an Islamic threat, many Arabs and Muslims believe there has also been a Western threat—of political, economic, and religiocultural imperialism, a political occupation accompanied by cultural invasion. As a result many in the Muslim world, like their counterparts in the West, opt for easy anti-imperialist slogans and demonization. At its worst, both sides have engaged in a process of "mutual satanization."[13]

The Islamic Threat Today

Fear of Islam is not new. The tendency to judge the actions of Muslims in isolation, to generalize from the actions of the few to the many, to disregard similar excesses committed in the name of other religions and ideologies (including freedom and democracy) is also not new.

At times it seems that the West's attitude toward communism is being transferred to or replicated in the elevation of a new threat, "Islamic fundamentalism."[14] In the nineties, this polarization is expressed by many governments in the Muslim world, Israel, and the West, as well as by the media and many political analysts, as they conclude, without regard to the diversity of Islamic organizations and specific social contexts, that "Islamic fundamentalism" is inherently a major global threat.[15]

Cognizant of a Western tendency to see Islam as a threat, many Muslim governments use the danger of Islamic radicalism or terrorism (equated with Islamic fundamentalism, Islamism, political Islam) as an excuse to control or suppress Islamic movements. They fan the fears of a monolithic Islamic radicalism both at home and in the West. Just as in the past many used anticommunism to excuse authoritarian rule and to win the support of Western powers. Banning Islamic organizations, imprisoning activists, and violating human rights are justified with the the same excuse: "We are facing young fanatics threatening our future."[16] Western stereotypes of a united, worldwide fundamentalist movement are exploited by Arab diplomats from states with strong Western ties, who declare: "Fundamentalism is international in scope. It has branches everywhere. . . . Fundamentalist expansion will eventually threaten the industrial nations when most Arab countries have been destabilized."[17] Whatever their differences, the concerns of some Arab and Muslim governments have found a ready ally in the leadership of Israel. Prime Minister Yitzak Rabin has said that "the Arab world, and the world in general, will pay if the cancer of radical fundamentalist Islam is not halted at the academy of Khomeini and his followers in Iran."[18] Similar arguments were put forth by Serbian leaders in Bosnia and Kosovo and by Russians in their war with Chechnya.

Focusing on radicalism and equating Islam with an extremism that threatens the West have become common in government and in the media. A selective (crises-oriented and headline-driven) analysis of Islam and events in the Muslim world by prominent scholars and political commentators too often informs articles and editorials on the Muslim world. Among them, "Don't Look for Moderates in the Islamist Revolution,"[19] "A Holy War Heads Our Way,"[20] "Clash of Cultures: Rise of Islam in France Rattles the Populace and Stirs a Backlash"[21] "Focus: Islamic Terror: Global Suicide Squad"[22] "American Jihad,"[23] "Algerians in London

Fund Islamic Terrorism,"[24] "Prince Charles Is Wrong—Islam Does Menace the West."[25]

A sensationalized monolithic approach reinforces facile generalizations and stereotypes instead of challenging our understanding of the "who" and the "why" of history, the causes or reasons behind the headlines. This selective analysis fails to tell the whole story; to provide the full context for Muslim attitudes, events, actions: and to account for the diversity of Muslim practice. Although it sheds some light, it is a partial light that obscures or distorts the full picture. As a result, Islam and Islamic revivalism are easily reduced to stereotypes of Islam against the West, Islam's war with modernity, or Muslim rage, extremism, fanaticism, and terrorism. Fundamentalism and terrorism have become inextricably linked in the minds of many. Selective (and therefore biased) analysis adds to our ignorance instead of our knowledge, narrows our perspective instead of broadening our understanding, and reinforces the problem instead of opening the way to new solutions. It contributes to a climate in which not simply dismissing Islamic activism is viewed as being biased or sympathetic toward the enemy, as communism was viewed in the McCarthy era.

Islam Against the West

According to many Western commentators, Islam and the West are on a collision course. Islam is a triple threat: political, civilizational, and demographic. The confrontation is often portrayed as a clash of civilizations. Two pieces have been particularly influential: Bernard Lewis's "The Roots of Muslim Rage" and Samuel P. Huntington's "The Clash of Civilizations."[26] Both have been seminal in defining the parameters of a debate that has gripped diplomats, policymakers, journalists, and academic analysts.

The image of Islam and Muslims as menacing militant fundamentalists was presented strikingly in Bernard Lewis's "Islamic Fundamentalism," which originated as the prestigious Jefferson Lecture of 1990, the highest honor accorded by the U.S. government to a scholar for achievement in the humanities. A revised version of the lecture, "The Roots of Muslim Rage," became the lead article in *Atlantic Monthly*. The packaging (new title, the magazine's cover, and the article's two illustrations) of "The Roots of Muslim Rage," exemplifies the pitfalls of a selective presentation. It reinforces stereotypes of Muslims and Islamic fundamentalism and predisposes the reader to view the relationship of Islam to the West in terms of rage, violence, hatred, and irrationality. Because of Lewis's international stature as a scholar and political commentator on the Middle East, his topic, and its prominent public platform, "The Roots of Muslim

Rage'' received widespread coverage nationally and internationally. It has had a significant impact both on Western perceptions of contemporary Islam and on Muslim perceptions of how Islam and Muslims are viewed in the West.

The message and impact of the title ''The Roots of Muslim Rage'' was reinforced by the front cover of *Atlantic Monthly*, which portrayed a scowling, bearded, turbaned Muslim with American flags in his glaring eyes. The threat motif and confrontation tone were supplemented by the two illustrations that accompanied the article, ostensibly presenting ''the'' Muslim perception of America as the enemy. The first was a serpent marked with stars and stripes seen crossing a desert (America's dominance of or threat to the Arab world); the second illustration showed the serpent poised behind an unsuspecting pious Muslim at prayer as if to attack. These illustrations perpetuated sensationalist stereotypes and were meant to provoke the reader and reinforce a myopic vision of reality. Muslims are attired in ''traditional'' dress, bearded and turbaned, despite the fact that most Muslims (and most ''fundamentalists'') do not dress in this way. This image portrays Islamic activists as ''medieval'' in life-style and mentality.

The title ''The Roots of Muslim Rage'' sets a tone and an expectation. Would we tolerate similar generalizations in analyzing and explaining Western activities and motives? Do we see articles that speak of Christian rage or Jewish rage? In a similar vein, the nuclear capability of Muslim countries such as Pakistan has often been spoken of in terms of an ''Islamic bomb'' rather than a Pakistani bomb, implying the existence of a monolithic Muslim world threatening Israel and the West. Do we expect Israel's or America's nuclear capabilities to be described in terms of a Jewish or a Christian bomb? Some Muslims have described Israeli bombings of Beirut in the eighties as ''Jewish boys dropping Christian bombs''—a description that most in the West would find offensive and inaccurate.

There is a lesson to be learned from the failure of the talented analysts who continued to warn of the dangers of a monolithic communist threat while the Soviet Union was in fact an economic basket case, breaking apart from within. Partial analysis that reinforces comfortable stereotypes and Western secular presuppositions must be transcended, if we are to avoid the ideological pitfalls and biases of a political analysis driven by an exaggerated threat factor.

The vision of an impending conflict between Islam and the West as but another stage in a historic (if not inevitable) pattern of confrontation is reinforced by Bernard Lewis:

The struggle between Islam and the West has now lasted fourteen centuries. It has consisted of [rather than included] a long series of attacks and counterattacks, jihads and crusades, conquests and reconquests. Today much of the Muslim world is again seized by an intense—and violent—resentment of the West. Suddenly, America had become the archenemy, the incarnation of evil, the diabolic opponent of all that is good, and specifically, for Muslims, of Islam. Why?[27]

Islam and Muslims are here portrayed as the instigators and protagonists in fourteen centuries of warfare. Islam is the aggressor. Islam and the acts of Muslims are held responsible for attacks, jihads, and conquests, whereas the West is described as defensive, responding with counterattacks, crusades, and reconquests. Despite the claim of fourteen continuous centuries of confrontation, the reader is informed that "suddenly" America has become the archenemy, evil personified, and so forth. If the contemporary threat is "sudden," then the reader will logically conclude that Muslims have a historic propensity to violence against and hatred for the West, or else that Muslims are emotional, irrational, and prone to war.

Most discussion of the "Islamic threat" or the roots of "Muslim rage" includes a surprising dearth of information and lack of discrimination concerning the nature and diversity of the Islamic resurgence. In "The Roots of Muslim Rage" Lewis explains the roots of Muslim rage but does not identify these angry Muslims and fails to recognize that Islamic organizations or activists, although sharing a general ideological commitment, differ among themselves. He gives little mention to specific organizations and includes scant discussion of the education, social backgrounds, and activities (other than violence and terrorism) of their members. Thus there is little to contradict the stereotype of strange, backward-looking figures from another age. The reader never learns why Islamic activism presents an attractive option for many educated Muslims. The predominant picture presented is that of radicalized, marginalized, and often violent revolutionaries, traditional in dress and at war with modernity. As an Israeli commentator remarked, "No matter how bad communism was, it was never a step back into the early Middle Ages, and what is hard to see is how democracies of the 21st century will be able to live in peace with forces determined to prove that the last thousand years did not happen."[28] Such descriptions prevent readers from realizing that the majority of so-called fundamentalist organizations functioned effectively within the political system because they are urban-based, led by well-educated leaders who attract students and educated followers, are well placed in the professions (engineering, science, medicine, law, education, the military), and organizations provide social and medical services.

The selective approach of most analyses of Islamic activism omits, downplays, or dismisses the reasons given by activists (and indeed many Arabs and Muslims) for their criticism and rejection of the West: imperialism, America's tilt toward Israel, Western governments' support for oppressive regimes (the Shah's Iran, Tunisia, Nimeiri's Sudan, Lebanon). The reader is never challenged to consider the reasons behind the attitudes and actions of activists rather than simply dismiss them as the product of a clash of civilizations or a blind, irrational clinging to faith.

Visions of Pan-Islam

The past and present fear of a monolithic Islamic threat has often been expressed in Pan-Islamic terminology. Triumphalist colonial Europe "saw all resistance to its domination as a sinister conspiracy. Such a plot could only be inspired by a cruel, Machiavellian spirit. . . . Whenever there was any show of anti-imperialism, even if it was a purely local reaction, pan-Islamic was blamed."[29] Despite the fractured nature of the Muslim world in the early twenties, at the time of the mandate period and continued European dominance, the tendency to generalize about a monolithic Pan-Islamic world—a "seething" Islamic ferment—remained firmly embedded in the consciousness of many in the West:

> In its very hour of apparent triumph, Western domination was challenged as never before. During those hundred years of Western conquest a mighty internal change had been coming over the Moslem world. The swelling tide of Western aggression had at last moved the "immovable" East. At last Islam became conscious of its decrepitude and with that consciousness a vast ferment, obscure yet profound, began to leaven the 250,000,000 followers of the Prophet from Morocco to China and from Turkestan to the Congo. . . . Today Islam is seething with mighty forces fashioning a new Moslem world.[30]

Anyone who doubted that Pan-Islam was a global threat to the West, a clash between civilizations, a rebellion fed by hatred only needed to listen to noted Orientalist Leone Caetani, who, speaking of the effect of World War I, warned.

> The convulsion has shaken Islamic and Oriental civilization to its foundation. The entire Oriental world, from China to the Mediterranean, is in ferment. Everywhere the hidden fire of anti-European hatred is burning. Riots in Morocco, risings in Algiers, discontent in Tripoli, so-called Nationalist attempts in Egypt, Arabia, and Libya are different manifestations of the same deep sentiment and have as their objective the rebellion of the Oriental world against European civilization.

The principal reason for this ferment is the report spread throughout the world that the Entente wishes to suppress the Ottoman Empire, dividing its territory among the powers and ceding Palestine to the Jews.[31]

Fear of a Pan-Islamic, global uprising persists today. In the wake of the Iranian Revolution, the Ayatollah Khomeini's call for other Islamic revolutions found ready believers not only in the Muslim world but also in the West. In France, Raymond Aron "warned of the Islamic 'revolutionary wave,' generated by 'the fanaticism of the prophet and the violence of the people,' which the Ayatullah Khumayni has unleashed."[32] In 1980, U.S. Secretary of State Cyrus Vance stated that a major reason for his opposition to a military mission to rescue American hostages in Iran was fear of an "Islamic-Western war . . . Khomeini and his followers, with a Shiite affinity for martyrdom, actually might welcome American military action as a way of uniting the Moslem world against the West."[33] A decade later, with the collapse of communism, Western and Muslim governments and commentators have echoed these concerns. M. J. Akbar, an Indian Muslim writer, declared that the West's "next confrontation is definitely going to come from the Muslim world. It is in the sweep of the Islamic nations from the Maghreb to Pakistan that the struggle for a new world order will begin."[34]

Some governments in the Muslim world, like those of Egypt, Tunisia, Algeria, Turkey, and Pakistan (under Benazir Bhutto), have used not only the regional fundamentalist threat but also the global threat to appeal for greater understanding and aid from the West and to justify their at times indiscriminate repression of Islamists. They fail to distinguish adequately between those who espouse violent revolution to overthrow the political system and those who, operating within the system, challenge the power of ruling elite. As I noted earlier, the Israeli government, no longer able to present itself as a bulwark against the spread of communism in the Middle East (a role that powerfully justified substantial American aid), found in political Islam not only a domestic threat but also a new, more virulent global threat:

> Our struggle against murderous Islamic terror is also meant to awaken the world, which is lying in slumber. . . . We call on all nations, all peoples to devote their attention to the great danger inherent in Islamic fundamentalism. . . . This is a real and serious danger that threatens world peace. . . . We stand on the line of fire against the danger of fundamentalist Islam.[35]

Similarly, the Turkish government, no longer able to portray itself a buffer state against the spread of communism to NATO's southern flank recast "itself as a buffer state and bulwark, only this time against revolutionary Islam."[36] Former prime minister Tansu Ciller warned that if

Turkey was not admitted to the European Economic Community, there "will be a confrontation in the world. . . . Fundamentalism will find a fertile land to flourish in, and then this will be the last fortress which will fall."[37]

Syndicated columnist Charles Krauthammer wrote that "history is being driven by another force as well: the political reawakening of the Islamic world."[38] It is a challenge all the more ominous because it is Pan-Islamic. It is a "global intifada," embracing not only the Islamic heartland but also the peripheries of the Muslim world in which Islam confronts the non-Muslim communities: Kashmir, Azerbaijan, Kosovo, Lebanon, and the West Bank. A similar attitude was expressed by Hirsh Goodman: "The incipient threat we see facing Egypt—the inexorable spread of radical, uncompromising, violent and militant Islamic fundamentalism—is by no means unique. Algeria, Tunisia, Jordan, some Gulf states, Turkey, Malaysia, Indonesia are, in varying degrees, all in similar crisis."[39]

Krauthammer's piece reflects the monolithic/reductionist threat approach to the Islamic world. Fundamentalism is equated with "fundamentalist Koran-waving Khomeiniism." Despite his recognition of multiple motives (religious and nonreligious) and differing political contexts, Krauthammer imposes a unity by asserting that "a deep historical current runs through" these random explosions, by speaking of a "pan-Islamic demand," and by emphasizing a shared political thread and geographical unity of this "global intifada."[40] The use of these terms yields an imagined rather than an empirical, transnational Islamic unity and reality.

Talk of a "global intifada" also distracts and detracts from the nature and real causes of discontent in the Palestinian intifada by implying that it was simply part of a transnational Islamic uprising rather than an Arab-Israeli problem. The intifada was first and foremost an uprising of Arabs, both Muslim and Christian. The primary cause of the intifada was not Islam or Islamic fundamentalism but continued Israeli occupation of the West Bank and Gaza and the desperation of young Palestinians in particular. The Islamic dimension (Hamas and Islamic Jihad) of the confrontation increased significantly when the Palestinian leadership proved unable to resolve the siutation effectively. (A similar situation continues in the post-Peace Accords period.) Moreover, the phrase "global intifada" imposes a superficial unity on events that occur in quite diverse contexts and obscures the profound differences between Kashmir and Kosovo, Azerbaijan and Lebanon.

Ironically, Krauthammer applauds the change of governments and political turmoil in Eastern Europe, the Balkans, and the Caucasus, which resulted from the collapse of communism, but he views Muslim demands for self-determination as a cause for concern. Krauthammer is in the curious position of raising the alarm over what he identifies as essentially twentieth-century independence movements in the Muslim world. The first phase occurred during the first half of the twentieth century, when the Islamic heartland "from Morocco to Pakistan . . . threw off European imperialism in a process that began earlier in the century and may be said to have culminated with the revolution in Iran." The second phase is "the further evolution of the Islamic awakening: the demand for local hegemony by Moslem populations at the borders of the Islamic world."[41] Are freedom and self-determination (or the use of violence to regain independence and sovereignty) less valid and more threatening if undertaken in the name of religious or ethnic nationalism? Is a Western secular profile (liberal secular nationalism) a requirement for freedom and acceptance within the international community?

The Pan-Islamic Myth

Monolithic Islam is a recurrent Western myth that has never been borne out by the reality of Muslim history. Indeed, when convenient, Western commentators have wasted little time in emphasizing the divisions and fratricidal relations of the Arab and Muslim world to underscore its intractable instability. Senator Albert Gore, now vice president, speaking of Syrian-Iraqi relations, noted, "Baathite Syrians are Alawites, a Shiite heresy, while the Iraqis are Sunnis. Reason enough in this part of the world for hatred and murder."[42] Yet Islam, the Arabs, and the Muslim world are also represented as a monolithic bloc poised against the West. Although the ideals of Arab nationalism or Islam speak of the unity and identity of a transnational community, history has proven otherwise. At best, some Muslims, as in the Iranian Revolution, have achieved a transient unity in the face of a common enemy. But it is a solidarity that dissipates as quickly as it was formed once the danger has subsided and competing interests again prevail. Arab nationalism, Arab socialism, Iran's Islamic Republic, and opposition to the Soviet Union's invasion of Afghanistan have all failed to produce a transnational or regional unity: even the Arab (Iraq and the Gulf states) coalition against Iran disintegrated after the Iran-Iraq war. As James Piscatori observed, "The problem with assuming a unified response is that it conceals the reality of . . . entrenched national differences and national interests among Muslims."[43]

Diversity rather than Pan-Islamic political unity is also reflected in foreign policy. The common "Islamic" orientation or claim of some governments reveals little unity of purpose in interstate and international relations due to conflicting national interests or priorities. Qaddafi was a bitter enemy of Sadat and Nimeiri even as all leaders were projecting an

"Islamic" image. Khomeini's Islamic Iran consistently called for the overthrow of the house of Saud on Islamic grounds, their rivalry even erupting during the annual pilgrimage to Mecca. Islamically identified governments also reflect differing relationships with the West. While Libya's and Iran's relationships with the West, and the United States in particular, were often confrontational, at the same time the U.S. has had strong allies in Saudi Arabia, Egypt, Morocco, Kuwait, Pakistan, and Bahrain. Despite its rhetoric, the Organization of the Islamic Conference has proven unable to mobilize an effective united Muslim response on issues from Palestine and Afghanistan to the Gulf War and Bosnia. National interest and regional politics rather than ideology or religion remain the primary determinants in the formulation of foreign policy.

Clash of Civilizations

The shift in Muslim attitudes toward the West from admiration and emulation to hostility and rejection is often reduced to a clash of separate and distinct (almost mutually exclusive) civilizations:

> Fundamentalist leaders are not mistaken in seeing in Western civilization the greatest challenge to the way of life that they wish to retain or restore for their people. . . . It should now be clear that we are facing a mood and a movement far transcending the level of issues and policies and the governments that pursue them. This is no less than a clash of civilizations—perhaps irrational but surely historic reaction of an ancient rival against our Judaeo-Christian heritage, our secular present, and the worldwide expansion of both.[44]

Stereotypical dichotomies are reinforced to obscure a complex reality: Islam against the West, fundamentalism against modernity, static tradition versus dynamic change, the desire to simply return to or preserve the past versus adaptation to modern life. All "fundamentalist leaders" are lumped together, obscuring the fact that many Islamists are modern, educated people who hold responsible professional positions and participate in the democratic process. Moreover, the causes of conflicts are facilely reduced to a clash of civilizations. The primacy of competing political interests, policies, and issues is dismissed or eclipsed by the vision of an age-old rivalry between "them" and "us." Once again, history witnesses Islam pitted against the West, against "our Judeo-Christian and secular West," a confrontation of competing and conflicting global visions and missions. This approach is as valid and useful as the attempts of Saddam Hussein (like the Ayatollah Khomeini before him) to reduce the West's antagonism toward him to Crusader imperialism against the oppressed masses of the Arab and Muslim worlds.

Denying the need to address specific political or socioeconomic issues also negates any notion of shared responsibility. How can the West respond to what is obviously emotional and "irrational," an assault upon it by peoples who are peculiarly driven by their passions and hatred? As James Piscatori observed:

> Whether it was the Ottoman attempt to thwart Christian nationalists or the Muslim attempt to gain independence from the West, Islam was fanatical because it ran counter to imperial interests. But it was the converse formulation that became the standard explanation of Muslim conduct: Islam was hostile to the West because it was fanatical. . . . Consequently, Muslims came to be seen as a uniformly emotional and sometimes illogical race that moved as one body and spoke with one voice.[45]

The pattern persists. As many in the past dismissed the political realities of Muslim-Christian relations by retreating to the bogey man of "Muslim fanaticism," so Muslims today are described as a people and civilization who, though courteous and possessing a rich religious tradition and civilization, harbor a propensity to hatred and rage when angered:

> And yet, in moments of upheaval and disruption, when the deeper passions are stirred, this dignity and courtesy toward others can give way to an explosive mixture of rage and hatred which impels even the government of an ancient and civilized country [Iran]—even the spokesman [Ayatollah Khomeini] of a great spiritual and ethical religion—to espouse kidnapping and assassination, and try to find, in the life of their Prophet, approval and indeed precedent for such actions.[46]

Many people—believers and nonbelievers, Muslims and Jews, Christians, Sikhs, and Hindus—become enraged when their survival or interests are threatened. And Muslims are not the only people who use religion to rationalize and legitimate actions. In reality, most "civilized" peoples, normally compassionate and kind, accept rage against evil and hatred of enemies as a normal response toward heinous crimes, wartime enemies, hostage taking, or terrorism. Moreover, have the lessons of the Crusades and the Inquisition, of the waves of European imperialism and colonialism, faded from memory—periods when popes and monarchs, clergy, civil servants, and soldiers often legitimated their actions in the name of religion: in the name of God and country, crown and cross?

Too often coverage of Islam and the Muslim world assumes the existence of a monolithic Islam in which all Muslims are the same, thinking and acting as one. To speak of "the spokesman of a great spiritual and ethical religion" perpetuates the image of a monolithic Muslim world seen through the lens of Iran and the Ayatollah Khomeini. The Ayatollah Khomeini was one spokesman, not *the* spokesman or voice of Islam. There is no pope of Islam. Seeing all Muslims and all events in the Muslim world through the prism of Khomeini and revolutionary Iran had profound effects upon American perceptions of Islam and the Middle East. It often obscured the divisions and differences in the Muslim world—the many countries and Muslims that did not follow his lead; Iran's failure or at best very limited success in exporting and inciting Islamic revolutions; and the many voices other than Khomeini's who spoke out on Salman Rushdie.

The creation of an imagined monolithic Islam leads to a religious reductionism that views political conflicts in the Sudan, Lebanon, Bosnia, and Azerbaijan in primarily religious terms as "Islamic-Christian conflicts." Although the communities in these areas may be broadly identified in religious or confessional terms as Christian and Muslim communities, it is nonetheless true, as with Northern Ireland's Catholic and Protestant communities, that local disputes and civil wars have more to do with political issues (e.g., ethnic nationalism, autonomy, and independence) and socioeconomic issues and grievances than with religion.

Beyond the Clash: Religious Resurgence and the Desecularization of Society

In the past the role of religion and culture was ignored or underestimated. Yet today recognition of its significance in international affairs has led to an exaggerated belief among some in an impending clash of civilizations. The clearest, most provocative, and influential articulation of this position is Samuel P. Huntington's "Clash of Civilizations." Huntington declares that in the post-Cold War period, "the clash of civilizations will dominate global politics. The fault lines between civilizations will be the battle lines of the future. . . . The next world war, if there is one, will be a war between civilizations."[47] For Huntington, the modern period has been dominated by conflicts between nations and ideologies—the superpowers during the Cold War. In contrast to civilizations, which have been more enduring sources of identity and conflict, nation-states are relatively new, as is their role as primary actors in global politics. In an increasingly smaller and interrelated world, one in which the nation-state as a source of identity is weaker, the fundamental differences among civilizations have become more prominent, as is evident in a world increasingly less secular and in which "a return to the roots phenomenon" has become more prominent.[48] All of this is occurring at a time in which, Huntington observes, a transition is occurring from a Western-dominated phase to one in which non-

Western civilizations are emerging as significant international players: "non-Western civilizations no longer remain objects of history as targets of Western colonialism but join the West as movers and shapers of history."[49] Huntington defines civilization as a "cultural entity . . . the highest cultural grouping . . . defined by both common objective elements, such as language, history, religion, customs, institutions, and by the subjective self-identification of people. . . . A civilization may include several nation states or only one."[50] Among the major civilizations are the West, Islam, Latin America, China, and Japan.

Huntington accepts an outdated monolithic notion of civilization and equally cites uncritically anti-Western voices. In reality, civilizations, like countries, are complex, encompassing diverse and often contradictory beliefs, values, and forces that belie facile generalizations. He fails to address seriously the great diversity and differences (political and cultural), the clashes, that exist not only among but also *within* Muslim (and for that matter Chinese) countries and societies. Moreover, although some common beliefs or characteristics (language, religion, or customs) may exist in the West, Latin America, or the Muslim world, their histories and politics reveal the extent to which national identities and interests, political and economic forces, often belie that unity. World Wars I and II, which pitted Germany against much of Europe and America, are testimony to the fragility of Western civilization. The Iran–Iraq war, the divisions within the Muslim world over support for the Gulf War of 1991, the conflicts among Muslim countries (particularly self-styled "Islamic" states and republics such as Saudi Arabia, Iran, and Libya) as well as among Islamic movements belie the existence of Huntington's monolithic threat, Islamic civilization, as it does Confucian civilization.

Belief in a monolithic notion of civilization results in the contention that some civilizations are diametrically opposed (the West vs. Islamic and Confucian civilizations), which creates the possibility of a clash of civilizations. In order to support his position, Huntington, astonishingly, is not content, as are many others, to see "Islamic fundamentalism" as a threat to the West but rather identifies Islam itself: "The underlying problem for the West is not Islamic fundamentalism. It is Islam, a different civilization whose people are convinced of the superiority of their culture, and are obsessed with the inferiority of their power."[51] Here again, "Muslim" or "Islamic civilization" rather than "Islam" would be the more comparable terminology, since Islam refers more properly and specifically to the religion of Islam, which is an important component of Muslim or Islamic civilization but is only one component of it. Over and against Islam, Huntington posits a monolithic West, whose difference puts it on a collision path with Islam: "The problem for Islam is not the CIA or the U.S.

Department of Defense. It is the West, a different civilization whose people are convinced of the universality of their culture and believe that their superior, if declining, power imposes the obligation to extend that culture throughout the world. These are the basic ingredients that fuel the conflict between Islam and the West.''[52] Huntington assumes that there is a monolithic West, Western civilization, that holds or accepts his definition of its worldview. France, like a number of European countries, has resisted the penetration of French culture by Arab culture and by American culture.

Huntington has replaced the underestimation of religion and culture in global politics and international affairs in the past with an emphasis on the power of cultural communality as an economic and political force and on its ability to unite transnationally to produce effective economic and political actors. Religion and ethnicity have always been a source of primary identification for many, especially the nonmodern elite. The extent to which secular presuppositions, in particular of the very modernization or development theory that he and others formulated in the 1960s, once overlooked these realities now results in Huntington's tendency to over-emphasize cultural differences. It contributes to an equally distorted vision that exaggerates the gap, or "fault lines," that divide civilizations. The result is a propensity to project transnational economic and political threats: "The Fault Lines between civilizations are replacing the political and ideological boundaries of the Cold War as the flash points for crisis and bloodshed.[53]

Huntington identifies a "Confucian-Islamic connection that has emerged to challenge Western interests, values, and power," concluding that "a central focus of conflict for the immediate future will be between the West and several Islamic-Confucian states.''[54] This view risks slipping into the racist perception of a cultural threat. Huntington characterizes Islam as the age-old enemy of the West, "Conflict along the fault line between Western and Islamic civilizations has been going on for 1300 years,''[55] and as being ideologically hostile to the West, "Western ideas of individualism, liberalism, constitutionalism, human rights, equality, liberty, the rule of law, democracy, free markets, the separation of church and state, often have little resonance in Islamic [and other] . . . cultures.''[56] Viewing the "crescent-shaped bloc of nations" from Africa to Central Asia and other conflicts between Muslims and Orthodox Serbs in the Balkans, Hindus in India, Jews in Israel, Catholics in the Philippines, he concludes that "Islam has bloody borders.''[57] Huntington's subsequent book, *The Clash of Civilizations and the Remaking of the World Order*, offered Huntington an opportunity to expand upon the thesis of his article and also to correct or alter it. However, he chose to entitle a section

"Islam's Bloody Borders" and also to state that "Islam's borders are bloody and so are its innards."[58] Thus he perpetuated the provocative and inaccurate phrase "Islam has bloody borders" instead of saying that Muslims have bloody borders or countries in the Muslim world have bloody borders. The phrase explicitly attributes the bloodshed to the religion of Islam and not simply to the actions of some Muslims. Moreover, it does not distinguish between legitimate and illegitimate use of force. Would it then be acceptable to indiscriminately characterize Israeli politics in the West Bank and Gaza and in Southern Lebanon as "Judaism has bloody borders" or to make similar statements about Buddhism in Sri Lanka or Hinduism in India?

Huntington is correct in noting that identification in terms of religion and ethnicity can contribute to an "us/them" outlook. Regrettably, Huntington himself, in his positing of different, almost diametrically opposed civilizations (Confucian, Islamic, and Western), contributes to the problem by providing intellectual justification. The tendency to view the world in bipolar terms is a human propensity that has always utilized any difference in identity in the process of self-definition, social relations, and international affairs—I belong to this family or village versus that family or village; I am secular versus religious; a believer versus a nonbeliever; capitalist versus communist; First World versus Third World. It is fed by a past tendency in our educational systems to either ignore other religious traditions and cultures or to treat them as mysterious, strange, foreign, inferior, or atavistic. As a result, both illiterate and highly educated people for different reasons are often ignorant of other traditions, more prone to view them in an "us" and "them" context, more likely to compare the ideals of their country, religion, or civilization with the negative realities of another. Moreover, as Huntington rightly notes, "A world of clashing civilizations, however, is inevitably a world of double standards: people apply one standard to their kin-countries and a different standard to others."[59]

The political as well as religious challenge today, even more than in the past, in an increasingly global, interdependent world is to recognize not only our competing interests but also our common interests. America's policy toward Japan or Saudi Arabia is not based upon a sense of shared culture, religion, or civilization but upon national or group interests. The transformation of Judaism and Christianity to accommodate pluralism was based upon historical experience and the ultimate recognition of the need to do so. Cooperation can result from common religious and ethnic backgrounds; however, more often than not it comes from the recognition of common national and strategic interests. Although a clash of civilizations can become the clarion call that justifies aggression and warfare, future global threats and wars will be due less to a clash of "civilizations" than a clash of interests—economic and otherwise.

Huntington's concern with and approach to civilizations is conditioned by a perspective that sees history in terms of sources of conflict—nation-state, ideology (liberal democracy versus communism), the Cold War—and thus, in looking for the source of future conflicts, he emphasizes differences in beliefs and values. But this is only one part of the reality. For example, although there are distinctive differences of doctrine, law, institutions, and values among Judaism, Christianity, and Islam, there are also a host of similarities. They all see themselves as children of Abraham, are monotheists, believe in prophethood and divine revelation, and have a concept of moral responsibility and accountability. This shared perspective has been recognized in recent years by the notion of a Judeo-Christian tradition, a concept that is slowly being extended by some who speak of a Judeo-Christian-Islamic tradition. Although major historic clashes and violent confrontations have occurred, they do not represent the total picture. In fact, positive interaction and influence have also taken place. Islamic civilization was indebted to "the West" for many of the sources that enabled it to borrow and translate and then to develop a high civilization that made its own remarkable contributions in philosophy, the sciences, and technology while the West went into eclipse in the Dark Ages. Similarly, the West in turn reclaimed a renovated philosophical and scientific heritage from Islamic civilization, retranslating and reappropriating that knowledge, which then became the foundation for its Renaissance. In the modern period, Muslims have freely appropriated the accomplishments of modern science and technology. In many ways, they face a period of reexamination, reformation, and revitalization. This process, like the Reformation in the West, involves not only intellectual ferment and religious debate but also religious and political unrest, violence, and revolution.

The issue of a clash of civilizations runs through a variety of phenomena and has been raised in multiple contexts, including the demographic threat resulting from growing Muslim populations in the West, from problems of assimilation to radical actions such as the World Trade Center bombing; the Rushdie affair with its issues of free speech versus a death sentence for blasphemy; Saddam Hussein's attempt to portray the Gulf War as yet another stage in the historic civilizational clash between the Muslim world and the West; and the claim that Islam and democracy as well as modernity are incompatible.

Islam in the West

> For a millenium, the struggle for mankind's destiny was between
> Christianity and Islam; in the 21st century, it may be so again. For,
> as the Shiites humiliate us, their co-religionists are filling up the
> countries of the West.[60]

For some, the linkage of the political and the demographic intensifies the nature of the Islamic threat. Thus Patrick Buchanan could write in "Rising Islam May Overwhelm the West" that while the West finds itself "negotiating for hostages with Shiite radicals who hate and detest us," their Muslim "co-religionists are filling up the countries of the West." The Muslim threat becomes global in nature as Muslims in Europe, the Soviet Union, and America "proliferate and prosper."[61] Even as the Soviet Union was unraveling, other observers, such as Charles Krauthammer, spoke of a global Islamic uprising, a vision of Muslims in the heartland and on the periphery of the Muslim world rising up in revolt: a new "arc of crisis."[62] In Britain, Charles Moore, in "Time for a More Liberal and 'Racist' Immigration Policy," wrote that "because of our obstinate refusal to have enough babies, Western European civilization will start to die at the point when it could have been revived with new blood. Then the hooded hordes will win, and the Koran will be taught, as Gibbon famously imagined, in the schools of Oxford."[63]

Much as observers in the past retreated to polemics and stereotypes of Arabs, Turks, or Muslims rather than address the specific causes of conflict and confrontation, observers today are witnessing the creation of a new myth. The impending confrontation between Islam and the West is presented as part of a historical pattern of Muslim belligerency and aggression that is now viewed not only as a global but also, given the significant presence and growth of Muslim communities in the West, as a potential domestic threat. Past images of a Christian West turning back the threat of Muslim armies seeking to overrun the West are conjured up and linked to demographic and political realities. Images of Charles Martel, who "halted the first Mohammedan advance preventing the crescent from closing over Christian Europe," the Crusaders' attempt to save Jerusalem, and the narrow defeat of "Islamic legions" at Vienna are linked to current realities and fears of the expansion of a resurgent Islam in Europe and America: "Contagion is precisely what some European countries are starting to fear. With Islamic fundamentalism gaining strength at Europe's doorstep, notably in Algeria and Turkey, they worry that it will spread to the large Muslim populations of Western Europe." Serbian leaders in Bosnia and then Kosovo have played on past history, portraying their genocidal war against Muslims as a struggle to turn back the tide of radical Islamic fundamentalism and prevent the creation of an Islamic state in the heart of Europe. France reacted out of fear that Algeria's crisis would lead to massive emigration from Algeria to France that would swell the ranks of its already sizable (4 million) and potentially combustible Muslim community, fostering a domestic fundamentalist threat. Some have warned that the combination of radicalism and spiraling population growth threaten to overrun East and West: "Clearly, Islam is in the ascent in Africa, Asia and the Middle East. In the West, devout Moslems are having children, while in our secular societies, the philosophy of Planned Parenthood takes hold and the condom is king."[64]

Events in the West reinforced the perspective of an impending demographic threat. As Europe experienced a new wave of immigration that supplemented its earlier migrant worker communities, settler workers from Romania, Albania, North Africa, and Turkey have become an explosive political issue. The impact and assimilation of Muslims is a particularly contentious issue in countries such as Great Britain, France, and Germany, among others. Earlier settled communities from the Middle East, Asia, and Africa have become significant, dominating local politics in cities and towns like Bradford, England, and Marseilles, France, and asserting their rights nationally and locally. These communities now are projected to grow significantly, supplemented by new waves of immigrants. The presence of significant Muslim minority populations puts strains on the social fabric of European societies like France, where Islam is the second largest religion, Germany, and Great Britain, where it is in third place. Anti-Arab/ Muslim sentiment in Western Europe is part of a growing combination of Islamaphobia and xenophobia. Muslim communities and indigenous groups have clashed over questions of continued immigration, citizenship, and the accommodation of Muslim belief and practice.

In England, debates from the Rushdie affair to local politics and school issues have raged. Muslims have demanded that Muslim schools be allowed to receive state subvention like that allowed for Catholic and Jewish schools. Such events have contributed to British Muslim politicization and have demonstrated the diversity of Muslim responses. Although some British Muslims created the Muslim Parliament of Great Britain, there has been considerable dissension within Muslim ranks in Britain. Some charged that creating a Muslim parliament is merely playing the Western game (i.e., "Parliament"), whereas others maintained that it constitutes a form of apartheid.[65] Still other Muslim leaders have objected to any notion of separatism as an alternative to integration into British society: "Many Muslims agreed with the grievances that Dr. Siddique [Kalim Siddique, the architect of the Muslim Parliament of Great Britain] identified—for instance, racism, an unequal share of unemployment, etc.; but the idea of separatism was anathema to most Muslims. Their real grievance was that they do not find it easy to get into the mainstream of British society."[66]

The British press (*The Times, Daily Telegraph, The Spectator*) reflected the deep-seated fears and prejudices of "Islamaphobia." Clare Hollingsworth, a defense correspondent, wrote that "Muslim fundamentalism is fast becoming the chief threat to global peace and security as well as a cause of national and local disturbance through terrorism. It is akin to the menace of Nazism and fascism in the 1930s and then by communism in the 1950s."[67] In the wake of the Oklahoma bombing, Bernard Levin warned in *The Times*, "We do not know who primed and put the Oklahoma bomb in its place; we do know that they were, in the fullest meaning of the word, fanatics. Unlike most of us, they do not in the least mind being killed; indeed, they are delighted, because they believe that they are going to a far, far better place. . . . Do you realize that in perhaps a half a century, not more and perhaps a good deal less, there will be wars, in which fanatical Muslims will be winning? As for Oklahoma, it will be called Khartoum-on-the-Mississippi, and woe betide anyone who calls it anything else."[68] When Prince Charles gave a speech calling for bridge building between Islam and the West, the *Daily Telegraph* responded, "Prince Charles is wrong—Islam does threaten the West."[69] In a major study, *Islamaphobia: A Challenge For Us All*, by the Runnymede Commission on British Muslims and Islamaphobia, the major sources identified were not the uneducated but "those sections of society who claim the mantle of secularism, liberalism, and tolerance. They are in the forefront of the fight against racism and against Islam and Muslims at the same time. They preach equality of opportunities for all, yet turn a blind eye to the fact that this society offers only unequal opportunities for Muslims."[70] Similar attitudes could be found in academia: "Not only is academia a bastion of orientalism and Islamaphobia but also a hothouse of cuturally formative influences which spill down through dinner parties and think tanks into political parties, journalism, the arts, popular culture, the professions, local authorities, and everyday thought and encounters in the workplace and on the street."[71] As the commission concluded, "Islamaphobic discourse, sometimes blatant but frequently subtle and coded, is part of the fabric of everyday life in modern Britain, in much the same ways that antisemitic discourse was taken for granted earlier in the century."[72]

In Germany and France, similar stereotypes and fears have been given free reign so that *Der Spiegel* could warn as the former Yugoslavia broke apart that a religious war could rally support from across the Muslim world. "Soon, Europe could have a fanatical theocratic state on its doorstep.''[73] German readers are also warned, ''Particularly in the Middle East, the cradle and cultural centre of Islam, bearded extremists are increasingly shaping the image of a militant Islam which is determined by 'Holy War' and blood sacrifice, fanaticism and violence, intolerance and the oppression of women.''[74] In France, the basic disposition of Muslims is characterized as antimodern and violent; it can be ''explained by the origins of their religion: it is warlike, conquest-hungry and full of contempt for the unbeliever.''[75] Often little distinction is made between Islam and fundamentalism or between violent and nonviolent fundamentalists. Thus, in one survey, ''three out of four French people questioned thought that the word 'fanatical' best applied to Islam.''[76] As in Britain, Islamaphobia combined with issues of demography and immigration. Calls for the expulsion of foreign workers were accompanied by celebrated cases in which Muslim girls in schools and universities were prohibited from wearing a head scarf (hejab) in school. The hejab issue ''exemplifies the widening gulf between French society and its Muslim minority. Nearly thirteen centuries after Charles Martel halted the Muslim conquest of Europe at this city, the new battle of Poitiers encapsulates the growing suspicion of—and sometimes hostility to—the Islamic faith in Europe.''[77] Ironically, political demagogues in France and elsewhere play on many of the same cultural fears of foreign cultural penetration and loss of identity that are so prevalent in the Muslim world: ''Europeans now feel threatened by so many things. . . . The Americanization of our culture, the drift to the left, a loss of identity, the rise of an ugly populist response to things foreign.''[78]

> Western European fears often express themselves in religiocultural as well as economic and political terms. While assimilation of other new Europeans occurred in the past, many today doubt the possibility or desirability of absorbing the new immigrants, especially Muslims who are both nationally and religioculturally alien: ''Our former immigrants were Europeans; these are not. Arab girls who insist on wearing chuddars [chador, veil or covering] in our schools are not French and don't want to be. . . . Europe's past was white and Judeo-Christian. The future is not. I doubt that our very old institutions and structures will be able to stand the pressure.''[79]

Some observers have seen the outcome of the current debate in potentially cataclysmic terms. ''While Europe has overcome the cold war . . . it now risks creating new divisions and conflicts, such as a white, wealthy and Christian ''Fortress Europe'' pitted against a largely poor, Islamic world. That could lead to terrorism and another forty years of small, hot wars.[80]

French Interior Department officials identified fundamentalism as a domestic threat and arrested Islamic militants suspected of supplying arms to Algerian Islamists. The more complex reality of Muslims in France was revealed in Lyons in 1994–95, where the building of the Grand Mosque reflected some people's fears but also hope for the future. The mosque was initially resisted as a breeding ground for extremists, especially by the extreme right National Front, which called for "active resistance against the danger of Islamic colonization."[81] However, within a short period after its opening, the mosque emerged as a symbol of reconciliation. As its Algerian-born grand mufti declared, "The protests have completely disappeared because we have shown that French Islam can be a force for moderation and integration. . . . Iran, Algeria, terrorists all blend into a simplistic and ignorant view that Islam means violence and fanaticism. I'm afraid we have a long, slow education process ahead of us."[82]

In a similar vein, a prominent German intellectual has noted that "what goes on before our eyes as regards policies on asylum seekers and refugees gives me greater reason for fear than Islamic fundamentalism or the growing number of asylum seekers. The image of the South as 'the enemy' does not only strengthen prejudice but also breeds racism and gives wide and effective support to sealing off fortress Europe. It is not Europe's military security, not its affluence that are threatened, it is its humanitarianism."[83]

The Muslim presence in Europe and North America does pose a challenge, though not in the sense that some have predicted. First and foremost, the challenge is to distinguish between a majority of its Muslim citizens and a minority of violent revolutionaries. Like many before them, the vast majority of Muslims who emigrate to the West come to escape authoritarian regimes or to seek a better future economically and educationally for themselves and their families. They wish to be and they are loyal citizens. Like many minorities, however, they face the challenge of assimilation versus total integration. Jews and Roman Catholics, like many ethnic and religious groups, have faced the problem of assimilation without a loss of identity. Responding to these concerns led to the construction of a vast educational system by Roman Catholics and Jews as well as religious and ethnic fraternal and social welfare societies. How to be American or British while retaining a sense of one's ethnic origins or faith is not a new issue. It is particularly acute for minorities. Indeed, the problem of national identity and multiculturalism and pluralism remains a contested issue, particularly in France.

The situation for Muslims in the West is compounded. Like Jews, they are a religious minority but they are also perceived to be a cultural minority. They are challenged to accommodate themselves to and thus find acceptance within societies that, however ethnically diverse, are culturally Western and Christian in origin. Yet this experience is not as unique as some would seem to believe when they speak of "our" Judeo-Christian tradition vis-à-vis Islam. References to a "Judeo-Christian tradition" obscure the fact that this term represents a twentieth-century understanding or interpretation of the relationship between Judaism and Christianity. Previously, both faiths were seen (and saw each other) as significantly different and separate in their theological outlook and values. In response to the realities (political, economic, social), experience, and necessity of living together, both Judaism and Christianity found ways to reinterpret and accommodate their traditions to new social conditions; in particular, they responded to the challenge of religious pluralism. This process required recognizing and identifying the differences between religions (the essentials of religious belief) and the diversity of cultural expressions or practices that came to be associated with religious traditions. As a result, Catholics today can see what they share in common with their worldwide faith community but also appreciate the extent to which cultural accommodation has also produced American, Canadian, French, Sudanese, or Malaysian Catholicism. The same could be said more broadly of the unity and diversity to be found among Sephardic and Ashkenazi or American, British, French, or Italian Jews. Within Judaism and Christianity, the process of religious change and accommodation has spanned the spectrum from conservative and traditional to reform and reconstructionist. The issues of continuity and change remain a challenge to faith communities everywhere.

Muslims in the West at first seem to differ from other immigrants or indigenous converts who, however ethnically diverse, possessed a shared Judeo-Christian culture. Muslims, like Jews in the past, find themselves in Western cultural contexts in which they are often regarded as completely ''other'' and thus as a threat. The *New Republic* reported that one ''cannot deny that there is also an Arab culture in Brooklyn and Jersey City and Detroit off which the criminals feed and which gets a grim thrill from them. Ours is not a country with which they identify or whose values they share.''[84] This is caused not only by ignorance of Islam or by equating it with extremism and terrorism but also by the failing to recognize the extent to which Islam is part of a Judeo-Christian-Islamic tradition. Too often categories that pit Islam against the West have been reinforced by an intellectual and religious outlook that has privileged a Judeo-Christian tradition over and against the ''other'' world religions. Islam, despite its monotheism and prophetic tradition, was grouped with ''foreign religions'' (Hinduism, Buddhism, Taoism, and so forth) in our scholarship, university curricula, libraries, and bookstores. Although there are significant differences among the three great monotheistic faiths, there is also a common theological outlook, or shared ethical monotheism, that can be a source of mutual respect and cooperation rather than confrontation and conflict.

A second and related issue is that of liberalism and pluralism: Will they adapt to our liberal agenda? This question is indeed important and cannot be dismissed. But there is another question: Will we adapt our own liberalism? Liberalism has long accepted ethnicity and race as inherent to the human condition and finds discrimination along these lines to be unacceptable. Yet the secularized mentality fails to appreciate that for many people in the world, religious faith is also a primary identity. It is a given, not a choice, and as such Muslim citizens in the West cannot be expected to forgo certain rights in society (e.g., school accommodation to dietary laws, dress codes, and holidays, and the right of workers to observe their Sabbath by attending the Friday congregational prayer). When we ask, What kind of democrats are they? we must also ask (and answer), What kind of democrats are we? To some extent it is now true that, increasingly in Western societies, "Islam and Muslims are us."[85]

But what of the domestic threat of violence and terrorism by Islamic fundamentalism? The violence and death threats that accompanied the Salman Rushdie affair in Europe, charges that Muslim citizens in Britain, France, and the United States have formed radical networks with international connections, the World Trade Center bombing, and the conviction of Shaykh Omar Abdur Rahman and others for conspiring to blow up major buildings and tunnels in America have raised questions about national security and immigration policies. Concerns are reflected in headline stories in major newspapers and the media, such as "Holy War Comes to America," "Islam under Siege," "The New Dawn for Islam: The Global Campaign against the Secular State," "Jihad in America."[86] Some warn that "Britain and the U.S. have become the bases for extremists seeking to turn Islam into an aggressive political movement. . . . Since the World Trade Center bombing, the F.B.I. is playing catch-up, even utilizing C.I.A. connections in meeting what is belatedly seen as a domestic threat."[87]

For some, the question Can they accommodate? is often joined to another, Can they be loyal and trusted citizens? Although these are legitimate questions, this approach risks painting all Muslims, and indeed Islam itself, as violent, when what is needed is to distinguish between a radical fringe and the mainstream, those who manipulate and distort religion to justify their actions and the Islamic tradition itself. The careful distinctions that have been made—between religious and ethnic communities and a minority of their members as applied to the activities of Puerto Rican terrorist groups in New York, the Jewish Defense League, the IRA, the Mafia, or Christian extremists calling themselves the Army of God who bomb abortion clinics—are not as sharply drawn when dealing with Muslim extremism. Nor are the distinctions between liberation or resistance movements and terrorist organizations. The situation is compounded by those who sharply contrast the Judeo-Christian tradition with Islam on such issues of peace, violence, holy war, and revenge. Others speak about religious and cultural differences or about diametrically opposed and thus irreconcilable differences in principles and values without any mention of shared beliefs and values. This tendency fosters a sense of alienation, marginalization, and radicalization on both sides. As one Muslim leader noted in France, "Our only ambition is to become at the same time good Muslims and good French citizens. . . . But as long as people wage campaigns on the peril of Islam, as long as we let rancors and frustrations accumulate, we will encourage all forms of radicalization."[88]

Islam and Democracy

Integral to the vision of an Islamic threat is the belief that Islam is inherently antidemocratic and intolerant or, at best, is "not hospitable to democracy."[89] In the wake of the Gulf War of 1991, the issue of political liberalization and democracy reemerged as an issue in the Middle East and in Western diplomacy.[90] Democracy has been slow in coming to the Middle East. Many Arab and Muslim governments, like many governments throughout the world, have found it useful to speak of democracy or "the people's" voice and role in government, whether or not it in fact exists. Despite Western influence and a facade of parliamentary government in some countries, the political reality has more often been one of authoritarianism—monarchies, dictatorships, societies, and parliaments dominated by one (the government's) political party. Arab states have been described as security (*mukhabarat*) states whose rulers' stability depends on a strong military and on security forces. Rulers have not found it embarrassing to report electoral victories with 95 to 99.91 percent of the vote. Political parties and trade unions are often banned or severely restricted, elections are often rigged, and the culture and institutions of civil society are weak.

Democracy movements and pressures on Muslim governments for greater liberalization predated the Gulf War. As the Soviet Union and Eastern Europe were swept along by the wave of democratization in 1989–90, Muslim nationalities in the Soviet Union demanded greater autonomy, the Palestinian intifada (uprising) occurred, and the Kashmiri Muslim demands for independence from India captured the attention of many in the Muslim world. Secular and Islamic activists increasingly couched their criticisms and demands in the language of political liberalization and democracy. As I pointed out in chapters 4 and 5, in many Muslim countries Islamic activists not only took to the streets but also turned to the ballot box. Both secular and Islamic organizations and political parties pressed for political reforms with limited success: elections in Egypt, Tunisia, Algeria, Jordan, and Pakistan, and, in the aftermath of the Gulf War, elections in Kuwait and Yemen and the formation of a consultative assembly in Saudi Arabia and Oman.

Talk of democratization troubles both autocratic rulers in the Muslim world and many Western governments. The former fear any opposition, let alone one that cloaks itself in values that its Western allies officially cherish and preach. For leaders in the West, democracy raises the prospect of old and reliable friends or client states being transformed into more independent and less predictable nations that might make Western access to oil less secure. Thus stability in the Middle East has often been defined in terms of preservation of the status quo.

The claim that both Arab culture and Islam are antidemocratic and the fear that Islamists will use the electoral process to seize power have been used to rationalize lack of enthusiasm or support for political liberalization in the Middle East. The lack of a democratic tradition and more specifically, the paucity of democracies in the Muslim world is mention in support of this claim. Why the glaring absence of democratic governments? The political realities of the Muslim world have not been conducive to the development of democratic traditions and institutions. European colonial rule and postindependence national governments headed by military officers, monarchs, and ex-military rulers have contributed to a legacy that has had little concern for political participation and building strong democratic institutions. National unity and stability as well as political legitimacy have been undermined by the artificial nature of modern states, whose national boundaries were often drawn by colonial powers and whose rulers were either placed on their thrones by Europe or simply seized power for themselves. Weak economies, illiteracy, and high unemployment, especially among the younger generation, exacerbate the situation, undermining confidence in governments and increasing the appeal of political Islam, or "Islamic fundamentalism."

Are Islam and democracy necessarily or inherently incompatible?[91] Among the arguments proffered by those who fear the promotion of a democratic process in the Muslim world is that it risks the "hijacking of democracy" by Islamic activists and furthers Islamic inroads into centers of power, threatening Western interests and fostering anti-Westernism and increased instability.

> Today in most Islamic countries, free elections would produce fundamentalist victories and validate the imposition of theocracy. . . . They have pressed for free elections in several Arab countries. Presenting themselves as the protectors of the oppressed, they have done quite well in these elec-

tions as they knew they would. But it is questionable that their real aim is to promote democracy. . . . Islam draws no line between religion and politics. As undemocratic as the present Saudi regime is, a total Islamic one—even with broader political participation—would be less free. It would have no neutral public space where people's views are treated as opinions, not as truth. Elections would become trivial in that environment.[92]

Many argue that Islamic values and democratic values are inherently antithetical, as seen in issues like the inequality of believers and unbelievers, as well as of men and women. History has shown that nations and religious traditions are capable of having multiple and major ideological interpretations or reorientations. A process of reinterpretation or reform accompanied the transformation of European principalities, whose rule was often justified in terms of divine right, into modern Western democratic states. Indeed, democracy itself has had multiple meanings for different peoples at different times, from ancient to modern notions of democracy, from direct to indirect democracy, from majority rule to majority vote.[93] The Judeo-Christian tradition, which once supported political absolutism and divine right monarchies, was reinterpreted to accommodate the democratic ideal. "Islam" also lends itself to multiple interpretations; it has been used to support democracy and dictatorship, republicanism and monarchy. The twentieth century has witnessed both tendencies.

Some Muslims and leaders of Islamic movements have spoken out against Western-style democracy and a parliamentary system of government. Their negative reaction has often been part of the general rejection of European colonial influence, a defense of Islam against further dependence on the West rather than a wholesale rejection of democracy. For others, Islam is totally self-sufficient, with a divinely mandated system based upon divine sovereignty and sacred law (Sharia), which is incompatible and irreconcilable with notions of popular sovereignty and civil law. Others insist that Muslims should generate their own forms of political participation or democracy from within Islam and have no need to look to Western forms of democracy. The range of those who distinguish between Islam and democracy is quite broad. It includes Islamists from the past like Sayyid Qutb and many of today's violent, anti-Western extremist organizations. But it also includes rulers such as King Fahd of Saudi Arabia, long regarded as an ally of the West, for whom democracy is a Western institution foreign to Islam, which has its own forms of participation: "the democratic system prevalent in the world is not appropriate in this region. . . . The election system has no place in the Islamic creed, which calls for a government of advice and consultation and for the shepherd's openness to his flock, and holds the ruler fully responsible before his people."[94]

In recent years, many Muslims have come to accept the notion of democracy but differ as to its precise meaning. They have sought to delineate Islamic forms of democracy, or popular political participation, seeking to provide an Islamic rationale and legitimacy rooted in tradition. The Islamization of democracy has been based on a modern process of reinterpretation of traditional Islamic concepts of political deliberation or consultation (*shura*), community consensus (*ijma*), and personal interpretation (*ijtihad*) or reinterpretation to support notions of parliamentary democracy, representative elections, and religious reform. Although radical revolutionaries reject any form of parliamentary democracy as Westernizing and un-Islamic, many Islamic activists have "Islamized" (asserted an Islamic rationale) parliamentary democracy and have appealed to democracy in their opposition to incumbent regimes. Islamic organizations such as the Muslim Brotherhoods in Egypt and Jordan, the Jamaat-i-Islami in Pakistan, Kashmir, India, and Bangladesh, Turkey's Welfare Party, as well as Algeria's Islamic Salvation Front, Tunisia's Renaissance Party, Kuwait's Jamiyyat al-Islah (Reform Society), Malaysia's ABIM and PAS, Indonesia's Muhammadiya and Nahdatul Ulama, among others, have advocated the principle of democratic elections and, where permitted, have participated in parliamentary elections.

There are differences between Western notions of democracy and Islamic traditions. These differences must be understood within a context that acknowledges that Western democracy itself has taken many forms from ancient Greece and applied them to the diverse democratic systems of government in modern France, Great Britain, and America. Thus, historically, democracy in the West has taken many forms, adapting itself to local conditions.[95] Increased emphasis on political liberalization, electoral politics, and democratization in the Muslim world does not necessarily imply uncritical acceptance of Western forms of democracy. In recent years, some have argued that Islamic forms of democracy have their limits. In contrast to Western democracy's unfettered popular sovereignty, Islamic democracy is a limited form of popular sovereignty, restricted or directed by the limits of God's law (Sharia). Thus both divine and popular sovereignty are affirmed in a delicate balance capable of producing multiple forms and configurations.

Not unexpectedly, the record of Islamo-democratic experiments has been diverse and incongruent. What is important is not that they are all consistent but that they are part of a process of real attempts at reconciling Islam and democracy. Some will no doubt fail. Others, as has been the case in the West, may lead to more meaningful indigenous versions of democracy.

Electoral successes of Islamic candidates (i.e., the emergence of Islamists as an effective opposition) in Algeria, Egypt, Jordan, Tunisia, Gaza, Turkey, and Kuwait have fed the fears of nervous rulers. In a climate in which most governments during the post-1979 period were traumatized by the specter of "Muslim fundamentalism," this fear provided an excuse for governments to limit political liberalization and/or close the door to democratization. Thus, as I have noted, Egypt's Hosni Mubarak not only moved effectively to control the radicalism of the Gamaa Islamiyya but also increasingly suppressed all Islamic opposition. The Muslim Brotherhood, which for more than two decades remained nonviolent and participated within the political system, came under sharp attack. Members of its leadership and rank and file have been intimidated and arrested. Because of the brotherhood's success in dominating professional associations for lawyers, engineers, and doctors, the government passed legislation to blunt their influence, leading Brotherhood leaders to charge that "the government can not beat us in elections, so they're hitting us below the belt."[96] Other Islamists have been arrested, including Adel Hussein, a prominent writer, former leftist turned Islamist, and secretary general of the Labor Party, which is linked to the Brotherhood. Although the government has reduced the threat from extremism, its indiscriminate use of state power to silence its opposition has had a cost: "Mr. Mubarak's claims of 'democratization' have been undermined by his brutally efficient crackdown on Islamic militants and more recently, political opponents who share their goal of an Islamic state. . . . The cost has been high in terms of abuses such as torture, extra-judicial killings, imprisonment without trial and mass arrests."[97]

The attitude of many rulers may be characterized, in the words of one Western diplomat, as an openness to "risk-free democracy" or, as another put it, "democracy without dissent." This approach is reflected in the Tunisian and Algerian governments' management of political liberalization. Both are open to government-controlled and government-dominated change, but not to a change of government that would bring Islamic activists (or any opposition) to power through democratic means. Recent years have shown that, at best, opposition parties and groups, whether secular or religious, are tolerated only as long as they remain relatively weak or accept government control and do not threaten the regime or ruling party at the ballot box.

Democracy has become an integral part of modern Islamic political thought and practice. It has become accepted in many Muslim countries as a litmus test by which both the openness of governments and the relevance of Islamic groups or other political parties are certified. It is a powerful symbol of legitimacy, legitimizing and delegitimizing precisely because it is seen to be a universal good. However, questions as to the specific nature and degree of popular participation remain unanswered. The extent to which practice will follow this evolution and what particular forms democratization might take in diverse Muslim political cultures remain difficult to predict. Muslim political traditions and institutions, like social conditions and class structures, continue to evolve and are critical to the future of democracy in the Middle East.

A major issue facing Islamic movements is their ability, if in power, to tolerate diversity and political dissent. The status of minorities in Muslim majority areas and freedom of speech remain serious issues. The record of Islamic experiments in Pakistan, Iran, the Sudan, and Afghanistan raises serious questions about the rights of women and minorities under Islamically oriented governments. The extent to which the growth of Islamic revivalism has been accompanied in some countries by attempts to restrict women's rights (to separate women and men in public, to impose and enforce veiling, and to restrict women's public roles in society) strikes fear in some segments of Muslim society and challenges the credibility of those who call for Islamization or re-Islamization of state and society. The record of discrimination against the Bahai in Iran and the Ahmadi in Pakistan as "deviant" groups ("heretical" offshoots of Islam), against Christians in Sudan and Pakistan, and Arab Jews in some countries, as well as communal sectarian conflict between Muslims and Christians in Egypt, Lebanon, and Nigeria, pose similar questions of religious pluralism and tolerance.

If many Muslims ignore these issues or facilely talk of tolerance and human rights in Islam, discussion of these questions in the West is often reduced to two contrasting blocs—the West, which preaches and practices freedom and tolerance, and the Muslim world, which does not. Muslim attitudes toward Christian minorities and the case of Salman Rushdie (and others in Egypt and Bangladesh) are marshaled to support the indictment that Islam is intolerant and antidemocratic. Thus Muslim demands for independence are regarded as deceptive and as a threat to minorities. "What is being pursued, therefore, is not Wilsonian self-determination (though many of these intifadas have adopted its language), because in the Islamic world self-determination is permitted only to Moslems. What instead is being pursued is a pan-Islamic demand for sovereignty over any territory where Moslems form a local majority."[98]

The charge of intolerance is supported by statements from some Christian church leaders that Muslim fundamentalists have no use for ecumenism or dialogue, which is considered a "betrayal to Allah. . . . For Islam, there is only one revelation, the final word has been spoken in the Quran, and Muhammad is the final Prophet."[99] This assertion, which fails to distinguish between what Islam teaches and what some Muslims do, is misleading. As I have noted earlier, Islam acknowledges God's revelation to the Jews and to Christians as it does biblical prophets, though it considers the Quran the final and complete revelation and Muhammad the last in a long line of prophets. Following the logic of the above statement, Christianity could present the same problem. Christians traditionally believed that they had the final, complete revelation, possessed not just a prophet but the Son of God, and had a universal mission to convert the world. In contrast to mainstream Christianity, some Christians today continue to espouse an exclusivist theological worldview. Anyone who has participated in local, national, and international ecumenical gatherings knows that Muslims are regular participants. This does not negate the fact that some Muslims and Islamic organizations, like some Christians and Jews, have little use for ecumenism and are intolerant in word and action. Although there are Muslims and Christians whose religious positions produce an inflexible blend of religion and self-righteousness, others, while affirming the truth of their own faith, are open to dialogue with other believers as they experience the realities of a pluralistic and interdependent world.

The status of non-Muslims and religious and political pluralism remain contemporary Islamic issues requiring reform. Without a reinterpretation of the classical Islamic legal doctrine regarding non-Muslim minorities as "protected people" (*dhimmi*), an ideologically oriented Islamic state would be at best a limited democracy. It would (and indeed has) restrict the participation of non-Muslims in key government positions and the existence of political parties that represent a competing ideology or orientation: secular, communist, socialist. Thus, by modern standards, non-Muslims would be second-class citizens with limited rights and opportunities, as is the case in countries such as Iran and Pakistan.

Muslims, like Christians, have grappled with religious pluralism and its implications in the twentieth century. Historically, the monotheistic vision of both Islam and Christianity, each believing that it possessed the final and complete revelation of God and was charged to call all to salvation, resulted in competing claims and missions and produced theological and political conflict. In the nineteenth and twentieth centuries, much of mainstream Christianity grappled with and came to grips with the realities of pluralism in the modern world. The outcome was the result of a process of reform in which doctrines were reexamined and reinterpreted. For example, Roman Catholicism in the late nineteenth and first half of the twentieth century resisted and condemned much of what was termed "modernism" (from popular sovereignty and elections to pluralism). However, at Vatican II, the church for the first time officially recognized and accepted pluralism.

For Muslims today the issue of pluralism is directly related to the status of non-Muslims in Islamic law as (*dhimmi*) protected minorities, as well as of Muslim minority communities living under non-Muslim rule. Historically, Islam often proved more flexible in tolerating non-Muslims (People of the Book) as minorities whose protected status enabled them to live and practice their faith under Muslim rule. But that status amounts to second-class citizenship in the modern world. The persecution and suppression of non-Muslims by some Muslim governments and by some Islamic movements underscores the need for reinterpretation and reform if the rights of all citizens are to be guaranteed.

For Muslim reformers, pluralism is a critical concern both for Muslim majority countries and for Muslim minority communities. Due to an unprecedented number of Muslim immigrants and refugees, there are more Muslim minority communities in existence across the globe than at any previous time in history. Although some wish to return someday, most face living in new, non-Muslim homelands. This reality raises many questions, from loyalty and political participation to living in societies whose laws are not based on (or reputed to be based on) Islamic law. From Egypt to Indonesia to the United States to Europe, scholars debate and reinterpret Islamic doctrines and laws. As with other faiths, the lines of the debate are often drawn between traditionalists, who wish to simply follow the authority of the past (i.e., retain the classical law intact), and modernists or reformers, who argue the need for and acceptability of a fresh interpretation of Islamic sources, a reformulation of Islam.

A diverse group of Muslim intellectuals and activists (Rashid Ghannoushi, Muhammad Selim al-Awa, Yusuf Qardawi, Mahmoud Ayoub, Kamal Aboul Magd, Fahmy Howeidy, Abdurahman Wahid, Nurcholish Madjid, Abdulaziz Sachedina, Fathi Osman, and Khalid Aboul Fadel) have produced a growing body of literature that reexamines Islamic traditions and addresses issues of pluralism at both theoretical and practical levels. Recognizing the need to open up prevailing one-party or authoritarian political systems as well as face the multireligious and multicultural demographic realities of their societies, they have both reinterpreted Islamic principles to reconcile Islam with democratization and multiparty political systems and recast and expanded traditional doctrine regarding the status (*dhimmi*) of non-Muslim minorities. In addition to employing traditional concepts like consultation (*shura*) and consensus (*ijma*) to limit the authority of rulers, words like party (*hizb*) have been reinterpreted in a way that acknowledges a positive connotation rather than difference and division, which undermine rather than promote the good of society.[100]

Islamists and other Muslim intellectuals have marshaled scripture and history to argue that Islam supports the equality and pluralism of the human community. Quranic passages which affirm that God chose to create the world with different nations and tribes (Sura 5:48; 30:22; 48:13) are emphasized. They argue that the pluralism of the Quran was in fact practiced by Muhammad and the early community in recognizing and extending freedom of religion, worship, and protection (*dhimmi*) to non-Muslims. Some assert that instead of implying a second-class citizenship, the word "dhimma" (which does not occur in the Quran but is found in the *hadith*) was intended to designate a special covenant of protection between Muslims, on the one hand, and Christians and Jews, on the other.[101] Still others note that the term "dhimma" refers to the form of a covenant, not its content, and that content can be redefined today in light of new realities.

Increasingly, both the writings of Muslim intellectuals and the experience of Islam in Southeast Asia become more relevant to the broader Muslim world. The multireligious and multiethnic societies of Malaysia and Indonesia provide a substantial example of pluralism—the issues, problems, and possibilities for change, accommodation, and coexistence.[102] Although Malaysia experienced Malay-Chinese riots in 1969, Malaysians continue to construct a Muslim majority society in which non-Muslims enjoy a degree of political and religious equality as well as democracy unknown in many parts of the Muslim world. Indonesia's depoliticization of Islam has ironically engendered both a deeper Islamization of Indonesian society and a diverse group of voices (Muslim and Christian) committed to a pluralist society.[103]

Despite democratic tendencies in the Muslim world and among some Islamic activists, multiple and conflicting attitudes toward democracy continue to exist and call the future into question. Only time will tell whether the espousal of democracy by many contemporary Islamic movements, as well as their participation in the electoral process, is simply a means to power or a truly embraced and internalized end goal, a transformation of tradition that is the product of a process of religious reinterpretation informed by both faith and experience. The record thus far suggests that when Islamic movements come into power, as they have in many governments in the Middle East, secular as well as "Islamic" issues of political pluralism and human rights will remain a source of tension and debate. Greater political liberalization and participation are part of a process of change that requires time and experience to develop new political traditions and institutions. However, if attempts to participate in the electoral process are blocked, crushed, or negated, as in Tunisia, Algeria, and Turkey, the currency of democracy as a viable mechanism for political and social change will be greatly devalued in the eyes of many. Equally important, failure to develop strong civil societies and democratic traditions perpetuates authoritarian regimes and a culture of authoritarianism, which, even if apparently successful in the short term (as in Tunisia), risks contributing to long-term radicalism and instability.

The Significance of the Rushdie Affair

Just as tolerance and freedom are equated with the West, so too is liberalism; illiberalism is imputed to Islam. The Salman Rushdie case has often been cited to illustrate that "the followers of Muhammad, even in the West, have little use for the liberalism of J. S. Mill."[104] Such judgments reduce the complexity of the Rushdie uproar to the issue of Islam's incompatibility with Western liberalism rather than the question of whether religious belief places limits on free speech. It also implies that all Muslims hold a single position or speak with one voice.

Any discussion of the Rushdie affair must be seen against the background of the past and must recognize the historical and international context in which the debate occurred. John Voll has noted that in regard to the complex history of Islam and the West,

> [a] long history of frequently hostile relations between Muslim and Western societies . . . involves the development on both sides of traditions of conscious defamation of "the enemy" as a part of the rivalry. Thus, we have to overcome a heritage of misunderstanding and prejudice that is deeply rooted in society. The "holy war mentalities" of Crusade and jihad in this heritage color many positions in the debate over *Satanic Verses*. American commentators speak of the threat to constitutional values in the United States, and Westerners often portray the Ayatollah as engaging in a holy war against Western values of tolerance and freedom of expression. At the same time, many Muslims view Mr. Rushdie's book as being in the Western tradition of defamation of Islam and as part of the West's Crusade against basic Islamic values of community responsibility and obedience to God.[105]

Equally important, although many Muslims repudiated Rushdie for blasphemy, all did not declare him an apostate or summarily condemn him to death. The variation in Muslim reactions was ignored by many Western commentators and the media. The multiple and diverse voices, official and unofficial, coming from the Muslim world were drowned out by more strident Western and Muslim voices and the fixation on Khomeini, which dominated media coverage.

The furor over Salman Rushdie's *Satanic Verses* quickly became an international event.[106] The book was condemned and burned by Muslims in many parts of the world. Orderly demonstrations and protest were overshadowed by crowds in the streets of Teheran calling for the death of the author, a demonstration in front of the American Center in Islamabad,

Pakistan, on February 12, 1989, which cost the lives of at least five Pakistanis, and riots and threats against the book's publishers and bookstores in Britain and the United States. The turmoil surrounding the book led to a further cooling of relations between Iran and the West as European nations condemned the Ayatollah Khomeini's call for Rushdie's execution and withdrew diplomats from Iran.

Many Muslims were offended by passages in the book that questioned the authenticity of the Quran, ridiculed the Prophet and the contents of the Quran and referred to Muhammad as "Mahound," a term used in the past by Christian authors to vilify Muhammad. The book also had prostitutes assuming the identity and names of Muhammad's wives, and the very Quranic symbol for their seclusion and protection, "the Curtain," is transformed into the image of a brothel, which men circumambulate as worshipers do the sacred shrine (Kaaba) during the pilgrimage to Mecca.

Muslim responses varied.[107] Most denounced the book as an attack on Islam. Many Muslims in the Muslim world and the West accused the author of blasphemy and sought to have *Satanic Verses* banned. The secretary-general of the Organization of the Islamic Conference (OIC) urged its member nations to ban the book and boycott the publishers. Many Muslim countries (as well as India, which has a significant Muslim minority) banned the book. Egypt had quietly done so in November 1988.

On February 14, 1989, the Ayatollah Khomeini issued a fatwah (religious decree or legal opinion) that condemned Rushdie to death and called for his execution. (Rushdie was born a Muslim but left the faith.) The mufti of Sokoto (Nigeria) also called for Rushdie's death. In contrast, religious scholars at Cairo's al-Azhar University, the oldest university in the world and a venerable center of Islamic learning, stated that according to Islamic law, Rushdie must first have a trial and must be given an opportunity to repent. Egyptian Nobel laureate Naguib Mahfouz, a strong proponent of freedom of expression, publicly backed Egypt's ban, stating that "different cultures have different attitudes towards freedom of speech. What might be endured in Western cultures might not be acceptable in Muslim countries."[108] Others noted that the issue arose in an age in which advocates of "political correctness" in academia and elsewhere have attempted to set boundaries on free speech. Many would proscribe certain forms of child pornography, depictions of gratuitous violence against women, and "hate speech" such as claims of racial inferiority and virulent anti-Semitism. Many Muslims asked, "Why the double standard? Why is blasphemy more acceptable or excusable?"

The Rushdie affair also had important policy implications. In the aftermath of the Iran–Iraq cease-fire in August 1988, Iran had taken notable steps to improve its image and relations internationally. Diplomatic and trade relations with Europe had been strengthened; the Ayatollah Khomeini had sent a personal message to Soviet leader Mikhail S. Gorbachev exhorting him to look to Islam instead of Marxism for a solution to his country's problems. The Iranian government had been taking steps to improve its image in general and the perception of its human rights policy in particular. Iran hosted and participated in a number of conferences that involved Europeans and Americans.

The more hard-line, anti-Western faction within Iran, however, was able to use the Rushdie affair to interrupt this turn toward normalization of relations with the West. It had found the right button to press in motivating Khomeini to respond as Iran's supreme religiopolitical leader. Thus he condemned the book and the author, denounced ''the devilish acts of the West,'' and approved Iran's severance of diplomatic relations with Britain.

Memories of the American embassy hostages in Iran, of the burning of the American embassy in Pakistan in 1979, of attacks against Americans in Lebanon and other countries in the aftermath of the Iranian revolution, and of the riot outside the American Center in Islamabad over the Rushdie book are vivid reminders of the treacherous pitfalls in relations between the United States and militant activists. In contrast to some European governments, the American administration responded more slowly and carefully. It distanced itself from the book (Vice President Quayle described it as offensive) while affirming the right of free speech and rejecting Khomeini's call for the assassination of the author.

One of the lessons of the Rushdie affair is that differences do exist in worldviews and values between the more secular culture of the West and Muslim cultures. The West's modern secular orientation can blind it to the reality to which many Muslims reacted—a book that many Muslims regarded as an attack on the most sacred bases of their faith. It would be equally unfortunate to lose sight of the complexity of Islam, of the multiple voices and diverse Muslim responses. Thus, for example, a group of Arab and Muslim intellectuals and writers did defend Rushdie in the name of free speech.[109] The Ayatollah Khomeini was not the sole spokesman of Islam, nor was it useful to place the Rushdie affair, like other issues, within the memory and emotions of the previous decade's contentious relationship with Iran.

For many Muslims, the Rushdie affair was primarily a religious matter. Yet for others in countries like Iran and Pakistan, religious outrage was often conveniently wedded to domestic politics, such as elite factionalism in Iran or anti-Benazir Bhutto sentiments in Pakistan. In the United Kingdom, the Rushdie affair was part of the larger questioning of a society that many Muslims believed did not seem to live up to its own commitment and standards for tolerance, religiously and politically. For example,

Muslims have repeatedly pointed out that the law against blasphemy protects only the Christian faith (in effect, the social and political establishment) and does not protect other religions (including Judaism and Islam). As Mashuq Ally of the University of Wales noted, "The Muslim community in this case saw itself as fighting a battle of principle: the injustice of the fact that the law of blasphemy applied only to a particular group within the society and not to other groups.[110] Both an insensitivity to cultural differences and a failure to appreciate differing political contexts limited the West's ability to understand the depth of Muslim anguish and, yes, rage. Acknowledging the offensiveness of *Satanic Verses* to many Muslims does not require agreeing with it but can include recognition that the limits of free speech may vary in different religiocultural contexts. On the other hand, the controversy raised by Pakistan's applying Islamic law on blasphemy to Christians who had been charged by Muslims reveal the complexities that attend setting religious limits on free speech.

Islam and the Gulf War of 1991

If Saddam Hussein had his way, Iraq would have emerged from the Gulf War as the defender of Islam against Western imperialism. However, the war again undermined stereotypical images of monolithic Arab and Muslim worlds gripped by Pan-Arabism or Pan-Islam. The Gulf crisis of 1990–91 divided the Arab and indeed Muslim worlds.[111] Similarly, it witnessed multiple appeals to Islam by Muslim political and religious leaders to legitimate each side in the conflict and tested the ideology and allegiances of Islamic movements.[112] The greatest incongruity, perhaps, was that Saddam Hussein, the head of a secularist regime who had ruthlessly suppressed Islamic movements at home and abroad, would cloak himself in the mantle of Islam and call for a jihad.

The Gulf crisis simultaneously presented an apparently united Arab response to a rapacious, expansionist Iraq and, at a deeper level, an Arab and indeed a Muslim world divided to an unparalleled extent. The Arab League and the Organization of the Islamic Conference, a Saudi-supported organization of forty-four Muslim states (today fifty-five states), condemned Saddam's invasion of Kuwait. Emphasis on Arab and Muslim government support for the alliance against Saddam Hussein obscured deeper divisions. Only twelve of the Arab League's twenty-one members supported the anti-Saddam forces. Moreover, as the crisis dragged on, Saddam came to enjoy a degree of popular sympathy often not fully appreciated by Westerners, who tended to equate the position of Arab and Muslim governments with their people and tended not to distinguish among the differing perspectives of the Western-led coalition supported by their Arab and Muslim allies and the views of a significant portion of the populace, whose deep-seated grievances were given a new voice and champion in Saddam Hussein.

Stunned by the unexpectedly quick and broadly based international condemnation, Saddam increasingly emphasized the Arab and Islamic rationales for his actions and thus created popular pressure on Arab and Muslim rulers. He stepped into a leadership vacuum in the Arab world. Although not a charismatic leader, he created a popular persona by appealing to Arab nationalism and Islam, shrewdly exploiting long-standing issues: the failures of Arab governments and societies (poverty, corruption, and the maldistribution of wealth), the plight of the Palestinians, and foreign intervention leading to Arab dependency. Like the Ayatollah Khomeini, Saddam appealed to Islam to enhance his image as the champion of the Palestinians, of the poor and oppressed, and the liberator of the holy places, as well as to legitimate his call for a holy war against Western (especially U.S.) occupation of Arab lands and control of Arab oil. In addition, he called for the overthrow of Arab regimes that opposed him. The espousal of populist causes, issues that transcend the individuals who champion them from time to time, enabled Saddam the secular despot to be transformed into a popular hero among many; the messenger was transformed by the message.

The deep divisions within the Muslim world were reflected in competing appeals to Islam and calls for jihad. Leading religious leaders in Saudi Arabia and Egypt legitimated the presence of foreign troops in Saudi Arabia—the home of Islam's holy sites and cities (Mecca and Medina), access to which is forbidden to non-Muslims. At the same time, Saddam Hussein, Iran's Ayatollah Khomeini, and the Jordanian ulama and Muslim Brotherhood called for a jihad against foreign intervention.[113]

Islamic movements, reflecting their societies, were initially pulled in several directions. At first, most condemned Saddam Hussein, the secular persecutor of Islamic movements, and denounced his invasion of Kuwait. But this initial rejection of Saddam gave way (despite the relationship that many had to supporters in Saudi Arabia) to a more populist, Arab nationalist, anti-imperialist support for Saddam and the condemnation of foreign intervention and "occupation" of Islam's homeland as large numbers of foreign troops poured into the Gulf. The key catalyst was the massive Western (especially U.S.) military buildup in the region and the threat of military action and a permanent Western presence.

For many in the Muslim world, the buildup of foreign troops, announced after the American elections in November 1990, transformed the nature of the conflict from a defensive operation to an offensive force.

Operation Desert Shield had been transformed into Operation Desert Storm, or what its Muslim critics called "Desert Sword"; the defense of Saudi Arabia and the liberation of Kuwait had become not just a war against Saddam Hussein but an all-out attempt to destroy Iraq politically and militarily. Who was thought to benefit most from the resulting power vacuum? America and its ally Israel.

Domestic politics—pressure not to run counter to popular sentiment more than religious conviction and ideology—influenced support for Saddam and his call for jihad by Islamic activists, as witnessed in Algeria, Tunisia, Morocco, Jordan, Pakistan, and Egypt. Thousands of Muslim activists in Algeria had initially demonstrated against Iraq's invasion of Kuwait; on a subsequent visit to Baghdad, however, Abbasi Madani, the leader of the Islamic Salvation Front, declared that "any aggression against Iraq will be confronted by Muslims everywhere."[114] In Jordan, the Muslim Brotherhood had also initially condemned the Iraqi invasion. However, after the deployment of American forces, it called for a jihad against "the new crusaders in defense of Iraq and the Islamic world." One American Muslim observer noted that "people forgot about Saddam's record and concentrated on America. . . . Saddam Hussein might be wrong, but it is not America who should correct him."[115] In Egypt, the Muslim Brotherhood denounced the Iraqi invasion and supported the government's anti-Saddam position. As the war continued, however, the brotherhood joined with other opposition groups and criticized the massive presence of foreign (Western) forces in Saudi Arabia.

Even in countries that sent forces to support the anti-Saddam "international alliance," popular sentiment often differed from that of the government. A majority in Pakistan had opposed the annexation of Kuwait, but in a poll taken by *The Herald*, a Pakistani magazine, 86.6 percent of those polled responded negatively when asked, "Should U.S. troops be defending the Muslim holy places in Saudi Arabia?"[116]

In Southeast Asia, Malaysian and Indonesian government support for U.N. resolutions was accompanied by general condemnation of Iraqi aggression in Kuwait. However, this did not translate into popular support for foreign troops or the threat of massive military action in the Gulf. Saddam Hussein's aggression and the Bush administration's portrayal of him as a new Hitler were not isolated, in the minds of many, from the turbulent politics of the Middle East or the obvious self-interest of the Western-led coalition and many of its allies. Defending Saudi Arabia and liberating Kuwait was one thing, attacking Iraq quite another. Many in Malaysia and Indonesia (reflecting or in solidarity with populist sentiment throughout much of the Muslim world), although critical of Saddam's annexation of Kuwait, were equally strong in their condemnation of the

U.S. "double standard," excoriating Saddam for violating international law and calling for vigorous enforcement of U.N. resolutions while continuing to refuse to take the very same stand with regard to U.N. resolutions condemning Israel's annexation and continued occupation of the West Bank and Gaza.[117] (Similar criticisms were made with regard to the West's failure to come to the defense of Bosnian Muslims.)

An independent Malaysian publication reflected the strong feelings of many in the Muslim world:

> Given the magnitude of the US military buildup in the Gulf and its past records of invasions of and interferences in Third World countries, it is likely that the situation in the Gulf will lead to full scale war. . . . It is indeed hypocritical for the US to come to the aid of Kuwait while it remains silent about Israel's invasion and occupation of the West Bank, Gaza Strip, Golan Heights, Lebanon and its bombing of Tyre, Sidon, and West Beirut, which wounded and killed hundreds of civilians. Instead of economic sanctions, Israel received an increasing amount of US aid. At present, Israel is receiving $4 billion a year from the US. $400 million of US aid goes to help settle Jews from the Soviet Union in Israel's occupied territories therefore legitimating Israel's territorial expansion. In addition, the US had consistently vetoed all attempts by the Security Council to condemn Israel for ignoring United Nations' demands that it withdraw from Lebanon. This double standard was again observed by the US in regard to the Palestinian intafada in which the Israeli military killed over 700 Palestinians including some 160 children. The UN resolution calling for international observers to investigate the situation in the occupied territories was vetoed by the US.[118]

Reluctance by the United States to link (or to acknowledge the linkage of) the two issues—enforcement of U.N. resolutions regarding Iraq's invasion and occupation of Kuwait and Israel's occupation of the West Bank and Gaza—in resolving the Gulf crisis was seen by many in the Muslim world as an attempt to disengage two already interlocked realities.

In Pakistan Qazi Hussein Ahmad, the leader of Pakistan's Jamaat-i-Islami and a member of Pakistan's senate, addressed a large anti-American rally, calling upon Pakistan's government to give up its pro-American foreign policy. Characterizing the American-European alliance as "anti-Islamic forces," he warned that the United States intended to establish its hegemony in the region, not liberate Kuwait. Europe and America had joined hands to "destroy the fighting power of the Islamic world."[119] Thus, he concluded, there would be no place for the Islamic world in the New World Order. Populist support for Saddam Hussein became more strident with pro-Saddam and anti-American rhetoric, demonstrations, protest marches, and, at times, violence across the Muslim world: in Algeria, Tunisia, Morocco, Mauritania, Sudan, Libya, Nigeria, Lebanon, Jordan, the West Bank and Gaza, Yemen, Egypt, India, Pakistan, Bangladesh, Iran, Malaysia, Indonesia, and even among South Africa's Muslim community. Scud missile attacks on Tel Aviv were celebrated by many Arab nationalists and Islamic activists alike. Saddam was seen as the first Arab leader to actually hit the heart of Israel. Those convinced that Israel supplied intelligence information on Iraq, fought its wars with the Arabs on Arab territory, and freely carried out retaliation attacks against Tunis, Baghdad, Beirut, and southern Lebanon, hailed Saddam for bringing the experience and human costs of war home to the Israelis. Algeria, Morocco, Tunisia, Mauritania, and the Sudan witnessed large demonstrations. Saddam's appeals to Arab Nationalism, Islam, and the Palestinian cause resonated with memories of French colonialism and the struggle of many to root their identity more indigenously in an Arab Islamic past. In Rabat on February 3, 1991, 300,000 demonstrators took to the streets demanding the withdrawal of Moroccan troops from the multinational coalition. Lebanon experienced some of the largest demonstrations since the beginning of the Lebanese civil war, along with bombings of Western banks and airline offices. In Iran anti-American demonstrations took place in many major cities. President Rafsanjani, while carefully maintaining Iran's official position of ''neutrality,'' was equally cautious, aligning himself with populist Muslim sentiment within both Iran and the broader Muslim world: ''the leader of imperialism is destroying a Muslim nation and ruining the resources of Muslims.''[120] The Indonesian government supported U.N. resolutions on the Gulf, and many Indonesians denounced the annexation of Kuwait. However, Saddam's linkage of his actions with resolution of the Palestinian problem, the presence of U.S. forces in the Gulf, and the subsequent devastation of Iraq produced a growing level of anti-American criticism in the press and among intellectuals, Muslim leaders, and student groups.[121]

Coalition members such as Morocco, Bangladesh, Egypt, Syria, and Pakistan, who had sent troops to the Gulf, were increasingly subjected to domestic pressure to remove their forces. Islamic activists joined with other opposition groups in protesting the war. In Egypt, the Muslim Brotherhood joined with the left and many professional associations. An antigovernment weekly carrying the headline ''Muslims! Your Brothers Are Being Annihilated. Hurry to Aid Iraq in Its Heroic Steadfastness'' sold out within hours.[122] Pakistan saw religious organizations like the Jamaat-i-Islami involved in massive public demonstrations throughout the country as hundreds flocked to centers to volunteer for the jihad.

As in other instances, the Gulf War revealed a diversity of positions within the Muslim world—a multiplicity of voices representing differing perspectives and priorities: differences among Muslim governments, between some governments and their people, among religious leaders and Islamic movements. Although images of the Crusades, imperialism, and a clash of civilizations were raised by Saddam in the name of Islam, they were rejected with equal force by other Muslim countries and religious leaders such as the official ulama of Egypt and Saudi Arabia.

The Islamic Threat: Issues of Interpretation

The ways in which people understand the nature of religion and the relationship of religion to politics and society greatly determine their presuppositions, expectations, and judgments. Why has the continued vitality of Islamic revivalism been underestimated? Conversely, why does it continue to be primarily perceived and responded to as a threat?

Despite greater interest and media coverage and a seemingly never ending stream of publications and conferences, understanding and appreciation of Islam and Islamic movements have remained limited and selective. Given the resources available, and the number of academic experts and government analysts, why did it take the Iranian Revolution of 1978–79 to draw attention to events that had been taking place previously throughout the seventies in Libya, Egypt, Pakistan, the Sudan, and the broader Muslim world? And even with the post factum "discovery" of Islamic revivalism, why did most analysts continue to underestimate the vitality and power of Islamic fundamentalism in countries like Algeria, Tunisia, Jordan, Egypt, and Turkey? Conversely, why has there been a persistent tendency to reduce Islam and Islamic activism to religious extremism and terrorism? Violence, warfare, terrorism, and injustice exist in the Muslim world, as in other places. They have been legitimated on occasion in the name of Islam, as they have in the name of Christianity, Judaism, and secular ideologies such as democracy and communism.

At the heart of Western misinterpretation, stereotyping, and exaggerated fears of Islam is a clash of viewpoints. Older stereotypes of "the Arab" and Islam in terms of Bedouin, desert, camel, polygamy, harem, and rich oil shaykhs have been replaced by those of gun-toting mullahs, bearded, anti-Western fundamentalists, and veiled women. Western fears and antipathy are not only fed by media reports and headline events but are also rooted in a secular outlook on life that is often antithetical to the perspective of Islamic activists. Modern, post-Enlightenment secular language and categories of thought often prejudice and distort understanding and judgment. The modern notion of religion as a system of personal belief makes an Islam (or any world religion or religious worldview) that is comprehensive in scope, in which religion is integral to politics and society, "abnormal" insofar as it departs from an accepted "modern" secular norm, and nonsensical. Thus Islam becomes incomprehensible, irrational, extremist, threatening.

Nevertheless, all the world's religions in their origins and histories were fairly comprehensive ways of living.[123] Although the relationship of religion to politics varies, religion is a path or a way of life with a strong emphasis on community as well as personal life: the way of the Torah, the straight path of Islam, the middle path of the Buddha, the righteous way (*dharma*) of Hinduism. It provides guidance for hygiene, diet, managing wealth, stages of life (birth, marriage, death), as well as for ritual and worship. The modern notion of religion has its origins in the post-Enlightenment West. Its restricted definition has become accepted as the norm or meaning of religion by many believers and unbelievers alike in the West. Bereft of a sense of history, few realize that the term "religion" as known and understood today is a modern and Western interpretation of it. The West then set about naming other religious systems or isms. Christianity and Judaism were joined by the newly named Hinduism, Buddhism, and Mohammedanism. Thus the nature and function of other religious traditions were categorized, studied, and judged in terms of modern Western, post-Enlightenment secular criteria, with its separation of church and state.

Even as our concept of religion is a modern construct, so too the Western notion of separation of church and state is relatively new. Historically, the dividing line between faith and politics among the Abrahamic faiths (Judaism, Christianity, and Islam) had been blurred from the Israelite conquests and the early Jewish kingdoms to imperial Christianity. As the Christian empires and Crusades demonstrated, although church and state were distinct, they were not always separate in Christianity. However, the modern notions of religion as a system of belief for personal life and of separation of church and state have become so accepted and internalized that they have obscured past beliefs and practice and have come to represent for many a self-evident and timeless truth. As a result, from a modern secular perspective (a form of "secular fundamentalism"), the mixing of religion and politics is regarded as necessarily abnormal, (departing from the norm), irrational, dangerous, and extremist. Those who do so are often dubbed "fundamentalists" (Christian, Jewish, or Muslim) or religious fanatics. Thus when secular-minded people (government officials, political analysts, journalists, and the bulk of the general public) in the West encounter Muslim individuals and groups who speak of Islam as a comprehensive way of life, they immediately dub them "fundamentalist" with the connotation that these are backward-looking individuals, zealots who are a threat. The attitude of many governments and of secular elites in the Muslim world is often similar. Images of militant mullahs and the violent actions of some individuals and groups are then taken as representative and proof of the inherent danger of mixing religion and politics.

Viewing Islam and events in the Muslim world primarily through the prism of violence and terrorism has resulted in a failure to see the breadth and depth of contemporary Islam, the multiplicity of orientations and diversity of expressions. In particular, many have overlooked the quiet revolution that has occurred in many parts of the Muslim world—the institutionalization of Islamic revivalism. As I have already noted, Islamic revivalism is no longer a movement of the marginalized few who exist on the periphery of society. It has become a part of mainstream Muslim life.

Secularization and Modernization: The Dangers of Secular Fundamentalism

Secular presuppositions—which inform our academic disciplines and outlook on life, our Western secular worldview—have been a major obstacle to understanding and analyzing Islamic politics and have consequently contributed to a tendency to reduce Islam to fundamentalism and fundamentalism to religious extremism. For much of the sixties, the received wisdom among many, from development experts to theologians, could be summarized in the adage: Every day in every way, things are and will continue to get more and more modern and secular. Integral to definitions of modernization was the progressive Westernization and secularization of society, including its institutions, organizations, and actors.[124] This attitude was reflected in analyses that viewed the choices in development in polar dichotomies: tradition and modernity, Mecca and mechanization. Religion and theology reflected the same presupposition and expectation as theologians spoke of demythologizing the scriptures, of a secular gospel for the modern age, of the triumph of the secular city (as distinguished from Augustine's City of God). A school of theological thought emerged that was dubbed the "Death of God Theology."[125] Religious faith was at best supposed to be a private matter. The degree of one's intellectual sophistication and objectivity in academia was often equated with a secular liberalism and relativism that seemed antithetical to religion. Although church or synagogue membership were recognized as useful, most political candidates avoided discussing their faith or religious issues.

Acceptance of the "enlightened" notion of separation of church and state and of Western, secular models of development relegated religion to the stockpile of traditional beliefs, valuable in understanding the past but irrelevant or an obstacle to modern political, economic, and social development. Neither development theory nor international relations considered religion a significant variable for political analysis. The separation of religion and politics overlooked the fact that religious traditions were established and developed in historical, political, social, and economic contexts. Their doctrines and laws were conditioned by these contexts. This was certainly true in the history of Islam and even more so in the belief of many Muslims. Ironically, some analysts became like conservative clerics the world over—they treated religious beliefs and practices as isolated, freestanding realities rather than as the product of the interplay of faith and history or, more accurately, faith-in-history.

Religious traditions, although characterized as conservative or traditional, are the product of a dynamic, changing process in which the Word of revelation is mediated through human interpretation or discourse in response to specific sociohistorical contexts. The post-Enlightenment tendency to define religion as a system of belief restricted to personal or private life, rather than as a way of life, has seriously hampered our ability to understand the nature of Islam and many of the world's religions. It has artificially compartmentalized religion, doing violence to its nature, and has reinforced a static, reified conception of religious traditions rather than revealed their inner dynamic nature. To that extent, a religion that does not seem to do so (a religion that mixes religion and politics) appears necessarily retrogressive, prone to religious extremism and fanaticism, and thus a potential threat.

Islam has generally been regarded in the West (and among many secular-minded Muslims) as a static phenomenon doctrinally and sociocuturally, and therefore antimodern and retrogressive. This attitude was supported by the prevailing tendency to emphasize such notions as the closing of the door of religious interpretation (*ijtihad*) or reform in the tenth century. Many experts were trained in area studies programs by professors (historians and social scientists) with little real expertise in Islamic religion. In history and politics courses Islam was treated primarily as part of a cultural legacy, historical baggage studied more for its relevance to the past than to the present. Islamic studies was textually and historically rather than contextually oriented, with little reliance on the social sciences and with minimal attention to the modern period. Coverage of the modern period, the nineteenth and twentieth centuries, was restricted to one chapter, often the shortest.[126] What judgments of vitality and relevance could be implied by courses and analyses of modern Islam, in particular Islamic modernism, which stopped with Muhammad Abduh, (who died in 1905) or Muhammad Iqbal (who died in 1938)?

A second factor that hindered analysis of the Islamic dimension and dynamic in Muslim societies and perpetuated images of an inherently retrogressive religion was its secular, elite orientation. Focusing on some governments and elites reflects a bias that hampers understanding of the nature of populist movements in general and Islamic movements in particular. It reinforces the notion that religion is the province of the tradition-bound cleric (*mullah*), religious scholars (*ulama*), and the uneducated or illiterate masses. Thus few scholars of the Middle East or other Muslim societies believed it necessary or relevant to know and meet with religious leaders, to visit their institutions, or to have some idea of their leadership roles in society. Too often the ulama were regarded as irrelevant or of marginal interest. Most Western scholars, as well as Western-trained Muslim scholars, were more comfortable working and studying with like-minded modern, and Westernized elites in urban settings. Much of Western scholarship viewed Muslim societies through the modern prism of a development theory that was secular and Western in its principles, values, and expectations. Experts analyzed and judged societies as their elites ran them—from the top down. As a result, academic and government analysts and the media often slipped into the same pitfalls: focusing on a narrow, albeit powerful, secular elite segment of society; and equating secularization with progress and religion with backwardness and conservatism, believing that modernization and Westernization are necessarily intertwined. As a result, the options available for the political and social development of Muslim societies were often seen in polarities, more recently characterized as a clash of civilizations: the tug between tradition and modernity, the past and the future, the madrasa (religious college or seminary) and the university, the chador (veil) and Western dress and values.

Edward Said's insightful critique of orientalism, though at times excessive, identified the deficiencies and biases in past scholarship. Today new forms of orientalism flourish in the hands of those who equate revivalism, fundamentalism, or Islamic movements solely with radical revolutionaries and focus on a radicalized minority rather than the vast majority of Islamically committed Muslims who belong to the moderate mainstream of society. Too often academia, government, and the media have focused on crises and headline events and thus on a violent radical fringe. Failing to see the forest for the trees, they have not studied sufficiently either moderate political on nonpolitical movements and organizations. This trend (and deficiency) has been reinforced by the realities of the marketplace. Publishing houses, journals, consulting firms, and the media key themselves to headlines, which all too often confirm fears of extremism and terrorism and reinforce stereotypes. Think how often any reference to an Islamic organization or activist includes adjectives like "fundamentalist," "radical," and "extremist."

Many who subscribe to a liberal secular or liberal Judeo-Christian tradition view any intrusion of religion into politics as potentially dangerous and "fundamentalist." This perception is heightened or intensified when our focus and knowledge of religious groups is limited to those who represent a radical minority. Compare coverage of Tabligh-i Jamaat and a myriad of jihad organizations. The former is a worldwide nonpolitical missionary Muslim organization with millions of members, whereas the latter are radical groups whose membership often only runs in the hundreds and whose sporadic violence, though dramatic at times, affects far fewer lives. Compare the number of substantive studies and media reports on Sufi (mystical) orders or brotherhoods, Islamic social welfare organizations, and moderate Islamic organizations such as the Egyptian Muslim Brotherhood, Pakistan's Jamaat-i-Islami, Kuwait's Jamiyyat al-Islah, Tunisia's Renaissance Party, or Malaysia's ABIM with those on radical Islamic movements.

The Politics of Underestimation

Why is it that the resurgence of Islam in many countries and its political implications have often been acknowledged only at the eleventh hour? When revivalism was growing in Egypt, Libya, Pakistan, Lebanon, and Malaysia in the early seventies, few noticed or gave it any attention. A presentation on Islam's potential role in sociopolitical development attracted fewer than ten people at an International Studies Association annual meeting. Today many professional meetings feature almost that number of participants on the panel alone. What was first described as an epiphenomenon was often later dismissed as a wave that had passed. This line of thought persisted during the eighties as we overlooked and then discovered or were forced to confront events in Iran, Pakistan, Lebanon, the Gulf, and now Turkey and North Africa. Many said it could happen in Pakistan but never in Iran, or in Iran but not in Egypt, or in Egypt but most assuredly never in Tunisia, Algeria, or especially "secular Turkey." As Islam has seemed to decline in the politics of one nation or region, it has risen in others. The 1988 Iran-Iraq cease-fire led many, forgetting the indigenous sources of the Islamic revival, to conclude that this signaled the discrediting of Khomeini and was thus a death blow to the "fundamentalist wave." For some, the death of the Ayatollah Khomeini meant a seeming end of a fundamentalist threat; others looked for new "Khomeinis" and new "Irans."

More often than not, Islamic movements have been lumped together and conclusions have been drawn that are based more on stereotyping or preconceived expectations than empirical research. This problem is due less to the secrecy of individuals and organizations than to more mundane factors:

1. The dearth of scholars in Middle East studies in general and Islamic studies in particular means that many attempt to cover (in their writings or as media commentators) vast geographic areas and such varied topics as politics, law, history, society, and oil.
2. Since many experts have come with a secular academic bias as well as limited training in Islam and the Islamic dimension of Muslim societies, there is a greater tendency to generalize or to draw deductive conclusions from secular presuppositions and prejudices. A shallow understanding of Islam and the dynamics of religious traditions compounds this problem.
3. Many scholars of Islam have training and work on past rather than modern or contemporary periods.
4. Most experts and commentators have limited training and even less actual direct contact and extended experience with Islamic activists and movements.

Analysis of modern Islamic movements and organizations requires more than generalizations or reliance on newspaper reports or movement-issued documents, isolated events, and government reports. Direct observation, interaction, and study are particularly critical, since many Islamic activists write comparatively little; what writings they do produce are often little more than ideological tracts or public relations documents. What they write or say must be placed within the context of what they actually do. Because of a combination of limited access and a tendency to respond to government concerns, media interest, and demands (headline events), the breadth, character, and activities of the moderate majority of contemporary organizations have often gone relatively unnoticed or downplayed.

Diversity and Change

The experience of the past two decades alerts us to the need to be mo⹁ attentive to the diversity that is behind the seeming unity of Islam, appreciate and more effectively analyze both the unity and diversity Islam and in Muslim affairs. In the past, the oneness of Islam (of G the Prophet, and the Book) gave rise to many diverse movements interpretations: Sunni, Shii, Kharaji, Wahhabi, and different schools law, theology, and mysticism. Today, similarly, differing contexts ⷉ spawned a variety of Islamically oriented nations, leaders, and orgar tions. The diversity of governments—the Saudi monarchy and Qadd populist state, Iran's clerically guided republic in Iran, the former mi⌁

regime of Zia ul-Haq and the current democratically elected government of Nawaz Sharif in Pakistan, the military regimes of Gaafar Muhammad Nimeiri and today Omar al-Bashir in Sudan, the Taliban government in Afghanistan, their differing relations with the West, as well as the variety of Islamic movements—has often been undercut and distorted by the univocal connotation of the term "Islamic fundamentalism."

Beyond the common reference to an Islamic alternative and to general ideological principles are multiple and diverse levels of discourse across the wide array of governments, societies, and Islamic organizations. There are as many differences as similarities in Muslim interpretations of the nature of the state, Islamic law, the status of women and minorities. Similarly, there are sharp differences regarding the methods (the ballot box, social service centers, violent confrontation, and terrorism) to be employed for the realization and implementation of an Islamic order or system of government. Thus there is today, as in the past, a rich diversity of interpretations, manifestations, and applications of Islam. No group epitomizes this more than Afghanistan's Taliban movement. Afghanistan witnessed he rise of a seemingly improbable militia that would go on to unite 90 ercent of the country and declare the Islamic Republic of Afghanistan.

In contrast to fear of the Islamic resurgence or "Islamic fundamental-'' in Iran and the Middle East throughout the eighties, Afghanistan's ahideien were seen as freedom fighters whose holy war (*jihad*) re-d substantial aid from the United States, Saudi Arabia, and other ries. However, the mujahidin victory did not bring peace. The com-slamic identity that had served to inspire, mobilize, and unify the din in their jihad against the Soviet Union was now eclipsed by istan's age-old tribal, ethnic, and religious (Sunni–Shii) differences lries. After almost eighteen years of civil war, a seemingly endless arnage and chaos was abruptly reversed.

ut of nowhere, a band of madrasa students (*taliban*) appeared in and within two years swept across the country. Denouncing all ling mujahidin militias, they claimed the mantle of moral lead-presentatives of the majority of Afghans who were victims of ine warfare. Although initially portrayed as young students drasas with no military background, in fact they were a force and taliban—religious leaders and students. The former was f veterans of the Afghan-Soviet war who had returned to the ter the Soviets departed.

initially hailed as liberators who secured towns, made the for ordinary citizens, and cleaned up corruption and graft, their of Islam soon became an issue. The Taliban subscribe to a vative (puritanical) interpretation of Islam. Their Wahhabi-like doctrines are close to those of Saudi Arabia's religious establishment and Pakistan's Jamaat-i-Islami, though more extreme. They banned women from school and the workplace, required that men wear beards and women chadors, banned music and television, and imposed strict physical punishments on deviators. Their intolerance of any ''deviation'' from their brand of Islam included the slaughter of many of Afghanistan's Shii minority, whom they disdained as heretics, when the Taliban overran Shii areas like Mazda al-Sharif

Many Muslim religious leaders denounced Taliban ''Islamic'' policies as aberrant. Muslim governments as diverse as Iran and Egypt, as well as Western governments and international human rights organizations, condemned Taliban violations of human rights. Despite their control of most of Afghanistan by fall 1998, neither the United Nations nor most of the global community (the Taliban government was recognized by only four nations) acknowledged their legitimacy.

As a romanticized notion of early Islamic history made many Muslims forget the dynamism and degree of change in the past, so too a Western secular tendency to pit modern change against a fixed tradition has obscured the degrees of difference and change in modern Islam and modern Muslim societies. Too often secular scholars and Muslim theologians alike have failed to appreciate the extent to which religious beliefs and laws are the product of human interpretation and application of revelation. A rigid, retrogressive Islam becomes a threat. Ironically, non-Muslim scholars sometimes themselves sound like mullahs. Faced with new interpretations or applications of Islam, they often critique such ideas from the vantage point of traditional belief and practice. On the one hand, Islam is regarded as fixed, and Muslims are seen as reluctant to accept change. On the other hand, when change occurs, it is dismissed as unorthodox, deceptive, sheer opportunism, or as an excuse for adopting that which is outside Islam. However, all we are witnessing is a natural process of reexamination and reinterpretation, difference and debate, tension and conflict, by and among individuals and communities, and another stage in the interpretation and development of the Islamic tradition. The reinterpretation (*ijtihad*) of traditional Islamic concepts such as consultation (*shura*) and community consensus (*ijma*) are excellent examples of this process. On the one hand, some scholars like to point out that Islam is antithetical to Western notions of democracy and parliamentary government, forgetting that the same could be said of traditional Judaism and Christianity. On the other hand, when Muslims attempt to adapt traditional Islamic concepts to contemporary needs and legitimate democratic forms of government, they are suspected of having a hidden agenda or are criticized for not being faithful to the original meaning of these concepts or ideals.

Change is a reality in contemporary Islam and in Muslim societies. It may be found at every level, in every quarter, and across social classes. The question is not change but the pace and direction of change. The questions facing many devout Muslims and their societies today are not whether there should be any change but rather how much change and what kinds of change are necessary and permissible. The flexibility of the Islamic tradition is not only demonstrated by those whom some regard as modern Islamic intellectuals or reformers. It is also clearly manifested in the Ayatollah Khomeini's interpretation of the doctrine of *vilayat-i-faqih* as well as the constitution of the Islamic Republic of Iran as it accepts a constitutional and parliamentary form of government.

Challenge or Threat?

Is there an Islamic threat? In the sense that there can be a Western threat or a Judeo-Christian threat, yes. Islam, like Christianity and Judaism, has provided a way of life and guidance that has transformed the lives of many. Yet some Muslims, like some Christians and Jews, have also used their religion to justify and legitimate aggression and warfare, conquest and persecution, in the past and the present. Political Islam, like the appeal to any religion or ideology, can be a positive effective force for change; it can also be a dangerous threat to Muslim societies and to the West. Secular ideologies (democracy, socialism, communism, and Arab nationalism) have proven equally vulnerable to manipulation and exploitation in the hands of demagogues. Noble ideals like spreading God's will and spreading democracy can be distorted and used to legitimate imperialism, oppression, and injustice in the name of God or the state.

Islam can also be a challenge or threat to the complacency of Western societies—spiritually, socially, and politically. It is, in some of its forms, a straightforward questioning of both the traditions that "we" seem to embrace—secularism, consumerism, unfettered individualism, though these may be a caricature of us—and also of our commitment to the values that we say we espouse: self-determination, pluralism, tolerance, freedom of expression. To be challenged to "walk the way you talk" may be unsettling but is not in itself unfair.

Likewise, political Islam is itself challenged. It is challenged by its own rhetoric and message to be self-critical: to live up to the standards and principles it espouses and demands of others; to move beyond slogans to practical programs; and to denounce acts of terrorism committed by governments and movements that identify themselves as Islamic. Finally, Islamic activists must accept Muslim responsibility and not simply blame the West for the failures of Muslim societies. In particular, many are challenged to avoid, in their zeal to Islamize state and society, a tendency to "kafirize." In many Muslim societies, advocates of the Islamization (or re-Islamization) of state and society have been prone to also engage in "kafirization," declaring others (Muslims and non-Muslims alike who disagree with them) to be infidels (kafirs). Any form of dissent makes the dissenters "the enemies of God," and thus persecution and warfare are justified. The results of this approach have ranged from public denunciation to physical attacks and assassinations. As in Egypt and Algeria, not only Christians and foreigners but also other Muslims (government officials, intellectuals, journalists, young women not deemed to be Islamically dressed) have been attacked and murdered. Similar forms of violence and terrorism in the name of Islam have paralleled charges of state authoritarianism, repression, and terrorism.

The reality of Muslim societies today contributes to a climate in which the influence of Islam and activist organizations on sociopolitical development will increase rather than diminish in most Muslim societies. Many Muslim states continue to exist in a climate of crisis in which many of their citizens experience and speak of the failure of the state and of secular forms of nationalism and socialism. Heads of state and ruling elites or classes possess tenuous legitimacy in the face of mounting disillusionment and opposition, among whom Islamic activists are often the most vocal and effective critics. The extent to which governments in predominantly Muslim countries fail to meet the socioeconomic needs of their societies, are corrupt, restrict political participation, fail to effectively incorporate Islam as a component in their national identity and ideology, or appear dependent on the West contributes to the appeal of an Islamic political alternative.

The political strength and durability of Islamic movements and their ideological impact are reflected in a variety of ways. They have forced government changes and, where permitted, successfully contested elections. Rulers from Morocco to Malaysia have become more Islamically sensitive and have sought to coopt religion or suppress Islamic organizations. Many have employed Islamic rhetoric and symbols more often, expanded support for Islamic institutions (mosques and schools), increased religious programming in the media, and have paid more attention to public religious observances such as the fast of Ramadan or restrictions on alcohol and gambling.

When free from government repression, Islamic candidates and organizations have worked within the political system and participated in elections in Tunisia, Turkey, Jordan, Egypt, Lebanon, Kuwait, Yemen, Pakistan, Indonesia, and Malaysia; activists have even held cabinet-level positions in the Sudan, Pakistan, Kuwait, Jordan, Yemen, and Malaysia. Islamic organizations are among the best-organized opposition forces and are often willing to form alliances or cooperate with political parties, professional syndicates, and voluntary associations to achieve shared political and socioeconomic reforms. Islamic student organizations successfully compete in student elections in the universities and lead student strikes and demonstrations.

Islamic movements face internal problems and challenges. Although they have often been able to identify and mobilize opposition against a common enemy or threat, once successful, internal power struggles and problems quickly emerge in defining and implementing an Islamic system of government. Islamic politics, like secular politics, is influenced by factionalism stemming from ideological interpretations or visions of Islam, internal power struggles for leadership, and the influence of family, ethnic, and tribal or regional ties. Yet it is constrained by the pragmatic demands and compromises of an interdependent global environment.

The challenge for Islamic activists today is one of personnel and resources, ideology and pluralism. Islam has proven an effective rallying cry to mobilize opposition to governments as in the Shah's Iran, Zulfikar Ali Bhutto's Pakistan, Soviet-occupied Afghanistan, and, most recently, in Turkey and Algeria. However, the real test is to produce an effective, representative government and program for sociopolitical change. Islamic movements continue to be challenged to move beyond slogans and vague promises to concrete political and socioeconomic programs. They need to bridge the gap between traditional Islamic beliefs and institutions and the sociopolitical realities of the contemporary world. The economic failures of governments in Sudan and Iran and their failure thus far to produce effective governments that enjoy widespread support at home have led many to speak of the failure of political Islam.[127] Substantive religious and intellectual reform have lagged behind and thus have not informed much of Islamic political and social activism. Political activists often have neither the time nor the temperament to undertake a process of Islamic reform that provides the intellectual foundations for political and socioeconomic change. And yet unlike their predecessors, they are no longer on the periphery of society but are often positioned to be key players in the political process and even to come to power. Moreover, the authority and Islamic legitimacy of their fresh interpretations of Islam will require the support of a critical mass of traditional religious leaders.

Islamic movements are increasingly required to demonstrate their ability to be effective problem solvers, not just social critics, who can transform ideological commitment and slogans into concrete policies and programs that respond to national and local concerns in diverse sociopolitical contexts. They must do this in a manner that is pluralistic enough in scope to enjoy the support of a broad and diverse constituency. These include fellow activists, secularists, religious and ethnic minorities, as well as that broad base majority of Muslims who, while wishing to be good Muslims, do not want to see the stability of their societies and their lives disrupted. The leadership of Islamic movements, like the rulers of Muslim countries, are particularly challenged to recognize that authoritarianism and repression, whether Islamic or secular, ultimately fails to respond to the temper and needs of the times. They will not offer the basis for political legitimacy, increased political participation, and national unity. Therefore, Islamists are challenged to demonstrate that they too can be self-critical and to denounce those Islamic movements and governments that engage in repression and terrorism in the name of Islam.

The examples of Islamically legitimated authoritarianism in Khomeini's Iran, Qaddafi's Libya, Zia ul-Haq's Pakistan, Bashir's Sudan, and the Taliban in Afghanistan, as well as the extremist activities of radical groups in Egypt, the West Bank and Gaza, and Algeria, reinforce fear of a "fundamentalist threat or takeover" and undermine the credibility of those who seek power in the name of Islam. The impact of Islamization on the status of women in many countries, attacks by Muslim extremists against Copts in Egypt, discrimination against Bahai in Iran and against Ahmadiyya in Pakistan, and the imposition of Islamic laws on non-Muslims in the Sudan and Pakistan raise grave concerns about the rights of minorities in an Islamically oriented state. In the wake of postrevolutionary Iran's example, the policies of Sudan's current Islamically backed government has led many to decry the dangers of Islamic (rather than secular) authoritarianism. Political fragmentation between the Muslim north and the non-Muslim (Christian and animist) south, imposition of Islamic law on non-Muslims, and the persecution of Christian churches are but several of the contentious issues. The sharp contrast between the reformist rhetoric of Hasan Turabi, leader of the National Islamic Front (NIF), when out of power, and the actual policies of Sudan's NIF-backed government tends to undermine the credibility of other Islamic leaders and movements. It also provides a primary example for those who emphasize that Islamic leaders say one thing when they are out of power and act quite differently when in office. Serious questions remain about whether or not Islamic movements, which insist upon their democratic rights and self-determination as fundamental human rights, would, if in power, extend those same rights to all citizens.

Islam and U.S. Policy

The nineties have tested the ability of political analysts and policymakers to distinguish between Islamic movements that are a threat and those that represent legitimate indigenous attempts to reform and redirect their societies. Of equal importance, it raises questions about the ability of policymakers to distinguish between short-term foreign policy goals and long-term interests, between fears of a monolithic Islamic threat and its diverse and diffuse reality. Although the vast majority of Islamic organizations seek to work within the system, clandestine radical organizations that advocate violence to seize power and establish an Islamic state continue to exist. A minority of militant Islamic organizations, with names like al-Jihad, the Gamaa Islamiyya, the Party of God, Salvation from Hell, the Army of God, Islamic Liberation Front, Turkish Revenge Brigade, and the Armed Islamic Group, continue to resort to violence and terrorism, threatening the stability of their societies as well as regional politics.

Stability and security interests in the oil countries of the Persian Gulf must be balanced by recognition that both the long-term stability of governments and societies in the region as well as the image and credibility of the United States may be affected in the next decade by (1) the ability of Muslim rulers to respond to domestic voices for change by fostering a political culture, values, and institutions that promote greater political participation and strengthen civil society and (2) the ability of Western policymakers to take a comparative perspective that recognizes and responds in diverse ways to the multiple forms of political Islam.

The Iranian Revolution dominated much of Middle East politics and Western perceptions of the Muslim world during the eighties and the nineties. It proved to be a decade of new alliances and alignments in which many Islamic movements challenged their societies and the West while a violent radical minority continued to directly threaten the stability of state and society. The massacre of tourists at Luxor, Egypt, the bombings and deaths of American servicemen in Saudi Arabia, and the carnage from the bombings of American embassies in Kenya and Tanzania were grim reminders of the threat posed by extremists and their global war against the West. The American cruise missile attack against suspected terrorist training bases and targets supported by Osama bin Laden raised the specter of a future struggle between international terrorists and the West in the twenty-first century.

Contemporary Islam is more a challenge than a threat. It challenges the West to know and understand the diversity of the Muslim experience. It challenges Muslim governments to be more responsive to popular demands for political liberalization and greater popular participation, to tolerate rather than repress nonviolent opposition movements, and to build viable democratic institutions, while containing violent extremism and terrorism. At the same time, it challenges Western powers to stand by the democratic values they embody, distinguish between authentic populist movements and violent revolutionaries, and recognize the right of all people to determine the nature of their government and leadership.

American and European support for repressive regimes intensifies anti-Westernism and anti-Americanism, as events in the Shah's Iran, Lebanon, Egypt, Algeria, and the West Bank and Gaza have demonstrated. A strong anti-Western, and especially anti-American, sentiment exists among many moderates as well as radicals, secular as well as Islamic. It is manifested in a tendency to regard the United States as anti-Islamic and uncritically pro-Israel and to blame the ills of Muslim societies upon Western political, economic, and sociocultural influences. At the same time, equating "Khomeinism" with "Islam" and "violent radicalism" with a monolithic "fundamentalism" results in the assumption that Islamic movements are naturally or inherently anti-Western. This detracts attention from the causes of anti-Americanism or radicalism. Movements are more often motivated by objection to specific Western policies and actions than by civilizational hostility. Differences between Western and Muslim societies (as between nation-states) can best be explained by competing political, socioeconomic, and cultural interests rather than a clash of civilizations. American presence and policy, not a generic hatred for Americans, is often the primary motivating force behind acts against American government, business, and military interests. American interests will best be served by policies that walk the fine line between selective, discreet cooperation with allies in the Muslim world balanced by contact with alternative political actors and opposition movements and, most importantly, a consistent human rights policy, including the right of citizens to determine their future.

The assumption that mixing religion and politics necessarily and inevitably leads to fanaticism and extremism has been a major factor in concluding that Islam and democracy are incompatible. Failure to differentiate between Islamic movements—between those that are moderate (nonviolent and willing to participate within the system) and those that are violent revolutionaries—is simplistic and counterproductive. Islamist movements or parties that participate in the system, engaging in social and political activism, do not necessarily threaten the political system as such but can be perceived as a threat by entrenched rulers and political elites when Islamists offer an attractive political alternative. The U.S. government (as well as the media) does not equate the actions of Jewish or Christian extremist leaders or groups with Judaism and Christianity. Whether it be the bombing of abortion clinics, the massacre of Muslims at prayer in a

Hebron mosque, or the Serbian (Christian) genocidal policy of ethnic cleansing in Bosnia, a sharp distinction is drawn between religious faiths and extremists who illegitimately exploit religion to justify their actions.

The U.S. government has not similarly condemned or regarded the mixing of religion and politics in South Africa, Israel, Poland, Eastern Europe, or Latin America as a necessary threat. A comparably evenhanded level of discrimination is too often absent when dealing with Islam. President Reagan's linking of Qaddafi and Libyan terrorism with a worldwide Muslim fundamentalist movement when he announced the U.S. bombing of Libya confirmed what many saw as America's monolithic, anti-Islamic approach to the Muslim world. Vice President Quayle's address to the 1990 graduating class of the naval academy in which he linked Nazism, communism, and radical Islamic fundamentalism, demonstrated a similarly ill-informed position.

The perception of a monolithic "Islamic threat" often motivates the United States to support repressive governments in the Muslim world and thus to a self-fulfilling prophecy. Governments that thwart a participatory process by cancelling elections or repressing populist Islamic movements that prove effective in electoral politics, as they have in Tunisia, Algeria, Egypt, and Turkey, encourage or risk the radicalization of moderate movements and the emergence of new forms of radicalism and extremism. At the very least, they inforce the belief that the United States has a double standard in its promotion and protection of democracy and human rights.

The history of Arab and non-Arab experiences, in particular the Muslim Brotherhood in Egypt and the Jamaat-i-Islami in Pakistan, are instructive regarding the linkage between state repression and radicalization. Gamal Abdel Nasser's repression of the Muslim Brotherhood, and the spiral of state violence and brotherhood counterviolence, spawned the more militant ideological interpretation of Sayyid Qutb and the ascendance of a radical wing within the Muslim Brotherhood. The suppression of the Brotherhood in the sixties led many to conclude that it had been effectively eradicated. In fact, prison experience and repression led more than a decade later to the formation of violent extremist splinter groups like Takfir wal-Hijra and Jamaat al-Jihad, the assassins of Anwar Sadat, and their offshoots today.

In contrast, Islamic movements such as the Jamaat-i-Islami in Pakistan (or PAS and ABIM in Malaysia) have been able to function within the system. The Jamaat has been politically influential, has participated in electoral politics, and has never been a violent, revolutionary threat. A more open political system in Pakistan, as in Malaysia, has enabled opposition parties, including a number of Islamic parties and organizations, to function within the political system. Although the Jamaat, like other Islamic leaders and organizations in Pakistan and Malaysia, has generally participated within the system, political pluralism has prevented it from monopolizing the role of political or religious opposition. It has been co-opted into government and has functioned in opposition, but it has never been able to dominate electoral politics. At the same time, its experience as a political party has forced it to become more pragmatic and flexible, a policy that has proven to be useful but also organizationally divisive.

Algeria provides a modern-day example of state repression and the resultant polarization and radicalization of society. The experience of regime violence, imprisonment, or torture drove many to withdraw from participation in the political process, convinced that force or violence is the only recourse against a repressive regime. In Egypt, Mohammed Al-Hodeiby, leader of the Muslim Brotherhood, responded to the Mubarak government when it blurred the distinction between the radical Gamaa Islamiyya and the Brotherhood and harassed the Brotherhood, warning that "if our supporters believe that we are not progressing in our causes, if they become frustrated with these setbacks, some may become radicalized."[128] The message was echoed by Fahmy Huweidi, a prominent, Islamically oriented Egyptian journalist (but not a member of the Brotherhood), who warned that a government crackdown against the leadership of the Brotherhood would lead the younger generation to turn to radical action to address social injustice.[129] New extremist groups will be spawned as a spiral of state violence and radical Islamist counterviolence polarizes and tears societies apart. Citizens are forced to choose between increasingly authoritarian governments and a "radical fundamentalist threat" as the middle ground erodes in a world in which one is either "for or against." Governments (as in Algeria, Tunisia, Egypt, and Turkey) no longer distinguish between radical surgery to counter or eradicate violent revolutionaries and the accommodation of a nonviolent opposition but instead lump all together, alleging a broad-based fundamentalist threat. The result, as in Algeria, can be a battle between a militant, authoritarian state and an equally militant and violent Islamic opposition in which the majority of the state's citizens become victims. The Algerian government's indiscriminate repression of Islamists is matched by radical Islamic militias, such as the Armed Islamic Group's deplorable acts of violence against intellectuals, journalists, foreigners, and women who fail to meet their self-styled Islamic standards.

Official U.S. or Western silence or economic, political, and military support for such regimes is read as complicity and a sign of the West's double standard for the implementation of democracy. Repressive regimes and the violation of human rights, along with a compliant Western policy toward such actions, can create conditions that lead to political confrontation and violence. They enable governments in the Muslim world and some Western policymakers to seemingly validate their prior contention and prophecy that Islamic movements are inherently violent and antidemocratic and constitute a threat to national and regional stability.

Contrary to what some have advised, the United States should not, in principle, object to the implementation of Islamic law or involvement of Islamic activists in government.[130] Islamically oriented political actors and groups should be evaluated by the same criteria that are applied to any other potential leaders or opposition party. Although some are rejectionists, many Islamically oriented leaders or governments will be critical and selective in their relations with the United States. However, they will generally operate on the basis of national interests and demonstrate a flexibility that reflects acceptance of the realities of a globally interdependent world. The United States must be willing to demonstrate by word and action its belief that the right of self-determination and representative government includes acceptance of an Islamically oriented state and society as long as it reflects the popular will and does not directly threaten U.S. interests.

As Muslim countries like Turkey, Iran, Pakistan, and Saudi Arabia compete for cultural and political influence in the emerging states of the Central Asian Muslim republics, the West in general, and the United States in particular, will need to balance its secular predisposition and thus seeming predilection for the promotion of Turkey's "secular Islam," a secular image challenged by municipal and parliamentary elections in which the pro-Islamic Welfare (Refah) Party emerged as a major political force. In municipal elections, Islamists swept local municipal elections and installed mayors in Istanbul and Ankara, the capital of Ataturk's secular state. Necmettin Erbakan subsequently took office in 1996 as Turkey's first Islamist prime minister. The U.S. and European response to the Turkish military–influenced resignation of Erbakan in 1998, followed by the dissolution of the Welfare Party, made Turkish-Western relations more sensitive. Although the United States and its European allies may wish to strengthen the Turkish government, they cannot afford to be seen as promoting a particular "brand" of Islam, a move that would lead to the dubbing of the Turkish secular model as yet another variant of "American Islam."

The United States should avoid being seen as intervening in state-initiated Islamization programs or as opposing the activities of Islamic organizations that pose no direct threat to it. American policy should, in short, be carried on in the context in which ideological differences between the West and Islam are recognized and, to the greatest extent possible, accepted or at least tolerated. Some Western leaders and officials have taken a sober stance. The Prince of Wales noted in a major address, "Islam and the West," that "the vast majority of Muslims, though personally pious, are moderate in their politics. . . . That which binds our two worlds together is so much more powerful than that which divides us."[131] Senior American foreign policy officials such as Edward Djerejian, assistant secretary of state for Near Eastern affairs during the Bush administration, and Robert H. Pelletreau, assistant secretary of state for Near Eastern affairs during the Clinton administration, made important contributions. Djerejian emphasized that the United States did not regard Islam or Islamic movements as the enemy. It recognized the right of movements to participate in the political process, provided that they not use democratic elections to seize power, that is, come to power motivated by the belief in "one man, one vote, one time."[132] Robert Pelletreau observed that the "image of Islam in the minds of the average newspaper reader is often one of an undifferentiated movement hostile to the West and ready to use violence and terrorism to achieve its ends." In contrast, he noted, "there are many legitimate, socially responsible Muslim groups with political goals. However, there are also Islamists who operate outside the bounds of law. . . . [Those] who espouse violence to achieve their aims, are properly called extremists, and extremists in the Middle East, as elsewhere, can be secular or religious."[133] Pelletreau acknowledged that some Islamic groups participate within their country's system and others use violence against existing governments and their citizens. Like his predecessor, Edward Djerejian, he noted, "We're suspicious of those who would use the democratic process to come to power only to destroy that process in order to retain power and political dominance."[134]

American policy toward Algeria reflects the difficult choices and ambivalence of policymakers. Djerejian's policy statement was tested shortly thereafter when the Algerian military intervened, annulled the election results, and suppressed the Islamic Salvation Front. The United States, like most Western governments, remained silent. Having been primarily concerned throughout the Reagan-Bush years with the export of Iran's revolution, American policymakers had not expected and thus were ill prepared to face the likelihood of an elected Islamic government. However, as time passed and the situation deteriorated in Algeria, the Clinton administration ostensibly developed a more consistent policy. In "Islam and U.S. Policy," Robert Pelletreau emphasized U.S. commitment to the development of democratic institutions and went on to note that "our views on Algeria, which is in the midst of an Islamist insurgency, provide a living example of our policy and practice. The U.S. government has long believed and has repeatedly stressed to Algerian leaders at the highest level that there is an urgent need for real political dialogue . . . to chart a new and democratic course for Algeria. We agree with the major Algerian parties, which insist that this process must involve a broadening of political participation to encompass all political forces in the country, including Islamist leaders who reject terrorism."[135] Unfortunately, this sentiment was not to be found in U.S. policy toward Tunisia. Tunisia's government used repression to decapitate the Renaissance Party, and as Pelletreau noted in testimony before Congress, "President Ben Ali was re-elected to a second 5-year term capturing 99.91 percent of the vote in what was widely regarded as a self-determined outcome. Political observers on the scene reported incidents of inappropriate election activities such as the removal or closure of some voting stations. Two presidential candidates were imprisoned for a period of time and then released."[136]

Clinton, Islam, and the War Against Global Terrorism

On August 7, 1998, American embassies in Kenya and Tanzania were bombed, killing 263 people and injuring more than 5,000, raising once again the specter of international terrorism. Once more the international community witnessed the extremist fringe of political Islam. The *Washington Post* headline read, "A Global, Pan-Islamic Network: Terrorism Entrepreneur Unifies Groups Financially, Politically."[137] On August 27 the United States attacked alleged terrorist militia training sites associated with Osama bin Laden in Sudan and Afghanistan in retaliation and as a preemptive strike against the threat of global terrorism. The U.S. response signaled a new phase of the war against terrorism that now focused on nonstate actors, in particular, a specific individual accused of supporting a network of terrorist organization.

Militias have played a significant role in Muslim politics in many countries. Although some are associated with organizations that seek to topple governments through violence, others are associated with organizations that function within their societies. The Armed Islamic Group in Algeria and the Gamaa Islamiyya and Islamic Jihad in Egypt are clear examples of violent revolutionaries. Hizbullah in Lebanon and Hamas in Israel/Palestine today function in mainstream society and also engage in armed struggle. The Taliban are a militia that has fought its way to rule in Afghanistan. The creation, existence, and histories of these organizations reflect their complexity and the issues that their existence and track record raise. If some would simply dismiss them as blindly, even mindlessly, anti-American or at war with the West, the reality is far more complex. Their origins, ideology, development, tactics, and agendas, though religiously legitimated, are often the product of political and economic factors as much as a theological–ideological worldview. Just as Hizbullah was a response to the Israeli invasion of Lebanon, inspired and supported by

Khomeini's revolutionary Iran, the Taliban of Afghanistan were the product of the American-supported mujahidin resistance movement to the Soviet invasion and the subsequent chaos and intertribal warfare. Hamas was a direct response to the Palestinian uprising (*intifada*) against Israeli occupation.

In what was the clearest presidential statement on Islam and terrorism, President Clinton, in announcing the air strikes, went out of his way to distinguish between Islam and terrorism, between the faith of Muslims and its distortion by those who committed acts of terrorism in the name of Islam. However, the critical point would be the relationship between a policy statement and the specific action undertaken by the United States. Although many American Muslim organizations and others applauded Clinton's distinction between Islam and terrorism, they also expressed concern that it not be a framework for an indefensible breaching of international law to engage in preemptive strikes within the borders of sovereign nations. Particularly contentious was the bombing of the Al-Shifa pharmaceutical plant in Khartoum, Sudan. The U.S. government claimed that it had hard evidence that this plant produced chemical weapons; the Sudanese protested that the plant produced 90 percent of Sudan's sorely needed medical supplies. In the aftermath, Sudan invited the United Nations to send an inspection team. Western diplomats and journalists in Khartoum who inspected the site could find no credible evidence that the plant produced dangerous chemicals, and eventually U.S. government spokespersons acknowledged that they had based their conclusion on an inadequate intelligence report.

As we have seen, Muslim politics in the nineties witnessed a series of attacks, bombings, and murders domestically and internationally. Tourists in Luxor, Egypt, and thousands of people in Algeria were massacred, the U.S. military was attacked in Riyadh and Dhahran, Saudi Arabia, and American embassies in Kenya and Tanzania were bombed. Such actions, for many U.S. government officials, personified a global war of terrorism waged by Islamic militants, particularly against the United States and its interests. The chief symbol for that war became Osama bin Laden, a Saudi millionaire long believed to be a "godfather" of international terrorism, a man whom some dubbed "the terrorism entrepreneur" for his support of radical groups and militias.[138] For some he represents a true mujahid, freedom fighter; for others a menace that supports a network of international terrorists. Bin Laden, like Hamas and Hizbullah, has had his admirers as well as his detractors. The many faces of militia leaders and militias reveal the causes and evidence for both facets of their image and character.

Osama bin Laden, the seemingly devout, well-educated, wealthy son of a prominent Saudi family, had gone off to fight against the Soviets in Afghanistan, a struggle that allied him with a cause supported by the United States, Saudi Arabia, Pakistan, and many others. He soon became a focal point for many of the "Arab Afghans," those from the Arab world who had also joined the jihad. After the war, he returned to Saudi Arabia. However, his militant objections to the Gulf War of 1991 and the U.S. military presence in Saudi Arabia put him on a collision course with his government. He bitterly criticized the House of Saud for permitting a foreign, non-Muslim military presence in the homeland of Islam's two most sacred sites, Mecca and Medina. Stripped of his Saudi citizenship, he moved to Sudan in 1994 and became more active in Islamist causes in the broader Muslim world. In 1996 Sudan asked him to leave in response to American charges that Bin Laden used Sudan as a base for his involvement in international terrorism. It was then that he returned to Afghanistan.

Bin Laden is regarded by the United States as a major funder of terrorist groups. He is suspected of funding groups involved in the bombing of the World Trade Center, a firefight in Somalia in 1993 that left eighteen Americans dead, bombings in Riyadh in 1995 and the Khobar Towers in Dhahran in 1996 (both of which he denies), the killing of fifty-eight tourists at Luxor, Egypt, in 1997, as well as the bombings in Tanzania and Kenya. He has admitted his complicity in the attacks in Somalia, expressed his admiration (though denying his involvement, he called them "heroes") for the bombings in Riyadh and Dhahran, threatened attacks against Americans who remain on Saudi soil, and promised retaliation internationally for Cruise missile attacks.[139] In February 1998, he announced the creation of a transnational coalition of extremist groups, the Islamic Front for Jihad against Jews and Crusaders.

Osama bin Laden's message and its causes resonate with the feelings of many in the Arab and Muslim world. A sharp critic of U.S. foreign policy toward the Muslim world, he denounces its support, "tilt," toward Israel, which he believes is responsible for the failure of the peace process, its refusal to condemn the Israeli shelling of civilians in Qana, Lebanon, in 1996, and U.S. insistence on continued sanctions against Iraq, which have resulted in the deaths of hundreds of thousands of civilians, especially children. He is equally critical of what he dismisses as the "new Crusades" in the Gulf, in particular the substantial U.S. (military and economic) presence and involvement in Saudi Arabia. To these are added other populist causes like Bosnia, Kosovo, Chechnya, and Kashmir.

Focusing on Osama bin Ladin risked catapulting one of many sources of terrorism to center stage, distorting both the diverse international sources (state and nonstate, non-Muslim and Muslim) of terrorism as well as the significance of a single individual. It risked turning America's stated defense of democracy and crusade against global terrorism into an incident that could transform Osama bin Laden from a mastermind of terrorism into a cult hero in many parts of the Muslim world. Members of the international community, including European diplomats and businesspersons with direct contact with the Al-Shifa plant, denied the U.S. claims. Members of the Clinton administration admitted that there was no evidence directly linking Bin Laden to the Al-Shifa factory in Khartoum or that it manufactured anything but pharmaceuticals (instead of being a "secret chemical weapons factory" as originally charged). Given Bin Laden's championing of popular causes, the need to provide hard evidence establishing the connection between Bin Laden and acts of terrorism became even more necessary. Although such evidence would not necessarily discredit him in the eyes of fellow extremists, it would destroy his credibility more broadly in the Muslim world as well as provide grounds for a more aggressive policy to capture him or destroy his network and training camps. Without it, the United States placed itself in the difficult position of engaging in a preemptive strike and violating international law and the borders of a sovereign nation. The action was taken without the cooperation of the international community, neither the United Nations nor its European allies. Without providing evidence for its actions, the United States became vulnerable to accusations of superpower arrogance or, worse, of state terrorism or of operating as a rogue state.

Violence, revolution and terrorism are particularly contentious and difficult issues. Although Osama bin Laden and those with whom he is associated, or for whom he has expressed admiration, present a clear picture of acts of violence and terrorism, many others do not. Distinguishing between the legitimate and illegitimate use of force, moderates and extremists, populist movements and terrorists can be difficult. Few people, whatever their actual track records, portray themselves as oppressors and exploiters. They reserve these judgments for others. Many Christians and Jews regard their traditions as committed to peace and social justice but are quick to believe that other traditions and peoples (such as Islam and Muslims) are more militant. Our wars are defensive and not offensive, "just wars" against aggressors. "Their" wars follow a tradition of holy war. The use of violence, distinguishing between moderates and extremists, between aggression and self-defense, resistance and terrorism often depends on where one stands. The line between movements of national liberation and terrorist organizations is often blurred or dependent upon one's political vantage point. The heroes of the American Revolution were rebels and terrorists for the British Crown, as were Menachem Begin and Yitzak Shamir, the Irgun and the Stern Gang. Nelson Mandela and the African National Congress and, until recently, Yasir Arafat and the PLO were regarded by their opposition as terrorists leading terrorist movements. Yesterday's terrorists may be just that—terrorists—or they may become today's statesmen. Soldier "peacekeepers" in an Israeli "security zone" in southern Lebanon are "forces of occupation" in the eyes of many Lebanese and Arabs. What some regard as a war of resistance and national liberation by Hamas in the West Bank and Gaza is regarded as a reign of terror by terrorists for many Israelis. The U.S. government refused to yield to repeated British requests that it rein in Irish-American involvement and support for the IRA, which the British government charged was a terrorist organization. It did yield to requests from Israeli and American Jewish organizations that action be taken to prevent similar support for "radical Islamic fundamentalist" organizations such as Hamas. Similar questions or issues exist elsewhere. Is Christian liberation theology and its derivative movements in Latin and Central America simply a crypto-Marxist revolutionary force or an authentic populist religious movement? The complexity of the situation is compounded by the tendency in the international system to regard those in power as legitimate rulers or governments, regardless of how they came to power or whether or not they are autocratic and repressive. Government agents (police, military, security forces) use "legitimate" force, whereas armed opposition groups are often portrayed as extremists or guerrilla organizations that engage in violence and terrorism. What is extremism? What is terrorism? Often the answer depends upon where one stands. A primary example of the real complexity of this issue is Hamas, whose history and actions raise key issues in their most acute form.

Hamas: The Islamic Resistance Movement in Palestine

Hamas, an acronym for the Islamic Resistance Movement, Harakat al-Muqawama al-Islamiyya, provides an equally controversial and complex example of a militant movement.[140] An offshoot of the Palestinian Muslim Brotherhood, Hamas was created in 1987 during the Palestinian intifada (uprising) against Israeli occupation and rule in Gaza and the West Bank. The founders of Hamas included Shaykh Ahmad Yasin, the charismatic paraplegic leader of the Muslim Brotherhood, and Palestinian professionals (physicians, teachers, and engineers). It provided a militant Islamic alternative whose success overshadowed the Brotherhood and challenged the leadership of the PLO in the struggle against Israeli occupation.

Hamas combines Islam with Palestinian and Arab nationalism. Its covenant declares that Palestine is a permanent Muslim territory, a religious endowment (*waqf*) given by God. Political and military activities are regarded as complementary and necessary components in the jihad (strug-

gle), incumbent upon all Muslims, to liberate Palestine from Israeli occupation.

Membership and Activities

Hamas is a religious, social, political, and military movement. Although
its leadership has included imams (religious officials), the majority of its
members are professionals and technocrats trained in medicine, engineering, science, and business. The combination of political and social activism
with guerrilla warfare has won financial and moral support from many
Palestinians and sympathetic supporters in the broader Arab and Muslim
world.

A primary reason for its popularity and following has been its extensive
network of community and charitable projects and programs: kindergar-
tens, schools, scholarships, support for students studying abroad, libraries,
social and sports clubs, and other social welfare services. Amid the poverty
and camps of the occupied territories, the network of services maintained
by Hamas has provided desperately needed services and has earned it
respect and admiration:

> HAMAS runs the best social services network in the Gaza Strip. . . . Struc-
> tured and well organized, HAMAS is trusted by the poor (Gaza's over-
> whelming majority) to deliver on its promises, and is perceived to be far
> less corrupt and subject to patronage than its secular nationalist counterparts,
> especially Fateh. . . . Some senior officials in UNRWA [United Nations Re-
> lief Works and Agency] in Gaza acknowledged that HAMAS is the only
> faction they trust to distribute UNRWA food donations to the people.[141]

Political Activism and Armed Struggle: Nationalist Movement or Terrorist Organization?

Hamas has engaged in political mobilization as well as armed struggle.
Political forums, mass demonstrations, and strikes have proven effective
political instruments. Always a minority of the population, Hamas receives
support from the broader population that has been linked to the progress
or failure of the peace process. The performance of its candidates in municipal, professional associations, chambers of commerce, and university
student elections have soared when relations between Israel and the Palestinians have deteriorated, as during the intifada. When the first municipal
elections in fifteen years were held in Hebron in 1992, Islamists sympathetic to Hamas won, as they did in 1993 in Ramallah, a city with a large
Palestinian Christian community. It took more than 40 percent of the vote
in professional association elections (Medical, Accountants, and Bar As-

sociations, Engineers Syndicate, and the Gaza Chamber of Commerce). Hamas' fortunes in university elections have also reflected the ups and downs of the peace process. In 1993, Hamas and its allies won 52 percent of the vote in Bir Zeit University student elections. In 1994, Hamas won overwhelmingly in strongholds like the Islamic University in Gaza and garnered 24 percent of the vote to Fateh's 64 percent at Al-Azhar University's branch campus, a Fateh stronghold.

Political and social activism has been accompanied by armed struggle. The military wing of Hamas, the Qassim Brigade (organized in 1991), engaged in well-planned selective attacks against Israeli military and police. Organized into small clandestine cells, it used guerrilla warfare, not random acts of violence. Responding to charges that it is a terrorist organization (a claim made by Israel, the United States, and others), Hamas has defended acts of violence as retaliation in a struggle against Israeli occupation and repression.

Although Hamas attacks were initially restricted to military targets in the occupied territories, that position changed dramatically after the Oslo Accords of 1993. Responding to specific events in Israel and the West Bank and Gaza, the Qassim Brigade undertook direct attacks in the heart of Israel against civilian as well as military targets. In particular, it adopted a new type of suicide bomber warfare in its struggle. Its deadly attacks increased exponentially after a Jewish settler (Baruch Goldstein) killed twenty-nine worshipers during the Friday congregational (*juma*) prayer at the Hebron Mosque of the Patriarch on February 25, 1994. The brigade promised swift revenge and retaliation for the ''massacre'' and undertook five anti-Israeli operations within Israel itself in cities like Galilee, Jerusalem, and Tel Aviv. The most deadly attack occurred on October 19, 1994, in the heart of Tel Aviv with the bombing of a bus, which killed twenty-three people and injured nearly fifty. Peace negotiations were again disrupted on July 30, 1997, when suicide bombers killed thirteen and wounded more than 150 in a Jerusalem market. The use of violence against civilians revealed deep cleavages within Hamas. If some of its leaders claimed that they were not able to control some members of the brigade, its critics rejected this distinction between its political and military wings as duplicitous.

Like many, Hamas, was caught off guard by Yasir Arafat's quietly and privately negotiated settlement, the Oslo Peace Accords (or Gaza-Jericho agreement) of September 13, 1993. Hamas opposition to Arafat and the accords and its call to continue to wage the Palestinian struggle against Israel put it at odds with both the PLO/PNA (the Palestinian National Authority) and Israel. Prior to the accords, both the PLO and Hamas were commonly dismissed as terrorist organizations. Now, the international community recognized Arafat, the former "terrorist," as a statesman, president of the Palestine Authority. Hamas became the common enemy (to both Israel and the PNA). The Likud government of Israel's Benjamin Netanyahu focused on terrorism and Hamas as the chief obstacle to peace, insisting that the PNA government of Yasir Arafat move effectively to suppress or dismantle HAMAS.

Like Lebanon's Hizbullah after the signing of the Taif Agreement ending Lebanon's civil war, Hamas after the signing of the Oslo Accords struggled with its response to new political realities. Its responses reflected the extent to which the agenda and tactics of most Islamic movements are shaped by the political context. Although it boycotted the Palestinian National Authority elections in which Yasir Arafat was elected president, the post-Oslo period saw divergent currents and growing divisions within Hamas. The Qassim Brigade wished to step up the armed struggle to strike further against continued Israeli occupation, undermine the peace process, and encourage a continuation of the intifada. The main political wing debated various forms of engagement. Some advocated participation in the political process, fearing that nonparticipation in elections would further marginalize Hamas from the majority of Palestinians who had participated in elections. Others went further, espousing the formation of a political party to assure that the voice of Hamas was present in the PNA government and Palestinian politics.

To conclude, with regard to U.S. policy and Islam, throughout the nineties, governments, policymakers, and experts have been divided in their assessment of political Islam and appropriate policy options. Some insist that there are no Islamic moderates and that all Islamic activists and organizations are a threat (whether overt or covert) and should be excluded from participation in the political process. Others distinguish between violent extremists and moderates, those who, if given the opportunity, participate within the system. The former charges that the difference between violent and nonviolent Islamists is one of strategy and tactics. The latter argue that nonviolent Islamists—those who participate within society—should be permitted (indeed have the right) to function as social and political organizations and parties. Those who advocate greater political liberalization and a policy of inclusion rather than exclusion of Islamic parties maintain that a more open system provides more competition and more options for voters. It also weakens the strength of Islamists who often attract not only their followers but also those who wish to cast a protest vote against failed or discredited governments. They believe that, faced with political reality, Islamists will prove more accommodating, both to survive politically and to act in the national interest. Inclusion also tests the capacity of Islamic activists to move beyond slogans, to prove or disprove their capacity for real political vision and leadership.

Both the track record of some Islamic regimes (Sudan, Iran, and Afghanistan) and the actions of more secular governments (Tunisia, Algeria, Turkey, and Egypt) reflect the authoritarianism, violence, and repression of Muslim politics and the need to strengthen political participation as well as the values and institutions of civil society.

Islam: Challenge or Threat?

For more than a decade "Islamic fundamentalism" has been increasingly identified as a threat to governments in the Muslim world and the West. This belief has been informed by the impact of the Iranian Revolution, the specter of the export of its revolution, the identification of Qaddafi and Khomeini with worldwide terrorism, and attacks against Western installations and personnel by shadowy extremist groups. Many watched and warned of other "Irans" or of radical groups seizing power through political assassination. Others soon dismissed Islamic revivalism as an epiphenomenon, a wave that had passed or was certainly receding, only to rediscover it as a threat when some new incident raised another alarm. The diversity and the many faces of contemporary Islamic revivalism tended to be subsumed under a monolith, "Islamic fundamentalism," which was simply equated with violence and religious extremism or fanaticism, with mullah-led theocracies or small, radical guerrilla groups.

The nineties challenged these assumptions and expectations. There have been no other Iranian-style Islamic revolutions, nor have any radical groups seized power. Yet neither the end of the Iran-Iraq war nor the death of the Ayatollah Khomeini signaled the death knell of Islamic revivalism. The resurgence of Islam in Muslim politics has been far more indigenously rooted. It has not receded; rather, its influence has been felt more deeply and pervasively. Its variety and diversity, its many faces and postures, have surfaced and will continue to do so. The impact of revivalism can now be seen by the extent to which it has become part of mainstream Muslim life and society and is not simply the province of marginalized and alienated groups. Secular institutions are now complemented or challenged by Islamically oriented schools, clinics, hospitals, banks, publishing houses, and social services. Their ability to provide much needed services is often taken by regimes as an implicit if not explicit critique or threat, underscoring their limitations and failures. Similarly, the emergence of an alternative elite, educated but more Islamically oriented, offers an alternative that challenges the Western, secular presuppositions and life-styles of many in the establishment. More ominously for some, many Islamic movements in recent years have joined the rising chorus of voices calling for political liberalization.

From North Africa to Southeast Asia, Islamic movements participated in electoral politics and, relative to the expectations of some, scored stunning successes. This created a political and analytical dilemma. The justification for the condemnation and suppression of Islamic movements was that they were violent extremists, small nonrepresentative groups on the margins of society that refused to work within the system and thus posed a threat to both society and regional stability. The vision of Islamic organizations working within the system ironically made them an even more formidable threat to regimes in the Muslim world and to some in the West. Those who once dismissed their claims as unrepresentative and denounced their radicalism as a threat to the system now accused them of an attempt to ''hijack democracy.'' This charge became the excuse for governments in Egypt, Turkey, Algeria, Tunisia, and Jordan to slow down or back away from political liberalization and democratization. Some experts (and governments) spoke of the need to first create, develop, or strengthen civil society. Others noted that a democratic framework is itself essential for the development of the nonstate space and institutions (professional associations, political parties, trade unions, a free press, private educational, medical, and social welfare institutions and services) of civil society.

In many Muslim societies, religion remains a pervasive, though at times diffuse, social force, and popular political culture is far less secular than is often presumed. The power of a religious idea or belief, when coupled with the economic and political failures of established governments, was neither anticipated nor comprehensible for those more accustomed to secular isms—nationalism, socialism, communism. As a result, the shock of the Iranian Revolution and of the electoral strength of Islamic movements in Algeria, Egypt, Jordan, and Turkey forced many to confront the inconceivable. Those who had feared Iran's export of its revolution and the creation of other ''Irans'' through violent revolution during the eighties were not reassured by the specter of an elected Islamic government. As one commentator asserted, ''Islamic fundamentalists . . . are the avowed enemies of democracy . . . their model of an Islamic polity is Ayatollah Khomeini's Islamic Republic, a regime that is ruled by clerical authority, torture and executions.''[142]

Islamic revivalism has challenged many of the presuppositions of Western liberal secularism and development theory: modernization means the inexorable or progressive secularization and Westernization of society.

Too often analysis and policymaking have been shaped by a liberal secularism that fails to recognize that it too represents a worldview that, when
assumed to be a self-evident truth, can take the form of a "secular fundamentalism." Secularism or liberal democracy is no longer regarded as
"a" way (one of many possible paradigms, albeit for some the best way)
but as "the" way, the only true path for political development. In the
name of enlightenment (reason, empiricism, pluralism), a new absolute, a
new norm, is subtly posited. Alternative paradigms, especially religious
ones, are necessarily judged as abnormal, irrational, and retrogressive—a
potential threat domestically and internationally.

This secular bias blinds many to the force and role of religion as a
source of faith and identity. Political economy is essential in understanding
the rise of social movements. However, the force of political Islam cannot
be simply reduced to the socioeconomic failures of societies. For many,
though certainly not all, activists, Islam is a motive force, a source of
guidance for this life as well as the next. We can not simply portray
"fundamentalism" as the child of poverty and unemployment. While support for the FIS came in large part from Algeria's unemployed younger
generation, the membership of Egypt's and Jordan's Muslim Brotherhoods, while also attracting disaffected youth, consists in large part of
middle- and upper-middle-class professionals (teachers, doctors, lawyers,
engineers).

Focus on "Islamic fundamentalism" as a global threat has reinforced
a tendency to equate violence and terrorism with Islam. It fails to distinguish between the legitimate use of force in self-defense and terrorism.
Most importantly, the illegitimate use or distortion of religion by individuals obscures the faith and practice of the majority of the world's Muslims.
Like believers in other religious traditions, they wish to live in peace. To
uncritically equate Islam and Islamic fundamentalism with extremism is
to judge Islam only by those who wreak havoc, a standard not applied to
Judaism and Christianity. Fear of fundamentalism creates a climate in
which Muslims and Islamic organizations are guilty until proven innocent.
Actions, however heinous, are attributed to Islam rather than to a twisted
or distorted interpretation of Islam. Christianity and Western countries
have a historic track record in conducting warfare, developing weapons
of mass destruction, and imposing their imperialist designs; yet Islam and
Muslim culture are portrayed as somehow peculiarly and inherently expansionist and prone to violence and warfare (*jihad*). The risk today is
that exaggerated fears will lead to a double standard in the promotion of
democracy and human rights in the Muslim world. Witness the volume
of Western democratic concern and action for the former Soviet Union
and Eastern Europe but the muted or ineffective response in promoting

democracy in the Middle East or defending Muslims in Bosnia-Herzegovina, Kosovo, and Chechnya.

For many governments in the Muslim world whose legitimacy is tenuous and whose power is based upon force and coercion, the combination of "uncontrolled democracy" and Islam is indeed a formidable threat. For Western governments, long accustomed to pragmatic alliances with regimes which, however undemocratic or repressive, were dominated by Western-oriented elites, the leap into the unknown of a potential fundamentalist government is far from attractive. This is especially true in light of the example of the Islamic republics of Iran, Afghanistan, and Sudan. As a result, the challenge of contemporary Islamic revivalism to the political and intellectual establishment is easily transformed into a threat.

The challenge of political Islam need not always result in a threat to regional stability or Western interests. Certainly, those groups, whether secular or Islamic, that attempt to impose their will through assassination and violent revolution are a direct threat. Furthermore, many contemporary Islamic movements today often appear to challenge the very principles of self-determination and intellectual and political pluralism we espouse. Therefore populist movements that participate in political life constitute a twofold challenge. On the one hand, governments in the Muslim world and in the West who espouse political liberalization or democracy are challenged to remain true to these very principles. On the other hand, Islamic movements, should they come to power, will be challenged to extend to their opposition and to minorities the very principles of political pluralism and participation that they demand for themselves.

Diversity rather than monolithic unity is more the norm than the exception in Islamic politics. Postrevolutionary Iran, Pakistan, Sudan, Lebanon, Egypt, Kuwait, and Malaysia have demonstrated that, as in secular politics, competing interests, agendas, and leadership exist, which, if permitted to emerge, often divide rather than unite Islamic groups within countries. Algeria's FIS was more a front or an umbrella organization for diverse currents of thought held together as much by its opposition to the ruling National Liberation Front and subsequently to government oppression as by common ideology. Islamic organizations in Pakistan such as the Jamaat-i-Islami have called for an Islamic state for decades, but they have proven incapable of producing and sustaining a unity of leadership, let alone an agenda. Despite a common Islamic commitment and marital ties, the Islamic organizations of Sudan's Hasan Turabi and Sadiq al-Mahdi have been in conflict more often than they have been united. Similarly, ABIM and PAS in Malaysia as well as the Muhammadiya and the Nahdatul Ulama in Indonesia, though Islamic organizations, differ significantly in their ideological vision and agenda.

Islamic organizations and parties constitute the only viable voice and vehicle for opposition in relatively closed political systems. The electoral strength of Tunisia's Renaissance Party, Algeria's FIS, or Jordan's Muslim Brotherhood came not only from a hard core of dedicated followers but also from the fact that they were the most credible and effective alternative "game in town." Thus they received support from those who voted for their Islamic agenda as well as those who simply wished to cast their vote against the government. Opening up the political system could foster the growth and strength of competing opposition parties and thus weaken the monopoly that Islamic parties hold on opposition voters. Importantly, the membership of Islamic organizations generally constitutes a numerical minority, not a majority of the population. The realities of a more open marketplace, having to compete for votes, and ruling amid diverse interests could force Islamic groups (as they often do secular political parties) to adapt or broaden their ideology and programs in response to domestic realities, diverse constituencies, and interests. The history of the Muslim Brotherhood, Jamaat-i-Islami, Refah, and other movements testifies to this reality.

All are challenged to recognize that political liberalization or democratization is a process that requires building institutions and cultivating a political culture and values for a strong civil society. This process entails experimentation and is necessarily accompanied by success and failure. The transformation of the West from feudal monarchies to democratic nation-states took time, trial, and error. It was accompanied by political as well as intellectual revolutions, which rocked both state and church. We tend to forget that the American and French democratic experiments emerged from revolutionary experiences. The nascent American democracy was then threatened by the horrendous Civil War. Throughout decades of democracy, equal rights remained an illusion for American blacks, Native Americans, and women. The transformation of political culture, values, and institutions does not happen overnight. It is a long, drawn-out process, accompanied by differences, debate, and battle among contending voices and factions with competing visions and interests.

Today we are witnessing a new historical transformation. Countries in the Muslim world, as in the former Soviet Union, Eastern Europe, and other parts of the world, are experiencing pressures and protests for greater political liberalization or democratization, prevented in the past by colonialism and more recently by authoritarian governments. Risks exist, for there can be no "risk-free democracy." Those who fear specific Islamic movements in power—what they will be like or how they will act—have a legitimate concern. However, government suppression and repression of its primary opposition, cancellation of elections, and massive violation of human rights may be found in current regimes such as Tunisia and Algeria, where the results of the Arab world's first free parliamentary elections were denied and the winners imprisoned. Their track records on political participation and pluralism and respect for human rights are well documented.

As some dream of the creation of a New World Order, and many millions in North Africa, the Middle East, Central Asia, and South and Southeast Asia aspire to greater political liberalization or democratization, the continued vitality of Islam represents a complex reality. Diverse movements cannot be reduced to a monolith and they cannot be evaluated or responded to by a preestablished, one-dimensional formula or strategy. Distinctions must be drawn between authentic populist movements that participate within the system and radical violent revolutionaries.

For many Muslims, Islamic revivalism is a social (rather than a political) movement whose goal is a more Islamically minded and oriented society but not necessarily the creation of an Islamic state. Indeed many, for pragmatic reasons (recognition of the power of authoritarian rulers) or out of disillusionment with the excesses of Islamic republics like Sudan, Iran, and Afghanistan, focus on Islamization of society rather than politics. For others, the establishment of an Islamic order requires the creation of an Islamic state. Although some advocate violent revolution, others do not. Islam and most Islamic movements are not necessarily anti-Western, anti-American, or antidemocratic. Although they challenge the outdated assumptions of the established order and autocratic regimes, they do not necessarily threaten U.S. interests. Our challenge is to better understand the history and realities of the Muslim world and to recognize the diversity and the many faces of Islam. This approach lessens the risk of creating self-fulfilling prophecies that augur the battle of the West against a radical Islam or a clash of civilizations. Guided by its stated ideals and goals of freedom and self-determination, the West has an ideal vantage point for appreciating the aspirations of many in the Muslim world as they seek to define and forge new paths for their future.

Notes

Introduction

1. Daniel Pipes, "Fundamentalist Muslims," *Foreign Affairs*, Summer 1986, pp. 939–59.

2. Strobe Talbott, "Living with Saddam," *Time*, February 25, 1991, p. 24.

3. Patrick J. Buchanan, "Is Islam an Enemy of the United States?," *New Hampshire Sunday News*, November 25, 1990.

4. "Islam and the West," *The Economist*, December 22, 1990, p. 18.

Chapter 1

1. John O. Voll, "Renewal and Reform in Islamic History: *Tajdid* and *Islah*," in John L. Esposito, ed., *Voices of Resurgent Islam* (New York: Oxford University Press, 1983); Nehemiah Levtzion and John O. Voll, eds., *Eighteenth-Century Renewal and Reform in Islam* (Syracuse, N.Y.: Syracuse University Press, 1987).

2. Donald Eugene Smith, ed., *Religion and Modernization* (New Haven, Conn.: Yale University Press, 1974), p. 4

3. Daniel Crecelius, "The Course of Secularization in Modern Egypt," in John L. Esposito, ed., *Islam and Development: Religion and Sociopolitical Change* (Syracuse, N.Y.: Syracuse University Press, 1980), p. 60.

4. For studies of the Islamic resurgence see Yvonne Y. Haddad, John O. Voll, and John L. Esposito, eds., *The Contemporary Islamic Revival: A Critical Survey and Bibliography* (New York: Greenwood Press, 1991); John L. Esposito, *Islam and Politics*, 3rd ed. (Syracuse, N.Y.: Syracuse University Press, 1991); John L. Esposito, ed., *Islam in Asia: Religion, Politics and Society* (New York: Oxford University Press, 1987); James P. Piscatori, ed., *Islam in the Political Process* (Cambridge: Cambridge University Press, 1983); and Nazih Ayubi, *Political Islam: Religion and Politics in the Arab World* (London: Routledge, 1991).

5. See John J. Donohue, "Islam and the Search for Identity in the Arab World," in Esposito, ed., *Voices of Resurgent Islam*, ch. 3; Ali Merad, "The Ideologisation of Islam in the Contemporary Arab World," in Alexander S. Cudsi

and Ali E. Hillal Dessouki, eds., *Islam and Power* (Baltimore, Md.: The Johns Hopkins University Press, 1981), ch. 3; Yvonne Y. Haddad, "The Arab–Israeli Wars, Nasserism, and the Affirmation of Islamic Identity," in John L. Esposito, ed., *Islam and Development: Religion and Sociopolitical Change* (Syracuse, N.Y.: Syracuse University Press, 1980), pp. 118–20.

6. Philip S. Khoury, "Islamic Revivalism and the Crisis of the Secular State in the Arab World," in I. Ibrahim, ed., *Arab Resources: The Transformation of a Society* (London: Croom Helm, 1983), pp. 213–34; Ayubi, *Political Islam*, pp. 164–74; Henry Munson, *Islam and Revolution* (New Haven, Conn.: Yale University Press, 1988), ch. 9.

7. James P. Piscatori, *Islam in a World of Nation States* (Cambridge: Cambridge University Press, 1986), p. 26.

8. The Islamic (Student) Association of Cairo University, "Lessons from Iran," in John J. Donohue and John L. Esposito, eds., *Islam in Transition: Muslim Perspectives* (New York: Oxford University Press, 1982), p. 246.

9. Ibid., p. 247.

10. See Michael C. Hudson, "The Islamic Factor in Syrian and Iraqi Politics," in James P. Piscatori, ed., *Islam in the Political Process* (Cambridge: Cambridge University Press, 1983), pp. 86ff.

11. Jacob Goldberg, "The Shii Minority in Saudi Arabia," in Juan R. I. Cole and Nikki R. Keddie, eds., *Shiism and Social Protest* (New Haven, Conn.: Yale University Press, 1986), p. 243.

12. William Ochsenwald, "Saudi Arabia and the Islamic Revival," *International Journal of Middle East Studies* 13:3 (August 1981): 271, 276–77; Joseph Kechichian, "The Role of the Ulama in the Politics of an Islamic State: The Case of Saudi Arabia," *International Journal of Middle East Studies* 18:1 (February 1986); 56–68; James P. Piscatori, "Ideological Politics in Saudi Arabia," in Piscatori, *Islam in the Political Process* (Cambridge: Cambridge University Press, 1983), p. 67.

13. Shaul Bakhash, *The Reign of the Ayatollahs: Iran and the Islamic Revolution* (New York: Basic Books, 1984), pp. 234–35.

14. Delip Hiro, *Iran Under the Ayatollahs* (London: Routledge and Kegan Paul, 1985), p. 340.

15. Joseph Kostiner, "Kuwait and Bahrain," in Shireen T. Hunter, ed., *The Politics of Islamic Revivalism* (Bloomington: Indiana University Press, 1988), pp. 121ff.

Chapter 2

1. For a Western scholar's perspective, see Francis E. Peters, *Children of Abraham* (Princeton, N.J.: Princeton University Press, 1982). To see the basic texts of these three religious systems juxtaposed on common issues, see Peters's *Judaism, Christianity, and Islam: The Classical Texts and Their Interpretation*, 3 vols. (Princeton, N.J.: Princeton University Press, 1990).

2. For an introduction to Islam from the formation of the early Muslim community to the present, see John L. Esposito, *Islam: The Straight Path*, expanded

ed. (New York: Oxford University Press, 1991); Frederick Mathewson Denny, *An Introduction to Islam* (New York: Macmillan, 1985); Fazlur Rahman, *Islam*, 2nd ed. (Chicago: University of Chicago Press, 1979).

3. For a translation of this classic, see A. Guillaume, *The Life of Muhammad: A Translation of Ishaq's Sirat Rasul Allah* (London: Oxford University Press, 1955).

4. The standard works in English remain W. Montgomery Watt, *Muhammad at Mecca* (Oxford: Clarendon Press, 1953), and *Muhammad at Medina* (Oxford: Clarendon Press, 1956). The two volumes were subsequently published in an abridged version, *Muhammad: Prophet and Statesman* (London: Oxford University Press, 1961).

5. Fred McGraw Donner, *The Early Islamic Conquests* (Princeton, N.J.: Princeton University Press, 1981), pp. 269ff.

6. Hugh Kennedy, *The Prophet and the Age of the Caliphates* (London: Longman, 1986).

7. Donner, *Early Islamic Conquests*, p. 269.

8. Bernard G. Weiss and Arnold H. Green, *A Survey of Arab History* (Cairo: The American University of Cairo Press, 1987), p. 59.

9. For the history of this period, see Ira Lapidus, *A History of Islamic Societies* (Cambridge: Cambridge University Press, 1988).

10. Patrick J. Bannerman, *Islam in Perspective* (London: Routledge, 1988), p. 86.

11. Marshall G. S. Hodgson, *The Venture of Islam*, 3 vols. (Chicago: University of Chicago Press, 1974), 1:235.

12. The standard works on Islamic law are Noel J. Coulson, *A History of Islamic Law* (Edinburgh: Edinburgh University Press, 1964), and Joseph Schacht, *An Introduction to Islamic Law* (Oxford: Clarendon Press, 1964).

13. For insightful introductions to Sufism, see Annemarie Schimmel, *The Mystical Dimensions of Islam* (Chapel Hill: University of North Carolina Press, 1975); A. J. Arberry, *An Introduction to the History of Sufism* (London: Longman, 1942); Martin Lings, *What Is Sufism?* (Berkeley: University of California Press, 1977).

14. Maxime Rodinson, "The Western Image and Western Studies of Islam," in Joseph Schacht and C. E. Bosworth, eds., *The Legacy of Islam* (Oxford: Oxford University Press, 1974), p. 9.

15. Albert Hourani, *Europe and the Middle East* (Berkeley: University of California Press, 1980), p. 9.

16. R. Stephen Humphreys, *Islamic History: A Framework for Inquiry* (Minneapolis, Minn.: Bibliotheca Islamica, 1988), p. 250.

17. Francis E. Peters, "The Early Muslim Empires: Umayyads, Abbasids, Fatimids," in Marjorie Kelly, ed., *Islam: The Religious and Political Life of a World Community* (New York: Praeger, 1984), p. 79.

18. For a history of the Crusades, see S. Runciman, *A History of the Crusades*, 3 vols. (Cambridge: Cambridge University Press, 1951–54), and J. Prawers, *Crusader Institutions* (Oxford: Oxford University Press, 1980).

19. J. J. Saunders, *A History of Medieval Islam* (London: Routledge and Kegan Paul, 1965), p. 154.

20. Peters, "Early Muslim Empires," p. 85.

21. Saunders, *History,* p. 161.

22. C. E. Bosworth, "The Historical Background of Islamic Civilization," in R. M. Savory, ed., *Introduction to Islamic Civilization* (New York: Cambridge University Press, 1980), p. 25.

23. Ira Lapidus, *A History of Islamic Societies* (New York: Cambridge University Press, 1988), p. 330.

24. Arthur Goldschmidt, Jr., *A Concise History of the Middle East*, 3rd ed. (Boulder, Colo.: Westview Press, 1988), p. 132.

25. Paul Coles, *The Ottoman Impact on Europe* (New York: Harcourt, Brace and World, 1968), pp. 146–47.

26. Ibid., p. 147.

27. Ibid., p. 151.

28. Ibid., p. 148.

29. Bosworth, "Historical Background," p. 25.

30. Ibid., p. 139.

31. Hourani, *Europe and the Middle East*, p. 10.

32. R. W. Southern, *Western Views of Islam and the Middle Ages* (Cambridge, Mass.: Harvard University Press, 1962), p. 2.

33. Ibid., p. 28.

34. Ibid., p. 31.

35. Rodinson, "Western Image," p. 14.

36. Hourani, *Europe and the Middle East*, p. 10.

37. Ibid., p. 2.

Chapter 3

1. Hichem Djait, *Europe and Islam: Cultures and Modernity* (Berkeley: University of California Press, 1985), p. 148.

2. Albert Hourani, *Europe and the Middle East* (Berkeley: University of California Press, 1980), pp. 12–13.

3. Maxime Rodinson, *Europe and the Mystique of Islam* (Seattle: University of Washington Press, 1987), p. 66.

4. John O. Voll, "Renewal and Reform in Islamic History: *Tajdid* and *Islah*," in John L. Esposito, ed., *Voices of Resurgent Islam* (New York: Oxford University Press, 1983), ch. 2.

5. John O. Voll, *Islam: Continuity and Change in the Modern World* (Boulder, Colo.: Westview Press, 1982), ch. 3.

6. Ibid., p. 33.

7. Wilfred Cantwell Smith, *Islam in Modern History* (Princeton, N.J.: Princeton University Press, 1957), p. 41.

8. As quoted in Asma Rashid, "A Critical Appraisal of James J. Cooke's 'Tricolour and Crescent: Franco-Muslim Relations in Colonial Algeria, 1880–1940,'" *Islamic Studies* 29:2 (Summer 1990): 203.

9. Arthur Goldschmidt, Jr., *A Concise History of the Middle East*, 3rd ed. (Boulder, Colo.: Westview Press, 1988), p. 231.

10. Ibid., p. 204.

11. Ibid., pp. 204–5.

12. William Wilson Hunter, *Indian Musulmans* (London, 1871), p. 184.

13. Hafeez Malik, *Sir Sayyid Ahmad Khan and Muslim Modernization in India and Pakistan* (New York: Columbia University Press, 1980), p. 172.

14. Albert Hourani, *Arabic Thought in the Liberal Age* (Oxford: Oxford University Press, 1970), especially chs. 2–7.

15. John O. Voll, "Islamic Renewal and the Failure of the West," in Richard T. Antoun and Mary Elaine Hegland, eds., *Religious Resurgence: Contemporary Cases in Islam, Christianity, and Judaism* (Syracuse, N.Y.: Syracuse University Press, 1987), ch. 6.

16. Hourani, *Arabic Thought*, p. 109.

17. Ibid., p. 122.

18. Muhammad Iqbal, *The Reconstruction of Religious Thought in Islam* (Lahore: Muhammad Ashraf, 1968), p. 8.

19. Ibid., p. 163.

20. Muhammad Iqbal, "Islam as a Social and Political Ideal," in S. A. Vahid, ed., *Thoughts and Reflections of Iqbal* (Lahore: Muhammad Ashraf, 1964), p. 35.

21. Taha Husayn, "The Future of Culture in Egypt," in John J. Donohue and John L. Esposito, eds., *Islam in Transition: Muslim Perspectives* (New York: Oxford University Press, 1982), pp. 74–75.

22. Ibid., p. 74.

23. Ibid., p. 75.

24. Albert Hourani, *A History of the Arab Peoples* (Cambridge, Mass.: Harvard University Press, 1990), pp. 308ff.

25. S. Abul Hasan Ali Nadwi, *Islam and the World* (n.d.; rpt. Lahore: Muhammad Ashraf, 1967), p. 139.

26. Abul Ala Mawdudi, *Nationalism and Islam* (Lahore: Islamic Publications, 1947), p. 10.

27. Ira M. Lapidus, *A History of Islamic Societies* (Cambridge: Cambridge University Press, 1988), pp. 625–26.

28. Richard P. Mitchell, *The Society of the Muslim Brothers* (London: Oxford University Press, 1969), p. 229.

29. Goldschmidt, *Concise History,* p. 278.

30. Ali E. Hillal Dessouki, "The Limits of Instrumentalism: Islam in Egypt's Foreign Policy," in Adeed Dawisha, ed., *Islam in Foreign Policy* (Cambridge: Cambridge University Press, 1984), p. 87.

Chapter 4

1. Quoted in Mahmoud Mustafa Ayoub, *Islam and the Third Universal Theory: The Religious Thought of Muammar al-Qadhdhafi* (London: KPI, 1987), p. 32. For a more extended analysis of the role of Islam in politics, see John L. Esposito, *Islam and Politics*, 3rd ed. (Syracuse, N.Y.: Syracuse University Press, 1991), which is a source for this discussion.

2. Raymond N. Habiby, "Muamar Qadhafi's New Islamic Scientific Socialist

Society," in Michael Curtis, ed., *Religion and Politics in the Middle East* (Boulder, Colo.: Westview Press, 1981), p. 247.

3. Lillian Craig Harris, *Libya: Qadhafi's Revolution and the Modern State* (Boulder, Colo.: Westview Press, 1986), p. 31.

4. Lisa Anderson, "Qaddafi's Islam," in John L. Esposito, ed., *Voices of Resurgent Islam* (New York: Oxford University Press, 1983), ch. 6, and Ann Elizabeth Mayer, "Islamic Resurgence or New Prophethood: The Role of Islam in Qaddafi's Ideology," in Ali E. Hillal Dessouki, ed., *Islamic Resurgence in the Arab World* (New York: Praeger, 1982), ch. 10.

5. "The Libyan Revolution in the Words of Its Leaders," *Middle East Journal* 24 (1970): 208.

6. Muammar al-Qdhadhafi, *The Green Book*, excerpted as the "Third Way," in John J. Donohue and John L. Esposito, eds., *Islam in Transition: Muslim Perspectives* (New York: Oxford University Press, 1982), p. 103.

7. Oriana Fallaci, "The Iranians Are Our Brothers: An Interview with Colonel Muammar al-Qaddafi of Libya," *New York Times Magazine*, December 16, 1979.

8. Ayoub, *Islam*, p. 94.

9. Dirk Vandewalle, "Qadhafi's Unfinished Revolution," *Mediterranean Quarterly*, Winter 1990, p. 72.

10. Lisa Anderson, "Tunisia and Libya: Responses to the Islamic Impulse," in John L. Esposito, ed., *The Iranian Revolution: Its Global Impact* (Miami: Florida International University Press, 1990), p. 171.

11. George Joffe, "Islamic Opposition in Libya," *Third World Quarterly* 10: 2 (April 1988): 624.

12. Anderson, "Qaddafi's Islam," p. 143.

13. Ibid., p. 629.

14. Jennifer Parmelee, "At Home, Gadhafi May Face Religious Turmoil," *International Herald Tribune*, January 11, 1989.

15. Adel Darwish, "Gaddafi's Garbled Message," *The Middle East*, December 1989, p. 14.

16. Vandewalle, "Qadhafi's Unfinished Revolution," p. 80.

17. B. Scarcia Amoretti, "Libyan Loneliness in Facing the World: The Challenge of Islam," in Adeed Dawisha, ed., *Islam in Foreign Policy* (Cambridge: Cambridge University Press, 1983), pp. 55ff.

18. Sulayman S. Nyang, "The Islamic Factor in Libya's Foreign Policy," *Africa and the World*, 1, no. 2 (1987), p. 20.

19. Lela Garner Noble, "The Philippines: Autonomy for Muslims," in John L. Esposito, ed., *Islam in Asia: Religion, Politics & Society* (New York: Oxford University Press, 1987), p. 101.

20. Nyang, "Islamic Factor," pp. 17–18.

21. *Al-Nahj al-Islami limadha* (Cairo: al-Maktab al Misri al-Hadith, 1980).

22. *The Arab News*, May 31, 1984.

23. Peter Bechtold, "The Sudan Since the Fall of Numayri," in Robert O. Freedman, ed., *The Middle East from the Iran-Contra-Affair to the Intifada* (Syracuse, N.Y.: Syracuse University Press, 1990), p. 371.

24. John O. Voll, "Political Crisis in the Sudan," *Current History* 89:546 (April 1990): 179.

25. Ann Lesch, "Khartoum Diary," *Middle East Report*, no. 161 (November–December, 1989), p. 37.

26. Voll, "Political Crisis," pp. 179–80.

27. Abdelwahab El-Effendi, *Turabi's Revolution: Islam and Power in Sudan* (London: Grey Seal Books, 1991), p. 162.

28. See John L. Esposito and John O. Voll, "Sudan: The Mahdi and the Military," in *Islam and Democracy* (New York: Oxford University Press, 1997), chap. 4, for a discussion of this and related issues.

29. Peter Woodward, "Sudan: Islamic Radicals in Power," in *Political Islam: Revolution, Radicalism or Reform?* (Boulder: Lynne Rienner, 1997), p. 101.

30. John Voll, "Political Crisis in the Sudan," *Current History* 89 (April 1990), pp. 179–80.

31. " 'Peace from within' Strategy Works: Rebels and Government from Bullet to Ballot," *Sudan Focus* Vol., 4, no. 4–5 (April-May 15, 1997), p. 1.

32. James C. McKinley Jr., "Sudan's Calamity: Only the Starving Favor Peace," *New York Times*, July 25, 1998.

33. Ibid.

34. Dessouki, *Islamic Resurgence*, p. 90.

35. Amira El-Azhary Sonbol, "Egypt," in Shireen T. Hunter, ed., *The Politics of Islamic Revivalism* (Bloomington: Indiana University Press, 1988), p. 25.

36. Gilles Kepel, *Muslim Extremism in Egypt: The Prophet and Pharaoh* (Berkeley: University of California Press, 1986), p. 192.

37. Johannes J. G. Jansen, *The Neglected Duty* (New York: Macmillan, 1986), p. 193.

38. Dessouki, *Islamic Resurgence*, p. 91.

39. John Kifner, "Egyptian Opposition Lionizes Guard Who Killed 7 Israelites," *New York Times*, December 27, 1985.

40. Jane Freedman, "Democratic Winds Blow in Cairo," *Christian Science Monitor*, January 17, 1990.

41. The discussion in this section draws on John L. Esposito, *Islam and Politics*, 4th ed. (Syracuse, N.Y.: Syracuse University Press, 1998), pp. 254–60.

42. Egyptian Organization for Human Rights, "A Statement of Recent [Incidents] of Communal/Religious Violence," April 3, 1990, p. 1.

43. "Assiut bears the brunt of Islamists' human rights abuse," *Middle East Times*, 16–22 May 1994, p. 2.

44. Christopher Hedges, "Seven Executed in Egypt in Move to Suppress Islamic Rebel Group," *New York Times*, July 9, 1993.

45. Ibid.

46. Virginia N. Sherry, "Egypt's Trampling of Rights Fosters Extremism," *New York Times*, April 15, 1993. For an analysis of the Egyptian Organization for Human Rights report for 1996, see "The Year in Review" *Civil Society* (July 1997), pp. 11–12.

47. Jane Freedman, "Democratic Winds Blow in Cairo," *The Christian Science Monitor*, January 17, 1990.

48. Chris Hedges, "Egypt Begins Crackdown on Strongest Opposition Group," *New York Times*, June 12, 1994, p. 3.

49. Raymond William Baker, "Invidious Comparisons: Realism, Postmodernism, and Centrist Islamic Movements in Egypt," *Political Islam: Revolution, Radicalism or Reform?* p. 124.

50. "Fugitive Lawyer Remains Defiant," *Middle East Times*, (June 27–July 3, 1994), p. 16.

51. Saad Eddin Ibrahim, "A Spring of Democracy," *Civil Society*, July 1997, p. 4.

52. Esmat Salaheddin, "A Report Shows Human Rights Deteriorating in Egypt," *Middle East Times*, June 28, 1998.

53. Steve Negus, "Brothers Found Guilty," *Middle East International*, December 1, 1995, p. 9.

54. Simon, Apiku, "Wasat Aims to Rebuild," *Middle East Times*, July 19, 1998.

55. CHRLA Document.

56. Robert Bianchi, "Islam and Democracy in Egypt," *Current History*, February 1989, p. 104.

57. Ervand Abrahamian, *Iran: Between Two Revolutions* (Princeton, N.J.: Princeton University Press, 1982), p. 448.

58. James A. Bill, *The Eagle and the Lion* (New Haven, Conn.: Yale University Press, 1988), p. 176.

59. In order of quotation, ibid., pp. 186, 184.

60. Ibid., p. 186.

61. As quoted in Ervand Abrahamian, "Ali Shariati: Ideologue of the Iranian Revolution," *MERIP Reports* 102 (January 1982): 26.

62. Dr. Ali Shariati. *Man and Islam* (Houston, Tex.: Free Islamic Literature, 1980), p. xi.

63. As quoted in Ali Shariati, *On the Sociology of Islam* (Berkeley, Calif.: Mizan Press, 1979), p. 23.

64. As quoted in Abrahamian, "Ali Shariati," p. 26.

65. Donohue and Esposito, eds., *Islam in Transition*, p. 302.

66. Ruhollah Khomeini, *Islam and Revolution: Writings and Declarations of Imam Khomeini* (Berkeley, Calif.: Mizan Press, 1981), pp. 249–50.

67. For an analysis of Khomeini's worldview, see Farhang Rajaee, *Islamic Values and the World: Khomeini on Man, the State and International Politics* (Washington, D.C.: University Press of America, 1983).

68. "Message to the Pilgrims," in *Islam and Revolution: Writings and Declarations of Imam Khomeini*, trans. Hamid Algar (Berkeley, Calif.: Mizan Press, 1981), p. 195.

69. Said Amir Arjomand, *The Turban for the Crown: The Islamic Revolution in Iran* (New York: Oxford University Press, 1987), p. 164.

70. Ibid.

71. For an analysis of the global impact of the Iranian Revolution and its implications for U.S. foreign policy, see John L. Esposito, ed., *The Iranian Revolution: Its Global Impact* (Miami: Florida International University Press, 1990).

72. John L. Esposito and James P. Piscatori, "The Global Impact of the Iranian Revolution: A Policy Perspective," ibid., p. 317.

73. "Constitution of the Islamic Republic of Iran," *Middle East Journal* 34 (1980): 185.

74. Ayatollah Khomeini as quoted in Esposito and Piscatori, "Global Impact," p. 322.

75. For divergent but overlapping analyses, see Ali Banuazizi, "Faltering Legitimacy: The Ruling Clerics and Civil Society in Contemporary Iran," *International Journal of Politics, Culture and Society* 8, no. 4, 1995, pp. 563–78; Mohsen M. Milani, "Political Participation in Revolutionary Iran," in *Political Islam: Revolution, Radicalism, or Reform?* ed. John L. Esposito, (Boulder: Lynne Rienner, 1997), pp. 77–94.

76. Barbara Crossette, "Iran Drops Rushdie Death Threat, and Britain Renews Teheran Ties," *The New York Times*, September 24, 1998.

Chapter 5

1. Robin Wright, *Scared Rage: The Wrath of Militant Islam* (New York: Simon and Schuster, 1985).

2. Richard Mitchell, *The Society of Muslim Brothers* (New York: Oxford University Press, 1969), and Charles J. Adams, "Mawdudi and the Islamic State," in John L. Esposito, ed., *Voices of Resurgent Islam* (New York: Oxford University Press, 1983), ch. 5.

3. John L. Esposito, *Islam and Politics*, 3rd ed. (Syracuse, N.Y.: Syracuse University Press, 1991), pp. 130–50.

4. Hassan al-Banna, "The New Renaissance," in John J. Donohue and John L. Esposito, eds., *Islam in Transition: Muslim Perspectives* (New York: Oxford University Press, 1982), p. 78.

5. Abul Ala Mawdudi, "Political Theory of Islam," in Donohue and Esposito, eds., *Islam in Transition*, p. 252.

6. Mitchell, *Society*, pp. 228–29.

7. Hassan al-Banna, "The New Renaissance," p. 78.

8. Muhammad Yusuf, *Maududi: A Formative Phase* (Karachi: The Universal Message, 1979), p. 35.

9. Sayyid Qutb, "Social Justice in Islam," in Donohue and Esposito, eds., *Islam in Transition*, pp. 125–26.

10. Yvonne Y. Haddad, "Sayyid Qutb: Ideologue of Islamic Revival," in Esposito, ed., *Voices of Resurgent Islam*, p. 69.

11. Adnan Ayyuh Musallam, "The Formative Stages of Sayyid Qutb's Intellectual Career and His Emergence as an Islamic Da'iyah, 1906–1952," Ph.D. diss., University of Michigan, 1983, p. 225. See also Gilles Kepel, *Muslim Extremism in Egypt: The Prophet and Pharaoh* (London: Al-Saqi Books, 1985), p. 41.

12. Yvonne Y. Haddad, "Sayyid Qutb," pp. 77ff.

13. Kepel, *Muslim Extremism in Egypt*; Emmanuel Sivan, *Radical Islam: Medieval Theology and Modern Politics* (New Haven, Conn.: Yale University Press,

1985); and Johannes Jansen, *The Neglected Duty: The Creed of Sadat's Assassins and Islamic Resurgence in the Middle East* (New York: Macmillan, 1986).

14. Kepel, *Muslim Extremism in Egypt*, pp. 31–32.

15. Saad Eddin Ibrahim, "Egypt's Islamic Activism in the 1980's," *Third World Quarterly*, April 1988, p. 643.

16. Saad Eddin Ibrahim, "Islamic Militancy as a Social Movement: The Case of Two Groups in Egypt," in Ali E. Hillal Dessouki, ed., *Islamic Resurgence in the Arab World* (New York: Praeger, 1982), p. 118.

17. Hamied N. Ansari, "The Islamic Militants in Egyptian Politics," *International Journal of Middle East Studies* 16:1 (March 1984): 123–44.

18. Johannes J. G. Jansen, *The Neglected Duty* (New York: Macmillan, 1986), p. 169.

19. Ibid., p. 161.

20. Ibid., p. 193.

21. *New York Times*, September 3, 1989.

22. Fouad Ajami, "In the Pharaoh's Shadow: Religion and Authority in Egypt," in James P. Piscatori, ed., *Islam in the Political Process* (Cambridge: Cambridge University Press, 1983), p. 29.

23. Ibid., p. 134.

24. Saad Eddin Ibrahim, "Egypt's Islamic Militants," in *MERIP Reports* 103 (February 1982): 11. See also Saad Eddin Ibrahim, "Islamic Militancy as a Social Movement," in Dessouki, ed., *Islamic Resurgence*, pp. 128–31, and Sivan, *Radical Islam*, pp. 118–19.

25. Louis J. Cantori, "The Islamic Revival as Conservatism and as Progress in Contemporary Egypt," in Emile Sahliyeh, ed., *Religious Resurgence and Politics in the Contemporary World* (Albany: SUNY Press, 1990), p. 191.

26. See Michael Hudson, *The Precarious Republic* (New York: Random House, 1968).

27. Augustus Richard Norton, "Religious Resurgence and Political Mobilization of the Shia in Lebanon," in Sahliyeh, ed., *Religious Resurgence*, p. 231.

28. Ralph E. Crow, "Religious Sectarianism in the Lebanese Political System," *Journal of Politics* 24 (August 1962): 489–520; and Albert Hourani, "Lebanon: The Development of a Political System," in Leonard Binder, ed., *Politics in Lebanon* (New York: John Wiley, 1966), pp. 13–29.

29. Joseph Olmert, "The Shiis and the Lebanese State," in Martin Kramer, ed., *Shiism, Resistance and Revolution* (Boulder, Colo.: Westview Press, 1987), p. 197.

30. Robin Wright, "Lebanon," in Shireen T. Hunter, ed., *The Politics of Islamic Revivalism* (Bloomington: Indiana University Press, 1988), pp. 62–63.

31. R. Augustus Norton, "Harakat AMAL—The Emergence of a New Lebanon Fantasy or Reality," in *Islamic Fundamentalism and Islamic Radicalism* (Washington, D.C.: U.S. Government Printing Office, 1985), p. 347.

32. Fouad Ajami, *The Vanished Imam* (Ithaca, N.Y.: Cornell University Press, 1986), p. 199.

33. Ibid., pp. 189–90.

34. Robin Wright, "Lebanon," in Shireen T. Hunter, ed., *The Politics of Islamic Revivalism* (Bloomington: Indiana University Press, 1988), p. 66.

35. Experts differ as to the actual origins of Hizbullah. While many date its beginning in 1982, Marius Deeb places it earlier. See Marius Deeb, *Militant Islamic Movements in Lebanon: Origins, Social Basis, and Ideology*, occasional papers (Washington, D.C.: Center for Contemporary Arab Studies, Georgetown University, 1986), pp. 13–14.

36. Shimon Shapira, 'The Origins of Hizbullah,''*Jerusalem Quarterly* 46, 1988: p. 130.

37. Augustus Richard Norton, "Lebanon: The Internal Conflict and the Iranian Connection," in John L. Esposito, ed., *The Iranian Revolution: Its Global Impact* (Miami: Florida International University Press, 1990), p. 23.

38. In contrast to many scholars, Marius Deeb regards Fadlallah as the political and religious leader of Hizbullah. See Marius Deeb, "Shia Movements in Lebanon," *Third World Quarterly*, p. 693.

39. Martin Kramer, "Muhammad Husayn Fadlallah," *Orient* 26:2 (1985): 147–48.

40. *The Middle East*, July 1989, p. 13.

41. Ibid.

42. Ibid.

43. "Iran Clamps Down on Hizbullah," *Christian Science Monitor*, October, 10, 1989, p. 3.

44. James P. Piscatori, "The Shia of Lebanon and Hizbullah: The Party of God," in Christie Jennett and Randal G. Stewart, eds., *Politics of the Future: The Role of Social Movements* (Melbourne: Macmillan, 1989), p. 301.

45. Fred Halliday, "Tunisia's Uncertain Future," *Middle East Report*, March–April 1990, p. 25.

46. "Nobody's Man—but a Man of Islam," in *The Movement of Islamic Tendency: The Facts* (Washington, D.C.: privately printed, 1987), p. 80. Similar comments appear in Abdelwahhab El-Effendi, "The Long March Forward," *Inquiry*, October 1987, p. 50.

47. "Nobody's Man," p. 84.

48. Interview with Ali Laridh, Tunis, 1989.

49. El-Effendi, "Long March," p. 51.

50. Interview with Ali Laridh, Tunis, 1989.

51. As quoted in Linda G. Jones, "Portrait of Rashid al-Ghannoushi," *Middle East Report*, July–August 1988, p. 20.

52. Clement Henry Moore, *Politics in North Africa* (Boston: Little, Brown, 1970), p. 108.

53. Dirk Vanderwalle, "From New State to the New Era: Toward a Second Republic in Tunisia," *Middle East Journal*, Autumn 1988, p. 612.

54. Dirk Vanderwalle, "Ben Ali's New Tunisia," *Field Staff Reports: Africa/Middle East*, 1989–90, no. 8.

55. Linda Jones, "Portrait," p. 22.

56. Vanderwalle, "From New State to the New Era," p. 603.

57. "Ben Ali Discusses Opposition Parties, Democracy,''*FBIS-NES*, no. 29 (December 1989).

58. Halliday, "Tunisia's Uncertain Future," p. 26.

59. "The Autocrat Computes," *The Economist*, May 18, 1991, pp. 47–48.

60. *The Middle East*, September 1991, p. 18.

61. "Useful Plot," *The Economist*, June 1, 1991, p. 38.

62. Robert Mortimer, "Islam and Multiparty Politics in Algeria," *Middle East Journal* 45:4 (Autumn 1991): 575.

63. Jean Claude Vatin, "Religious Resistance and State Power in Algeria," in Alexander. S. Cudsi and Ali E. Hillal Dessouki, eds., *Islam and Power* (Baltimore: Johns Hopkins University Press, 1981), p. 146.

64. Ibid., p. 575.

65. Charte Nationale (République Algérienne, 1976), p. 21.

66. Francois Burgat, *The Islamic Movement in North Africa*, trans. William Dowell (Austin: Center for Middle Eastern Studies, University of Texas, 1993), p. 261.

67. "Human Rights in Algeria Since the Halt of the Electoral Process," *Middle East Watch* 4:2 (February 1992), p. 11.

68. Daniel Brumberg, "Islam, Elections, and Reform in Algeria," *Journal of Democracy* 2:1 (Winter 1991): 59. See also Saad Eddin Ibrahim, "Crises, Elites, and Democratization in the Arab World," *Middle East Journal*: 1:2 (Spring 1993): 293.

69. "Algeria's Facade of Democracy," *Middle East Report* (March–April, 1990), p. 17.

70. Burgat, *The Islamic Movement*, p. 276.

71. "Transcript: Interview With Abassi Madani" (Los Angeles: Pontifex Media Center, 1991), p. 4.

72. Ibid., p. 5.

73. Ibid.

74. Ibid., p. 6.

75. Ibid., p. 8.

76. Ibid., p. 10.

77. Ibid.

78. Ibid., p. 11.

79. Ibid.

80. Ibid., p. 14.

81. Ibid., p. 16.

82. Burgat, p. 279.

83. Mohamed Esseghir, "Islam Comes to Rescue Algeria," *The Message International* (August 1991), p. 13.

84. Burhan Ghalyoun in *Al-Yawm Al-Sabi*, "Algeria: Democratization at Home, Inspiration Abroad," *The Message International* (August 1991), p. 19.

85. For an example of this kind of activity, see "Taking Space in Tlemcen: The Islamist Occupation of Urban Algeria," *Middle East Report* 22:6 (November–December 1992): 12–13.

86. John P. Entelis and Lisa J. Arone, "Algeria in Turmoil: Islam, Democracy and the State," *Middle East Policy*, 1:2 (1992), p. 29.

87. John P. Entelis, as quoted in *Maghreb Report* (March–April 1993), p. 6.

88. Ibid., p. 31.

89. Brumberg, p. 69.

90. *Middle East Watch*, p. 2.

91. "Amid Praise for Algerian System: Hopes for an Islamic Government," *The Message International* (August 1991), p. 16.

92. David Hirst, "Algiers Militants Urge Care at the Gates of Victory," *The Guardian*, January 18, 1992.

93. *Middle East Watch*, p. 13.

94. *Middle East Times*, June 19–25, 1990; and *Middle East Watch*, p. 13.

95. Vanderwalle, "Ben Ali's New Tunisia," p. 3.

96. Jonathan C. Randal, "Algerian Elections Cancelled," *Washington Post*, January 13, 1994.

97. Ibid.

98. "Algeria: Dusting Off the Iron Glove," *The Middle East* (April 1993), p. 19.

99. Entelis and Arone, "Algeria in Turmoil," p. 35.

100. Jonathan C. Randal, "Fundamentalist Leader in Algeria Is Arrested," *Washington Post*, January 22, 1994.

101. Randal, "Algerian Elections Cancelled."

102. *Middle East Watch*, p. 1.

103. "Algeria: The Army Tightens Its Grip," *The Economist*, July 17, 1993, p. 37.

104. "Algeria: A Kite for Peace," *The Economist*, March 5, 1994, p. 45.

105. "Algeria: Looking for Scapegoats," *The Middle East* (May 1994), p. 20.

106. Ibid., p. 21.

107. Ibid.

108. John P. Entelis, "Political Islam in Algeria," *Current History* (January 1995), p. 17.

109. Dirk Vandewalle, "Islam in Algeria: Religion, Culture and Opposition in a Rentier State," *Political Islam: Revolution, Radicalism or Reform?* p. 48.

110. Ian Williams, "Algeria: A Deaf Ear to Amnesty," *Middle East International*, November 21, 1997, p. 15.

111. Ibid.

112. Nilufer Gole, "Authoritarian Secularism and Islamist Politics," in *Civil Society in the Middle East*, vol. 2, ed. Augustus Richard Norton (Leiden: E. J. Brill, 1996), p. 20.

113. Feroz Ahmad, "Turkey," in *The Oxford Encyclopedia of the Modern Islamic World*, 4: 244.

114. Feroz Ahmad, "Political Islam in Modern Turkey," *Middle East Studies* 27, (January 1991), p. 14–15.

115. Ibid., p. 14.

116. Ibid., p. 15.

117. Binnaz Toprak, "Refah Partisi," in *The Oxford Encyclopedia of the Modern Islamic World*," 3:414.

118. Kurkcu, Ertugrul, "The Crisis of the Turkish State, *Middle East Report*, April–June 1996, 3.

119. For a fuller discussion, see M. Hakan Yavuz, "Political Islam and the

Welfare Party in Turkey," *Journal of Comparative Politics.* 30, no. 1 (October 1997), pp. 63–82.

120. Howard Reed, "A Turgut Ozal," in *The Oxford Encyclopedia of the Modern Islamic World,* 3: 277.

121. David Kushner, "Self-Perception and Identity in Contemporary Turkey," *Journal of Contemporary History* 32, no. 2 (April 1997), p. 230.

122. Jeremy Salt, "Nationalism and the Rise of Muslim Sentiment in Turkey," *Middle Eastern Studies* 31, no. 1 (January 1995), p. 18.

123. See Bulent Aras, "Turkish Islam's Moderate Face," *Middle East Quarterly* 5, no. 3 (September 1998), pp. 23–29.

124. For more on Nurcu political activism, see M. Hakan Yavuz, *Print-Based Islamic Discourse and Modernity: The Nur Movement*, Third International Symposium on Bediuzzaman Said Nursi (Istanbul: Sozler, 1995), 2: 324–50.

125. Sencer Ayata, "Patronage, Party, the State: The Politicization of Islam in Turkey," *Middle East Journal* 50, no. 1 (Winter 1996), p. 51.

126. Jenny White, "Islam and Democracy: The Turkish Experience," *Current History* 94, no. 588 (January 1995), p. 8.

127. Umit Cizre Sakallioglu, "Liberalism, Democracy, and the Turkish Centre-Right: Identity Crisis of the True Path Party," *Middle East Studies*, April 1996, p. 154.

128. M. Hakan Yavuz, "Turkey's 'Imagined Enemies: Kurds and Islamists,' " *The World Today* 52, no. 2 (April 1996), pp. 99–101.

129. Ayse Saktanber, "Becoming the 'Other' as a Muslim in Turkey: Turkish Women vs. Islamist Women," *New Perspectives on Turkey* 11 (Fall 1994), p. 105.

130. Ibid., pp. 43–44.

131. Metin Heper, "Islam and Democracy in Turkey: Towards a Reconciliation," *Middle East Journal* 51 no.1 (Winter 1997), p. 35.

132. Eric Rouleau, Turkey: Beyond Ataturk," *Foreign Policy* 103 (Summer 1996), p. 77.

133. Yavuz, "Turkey's 'Imagined Enemies,' " p. 100.

134. Stephen Kinzer, "The Islamist Who Runs Turkey, Delicately," *New York Times*, February 23, 1997, p. 29.

135. Ibid., p. 30.

136. Ibid.

137. *Der Spiegel*, October 14, 1991; Kushner, "Self-Perception and Identity," pp. 231–32.

138. Kelly Couturier, "Anti-Secularism Eclipses Insurgency as Army's No. 1 Concern," *Washington Post*, April 5, 1997, p. A22.

139. *The Economist*, July 19, 1997, p. 23.

140. Martin Heper, "Islam and Democracy in Turkey: Towards a Reconciliation," p. 45.

141. Adnan Adiver, "Interaction of Islamic and Western Thought in Turkey," in *Near Eastern Culture and Society*, ed. T. C. Young (Princeton: Princeton University Press, 1951), p. 126.

142. Ayse Kadioglu, "Republican Epistemology and Islamic Discourses in Turkey in the 1990s," *Muslim World* 84, no. 1 (January 1998), p. 11.

143. For a discussion of this phenomenon, see Sherif Mardin, "Ideology and Religion in the Turkish Revolution," *International Journal of Middle East Studies* 2 (1971), pp. 208–9.

144. Hakan Yavuz, "Political Islam and the Welfare (Refah) Party in Turkey," *Comparative Politics* 30, no. 1 (October 1997), p. 65.

145. Stephen Kinzer, "The Islamist Who Runs Turkey, Delicately," p. 29.

Chapter 6

1. William Pfaff, "Still Fighting the Crusades," *Foster's Daily Democrat*, November 27, 1990.

2. When I first wrote this phrase, I feared that some might think the statement a bit outrageous. I discovered subsequently that the *National Review* had published Daniel Pipes's "The Muslims Are Coming! The Muslims Are Coming!" November 19, 1990, pp. 28–31.

3. Edward Said, *Covering Islam* (New York: Pantheon, 1981), p. 136.

4. *Boston Globe*, July, 27, 1991.

5. Frederic Bichon, "U.S. Drive against Terrorism has Muslims Worried," *Middle East Times* February 19–25, 1995, p. 8.

6. David Hirst, "France Back on the Rack: As Algeria's Rage Targets Its Tormented Former Oppressor the Rest of Europe Could Be in Its Sights," *The Guardian*, December 28, 1994.

7. Patrick Bannerman, *Islam in Perspective: A Guide to Islamic Society Politics and Law* (London: Routledge, 1988), p. 219.

8. Amos Perlmutter, "Wishful Thinking about Fundamentalism," *Washington Post*, January 19, 1992; David Pryce-Jones, *At War with Modernity: Islam's Challenge to the West* (London: Alliance Publishers for the Institute for European Defense and Strategic Studies, 1992); Michael Youssef, *Revolt against Modernity: Muslim Zealots and the West* (Leiden: E. J. Brill, 1985); Samuel P. Huntington, "Will More Countries Become Democratic," in *Global Dilemmas*, ed. Samuel P. Huntington and Joseph Nye Jr. (Cambridge: Harvard University Press, 1985), pp. 253–79; Bernard Lewis, "Islam and Democracy," *Atlantic*, February 1993, pp. 87–98; Martin Kramer, "Islam vs. Democracy," *Commentary*, January 1993, pp. 35–42; and Yahya Sadowski, "The New Orientalism and the Democracy Debate," *Middle East Report* July–August 1993.

9. "People Direct Islam in Any Direction They Wish," *Middle East Times*, 28 May–June 3, 1991, p. 15.

10. For an analysis of the role of Islamic movements in the Gulf War, see James Piscatori, ed., *Islamic Fundamentalisms and the Gulf War* (Chicago: University of Chicago Press, 1993).

11. Fouad Ajami, "Bush's Middle East Memo," *U.S. News and World Report*, December 26, 1988–January 2, 1989, p. 75; Oliver Roy, *The Failure of Political Islam* (Cambridge: Harvard University Press, 1994).

12. "Can Islam, Democracy, and Modernization Co-Exist?" *Africa Report*, September–October 1990, p. 9.

13. I am indebted to professor Ramazani of the University of Virginia for this phrase.

14. This attitude is exemplified in Hirsh Goodman, "The Green Curtain," *The Jerusalem Report*, June 3, 1993.

15. Judith Miller, "The Challenge of Radical Islam," *Foreign Affairs* 72, no. 2 (Spring 1993). For an alternative perspective, see Leon Hadar, "What Green Peril?" *Foreign Affairs* 72, no. 2 (Spring 1993).

16. "Tunisia Warns of Islamic Radicals," *Washington Times*, October 25, 1991.

17. Ibid.

18. Michael Parks, "Israel Sees Self Defending West Again," *Los Angeles Times*, January 2, 1993.

19. Peter Rodman, "Don't Look for Moderates in the Islamic Revolution," *International Herald Tribune*, January 4, 1995.

20. Fergus M. Bordewich, "A Holy War Heads Our Way," *Readers Digest*, January 1995, pp. 76–80.

21. Thomas Kamm, "Clash of Cultures: Rise of Islam in France Rattles the Populace and Stirs a Backlash," *Wall Street Journal*, January 5, 1995.

22. "Focus: Islamic Terror: Global Suicide Squad," *Sunday Telegraph*, January 1, 1995.

23. Steven Emmerson, "Jihad in America," PB8 1994.

24. "Algerians in London Fund Islamic Terrorism," *Sunday Times*, January 1, 1995.

25. Patrick Sookhdeo, "Prince Charles Is Wrong—Islam Does Menace the West," *Daily Telegraph*, December 19, 1996.

26. Bernard Lewis, "The Roots of Muslim Rage," *Atlantic Monthly*, September 1990, Samuel P. Huntington, "The Clash of Civilizations," *Foreign Affairs* 72, no. 3 (Summer 1993).

27. Lewis, "Roots of Muslim Rage."

28. Lewis, "Roots of Muslim Rage," p. 2.

29. Goodman, "The Green Curtain."

30. Rodinson, "The Western Image and Western Studies of Islam," in Joseph Schacht and C. E. Bosworth, eds., *The Legacy of Islam* (Oxford: Oxford U. Press, 1974), p. 67.

31. Lothrop Stoddard, *The New World of Islam* (New York: Scribner's, 1921), pp. 23–24.

32. As quoted in *New York Times*, June 1, 1919, p. 9.

33. Raymond Aron, "L'Incendie," *L'Express*, December 1, 1979, as quoted in James Piscatori, *Islam in a World of Nation States* (Cambridge: Cambridge University Press, 1986), p. 39.

34. Cyrus Vance, *Hard Choices: Critical Years in American Foreign Policy* (New York: Simon & Schuster, 1983), pp. 408, 410, as quoted in Piscatori, *Islam in a World of Nation States*.

35. As quoted in Huntington, "Clash of Civilizations," p. 32.

36. Parks, "Israel Sees Self Defending West Again."

37. John Darton, "Islamic Fundamentalism Is on the Rise in Turkey," *International Herald Tribune*, March 3, 1995, p. 2.

38. Charles Krauthammer, "The New Crescent of Crisis: Global Intifada," *Washington Post*, February 16, 1990.

39. Goodman, "Green Curtain."

40. Krauthammer, "New Crescent of Crisis."

41. Ibid.

42. "Exit Lebanon," *New Republic*, November 12, 1990.

43. For a discussion of this point, see Piscatori, *Islam in a World of Nation States*, p. 149.

44. Lewis, "Roots of Muslim Rage," pp. 56–60.

45. Piscatori, *"Islam in a World of Nation States*, p. 38.

46. Lewis, "Roots of Muslim Rage," p. 59.

47. Huntington, "Clash of Civilizations?" pp. 22, 39.

48. Ibid., p. 26.

49. Ibid., p. 23.

50. Ibid., p. 24.

51. Huntington, *The Clash of Civilizations and the Remaking of World Order* (New York: Simon & Schuster, 1997), p. 217.

52. Ibid., p. 218.

53. Huntington, "Clash of Civilizations?"

54. Ibid., pp. 45–48.

55. Ibid., p. 31.

56. Ibid., p. 40.

57. Ibid., pp. 34–35. P. 254 name of section (Islam's Bloody Borders) and phrase," Islam's borders are bloody and so are its innards" p. 258.

58. Huntington, *Clash of Civilizations and the Remaking of World Order*, p. 258.

59. Huntington, "Clash of Civilizations," p. 36.

60. Patrick Buchanan, "Rising Islam May Overwhelm the West," *New Hampshire Sunday News*, August 20, 1989.

61. Ibid.

62. Krauthammer, "New Crescent of Crisis."

63. Charles Moore, "Time for a More Liberal and 'Racist' Immigration Policy," *The Spectator*, October 19, 1991.

64. Buchanan, "Rising Islam."

65. Tariq Azim-Khan, a member of the Muslim Forum, as quoted in *The Independent*, October 29, 1991.

66. Hesham El-Essawy, chairman of the Islamic Society for the Promotion of Religious Tolerance, as quoted in *The Independent*.

67. Claire Hollingsworth, *International Herald Tribune* November 9, 1993.

68. Bernard Levin, *The Times*, April 21, 1995.

69. Patrick Sookhedo, "Prince Charles Is Wrong.

70. *Islamaphobia: A Challenge for Us all* (London: Runnymede Trust, 1997), p. 10.

71. Ibid.

72. Ibid.

73. As quoted in *The Next Threat: Western Perceptions of Islam*, ed. Jochen Heppler and Andrea Lueg, (London: Pluto Press, 1955), p. 9.

74. Ibid., p. 13.

75. Ibid., p. 9.

76. Ibid., p. 16.

77. Kamm, "Clash of Cultures."

78. Dominque Moisi, of France's Institute of International Relations, as quoted in Judith Miller, "Strangers at the Gate: Europe's Immigration Crisis," *New York Times Magazine*, September 15, 1991, p. 86.

79. Ibid., p. 80.

80. Ibid., p. 86.

81. William Drozdiak, "Once Feared, Lyon's Mosque Emerges as Symbol of Tolerance," *International Herald Tribune*, March 6, 1995, p. 2.

82. Ibid.

83. *The Next Threat*, p. 29.

84. "The Immigrants," *The New Republic*, April 19, 1993, p. 7.

85. I am indebted to James Piscatori for bringing these important points to my attention.

86. Lisa Anderson, "Holy War Comes to America," *Chicago Tribune*, July 12, 1993; William Safire, "Islam under Siege," *New York Times*, March 18, 1993; "The New Dawn for Islam: The Global Campaign against the Secular State," *El Pais*, reprinted in *World Press Review*, June 1993, p. 19.

87. Safire, "Islam under Siege."

88. Kamm, "Clash of Cultures."

89. Perlmutter, "Wishful Thinking about Fundamentalism"; and Huntington, "Will More Countries Become Democratic?" p. 226.

90. "Democratization in the Middle East," *American-Arab Affairs* 36 (Spring 1991), pp. 1–47; Michael Hudson, "After the Gulf War: Prospects for Democratization in the Arab World," *Middle East Journal* 45 (Summer 1991), pp. 407–26.

91. For an analysis of this issue, see John L. Esposito and John O. Voll, *Islam and Democracy* (New York: Oxford University Press, 1997); John L. Esposito and James P. Piscatori, "Democratization and Islam," *Middle East Journal* 45 (Summer 1991), pp. 427–40; John O. Voll and John Esposito, "Islam's Democratic Essence," *Middle East Quarterly*, September 1994, pp. 3–11 with ripostes, pp. 12–19, and Voll and Esposito reply, *Middle East Quarterly*. December 1994, pp. 71–72; Mahmoud Monshipouri and Christopher G. Kukla, "Islam and Democracy and Human Rights," *Middle East Policy* 3 (1994), pp. 22–39; and Robin Wright, "Islam, Democracy and the West" *Foreign Affairs*, Summer 1992, pp. 131–45.

92. Leslie Gelb, "The Free Elections Trap," *New York Times*, May 29, 1991.

93. Voll and Esposito, "Islam's Democratic Essence."

94. *Mideast Mirror*, March 30, 1992, p. 12.

95. Esposito and Voll, *Islam and Democracy*.

96. John Lancaster, "Despite Plaudits of West, Mubarak Regime Is Stumbling," *International Herald Tribune*, March 15, 1995, p. 2.

97. Ibid.

98. Krauthammer, "New Crescent of Crisis," p. 2.

99. Buchanan, "Rising Islam."

100. For a summary discussion of Arab Islamists and pluralism, see Yvonne Y. Haddad, "Islamists and the Challenge of Pluralism," Occasional Paper (Washington, D.C.: Center For Contemporary Arab Studies and the Center for Muslim-Christian Understanding, 1995).

101. Mahmoud Ayoub, "Islam and Christianity: Between Tolerance and Acceptance," in *Religions of the Book: The Annual Publication of the College Theology Society*, ed. Gerard Sloyan (Landham, Md.: College Theology Society, 1992), 38:28.

102. See, for example, Robert Heffner, "Modernity and the Challenge of Pluralism: Some Indonesian Lessons," *Studia Islamika* 2, no. 4 (1995), p. 25.

103. Nurcholish Madjid, "In Search of Islamic Roots for Modern Pluralism: The Indonesian Experience," in *Toward a New Paradigm: Recent Developments in Indonesian Thought*, ed. Mark R. Woodward (Tempe: Arizona State University, 1996), p. 90; and Olaf-Schumann, "Christian-Muslim Encounter in Indonesia," in *Christian-Muslim Encounters* ed. Yvonne Y. Haddad and Wadi Z. Haddad, (Gainesville: University of Florida Press, 1995).

104. *Middle East Times,* June 19–25, 1990.

105. John O. Voll, "For Scholars of Islam, Interpretation Need Not Be Advocacy," *Chronicle of Higher Education*, March 22, 1989, p. 2.

106. For a sampling of international reactions, see Lisa Appignanesi and Sara Maitland, eds., *The Rushdie File* (Syracuse: Syracuse University Press, 1990).

107. James Piscatori, "The Rushdie Affair and the Politics of Ambiguity," *International Affairs* 66 (1990): 767–89.

108. "Repeating an Apostasy Is an Apostasy: Religious Leaders Urge Muslims to Ignore Rushdie Issue," *Middle East Times*, March 7–13, 1989, p. 14.

109. *For Rushdie: Essays by Arab and Muslim Writers in the Defense of Free Speech* (New York: George Braziller, 1994).

110. *Law, Blasphemy and the Multi-Faith Society: Report of a Seminar*, Discussion Papers 1 (London: Commission of Racial Equality, 1990), p. 53.

111. See John L. Esposito, "Jihad in a World of Shattered Dreams: Islam, Arab Politics, and the Gulf Crisis, *The World and I*, February 1991, pp. 512–27.

112. Piscatori, ed. *Islamic Fundamentalisms and the Gulf Crisis*; Yvonne Y. Haddad, "Operation Desert Shield/Desert Storm: The Islamist Perspective," in *Beyond Desert Storm: The Gulf Crisis Reader*, ed. Phyllis Bennis and Michel Moushabeck (New York: Olive Branch Press, 1991), chapter 23.

113. See *Washington Post*, September 14, 1990; and *Los Angeles Times*, September 22, 1990.

114. "Islam Divided," *The Economist*, September 22, 1990, p. 47.

115. Abdurrahman Alamoudi in *The Washington Report on Middle East Affairs*, October 1990, p. 69.

116. *The Herald*, September 1990, p. 30.

117. "The Gulf Crisis," *Aliran* 10, no. 8 (1990), p. 32.

118. "Exposing US Motives: A Third World View," *Aliran* 10, no. 11 (1990), p. 38.

119. *Dawn*, February 1, 1991.

120. *Christian Science Monitor*, January 24, 1991.

121. *Far Eastern Economic Review*, January 24, 1991.

122. *The Economist*, January 26, 1991.

123. For an early and insightful analysis of the origins of the modern construct of religion, see Wilfred Cantwell Smith, *The Meaning and End of Religion* (New York: Harper & Row, 1962).

124. See, for example, Daniel Lerner, *The Passing of Traditional Society: Modernizing the Middle East* (New York: Free Press, 1958); and Manfield Halpren, *The Politics of Social Change in the Middle East and North Africa* (Princeton: Princeton University Press, 1963). For an analysis and critique of the factors that influenced the development of modernization theory, see Fred R. von der Mehden, *Religion and Modernization in Southeast Asia* (Syracuse: Syracuse University Press, 1988).

125. See, for example, Harvey Cox, *The Secular City: Urbanization and Secularization in Theological Perspective* (New York: Macmillan, 1965); and Cox *Religion in the Secular City: Toward a Post Modern Theology* (New York: Simon & Schuster, 1984); Dietrich Bonhoeffer, *Letters and Papers from Prison*, rev. ed. (New York: Macmillan, 1967); and William Hamilton and Thomas Altizer, *Radical Theology and the Death of God* (Indianapolis: Bobbs Merrill, 1966).

126. See, for example, the influential introduction of H. A. R. Gibb, *Mohammedanism* (Oxford: Oxford University Press, 1962); or John B. Christopher, *The Islamic Tradition* (New York: Harper & Row, 1972).

127. See, for example, Olivier Roy, *The Failure of Political Islam* (Cambridge: Harvard University Press).

128. "Squeezing Islam's Moderates," *The Middle East*, June 1993, p. 11.

129. Ibid.

130. Daniel Pipes, "Fundamentalist Muslims between America and Russia," *Foreign Affairs*, Summer 1986, pp. 939–59; and Robert H. Pelletreau, Jr., Daniel Pipes, and John L. Esposito, "Political Islam Symposium: Resurgent Islam in the Middle East," *Middle East Policy* 3 (1994), pp. 7–8.

131. Andrew Brown, "How English Can a Muslim Be?" *The Independent*, October 28, 1993.

132. Edward P. Djerejian, *The U.S. and the Middle East in a Changing World* (Washington, D.C.: Meridien House International, June 2, 1992).

133. Robert Pelletreau, "Islam and U.S. Policy," an edited version of which appeared in Pelletreau, Pipes, and Esposito, "Political Islam Symposium" p. 2.

134. Ibid., p. 3.

135. Ibid., p. 4.

136. "Statement of the Assistant Secretary of State for Near Eastern Affairs Robert H. Pelletreau before the House Foreign Affairs Committee Subcommittee on North Africa," September 28, 1994, pp. 8–9.

137. Vernon Loeb, "A Global, Pan-Islamic Network: Terrorism Entrepreneur Unifies Groups Financially, Politically," *Washington Post* August 23, 1998.

138. Ibid.

139. Transcript of Osama bin Laden interview, CNN/Time *Impact: Holy Terror?* August 25, 1998.

140. The discussion of Hamas draws on materials in John L. Esposito, *Islam and Politics* 4th ed. (Syracuse: Syracuse University Press, 1998), pp. 228–232.

141. Sara Roy, "Gaza: New Dynamics of Civic Disintegration," *Journal of Palestine Studies*, Volume 22, no. 4, Summer 1993, 20–21, page 25.

142. "The Tough Dilemma in Algeria," *Boston Globe*, February 16, 1992.

Select Bibliography

For a comprehensive bibliography on the role of Islam in contemporary history and politics, see Yvonne Yazbeck Haddad, John Obert Voll, and John L. Esposito, eds., *The Contemporary Islamic Revival: A Critical Survey and Bibliography* (New York: Greenwood Press, 1991).

Abdillah, Masykuri. *Responses of Indonesian Muslim Intellectuals to the Concept of Democracy (1966–1993)*. Hamburg: Avera Verlag Meyer, 1997.

Abrahamian, Ervand. *Iran Between Two Revolutions*. Princeton, N.J.: Princeton University Press, 1982.

Ahmed, Akbar S. *Postmodernism and Islam: Predicament and Promise*. London: Routledge, 1992.

Ajami, Fouad. *The Arab Predicament*. New York: Cambridge University Press, 1982.

———. *The Vanished Imam: Musa Sadr and the Shia of Lebanon*. Ithaca, N.Y.: Cornell University Press, 1986.

Akhavi, Sharough, *Religion and Politics in Contemporary Iran*. Albany: SUNY Press, 1980.

Al-e-Ahmad, Jalal. *Gharbzadegi*. Lexington, Ky.: Mazda, 1982.

Algar, Hamid, trans. *Islam and Revolution: Writings and Declarations of Imam Khomeini*. Berkeley, Calif.: Mizan Press, 1981.

Antoun, Richard T., and Mary Elaine Hegland, eds. *Religious Resurgence: Contemporary Cases in Islam, Christianity, and Judaism*. Syracuse, N.Y.: Syracuse University Press, 1987.

Arjomand, Said Amir. *The Turban for the Crown: The Islamic Revolution in Iran*. New York: Oxford University Press, 1988.

———, ed. *Authority and Political Culture in Islam*. Albany: SUNY Press, 1988.

Ayoob, Mohammed, ed. *The Politics of Islamic Reassertion*. New York: St. Martin's Press, 1981.

Ayoub, Mahmoud M. *Islam and the Third Universal Theory: The Religious Thought of Muammar al-Qadhdhafi*. London: KPI, 1987.

313

Ayubi, Nazih. *Political Islam: Religion and Politics in the Arab World*. London: Routledge, 1991.

Baker, Raymond. *Sadat and After: Struggles for Egypt's Political Soul*. Cambridge, Mass.: Harvard University Press, 1990.

Bakhash, Shaul. *The Reign of the Ayatollahs: Iran and the Islamic Revolution*. New York: Basic Books, 1984.

Bannerman, Patrick. *Islam in Perspective*. London: Routledge, 1988.

Banuazizi, Ali, and Myron Weiner, eds. *The State, Religion, and Ethnic Politics*. Syracuse, N.Y.: Syracuse University Press, 1986.

Bennigsen, Alexandre, and Marie Boxup. *The Islamic Threat to the Soviet State*. New York: St. Martin's Press, 1983.

Bill, James A. *The Eagle and the Lion*. New Haven, Conn.: Yale University Press, 1988.

Binder, Leonard. *Islamic Liberalism: A Critique of Development Ideologies*. Chicago: University of Chicago Press, 1988.

Burgat, Francois. *The Islamic Movement in North Africa*. 2d ed. Translated by William Dowel. Austin: University of Texas, 1997.

Burke, Edmund, and Ira M. Lapidus, eds. *Islam, Politics, and Social Movements*. Berkeley: University of California Press, 1988.

Cole, Juan R. I., and Nikki R. Keddie, eds. *Shiism and Social Protest*. New Haven, Conn.: Yale University Press, 1986.

Curtis, Michael, ed. *Religion and Politics in the Middle East*. Boulder, Colo.: Westview Press, 1982.

Daniel, Norman. *Islam: Europe and Empire*. Edinburgh: Edinburgh University Press, 1966.

Dekmejian, R. Hrair. *Islam in Revolution: Fundamentalism in the Arab World*. Syracuse, N.Y.: Syracuse University Press, 1985.

Dessouki, Ali E. Hillal, ed. *Islamic Resurgence in the Arab World*. New York: Praeger, 1982.

Djait, Hichem, *Europe and Islam: Cultures and Modernity*. Berkeley: University of California Press, 1985.

Donohue, John J., and John L. Esposito, eds. *Islam in Transition: Muslim Perspectives*. New York: Oxford University Press, 1982.

Eickelman, Dale F. *The Middle East: An Anthropological Approach*. 2nd ed. Englewood Cliffs, N.J.: Prentice Hall, 1989.

Enayat, Hamid. *Modern Islamic Political Thought*. Austin: University of Texas Press, 1982.

Esposito, John L. *Islam: The Straight Path*. 3d ed. New York: Oxford University Press, 1997.

———. *Political Islam*. Boulder, Colo.: Lynne Rienner, 1997.

———. *Islam and Politics*. 3rd ed. Syracuse, N.Y.: Syracuse University Press, 1991.

———. *Islam in Asia: Religion, Politics and Society*. New York: Oxford University Press, 1987.

———. *Islam: The Straight Path*. Expanded ed. New York: Oxford University Press, 1991.

————, ed. *The Iranian Revolution: Its Global Impact*. Miami: Florida International University Press, 1990.

————, ed. *The Oxford Encyclopedia of the Modern Islamic World*, 4 vols. New York: Oxford University Press, 1995.

————, ed. *Voices of Resurgent Islam*. New York: Oxford University Press, 1983.

Esposito, John L., and John Obert Voll. *Islam and Democracy*. New York: Oxford University Press, 1996.

Fischer, Michael M. J. *Iran: From Religious Discourse to Revolution*. Cambridge, Mass.: Harvard University Press, 1980.

Gibb, Hamilton A. R., and Harold Bowen. *Islamic Society and the West*. Oxford: Oxford University Press, 1960.

Gilsenan, Michael. *Recognizing Islam: Religion and Society in the Modern Arab World*. New York: Pantheon, 1983.

Goldschmidt, Arthur, Jr. *A Concise History of the Middle East*. 3rd ed. Boulder, Colo.: Westview Press, 1991.

Haddad, Yvonne Y. *Contemporary Islam and the Challenge of History*. Albany: SUNY Press, 1982.

————, ed. *The Islamic Impact*. Syracuse, N.Y.: Syracuse University Press, 1984.

Haddad, Yvonne Y., and John L. Esposito, et al. *The Islamic Revival Since 1988: A Critical Survey and Bibliography*. Westport, Conn.: Greenwood Press, 1997.

Haddad, Yvonne Y., and John L. Esposito, eds. *Islam, Gender and Social Change*. New York: Oxford University Press, 1997.

Hippler, Jochen and Andrea Lueg. *The Next Threat: Western Perceptions of Islam* (London: Pluto Press, 1995).

Hiro, Delip. *Holy Wars: The Rise of Islamic Fundamentalism*. New York: Paladin, 1989.

Hodgson, Marshall G. S. *The Venture of Islam*. 3 vols. Chicago: University of Chicago Press, 1974.

Hourani, Albert. *Arabic Thought in the Liberal Age, 1798–1939*. New York: Cambridge University Press, 1983.

————. *Europe and the Middle East*. Berkeley: University of California Press, 1980.

————. *A History of the Arab Peoples*. Cambridge, Mass.: Harvard University Press, 1991.

Hudson, Michael C. *Arab Politics: The Search for Legitimacy*. New Haven, Conn.: Yale University Press, 1977.

Hunter, Shireen T., ed. *The Politics of Islamic Revivalism: Diversity and Unity*. Bloomington: Indiana University Press, 1988.

Islamic Fundamentalism and Islamic Radicalism. Committee on Foreign Affairs, House of Representatives, Washington, D.C.: U.S. Government Printing Office, 1985.

Johnson, Nels. *Islam and the Politics of Meaning in Palestinian Nationalism*. London: Kegan Paul, 1983.

Keddie, Nikki R. *Iran: Religion, Politics and Society*. London: Frank Cass, 1980.

————. *Roots of Revolution: An Interpretive History of Modern Iran.* New Haven, Conn.: Yale University Press, 1981.

Kepel, Gilles. *Muslim Extremism in Egypt: The Prophet and Pharaoh.* Berkeley: University of California Press, 1986.

Kramer, Martin. *Political Islam.* Beverly Hills, Calif.: Sage Publications, 1980.

————. *Shiism, Resistance and Revolution.* Boulder, Colo.: Westview Press, 1987.

Lapidus, Ira M. *A History of Islamic Societies.* Cambridge: Cambridge University Press, 1988.

Lawrence, Bruce. *Defenders of God: The Fundamentalist Revolt Against the Modern Age.* New York: Harper and Row, 1989.

Lee, Robert D. *Overcoming Tradition and Modernity: The Search for Islamic Authenticity.* Boulder, Colo.: Westview Press, 1997.

Lewis, Bernard. *The Middle East and the West.* New York: Harper and Row, 1968.

————. *The Muslim Discovery of Europe.* New York: W. W. Norton, 1982.

————. *The Political Language of Islam.* Chicago: University of Chicago Press, 1988.

Masr, Seyyed Vali. *The Vanguard of the Islamic Revolution: The Jamaat-i Islami of Pakistan* (Berkeley, University of California Press, 1994).

Mayer, Ann Elizabeth. *Islam and Human Rights: Tradition and Politics.* Boulder, Colo.: Westview Press, 1991.

Milton-Edwards, Beverly. *Islamic Politics in Palestine.* London: Tauris Academic Studies, 1996.

Mitchell, Richard. *The Society of Muslim Brothers.* New York: Oxford University Press, 1969.

Mortimer, Edward. *Faith and Power.* New York: Random House, 1982.

Mottahedeh, Roy P. *The Mantle of the Prophet: Religion and Politics in Iran.* New York: Random House, Pantheon, 1986.

Munson, Henry. *Islam and Revolution in the Middle East.* New Haven, Conn.: Yale University Press, 1988.

Nasr, Seyyed Vali Reza. *Mawdudi and the Making of Islamic Revivalism.* New York: Oxford University Press, 1996.

Norton, Augustus Richard. *AMAL and the Shia: Struggle for the Soul of Lebanon.* Austin: University of Texas Press, 1987.

Peters, Rudolph. *Islam and Colonialism: The Doctrine of Jihad in Modern History.* The Hague: Mouton, 1979.

Pipes, Daniel. *The Rushdie Affair: The Novel, the Ayatollah, and the West.* New York: Birch Lane Press, 1990.

Piscatori, James P. *Islam in a World of Nation States.* Cambridge: Cambridge University Press, 1986.

————, ed. *Islam in the Political Process.* Cambridge: Cambridge University Press, 1983.

————, ed. *Islamic Fundamentalisms and the Gulf Crisis.* Chicago: University of Chicago Press, 1991.

Piscatori, James P., and Dale Eickelman. *Muslim Politics.* Princeton: Princeton: University Press, 1996.

Rahman, Fazlur. *Islam and Modernity.* Chicago: University of Chicago Press, 1982.

Rodinson, Maxime. *Europe and the Mystique of Islam.* Seattle: University of Washington Press, 1987.

Roff, William, ed. *Islam and the Political Economy of Meaning.* London: Croom Helm, 1987.

Roy, Olivier. *The Failure of Political Islam* (Cambridge: Harvard University Press, 1994).

———. *Islam and Resistance in Afghanistan.* Cambridge: Cambridge University Press, 1986.

Sahliyeh, Emile, ed. *Religious Resurgence and Politics in the Modern World.* Albany: SUNY Press, 1990.

Said, Edward W. *Covering Islam.* New York: Pantheon, 1981.

———. *Orientalism.* New York: Vintage, 1979.

Shariati, Ali. *On the Sociology of Islam.* Berkeley, Calif.: Mizan Press, 1979.

Sivan, Emmanuel. *Radical Islam: Medieval Theology and Modern Politics.* New Haven, Conn.: Yale University Press, 1985.

Sivan, Emmanuel, and Menachem Friedman, eds. *Religious Radicalism and Politics in the Middle East.* Albany: SUNY Press, 1990.

Smith, Donald E., ed. *Religion and Political Modernization.* New Haven, Conn.: Yale University Press, 1974.

Sonn, Tamara. *Between Quran and Crown.* Boulder, Colo.: Westview Press, 1990.

Southern, R. W. *Western Views of Islam in the Middle Ages.* Cambridge, Mass.: Harvard University Press, 1962.

Stowasser, Barbara, ed. *The Islamic Impulse.* London: Croom Helm, 1987.

Voll, John Obert. *Islam: Continuity and Change in the Modern World,* 2nd ed. (Syracuse, N.Y.: Syracuse University Press, 1994).

Watt, W. Montgomery. *Islamic Political Thought.* New York: Columbia University Press, 1980.

Weiss, Anita, ed. *Islamic Reassertion in Pakistan: The Application of Islamic Laws in a Modern State.* Syracuse, N.Y.: Syracuse University Press, 1986.

Wright, Robin. *Sacred Rage: The Wrath of Militant Islam.* New York: Simon and Schuster, 1985.

———. *In the Name of God: The Khomeini Decade.* New York: Simon and Schuster, 1989.

Index

319